RAY ALLEN BILLINGTON

HENRY E. HUNTINGTON LIBRARY AND ART GALLERY

AMERICA'S FRONTIER HERITAGE

Ray Allen Billington

HISTORIES OF THE AMERICAN FRONTIER
Ray Allen Billington, General Editor
Howard R. Lamar, Coeditor

UNIVERSITY OF NEW MEXICO PRESS
Albuquerque

Preface

IF THE HYPOTHESIS advanced by Frederick Jackson Turner in his famous 1893 essay on "The Significance of the Frontier in American History" is valid, its importance today is greater than at any time in the past. The pioneering experience, Professor Turner suggested, helped account for some of the distinctive characteristics of the American people; during three centuries of expansion their attitudes toward democracy and nationalism and individualism were altered, and they developed identifiable traits not shared in like degree by their European ancestors: wastefulness, inventiveness, mobility, and a dozen more. If these distinctions do exist, they should be known to the American people and the international community. In the contracted world of the post-World War II era, men and nations can live in harmony only if they recognize each other's similarities and differences. The misconception that mankind has been cast in a common mold and that the institutions of one nation can be transplanted unchanged to another with a different cultural heritage is as destructive of international tranquility as the equally false belief that variations in culture are irreconcilable. If peoples everywhere can recognize that other peoples must behave in differing ways world frictions will be lessened.

Since the frontier hypothesis was pronounced as one—but only one —explanation of distinctive American behavioral patterns, it has endured an experience of overenthusiastic acceptance and one of unjustified rejection. Each did it harm. Until Turner's death in 1932 the thesis was almost universally viewed as the sole valid interpretation of the nation's history; students in many disciplines restudied the past and concluded that expansion had been responsible for shaping the thought and behavior and values of the people of the United States. During the 1930's and 1940's the thesis endured a series of attacks that were often as unreasonable as the overextravagant praise that it had inspired during the previous decades. More recently historians have entered into what one of them has called the "third generation of the frontier hypothesis." Their attitude is still one of doubt, but scholars in a variety of fields are increasingly showing a willingness to test aspects of the thesis, rather than accept or condemn it as a whole.

This book attempts not only to summarize their findings, but to reappraise the entire hypothesis in the light of modern research in both history and the social sciences. Its purpose is neither to praise nor attack Professor Turner's statement of that thesis; his name and his ideas seldom appear after the first chapter, which recounts the history of the theory that he evolved. Its concern is solely with the validity of the thesis, to the degree that that validity can be tested with tools available to today's historian. This approach would have been heartily endorsed by Professor Turner. "Each age," he wrote in his essay on "The Significance of History," "writes the history of the past anew with reference to conditions uppermost in its own time." As a pioneer in popularizing the concept of relativism and as a trail breaker in the employment of interdisciplinary techniques, he would favor retesting every historical theory periodically with every technique that the world of scholarship could muster.

A word on my own methodology seems appropriate. My first task was to attempt to identify the attitudes and behavioral traits that were judged to be most distinctly "American" by visitors from overseas. This quest led to the reading of several hundred travel accounts, written largely during the eighteenth and nineteenth centuries, with an eye always for the characteristics that were considered "different" by the authors. An attempt was made to select visitors who had included the frontier in their itineraries and who paid particular attention to the characteristics of the pioneers. The result was rewarding. Not only did a majority of the visitors agree on a number of traits that they viewed as distinctly American, but a sizable proportion believed that these were most strongly exhibited in the successive Wests. Thus they found Americans everywhere were wasteful, democratic, and inquisitive, but they found that Westerners were more wasteful, more democratic, and more inquisitive than their counterparts along the Atlantic seaboard. Moreover these traits were noted on each new frontier; travelers observed them among the pioneers who peopled the Trans-Appalachian country just after the Revolution, among the frontiersmen who conquered the Mississippi Valley backwoods a generation later, among the homesteaders who overran the Great Plains late in the nineteenth century. These findings suggested, ·but by no means proved, that some connection existed between identifiable characteristics of the American people and their pioneering heritage.

The question remained: How could the frontiering experience alter the behavior not only of frontiersmen, but of their descendents? In seeking an answer, I found the studies of sociologists, anthropologists, social psychologists, and demographers extremely valuable. The results of this investigation will be found on the pages that follow, for they are too extensive even to be summarized here. Sufficient to say that the findings of social scientists, particularly in the fields of motivation, personality, culture, and spatial mobility, do suggest logical means whereby three centuries of expansion did alter the behavioral patterns of the frontiersmen, and to a lessening degree of their descendents of the twentieth century.

The reading necessary before reaching these conclusions was done largely in three libraries, to whose staffs I am forever indebted. The Deering Library of Northwestern University allowed me access to its extensive holdings in the social sciences, while three friends on the faculty—Professor Kimball Young of the Department of Sociology, Professor Francis L. K. Hsu of the Department of Anthropology, and Professor Lee B. Sechrest of the Department of Psychology—were kind enough to give me invaluable advice on the literature of their respective fields. At the Newberry Library I was privileged to spend many months immersed in travel accounts, most of them rare volumes housed in the Edward E. Ayer and Everett D. Graff collections. To Ruth L. Butler and Colton Storm, custodians of those collections, and to Stanley Pargellis, director of the library until his retirement in 1962, I am grateful for invaluable aid and countless courtesies. Finally, this book was written amidst the unrivaled comforts and literary riches of the Henry E. Huntington Library and Art Gallery, where much of the research was also done. For an opportunity to be permanently associated with that academic Valhalla, as well as for generous help and wise counsel, I am indebted to John E. Pomfret the director and his staff.

Pleasant periods of research at these institutions were made possible by a Faculty Research Grant from the Social Science Research Council during the academic year 1959–1960, and by a grant-in-aid from the Huntington Library during the summer of 1961. For both I am grateful, for without them I could not have broadened my knowledge of frontier theory by the study of the Frederick Jackson Turner papers at the latter institution.

My debts extend also to three good friends—Professor Merle Curti of the University of Wisconsin, Professor Earl Pomeroy of the University of Oregon, and Professor Martin Ridge of San Diego State College—who were not only kind enough to read the entire manuscript but frank enough to give me the benefit of their vast critical knowledge. Their expert advice not only saved me from embarrassing errors but contributed materially to the form and content of this book. Portions of the manuscript were also read by Professor Rodman W. Paul of the California Institute of Technology, and by two of his colleagues who were generous enough to share with me their knowledge in two specialized disciplines: Professor Norman H. Horowitz in genetics, and Professor Thayer Scudder in anthropology. The generosity of these competent scholars saved me from many mistakes of judgment as well as fact; for the many that almost certainly remain I assume sole responsibility.

Any catalogue of credits for this book, or any other volume that I have written or will write, would be woefully incomplete without inclusion of the name of the late Professor Arthur Meier Schlesinger of Harvard University. From Professor Schlesinger I learned both the techniques and the joys of historical research. Until his death in October 1965 he remained not only a generous counselor and warm friend but a continuing inspiration. To his memory I gratefully dedicate this book.

RAY ALLEN BILLINGTON

San Marino, California

Contents

Preface   v

1   The History of a Theory   1

2   Why and How Pioneers Moved Westward   23

3   The Frontier and the American Character   47

4   The Frontier: Cradle of Barbarism or Civilization?   69

5   The Structure of Frontier Society   97

6   Frontier Democracy: Political Aspects   117

7   Frontier Democracy: Social Aspects   139

8   The Economic Impact of the Frontier   159

9   The Frontier and the Migratory Compulsion   181

10   The Frontier and American Behavioral Patterns   199

11   The Persistence of Frontier Traits   219

Notes   237

Bibliographical Notes   285

Index   303

1

The

History

of a Theory

IF THE HUNDREDS of visitors from overseas who have written about the United States can be believed, we Americans are a strange and inexplicable lot. We work too hard; even our games are played with a grim determination to have a good time. We are forever moving about, showing none of the attachment to place and family of normal human beings. We rebel against tradition, even to experimenting with the new when the old is still useful. We are shockingly wasteful, addicted to such extravagances as disposable tissues, throw-away beer cans, and automobiles cunningly contrived to wear out after a few years of use. We venerate our wives, shower them with adulation, burden them with authority, and reduce the mere male to a henpecked nonentity. We are crassly materialistic, absorbed in pursuing the Almighty Dollar, and blind to cultural values. We are so unrealistically optimistic that we would refuse to recognize the day of doom were its shadow already upon us.

A few more astute visitors—those probing beneath the surface behavior to explore that mystical ethos known as a "national character"—have added to this list of particulars. Americans, they say, display a naïve nationalism; they magnify minor incidents into wars (as they did the unpleasantness in Korea in 1950), and they flex their military muscles whenever another nation indulges in a bit of diplomatic bluffing (as did Russia in an annoying number of cases during the Cold War). Americans have been and are wedded to a brand of "rugged individualism" already proved obsolescent in the urban-industrial world of the twentieth century. And Americans, they argue, have such an emotional attachment to democracy that they refuse to see virtue in any other form of government, encourage those of humblest birth to become Presidents, and call servants "gentlemen" and masters "hey you."

Putting aside for the moment the truth or falsity of these appraisals, the fact remains that a good many hundred travelers have isolated these traits as peculiarly American; so many, indeed, that their chorus of assent becomes convincing. We Americans do exhibit characteristics not shared by our cousins beyond the seas. This does not mean that we are the sole owners of an entirely unique character; many "uniquely" American traits are exhibited elsewhere in the western world today as mounting prosperity encourages mobility, democracy, optimism, materialism, and even a touch of wastefulness. It does mean that over the past two centuries European visitors have found those characteristics so exaggerated in the United States that they have branded Americans a different people. The Londoner who remarks, as many have, that he feels more at home in Paris than Chicago is only mirroring a belief that the Americans have been transmuted into a different species from the English pioneers who planted their civilization at Jamestown and Plymouth three centuries ago.

Why this transmutation? Historians have proposed a number of answers, all more or less true. Some have gone so far as to deny that differences exist, and have argued learnedly if ineffectively that man's character is unchangeable. Others have ascribed uniquely American traits to the ethnic hodgepodge created by immigration; they dwell on the effect of acculturation and on the results of borrowing from many cultures. Still others see American distinctiveness as a by-product of the nation's abundant natural resources or of the physical mobility that keeps the people forever on the move.[1] That there is a kernel of truth in each of these explanations is indisputable. Historians have long realized that events occur and characteristics emerge through the operation of many forces; human behavior is too infinitely complex to be explained by any single cause. We must visualize the distinctive features of American civilization as the product of the multitudinous forces contributing to the country's heritage.

To this list, however, one more must be added, and this book will argue that it has been of major importance. It will maintain that some—but by no means all—of the characteristics that Europeans brand uniquely American were the product of the three centuries of pioneering needed to settle the continent. It will defend what scholars call the "frontier hypothesis."

This hypothesis may be stated thus: The Europeans who founded the New World settlements in the seventeenth century and the later pioneers who were lured ever westward by the thirst for furs or cheap land or gold or adventure found themselves in an unfamiliar environment. In Europe and the East men were many and land was scarce; on the frontiers men were few and land was abundant. There the old laws governing compact societies no longer applied. Traditional techniques of production were unsuited to an environment where resources were more plentiful than manpower; innovation and experimentation became a way of life. Attachment to place diminished in a land where more attractive places lay ahead; mobility came to be a habit. Pinchpenny Easterners so profited by exploiting nature's abundance that their thrifty ways were outmoded; wastefulness was a natural consequence. Cultural creativity lost its appeal to men burdened with the task of clearing a continent; materialism emerged as a desirable creed no less than an economic necessity. Leisure was nonexistent in frontier communities; hard work became a persistent habit. Inherited titles seemed archaic and traditional class distinctions less meaningful in a land where a man's worth to society was judged by his own skills; a democratic social system with greater possibilities for upward mobility followed naturally. And, most important of all, men found that the man-land ratio on the frontier provided so much opportunity for the individual to better himself that external controls were not necessary; individualism and political democracy were enshrined as their ideals. These were the traits which were revitalized over and over again as the frontier moved westward, eventually creating an American way of life and thought that was distinct.

This is the argument of those who uphold the "frontier hypothesis" as one—but only one—of the several forces shaping the civilization of the United States.

✎§✎§ WHENCE CAME this most American of all explanations of the nation's distinctiveness? Virtually from the beginning of the Republic observers noted that the frontier was a unique feature in the nation's growth, and that it was leaving a mark on the national character. Benjamin Franklin and Thomas Jefferson realized that as long as cheap lands lasted, the continual drain of men westward would retard the growth of industry and cities, thus strengthening rural democracy and postponing the day when autocratic controls would be necessary.[2] Francis Parkman, historian of the Golden Age, similarly viewed the West as "a counter influence" against "absolute authority," and believed that contact with the wilderness endowed Europeans with "a rugged independence, a self-sustaining energy, and powers of action and perception before unthought of."[3] To James Russell Lowell the unique democracy of the United States was "a gift of the sky and of the forest."[4] These intellectual pioneers, and dozens like them who expressed similar views, clearly recognized that the frontier experience was a force in American life, and just as certainly based their beliefs on their own capable observations of the pioneering process.

These impressions were refined and given substance by more searching observers. Alexis de Tocqueville linked American democracy with the recurring exploitation of natural resources by the westward-surging population, a theme also in the mind of Lord Bryce when he wrote in his *American Commonwealth* that "the West is the most American part of America." "What Europe is to Asia," he went on, "what England is to the rest of Europe, what America is to England, that the Western States and Territories are to the Atlantic States."[5] The nation's democracy, others pointed out, rested not only on frontier-fed prosperity but on the ability of the working man to use the West as an economic escalator. "When population is low in proportion to the amount of land," wrote William Graham Sumner, "life is easy, competition weak, . . . the average condition is comfort and the society will be democratic." Even Karl Marx, writing in 1869, recognized that in the United States "the wage earner of today is tomorrow an independent peasant or artisan, working for himself," and forever lost to the forces of labor.[6] Henry George only echoed these sentiments when he prophesied that "when we cease to have cheap land we shall realize in full force the social evils which affect Europe."[7]

While these learned men pontificated on the democratizing of frontier America, others saw in the pioneering process an explanation for many of their country's characteristics. As early as 1834 one guidebook author viewed the West as a spawning ground for independence of thought and action, an adventurous spirit, and rudeness of manners. To this list a reviewer in the *American Quarterly Review* added bravery, indolence, generosity, sagaciousness, and a tendency toward "powerful bodily exertions." Westerners were said to exhibit "great energy, and the spirit of enterprise," intense patriotism, and a universal spirit of improvement; they were "endowed with great boldness and originality of mind, from the circumstances under which they are placed."[8] The typical frontiersman was more inventive than a man living in a social order "with fixed habits."[9] These scattered observations suggest that a number of nineteenth-century writers were aware that pioneering was gradually transforming Europeans into Americans.

Of those who speculated along these lines, the most searching was E. L. Godkin, editor of the *Nation*, whose essay on "Aristocratic Opinions of Democracy" (1865) was the first systematic attempt to link the frontier with basic American traits.[10] Godkin argued that the phenomena that distinguish American society from the niceties of older countries could be attributed largely to what he called "the frontier life." Democracy came from neither the Revolution nor the decline of English nobility in America, but from the disruption of society as it moved westward, breeding individualism and a tendency for men to look to their own interests rather than to those of the community. As a corollary to this change, Godkin saw Americans developing "a prodigious contempt for experience and for theory" as they learned to solve their own problems in their own ways. He also traced to the pioneering experience a whole scratch pad full of characteristics: materialism stemming from the vast richness of the West and breeding disrespect for art and literature; originality in thought and action; an absence of a strong sense of social or national continuity; and a distrust of history as a guide to the future. Cultural progress would come when energies were no longer absorbed in the taming of a continent, but the love of democracy bred into the people by centuries of pioneering would endure forever. So Godkin believed, and so he wrote in 1865.

His views, and those of others who preached his message, had little impact on the popular mind, for when he and his contemporaries wrote, the United States was not yet ready to receive the "frontier hypothesis." During the last two decades of the nineteenth century this situation changed. An altered intellectual atmosphere created a climate of opinion suited to receive and nurture the frontier theory. And, through a happy conjunction of circumstances, those years produced a prophet capable of formulating the hypothesis in terms understandable to the public.

The changed intellectual environment was created by publicists who during the 1880s awakened to the fact that an era of history was closing with the exhaustion of the public domain. Their first impulse was to pay more attention to the role of land in man's social evolution; the works of Adam Smith, John Stuart Mill, and Karl Marx were widely read and freely discussed, while commentators such as Josiah Strong and James Bryce showed increasing awareness of the relationship between land and society. The question was catapulted into the public conscience by the great depression of the 1890s. Searchers after causes and cures inevitably stumbled upon the fact that the frontier was closing and that Americans would be forced to live within a closed space. Some, such as C. Wood Davis who published a whole battalion of articles in the *Country Gentleman* and elsewhere, saw the exhaustion of cheap land as a panacea for the farmer, whose food prices would inevitably rise, and as the doom of the worker, who could no longer flee westward to escape exploitation. Others, writing principally in the *Review of Reviews,* preached that the end of the frontier justified the restriction of immigration insomuch as the West no longer provided a haven for newcomers. Racists whose crusade for Anglo-Saxon supremacy attracted a disgraceful amount of support in the 1890s persuaded thousands of Americans that the gates must be closed against Orientals and southern Europeans if the nation's blood was to remain pure. All of these propagandists made the nation aware that its era of expansion was at an end.[11]

The prophet who capitalized on this newborn concern with the West was Frederick Jackson Turner. Born in the village of Portage, Wisconsin, in 1861, Turner had as a boy witnessed wilderness scenes that he would never forget: army officers marching Indians through the streets on their way to a Western reservation, camps of the red men along the Wisconsin River "where dried pumpkins were hung up, and cooking muskrats were in the kettle," gangs of red-shirted raftsmen who left their lumber rafts to "take over" Portage. He had observed firsthand the mingling of peoples that took place in all new communities; "it was a town," he later recalled, "with a real collection of types from all the world, Yankees from Maine & Vermont, New York Yankees, Dutchmen from the Mohawk, braw curlers from the Highlands, Southerners—all kinds. They mixed, too. And respected and fought each other."[12] These boyhood scenes made an indelible impression. Turner carried them with him when he entered the University of Wisconsin to begin the serious study of history under a remarkable teacher, William Francis Allen.

There he was superbly trained as he progressed toward the bachelor's and master's degrees between 1881 and 1888. Allen instilled in his young protégé a respect for the principles of historical criticism, a belief in the use of sources, and the concept of society as a continuously evolving organism. His own interests were in classical and medieval history, but Turner was instinctively drawn to the study of the United States. "The more I dip into American history," he wrote his fiancée in 1887, "the more I can see what a great field there is here for a life study. One must specialize even here. I think I shall spend my study chiefly upon the Northwest and more generally on the Mississippi Valley."[13] A few months later he was still bubbling with excitement. "I do not talk anything now but Western history," he wrote. ". . . I have taken a fever of enthusiasm over the possibilities of the study of the great west and of the magnificent scope of United States history in general."[14] His Commonplace Books—notebooks filled in the tradition of his day with scribbled thoughts and quotations—show that he was already asking searching questions about the differences between American and European societies. "Need of Study of foreign groups," he jotted on one occasion. ". . . Why are Nor[wegians] rep[ublicans]. Irish dem[ocrats]?"[15] Did the mingling of peoples in new communities alter traditional social behavior?

Answers to these questions required more training, and in 1888 at Allen's urging young Turner enrolled at the Johns Hopkins University, where he spent a year that was both challenging and disturbing. The challenges came from such great teachers as Richard T. Ely and Woodrow Wilson, who sharpened his interest in economic and regional history. His principal instructor, Professor Herbert Baxter Adams, played a more disquieting role in Turner's training. Adams was an exponent of the theory that the roots of all American institutions could be traced to their beginnings in the folkmoots of medieval Germany; at one point he told his students that the origins of every institution had been so thoroughly studied that the subject was exhausted and urged them to turn to the investigation of European history. Turner refused to accept either the advice or a concept that recognized no differences between European and American culture, and that offended his belief in social evolution. "The Frontier theory," he later recalled, "was pretty much a *reaction* from that due to my indignation."[16]

He harbored these thoughts when he returned to the University of

Wisconsin in 1889, and there gave himself over to the reading and speculation that ended with the announcement of the frontier hypothesis four years later. What was the genesis of this new concept? Creative thought, some psychologists hold, usually emerges in four definable stages: first a period of preparation in which random ideas are haphazardly tested and rejected as attention focuses more and more on the problem to be solved, next a time of incubation in which the problem is laid aside consciously but continues to generate subconscious flashes of insight, third a period of illumination with the conscious and unconscious reformulation of the problem in a form that allows blocks to be surmounted and a solution to be sighted either slowly or in a burst of insight known as the "Aha Experience," and finally a stage of verification as the solution is formulated and tested.[17] Only a little imagination is needed to trace these stages in the evolution of the frontier theory.

The period of preparation coincided with Turner's undergraduate and graduate years as he interested himself in the American West, realized that migration had been a fact for two centuries, and recognized that the process created an environment different from that of Europe. As yet he was only partly aware that a frontier had existed, and largely unconcerned with its impact on the national character. The stage of incubation lasted during his first years of teaching at the University of Wisconsin, as he busied himself with the tasks necessary in launching a university career. Classes must be arranged, lectures prepared, and departmental matters tended. Above all there were books to be read if he was to be properly prepared to meet his students. Especially did he seek information on the West, for his interest in that area could now be expressed. The university catalogues of that era mirror his increasing concern; an inherited course in "Constitutional and Political History" was sacrificed in 1891–1892 for one on "Economic and Social History." This focused more and more on the West; in 1892–1893 students were told that "particular attention will be paid to the spread of settlement across the continent."[18] If lectures on that subject were to be prepared, Turner must read in widely scattered materials, for books on the West were few in that day.

His quest for knowledge led him into two areas that helped clarify his thinking on the frontier. From the study of statistical and geographical publications originating in the Census Bureau he learned how and where the westward movement of peoples occurred; from scattered works by dozens of American and European authors he realized that the frontier had been a moulding force in the evolution of the civilization of the United States.

A pivotal book in shaping Turner's thoughts on the nature of westward migration was the *Statistical Atlas of the United States Based on the Results of the Ninth Census 1870,* prepared by the eminent statistician Francis A. Walker and published in 1874. There the young historian studied a series of maps based on census returns from 1790 to 1870 showing the concentration of population in five degrees from less than two persons to the square mile to more than ninety.[19] In these, as one reviewer put it, "the movement of the population seems to take place under our very eyes."[20] In a suggestive essay accompanying the maps, Walker spoke of "the line of continuous settlement," and "the frontier line"; he noted that on the outer fringes primitive economies based on fur trapping or ranching predominated, and that as population thickened the degree of economic complexity steadily increased. This lesson in social evolution was not lost on Turner.

His interest was whetted and his knowledge broadened when he dipped into a similar volume based on the census of 1880, the monumental statistical work by Henry Gannett and Fletcher W. Hewes entitled *Scribner's Statistical Atlas of the United States,* published in 1885.[21] Once more the westward movement was graphically represented, but now with greater sophistication than in the 1874 volume; the shaded maps had been refined to show the pattern of migration in relation to natural barriers. Once more the sequential nature of the frontier process was revealed; "there are to be seen in the United States," wrote Gannett, "nearly all conditions of industry attendant upon different degrees of density of population."[22] This evolution was spelled out by Gannett in a later bulletin of the census bureau when he noted that "in the course of settlement and development of a new country, the industries commonly follow one another in a certain order. After the hunter, trapper, and prospector, who are commonly the pioneers, the herdsman follows, and for a time the raising of cattle is the leading industry. As settlement becomes less sparse, this is followed by agriculture, which in its turn, as the population becomes more dense, is succeeded by manufactures."[23] Here, hand-tailored for Turner's use, was a clear statement of the evolution of society that occurred as a frontier moved westward.

The significance of all this information was brought home to him when in 1892 the bulky *Compendium of the Eleventh Census: 1890* arrived at the library of the Wisconsin State Historical Society. As

Turner scanned the pages of the usual essay on "Progress of the Nation" his eye certainly fastened on the now-famous words: "Up to and including 1890 the country had a frontier of settlement, but at present the unsettled area has been so broken into by isolated bodies of settlement that there can hardly be said to be a frontier line."[24] What speculations did this prophetic announcement spark in Turner's mind? As he read did he experience that flash of insight—that "Aha Experience"—so often associated with creative thought? Did he realize that an era of history was drawing to a close, and that American society must now follow a new evolutionary course in the future? Did he ask himself what the past, the frontier era, had bequeathed to the nation's culture? Did he ponder over the course that society would have to follow as it adjusted to a closed-space world?[25] We will never know the answers to these questions, but we do know that only a few months later Turner penned an essay that revealed with startling clarity the frontier's significance and for the first time explained its impact on American institutions and character.

He could do so, for his reading over the past few years had filled his mind with tidbits of information that fell into an orderly pattern as he pondered the effects of the passing of the frontier age. We can salvage some of those scraps from the 3-by-5 cards on which he scrawled his thoughts as he prepared his course on "Economic and Social History" in 1891 and 1892. "Am. the 'most mechanical of nations' (Why? frontier experiences!)" read one. On another he wrote: "West. Influence on Am. Breaker of *Custom*." And on another: "West Infl on US—Custom. It stood to East as the Sea to Phoenicia, to Egypt, to Greece."[26] Clearly he was groping toward a major thesis that would explain some of America's unique heritage.

The explanation that finally emerged was certainly not original; it was formed by fitting together a variety of scattered concepts and ideas to form a unified interpretation of one phase of American history. Turner's contribution was to weld a set of demographic and historical facts into a meaningful pattern; his insight revealed a series of relationships that had escaped others. That many of the ideas contributing to that relationship were borrowed does not detract from his genius, for most of the great inventions in history have been built upon the concepts of many men.

To trace Turner's course through the books that he read, and to identify the ideas and phrases that he later combined into his "frontier hypothesis" would require the patience of Job. His catholic tastes led him into every field of literature, from guidebooks to treatises on economic theory, and from countless volumes he distilled ideas or appropriated phrases. His notes suggest, however, that his principal reliance was on a relatively few germinal books that he read between 1889 and 1892.[27] These provided the skeleton of his frontier theory.

From Achille Loria, an Italian political economist whose *Analisi della Proprietà Capitalista* Turner probably read soon after its publication in 1889, he borrowed the concept that "free" (meaning unoccupied) land was the key to a nation's economic growth and that with a thickening of population the economy inevitably shifted to more complex forms.[28] From the American reformer Henry George he learned that environmental forces in the form of free land could alter a people's cultural traits.[29] From the English social philosopher, Walter Bagehot, who published his *Physics and Politics* in 1880, Turner discovered that the "cake of custom" was broken when incoming peoples occupied virgin areas and that their cultural borrowings laid the basis for a new national character.[30] From a Phi Beta Kappa address delivered at Brown University in 1889 by Francis A. Walker he gained the impression that such basic traits as inventiveness and nationalism could be traced to the frontier's influence.[31] From the French scholar Emile Boutmy whose *Studies in Constitutional Law* were translated in 1891, Turner learned that intense energy, adventurous enterprise, independence of action, materialism, and surface roughness were characteristic of frontiersmen who transmitted these traits to the American character.[32] From a French traveler named André Churillon, who published an essay on "American Life from the French Point of View" in the *Review of Reviews* (1892), he borrowed the belief that mobility and disrespect for tradition were Western traits that had been adopted by the American people as a whole.[33] Turner's unique contribution was to weld these scattered bits of information into a workable theory that would help explain the distinctiveness of the American historical experience.[34]

The evolution of his own thought as his reading increasingly focused his attention on the frontier can be traced in the essays and reviews that he wrote during his first years on the Universty of Wisconsin faculty. In a review that berated Theodore Roosevelt for ignoring the broader significance of the frontier in the *Winning of the West*, in an unpublished essay attacking Hermann Von Holst for distorting American history by ignoring Western influences in his multivolume *Constitutional and Political History of the United States*, in a brilliant lecture on "American Colonization" before the Madison Literary Club in the spring of 1891, he revealed a steadily mounting faith in the West as a key to the American character.[35] When Turner could write, as he did in the essay on Von Holst that American democracy "came not from the political theorists' dreams of the primitive German forest. It came stark and strong and full of life from the American forest," he had moved far along the path to developing his frontier thesis.

This found expression first in an essay called "Problems in American History" published in the student newspaper, *The Aegis*, in November, 1892,[36] and a year later expanded into his famous paper on "The Significance of the Frontier in American History."[37] Drawing his text from the announcement of the superintendent of the census that a frontier line no longer existed, Turner noted the end of an historic epoch. "Up to our own day," he wrote, "American history has been in a large degree the history of the colonization of the Great West. The existence of an area of free land, its continuous recession, and the advance of American settlement westward, explain American development."[38] This was so because "the peculiarity of American institutions is, the fact that they have been compelled to adapt themselves to the changes of an expanding people." Each move westward meant a "return to primitive conditions on a continually advancing frontier line," a "continual beginning over again" in the process of social evolution. First the wilderness mastered the colonist, stripping off the garments of civilization, and returning him to a state of near savagery. Then came the climb back toward social maturity, but a different maturity than that known in the East. The "bonds of custom" had been broken; in the repeated rebirth of civilization an Americanization of men and institutions had occurred.

The result, Turner believed, was a new society, based on borrowings from the old, but markedly different. One significant result was the "formation of a composite nationality" as immigrants were Americanized in the "crucible of the frontier." Another was "the promotion of democracy here and in Europe" as frontiersmen rebelled against external controls or responded to the individualizing influence of cheap land and abundant resources. "To the frontier," Turner went on, "the American intellect owes its striking characteristics. That coarseness and strength combined with acuteness and inquisitiveness; that practical, inventive turn of mind, quick to find expedients; that masterful grasp of material things, lacking in the artistic but powerful to effect great ends; that restless, nervous energy; that dominant individualism, working for good and for evil, and withal that buoyancy and exuberance which comes with freedom—these are traits of the frontier, or traits called out elsewhere because of the existence of the frontier."

When Frederick Jackson Turner read these challenging phrases to his fellow historians in Chicago during the summer of 1893 they attracted but perfunctory notice. Only one newspaper deigned his paper worthy of mention—on page three—and even his father, who was visiting there, wrote glowingly of everything but his son's performance.[39] Nor did the distribution of the essay in printed form inspire any chorus of acclaim. Edward Everett Hale acknowledged receipt of "your curious and interesting paper"; Francis A. Walker believed the title "a success in itself" but probed no deeper; Charles M. Andrews felt it "interesting" because of the "elements of romance" that it contained; and Theodore Roosevelt wrote that Turner had "struck some first class ideas, and . . . put into definite shape a good deal of thought which has been floating around rather loosely."[40] Faint praise indeed for a concept that was to revolutionize the understanding of the American past, but each in its way partially correct.

Gradually, however, Turner received his due. He helped popularize his own findings by a small but significant stream of publications. His original essay appeared not only in historical journals, but in the yearbook of the National Herbart Society in 1899 and the *International Socialist Review* in 1905. An article on "The Problem of the West" in the *Atlantic Monthly* for September 1896, was deliberately designed to catch the public eye, and did so; editorial writers across the nation commented favorably on a study that made the Western problem of that day meaningful.[41] A few months later he duplicated this success with an essay on "Dominant Forces in Western Life" in the *Atlantic Monthly,* to be followed by one on "The Middle West" in the *International Monthly* and another on "Contributions of the West to American Democracy" for the *Atlantic Monthly.*[42] Within a decade after its appearance, the "frontier hypothesis" was known to every competent historian and to a respectable portion of the lay public.

As Turner's fame spread, students flocked to his University of Wisconsin seminars, then returned to preach "the word" in classrooms across the nation.[43] Textbook writers sensed an opportunity to liven their political narratives with blood-chilling tales of frontier life, and the West began to push constitutional details from schoolbooks.[44] Semipopular authors rallied to the cause; Woodrow Wilson penned several articles for popular journals in which he glorified the frontier as "the central and determining fact of our national history."[45] Public lecturers discovered the theme; by 1895 the well-known John Fiske was telling audiences of "The Influence of the Frontier upon American Life."[46] A generation concerned with the wild-eyed Westerners who had rallied beneath the banner of the Populist Party, and uncertain of itself, as the nation blundered upon the international scene as a major power, was receptive to a theory that made the West understandable and that glorified nationalism and democracy as American virtues.

The results were both good and bad. Turner had not decreed an infallible new formula for the interpretation of the nation's past; he had merely advanced an untested hypothesis for the consideration of his brethren. Unfortunately neither the general public nor his scholarly disciples shared his modesty or respect for the truth. To most of them the frontier theory was Holy Writ, descended from on high. The hypothesis was no hypothesis at all but *the* unassailable key to America's past, capable of unlocking every door and essential to the interpretation of every form of human behavior. As American historians rewrote their lectures to preach that the frontier was the sole molding force shaping the national character, European historians caught the infection. Medievalists, led by the eminent James Westfall Thompson, discovered that "with scarcely more than a change of dates and proper names many of the paragraphs in Professor Turner's essay may be applied to German medieval history."[47] Although a handful of leaders in the profession failed to leap upon the bandwagon (Edward Channing, A. C. McLaughlin, Charles M. Andrews, Charles Beard, and W. A. Dunning remained skeptical) enough did that the American Historical Association, as one critic noted, was converted into "One Big Turner Verein." "I think," Turner later wrote as he looked back upon this acclaim, "that some of my students have apprehended only certain aspects of my work and have not always seen that in *relation*."[48]

Nor were scholars in other fields of learning immune. Political scientists, economists, and geographers began a new search of the past to demonstrate the frontier's influence on constitution making, commercial growth, and the settlement pattern. Students of literature under the inspiration of Norman Foerster poured forth books on *The Literature of the Middle Western Frontier, The Prairie and the Making of Middle America,* and *The Frontier in American Literature.*[49] From the dawn of the century to the end of the 1920s much of the scholarly world worshipped at Turner's shrine and glorified the frontier as a molding force that had reshaped the course of civilization.

Politicians and diplomats found the interpretation useful in their public utterances. Tub-thumpers for greater governmental powers saw the passing of the frontier as a reason to extend controls over the nation's industrial machine. "The end of free lands meant, to an important degree, the end of free movement to new opportunity," declared Philip La Follette in his inaugural address as governor of Wisconsin in 1931, as he pleaded for authority to enlarge the social services of the government.[50] He was echoed in the national arena by Franklin D. Roosevelt who pointed out that there was no longer a "safety valve in the form of a Western prairie to which those thrown out of work by the Eastern Economic Machines can go for a new start."[51] Roosevelt's opponents, not to be outdone, saw in the frontier thesis proof that rugged individualism was the American way of life and should not be discarded.[52] Similarly, imperialists found in the closing of the frontier an argument for overseas expansion, while anti-imperialists answered that this would be fatal to the frontier democracy and individualism on which the United States based its strength.[53] So the arguments raged, and with each, new testimony that the Turner doctrine had become the Holy Word for scholars and politicians alike.

This was unfortunate. Disciples bent on preaching the gospel forgot that their master had made no false claims to the validity of his hypothesis. Had they been less blind to this essential fact, they would have used their time testing aspects of the frontier thesis rather than proclaiming its inviolability.

The day of reckoning found them unprepared to repel the inevitable attack. This began shortly after Turner's death in 1932, for by this time the intellectual climate of the United States was changing under the impact of the Great Depression and the time was ripe for an assault on his theories. An interpretation of the American past that stressed agrarianism rather than industrialism, rugged individualism rather than state planning, and optimistic nationalism rather than political internationalism seemed outmoded in a one-world of machines and cities suddenly beset by a bewildering economic cataclysm. Younger scholars, impatient with what they regarded as Turner's faulty methodology and resentful of an interpretation that they believed stressed a single causal force at a time when multiple causation was the by-word of social scientists, were ready to rebel against over-glorification of the useless agrarian past, ready to demand a reinterpretation in terms of a usable recent past that would help them understand the complexities of an urban culture at a time when civilization seemed out of joint.[54]

~§~§ THE ATTACK took two forms. One group of critics condemned Turner for his *statement* of the thesis, indicting him for creating a Pandora's box of troubles by failing to define the "frontier" exactly, for the haziness of his language, his inability to explain how migration accomplished the changes ascribed to it, his methodology, and his indifference to other forces even more important in shaping the American culture. Another group questioned the hypothesis itself; they charged that the frontier had not fostered democracy, that it had been no spawning bed for nationalism, that it had failed to stimulate social mobility, and that it had never served as a "safety valve" through which displaced Easterners could escape to a new affluence. Later in this book we will examine in detail the attacks on the thesis; let us look now at the assault on Turner's statement of the thesis.[55]

That he twisted the meaning of the word "frontier" to suit a variety of moods is unquestionable. At times the frontier was the edge of the settled territory, the hither edge of free land, the line of settlement; at others it was the "West," or a "form of society" rather than an area, or a "process." This vagueness provided a happy hunting ground for his critics. How, they asked, could a thin line of settlers alter a whole civilization as Turner claimed? How could a handful of illiterate trappers, herdsmen, and small farmers tear down and rebuild a nation's institutions? In their minds the whole hypothesis collapsed because the frontier in Turner's essays wore too many disguises to be recognizable.[56]

He was even more violently condemned for his often contradictory language. How, his attackers asked, could the frontier be responsible for nationalism and sectionalism, individualism and cooperation, materialism and idealism, innovation and conformity, coarseness of character and optimism, equalitarianism and upward social mobility? How could pioneers improve civilization by abandoning civilization?[57] This was no mean trick, they charged. That Turner was guilty of semantic sins is unquestionable. He was by nature a poet, incapable of marring his text with scientific definition, and inclined to be swept along on a tide of metaphors until trapped by his own imagery. Had he been less gifted in the use of language, or the product of an age given to scientific precision, he would have been more clearly understood—and less widely read.[58]

Turner was also accused, and rightly, of failure to explain how migration westward altered people and institutions. Did the mere process of moving affect a change, as he hinted when he spoke of discarding "cultural baggage"? Nonsense, cried the critics. Had that been so, similar transmutations would have occurred among the Norsemen who occupied Iceland or the Chinese who settled in Manchuria. Did the pioneers undergo some magic transformation through contact with raw nature in their new homes? Absurd, said his detractors. To believe this was to assume that a nature-made product was more essential to humans than a man-made product when the opposite was true; frontier resources were nonusable until changed by men trained for generations in Europe's economic traditions. Pioneers made the frontier attractive, not nature's abundance.[59] To believe the opposite, Turner's critics charged, was to court the label of "geographic determinist." It was also to accept such untruths as the idea that the frontier had closed in 1890, when actually improvements in technology and the increasing mobility of twentieth-century man allowed the resources of an ever-expanding series of frontiers to be tapped.[60] The United States, some critics stoutly maintained, faced no "closed-space" future in which governmental largess provided security formerly offered by free land.

If Turner stood indicted for the vagueness of his language and the inexactness of his understanding of the frontier process, he was also branded the victim of faulty methodology. His critics charged that his misuse of statistics obscured the operation of nongeographic forces in stimulating migration westward. They insisted that he based his examples on the Old Northwest, and that his theory collapsed if applied to other sections of the country. In the arid Southwest, they pointed out, cooperative enterprise needed for irrigation projects displaced individualism, law enforcement devices were copied from the East, and frontiersmen showed no tendency to innovate as they applied irrigation techniques handed down unchanged from the Moors. Critics also charged that Turner's "stages" of social evolution—with trapper, herdsman, small farmer, and equipped farmer marching in orderly procession across the continent—not only failed to describe the actual patterns but obscured the contribution of a variety of Westerners (such as land speculators) who played just as essential a role in the conquest of the West.[61]

An even more serious accusation identified Turner as a "mono-causationist" whose blind reliance on the frontier as the *only* causal force shaping American civilization ignored other forces even more important. To think in geographic terms as Turner did, critics insisted, was to conceal the fact that Eastern-created economic forces played a more prominent role in national evolution than western-created agrarian forces. These were ticked off by his critics: capital accumulation, spread of a transportation network, the opening of domestic and foreign markets, the rise of a planter economy, industrialization.[62] Turner, they argued, failed to recognize that the prosperity of the United States could obviously not be traced to the exploitation of a narrow frontier zone by a handful of pioneers; instead it came from the sequential utilization of resources everywhere as technological innovations were applied to the country's wealth.[63] He had been unable to see that urbanization was a major force in American life, even though by 1860 one in every six people lived in a city.[64] He had ignored the obvious fact that class divisions had marred national harmony since the end of the eighteenth century, and that much of the nation's history could be explained as a conflict between capital and labor rather than between West and East.[65]

What, asked the critics, was the result of this sin against history of which Frederick Jackson Turner was guilty? Not only had he ravaged Clio, they answered, but he had endangered the future of the United States. By preaching the uniqueness of America and its institutions, he had blinded a whole generation to the essential unity of the peoples of the western world. He had obscured the fact that the nation's basic institutions and values—the Protestant ethic, democracy, the laissez-faire tradition, industrialization and urbanization—transcended national boundaries and tied Americans to their cousins beyond the seas. He had not only fostered isolationism, but had directed attention to local problems and away from the broader issues that linked the United States with its cultural ancestors in England. Only by abandoning the Turnerian viewpoint could the American people realize their kinship to people everywhere in the emerging "one world" of the twentieth century. Only then could they discover that "the abiding heritage of traditional civilization outweighed, in a relatively brief period, the novelties acquired from Indians and wilderness."[66]

⋐§⋐§ THUS DID Frederick Jackson Turner stand indicted at the bar of historical criticism. Was he guilty? Only one man could have put the case for the defense, and this Turner never bothered to do. He was deeply wounded by the few attacks launched before his death in 1932, and would have been more deeply hurt had he lived to see the assault gather momentum. "I find myself," he wrote a friend, "like a great grandfather in reference to the essay on the frontier, quite ready to see its imperfections myself, but disposed to pick up the cudgels when someone else finds flaws in its features."[67] Yet he never did take up those cudgels, despite the urging of his friends.

The truth of the matter is that Turner hated to write, and hated even more to rerake burned-over coals. His mind was mercurial, capable of flashes of brilliance that could best be recorded in an essay. He was happy when blazing new intellectual trails, developing new hypotheses, constructing new theories to illuminate the past. But to add wearisome details to a study already completed, or to amass evidence to substantiate a thesis already postulated, was something that he could not drive himself to do. His critics were never publicly answered. Yet in letters to friends, and in fragments of unpublished lectures and essays, Turner did marshal evidence that proves him far less culpable than his enemies believed.

That he was a monocausationist, explaining all the American past as a by-product of the frontier, is patently false. Turner might better be glorified as the father of multiple causation as applied to American historical studies; he learned that doctrine at the feet of the eminent geologist Thomas C. Chamberlin, when still a student, and never wavered in paying it his complete respect.[68] "In truth," he told an audience at the height of his career, "there is no single key to American history. In history, as in science, we are learning that a complex result is the outcome of the interplay of many forces. Simple explanations fail to meet the case."[69] Students remembered that the point most stressed in his seminars was that "no single factor is determinative in explaining causes, even proximate causes."[70] His own interest in the total past is attested by the thirty-four file drawers of reading and research notes that he accumulated on every phase of the American history from Columbus to Herbert Hoover. "I sometimes wonder," he confided to Carl Becker in 1926, "if after all I have not been simply, rather blindly, trying to explain America to myself instead of writing history! or writing agriculture, or geography, or diplomacy, or economics, land, transportation, etc., or literature, or religion."[71]

At the very beginning of his career Turner summed up his thought in words that might have been written today: "All kinds of history are essential—history as politics, history as art, history as economics, history as religion—all are truly parts of society's endeavor to understand itself by understanding its past."[72] From this creed he never deviated. Immigration history fascinated him; "one cannot understand 'Anglo-Am[erican] Civilization' apart from the influence of the immigrant stocks," he wrote a friend. One of his last academic acts was to urge several midwestern universities to create chairs in this field.[73] Urban history was equally intriguing; he felt that too little attention had been paid "to the phenomena of great city development and the results and problems in many fields incident thereto," and believed that there would soon be "an urban reinterpretation of our history."[74] Buried among his papers is the outline for an essay on "The Significance of the City in American History" prepared in 1922, and never written. But the history of ideas he felt to be the wave of the future, and a badly needed one. Late in life he confessed that should he ever again be asked to give a general course in American history "I should find some of the best in the literary, religious, and idealistic aspects of it and enjoy them the most too!"[75]

Turner's broad historical interests mirrored his belief that mankind's behavior was explainable only in terms of a complex of forces. He stressed the frontier because some specialization was necessary, even in his generation. "I do not," he wrote a friend in 1925, "think of myself as primarily either a western historian, or a human geographer. I have stressed those two factors, because it seemed to me that they had been neglected."[76] Certainly he had no intention of explaining the past in such simple terms. Only a few months before his death he bemoaned the fact that some people believed incorrectly that he "had made the frontier phenomenon the one key to American history. It *was* a key, and a neglected one."[77] This is a statement with which no modern historian can quarrel.

Nor can those familiar with his published and unpublished works censure him for unscientific methodology. History as a scientific discipline in America was still in its swaddling clothes when he began writing, yet he showed a firm grasp of internal and external criticism and employed techniques that are surprisingly modern. Overstatement, although appearing in his works, is relatively rare; he showed far more caution than most of his contemporaries in generalizing from inadequate factual material. His method, he once explained, was to dig deeply in spots, knowing where to dig and how to test others' diggings, and then to try to envisage the whole historical landscape.[78] He was always careful to sink those holes wisely and often; once, on reading books on the settlement process in Illinois and Missouri, he remarked that "when we get similar studies for all of the Western States we shall better understand the evolution of institutions."[79]

Turner's allegiance to scientific history was made just as apparent by his application of interdisciplinary techniques. Recognizing the complexity of human behavior no less than do modern behavioral scientists, he believed as early as 1901 that "no satisfactory understanding of the evolution of . . . people is possible without calling into cooperation many sciences and methods hitherto little used by the American historian." Few men of his day could speak so firmly for "Geo-history," and "Geo-economics" as he; few believed so devoutly that "all the social sciences were one, and related to physical science."[80] In all disciplines he found the evolutionary process illustrated, and in Turner's stress on social change lies further evidence of the modernity of his views. To him "society is an organism, ever growing." This accounted for his love affair with American history, where "we may trace the evolution of a vast population, almost under our gaze, from a handful of colonists lodged in the wilderness."[81] This capsulizing of the past allowed him to compress a whole evolutionary development into a subject for manageable study. No historian of his day had a more exact impression of his subject.

Finally, Turner was no economic or geographic determinist. Through his lifetime he clung to the belief that human behavior was molded by both environmental and cultural forces. "I think it clear," he maintained, "that those who believe in geographic determinism, go too far."[82] Instead, American history was a complex equation, determining "the interaction of the various migratory stocks . . . adjusting to new social types." These came bearing with them "a variety of institutions, customs, ideals, ethnic spirit" which were to be fused into a new society in the "great geographic melting pot" of the West. The imported ideas and ideals were fully as important as the environment that altered them. "I like to believe," Turner wrote in 1928, "that inherited ideals persist long after the environmental influence has been changed; but the environment does change, and society changes —otherwise no history."[83] If these words can be half believed, his understanding of the evolution of society in new lands differed little from that of today's historian.

THAT TURNER deserved only a few of the shafts launched by his critics seems clear. Equally clear is the fact that the whole conflict over his views that raged during the 1930s and 1940s was partly specious. Attackers and defenders alike squandered their energies on an academic trifle, for the validity of the frontier hypothesis had nothing whatever to do with Turner's *statement* of that hypothesis. If biologists had followed the same path they would still be quarreling over the meaning of semantic mysteries in Darwin's *Origin of Species*. Instead they turned to testing his theory of the evolution of living forms. Turner made an enduring contribution to the understanding of the American past by advancing a working hypothesis. Others should have employed his thesis where it was productive of results and discarded those portions that proved untenable. Only in this way could the hypothesis be actually tested.

Since the 1940s scholars in a variety of disciplines have turned their attention to this challenging task. The chapters that follow will summarize their findings and draw certain conclusions. Did the three-centuries-long process of expansion that peopled the continent endow Americans with traits and institutions distinguishable from those of Europe? If so, how? And to what degree were they altered. These are the questions that will be explored and (hopefully) partially answered in this book.

2

Why and How
Pioneers
Moved Westward

THE PAGES that follow will deal with the American "frontier," not necessarily as Frederick Jackson Turner used the word, but as it would be defined by a social scientist seeking a rational explanation of one aspect of the national past. What does that word mean, and what has it meant to prior generations in the United States and Europe? To use the term with precision means to realize that its denotation has changed radically since the eighteenth century, and that those changes have confused historians.

Traditionally a "frontier" in England was either a remote border-land or a boundary; in 1755 Dr. Samuel Johnson recognized both meanings when in his learned dictionary he referred to "the marshes . . . the utmost verge of any territory," and also to "the border . . . which fronts another country."[1] During the nineteenth century, usage in the United States tended to emphasize the second meaning; to the American of the 1880s a "frontier" was a "line" separating two nations or peoples. Implicit in this meaning was the concept of confrontation,

23

for the frontier was the boundary where advancing settlers confronted hostile Indians. As the century drew to a close this situation changed, and with it the whole concept of the frontier in the popular mind. As Indian resistance vanished, the unsettled West was seen as an attractive borderland, and not a barrier. A dictionary printed between 1889 and 1891 defined the frontier as "that part of a country which forms the border of its settled or uninhabited regions"; another published in 1890 spoke of the "border of the settled or civilized parts of any country; as, the *frontier* of civilization."[2]

The point is that when Turner developed his frontier thesis, the meaning of the word "frontier" was not only vague, but was rapidly changing. Perhaps as a result, he used the term in a variety of ways. In his published essays it appeared as "the hither edge of free land," "the line of most rapid and effective Americanization," "the outskirts of civilization," "the graphic line which records the expanding energies of the people behind it," "a migrating region," "the mere edge of settlement," "the belt of territory occupied" by frontier types, and "a form of society, rather than an area."[3] Turner was more lucid in the letters to friends written during his latest years. "I have," he confessed in 1926, "never published an adequate discussion of this phase [a definition] of the 'frontier,' with the result that some readers of my first essay seem to think that I imagined all that is significant in American life as having been born on the extreme edge of things." Nothing, he went on, could be further from the case, His concern was with "the *movement of population into unsettled geographic provinces,* thus creating a dynamic force in American History and influencing the East by the economic, political, and social development of these new lands."[4]

Neither Turner's later speculations nor those of his disciples produced a definition of the term that would stand the rigorous scrutiny of modern scholarship. All were deficient in at least three respects. First they suggested a continuous line advancing systematically across the map; actually the frontier seldom moved in orderly fashion but twisted awkwardly, leaving islands of wilderness amidst settlements or thrusting peninsulas of occupation into unsettled regions.[5] Secondly, they confused the frontier as a geographic region, and as a process through which a primitive society was transformed into a complex social order. Finally, all of the definitions implied a relatively narrow frontier "line" or "zone"; actually pioneer conditions influenced a relatively wide band of countryside peopled by various exploiters and sufficiently enduring to make its influence felt over an extended time period. Keeping these defects in mind, let us try to construct two definitions of the frontier—one as *place* and the other as *process*—that will be both exact and meaningful.

A definition of the frontier as *place* must not only recognize the altered man-land ratio, but must reveal a relativistic concept; Missouri farmers in the 1840s might feel overcrowded even though an Easterner would consider the land thinly occupied. It must also show that the frontier was an area of unusually abundant natural resources even in the eyes of newcomers who had been accustomed to varying degrees of abundance in the "Easts" they had left behind. Finally, it must make clear that these resources were exploitable by the small-propertied newcomer, at least in their primary form. Modern "frontiers" of technology or space, although benefiting society, do not provide individuals with a chance to begin over again as did the cheap lands of the West in the eighteenth and nineteenth centuries. The frontier as place, then, may be defined as *a geographic region adjacent to the unsettled portions of the continent in which a low man-land ratio and unusually abundant, unexploited, natural resources provide an exceptional opportunity for social and economic betterment to the small-propertied individual.*

A definition of the frontier as *process* must also be based on certain assumptions. It must assume that men and their institutions were in some manner altered by moving to the unique environment of the geographic frontier, but it must recognize that these alterations were slight and that they varied with the newcomers; men of differing traditions and culture responded in wholly different ways to pioneer conditions. Finally, any definition must reveal the influence of the "Easts" bordering the frontier areas, for both the migrations westward and the reaction of the pioneers to their new environment were governed in part by continuing relationships with the social orders adjacent to their settlements. With these requirements in mind, let us define the frontier process as: *the process through which the socioeconomic-political experiences and standards of individuals were altered by an environment where a low man-land ratio and the presence of untapped natural resources provided an unusual opportunity for individual self-advancement.* These are the definitions that will be used when the frontier, as place or process, is mentioned in this book.[6]

ⴰ§ⴰ§ ADEQUATE THOUGH these definitions may be, neither the frontier's influence nor the impact of pioneering on individuals can be comprehended without exploring the process of migration that peopled the West. Frontiering was selective, attracting some and repelling others. If we realize this, and isolate certain types who consistently occupied the successive frontiers, we can better understand the peopling of the continent.

Demographers, studying modern migrations, have determined that men respond to a complex of factors that repel them from their old homes or attract them to their new, with transportation facilities playing a secondary role in determining the direction of movement. Psychologists have grouped these factors under two general headings: "deficiency motivation," and "abundancy motivation." Deficiency motivation is a response to man's basic urge for survival and security; some men move to escape dangers, or anxieties, or discomforts. Abundancy motivation is a desire to find new pleasures, gratifications, experiences, and achievements; a migrant with such a motivation is in quest of adventure or a better life or a richer society. Both "deficiency" and "abundancy" motivation are combined within every person who migrates, with the relative weight of the two varying greatly from individual to individual. This was the case with the pioneers who peopled America's frontiers. They differed from their stay-at-home neighbors in an exaggerated need for security or in an unusual urge for self-betterment.[7]

Those who craved security and acceptance were driven westward by a number of expelling forces: lack of economic success, changing means of making a living in the homeland, catastrophes such as droughts or floods, overcrowding, an uncongenial social or political atmosphere, and just plain dislike of their neighbors. Those with an unusual "abundancy motivation" were attracted to the frontiers by the hope of economic and social advancement, the quest for health, a desire for change, a thirst for adventure, and the mystical lure of the unknown, the call of the primitive, the dominance of the explorer impulse. These were the men "with the West in their eyes" who were impelled to move, they knew not why. Curiosity and the urge to adventure are common in all higher organisms, from rats who will endure a severe shock to investigate a new maze to today's spacemen, but they are by no means universal; psychological tests reveal least curiosity among the underprivileged who are so preoccupied with survival that they have no time for anything else. The frontier attracted the adventuresome and the ambitious, leaving others behind.

If we may believe the pioneers themselves, as they recorded their thoughts in letters or diaries, the principal expelling forces driving men westward were overcrowding and the urge to escape an uncongenial environment. Timothy Dwight noted in the eighteenth century that New Englanders, "having large families and small farms, are induced, for the sake of settling their children comfortably, to seek for new and cheaper lands";[8] generations later this same explanation was even more commonplace, for the urge to provide for children remained constant and powerful. Others moved to escape what William Ellery Channing called "the yoke of opinion" as they found their political views unpopular; one old man leaving Pennsylvania in 1833 told a traveler that his wife "took such a horror of the little bit of mobbing" he had suffered in a tavern argument that she had made him head for the West.[9] Still others fled the loneliness of homes when children had departed, or left because of plain ordinary cussedness. "I'm going to the mines," wrote one would-be miner in 1849, "so I can be independent of the darned fools that feel themselves above me back home because I'm a poor cuss—damn their stinking hides."[10]

The most compelling attraction of the frontier was the hope of economic betterment, the feeling that "I ought to do better." This was an uncontrollable passion with the true frontiersmen. Moses Austin, later to gain fame as a Texas pioneer, observed the hordes streaming westward in 1796 and recorded: "Can any thing be more Absurd than the Conduct of man, here is hundreds Travelling hundreds of Miles, they Know not for what Nor Whither, except its to Kentucky, passing land almost as good and easy obtain'd."[11] One immigrant touched on the frontier spirit when he noted the rich fields along the way and wrote that "this is a land of plenty, but we are proceeding to a land of abundance."[12] Some wanted better land, others larger farms, others the speculative profits that would come when surplus acres were sold, but most sought wealth that their old homes had denied them. Wrote Henry Schoolcraft in the early nineteenth century:

> One object impels them, one passion inspires—
> The rage for improvement, for wealth the desires;
> And alike in all countries, conditions, and states
> This passion is cherished, prevails and inflates.[13]

The West to the pioneer was wealth and affluence.

But the West was more. There better health could be found in nature's fresh air.[14] There adventure beckoned; one English visitor who talked with dozens of pioneers believed them governed by the same impulses that drove men into war in the age of chivalry. In the newer settlements, some believed, could be found "a theatre where small talents and learning may figure to better advantage."[15] But above all, the frontier was a land of rebirth, of beginning again, of exuberant hope. There they could find, Timothy Flint realized, "in a new country, and in new views and combinations of things, something that we crave but have not." Idealism drove the pioneers onward no less than the hope of material gain; they were dreamers who found in westering a road to the foot of the rainbow. Even Henry David Thoreau, protected from the buffetings of opinion in placid Concord, found that in his daily walks he invariably turned southwest or west; "Eastward I go only by force; but westward I go free."[16] That the motives of the pioneers were often contradictory or ambivalent is not surprising; human nature is seldom logical.

Whether men went west in search of adventure or wealth, they were driven by impulses that failed to motivate their neighbors who stayed behind. In every pioneer there was a touch of the gambler. Those who did not respond to the lure of the frontier were the contented, the cautious, and the secure. Wealth and poverty were not the deciding factors; the cost of migrating kept the very poor at home, while many with fortunes responded to the lure of the world of the setting sun.[17] Whatever their status in life, they were a breed different from their fellows who stayed behind. Lands peopled by this selective process would develop societies somewhat altered from those of the Easts from which the migrants came.

Differences between the older and newer social orders were accentuated by the groupings of population that took place in the successive Wests. Pioneers normally chose to settle where they believed they could continue their traditional ways of life and thought without serious disruption, but where their own status in the social group would be elevated. Thus a migrating slaveholder would not only move to a region where he could keep his slaves but where the climate of opinion would be congenial to his own thoughts on servitude. He would construct for himself an imaged situation where his value expectations would be fulfilled. If he found that the spot lived up to this image he remained, and immediately began recruiting others who shared his judgments and values. Through letters home, by word of mouth, in the columns of local newspapers, he projected the image that he had formed of his new home to persons of similar predilections. This image would attract them as it had him. This process tended to form in the West communities of persons having common interests and values, distinguished from persons in other communities where the same process had been attracting different types.[18] "The migrations of men," wrote an eighteenth-century emigrant as he watched the wagon trains roll westward, "are like the movements of a flock of sheep, where one goes the flock follows, without knowing why."[19] These groupings served to accentuate characteristics that had been found in the Easts, but that in isolation tended to grow more dominant.

ᘏᔓᘏᔓ WE HAVE DISCUSSED why pioneers move westward and how they grouped themselves when they arrived, seeking in both instances to emphasize the impact of these processes on the new social orders emerging along the frontiers. One question remains before we are through with migration. When did movements of population take place? Through the three centuries required to settle the continent, the westward moving tide ebbed and flowed constantly. At times a "Kentucky fever" or an "Illinois fever" or a "Dakota boom" would crowd the trails with eager home seekers. At others the flow would trickle to a halt. What accounted for these fluctuations? What light do they shed on the character of the pioneers?

Economic statisticians have summoned columns of figures to prove a rather obvious point: pioneers moved westward when times were good and did not when times were bad. They have established a direct relationship between land sales in the West and commodity prices in England and on the Continent; when prices soared settlers or speculators bought land heavily. Thus between 1815 and 1820 booming demands for cotton from British textile mills stimulated expansion in the Southwest where the commodity could be grown, and in the old Northwest where corn and wheat and hogs could be produced to feed plantation hands. In 1820 cotton prices slumped, and with them the demand for southern lands, but wheat prices continued high until 1827 and land sales remained brisk in the Northwest until that time.[20] Prosperity stimulated migration; depressions halted the westward-flowing stream.

This simple fact contradicts one of the basic assumptions in the folklore of American expansion. From the dawn-days of the Republic, and even before, the frontier was believed to be a "safety valve" through which the dispossessed and unfortunate could escape the buffetings of economic storms. In bad times, so the theory held, the unemployed had only to pack their bags, move westward where cheap lands could be purchased, and start farms of their own. This constant exodus drained excess workers from the Eastern labor market, especially when that market was most overcrowded, forcing wages up as employers bid for the services of those remaining, and preventing the growth of a militant labor class in the United States.

Belief in a frontier safety valve originated in the seventeenth century, and persisted until well into the twentieth. As early as 1634 Governor John Winthrop of the Massachusetts Bay colony favored limiting the land holdings of poorer colonists to prevent "the neglect of the trades" by those who found independent farming more satisfactory than artisanship. His views were echoed by Benjamin Franklin, who believed that labor would never be cheap in America where "no Man continues long a Labourer for others, but gets a Plantation of his own," and by George Washington, who viewed the Ohio Valley as a "Land of Promise" where anyone "who is heavy laden and wants land to cultivate" could find new prosperity. Thomas Jefferson and Alexander Hamilton, although at swords' points on most issues, agreed that as long as vacant lands availed class feeling would be minimal in the United States because, in Jefferson's words, "whenever it shall be attempted by the other classes to reduce them to a minimum of subsistence, they will quit their trades and go to labouring the earth."[21]

During the nineteenth century the safety-valve concept was so firmly fastened in the public mind, at home and abroad, that it became a part of the American creed. Englishmen built their colonization schemes on the belief that the poor could always escape to the frontiers; Karl Marx based aspects of his teachings on this seemingly indisputable fact. Thomas Carlyle saw the cheap lands of the United States as "verily the Door of Hope to a distracted Europe; which otherwise I should see crumbling down into the blackness of darkness."[22] His words were echoed in Germany by Wilhelm Friedrich Hegel, who wrote in his famous essay on the philosophy of history that through repeated migrations westward, "the chief source of discontent is removed, and the continuation of the existing social condition is guaranteed."[23] Travelers by the score filled their accounts of life in the United States with hymns of praise for a frontier that stabilized society by equalizing economic opportunity as nowhere else in the world.[24]

Americans subscribed to these sentiments with no less enthusiasm than Europeans. Easterners took pious solace in the belief that the West was, as Edward Everett put it, "the safety-valve of states," and that workers who disliked low wages or miserable factory conditions could escape if they wished. Westerners were just as convinced; "no poor man in the Eastern states," wrote an Illinois editor in 1832, "who has feet and legs, and can use them has any excuse for remaining poor where he is."[25] Horace Greeley voiced his famous "Go West, young man, go forth into the Country" because he believed unquestioningly that the drainage of excess laborers would improve the lot of those left behind.[26] His philosophy underlay the efforts of land reformers who during the 1850s agitated for a homestead act that would grant free plots to all actual settlers. "My point," one advocate of that measure told his Congressional colleagues, "is that this 'homestead bill' will take labor from the manufacturing states to the land states—from the manufactures of the East to the farms of the West—and thereby increase the cost of labor."[27] Post-Civil War industrialization only strengthened faith in the operation of a safety valve, as sharpening class antagonisms heightened fears that the end of the era of free lands would usher in a period of class warfare.[28] By the 1890s this was the universal belief of the American people, often popularly expressed, and never questioned.

Not surprisingly, in view of this climate of opinion, Frederick Jackson Turner incorporated the safety-valve concept into his frontier hypothesis, but with a lack of emphasis that suggested his own doubts of its validity. In early writings he was inclined to follow the traditional interpretation, observing that whenever capital tended to press upon labor or impede political freedom "there was this gate of escape to the free conditions of the frontier," and that "the freedom and abundance of land in the Great Valley opened a refuge to the oppressed of all regions."[29] In his lectures of that era, too, he referred to the West as "always open as a gate of escape to the discontented and unprosperous in the older areas."[30] During his later years he apparently became skeptical of the doctrine's validity, as more extended research convinced him that a safety valve never operated exactly as its proponents claimed.[31] Until the coming of the transcontinental railroads, he wrote in his last book, "the opportunity of direct access to cheap Western lands was not open to the poorer people of the Northeastern states and of Europe."[32] Few scholars of his generation, however, exhibited such restraint. To them, as to Americans in general, the frontier was a safety valve operating successfully to keep the national economy on an even keel, elevate wages, and stifle class discontent.[33]

If we are to judge the validity of their conclusion, we must recognize that no less than four types of "safety valves" have been said to operate in the United States. One was a "direct" safety valve of the sort popularized by Horace Greeley who believed that Eastern workers could escape to the West's cheap lands in time of depression. A second was "indirect"; Eastern farmers dislodged by competition with Western farmers went west themselves, rather than competing with Eastern workers for factory jobs. A third was a "resources" safety valve through which the successive development of the rich reservoir of natural resources kept wages high and prevented the growth of unrest or radical thought among laborers. Finally, a "socio-psychological" safety valve has been recognized; as long as workers *believed* that the frontier offered a haven from economic storms, they were less inclined to develop class consciousness and proletarian philosophy.[34] Did one or all of these safety valves operate during America's frontier era? Economists and historians have weighed this question carefully since the 1930s, and have reached conclusions that Horace Greeley would find bewildering but comforting.

One is that a "direct" safety valve—draining Eastern wage earners directly to frontier farms in periods of depression—never functioned during the nineteenth century. This does *not* mean that workers from seaboard cities never moved west; many migrated from Eastern cities to Western towns and villages where they could find jobs suitable to their training, and at higher wages than they had earned at home. Travelers along the western roads often noted "a company of tinners" or other craftsmen bound for the frontier.[35] It *does* mean that Eastern wage earners almost never moved directly to the cheap lands of the West, for farming was a profession requiring skills, training, and capital largely unavailable to the urban workman; even Horace Greeley admitted that "no man born and reared in the city can remove to a farm at thirty or forty years of age and become immediately an efficient, thrifty, successful farmer."[36] Even those workers with an urge to become pioneer farmers were prohibited from making the transition by the cost of moving and placing land under cultivation. In the middle nineteenth century, transportation westward to the Illinois frontier from New York by coach or canal boat approximated $30 a person, even the cheapest government land sold for $1.25 an acre, and the charges for needed farm equipment, livestock, fencing, and housing were seldom less than $500. The most frugal manager required some $1,500 to bring a 40-acre farm into production, a sum far beyond the reach of Eastern workers whose wages ranged between $1.00 and $2.00 a day.[37] Nor were these high costs unknown to Easterners; they were prominently mentioned in many guidebooks used by immigrants to the West.[38]

Further evidence that workers displaced by the East's industrial storms seldom fled toward the West's cheap lands—either as independent farmers or as hired farm laborers—is provided by migration statistics. These reveal that throughout the nineteenth century the westward-moving population tide swelled during good times and diminished in depression periods when the safety valve should have been operating. This is not surprising; spiraling prices in the boom eras preceding panics usually wiped out such savings as workers had accumulated, depriving them of the resources needed to move. Fragmentary data show that train travel westward in the 1850s declined by one half in depression years, that labor turnover in Eastern factories multiplied in periods of prosperity and declined during hard times, and that Western communities increased their population in almost direct proportion to the nation's well-being. Thus Michigan's settlers doubled in the boom years between 1834 and 1837, but increased only 22 percent in the three years of the panic that followed.[39] No rush of artisans to the West occurred in bad times. Nor did philanthropic societies formed to finance the movement of workers to the frontier during depressions play a significant role; while a number operated during the 1830s and 1850s, they apparently transported only about 500 Easterners to the West each year.[40] Even those who moved did not always remain. A random sample of migration from New England and New York towns shows that seven of every ten who tried the West returned within a few years.[41]

There seems little doubt that very few actual wage earners left Eastern cities to become frontier farmers; the rural frontier was settled largely by experienced farmers or younger sons of farmers, most of them from adjacent or nearby areas. After 1865 their numbers were supplemented by farmer-immigrants who came directly from abroad. In thirty of the thirty-four states, the superintendent of the census noted in 1860, *"native emigrants have chiefly preferred to locate in a State immediately adjacent to that of their birth."*[42] The frontier fattened on itself, rather than on an influx of depression-lashed factory workers from the East. A "direct" safety valve in the sense understood by the nineteenth century never operated.

The answer to the question of whether an "indirect" safety valve operated to drain westward Eastern farmers who might otherwise have entered factories as competitors for jobs is less clear. Before the Civil War many farmers from the Northeastern states did move westward to occupy much of the eastern half of the Mississippi Valley, for expelling forces in the seaboard states sparked a migration not entirely typical of the usual settlement pattern. Responsible was the completion of the Erie Canal in 1825 and the construction of the network of branch waterways that brought the Great Lakes and Ohio River within commercial reach of New York and Philadelphia. Farmers in the Northeast found that the products of their worn soils could not compete in Eastern markets with produce grown on the virgin lands of the Old Northwest. Thousands upon thousands of them abandoned their exhausted fields and joined the exodus westward, leaping across the adjacent occupied areas of New York and Pennsylvania to settle in Ohio, Indiana, Illinois, Michigan, Wisconsin, and eventually Iowa. Had no such outlet existed, many would have sought factory employment in the Northeast, competing for jobs and depressing wages. During this period an "indirect" safety valve did operate.

After the Civil War the question becomes more confused; economists have variously employed statistical evidence to "prove" that the frontier both was and was not an outlet for surplus Eastern laborers. On the one hand some argue that the total immigration from East to West between 1860 and 1900 was insufficient to alter the labor market appreciably. During those years, say the anti-safety-valvers, the nineteen million farmers in the United States should have increased to forty-six million if the normal growth rate had been projected; instead the total farm population numbered only twenty-eight million in 1900. This proves, they maintain, that nearly twenty farmers moved to towns or cities for every one industrial worker who moved to the land; the city served as a safety valve for rural discontent rather than the opposite.[43] Using somewhat different statistics, the pro-safety-valvers insist that if twenty million discontented farmers left the rural areas, then over forty million persons must have taken their place, for the total population of this sector increased from twenty-five million in 1860 to nearly forty-six million in 1900. This number was sufficient to affect the labor market and create an actual safety-valve situation.[44] The frontier even after 1860, they argue, served as an "indirect" safety valve, even though not as a "direct" safety valve.

All of this speculation, figure juggling, and manipulation of fragments of evidence fails to come to grips with the basic problem of who went west and how the national economy was altered as a result. The actual importance of the frontier as a safety valve can be understood only if *all* aspects of the nation's economy are surveyed, not simply this or that segment of the population. If this is done, the concept of the frontier as a "resources" safety valve and a "socio-psychological" safety valve is endowed with new significance.

Preliminary to exploring this theme, certain stipulations must be made. First, what the Eastern wage earner did when he reached the West has nothing to do with proving or disproving the thesis; what is important is that his departure from the East changed the labor market there, whether he continued as a wage earner in a frontier town or became a farmer or farm laborer. We know that mechanics and craftsmen did move, for Western communities were furnished with millers, blacksmiths, carpenters, and dozens of other skilled workmen. We know also that by moving these workers increased their income relative to what it would have been in the East, and that a higher national wage level was the result. Second, the fact that workers were not drained westward during economic depressions does not invalidate the safety-valve thesis; solely important is the fact that they moved, whether in good or bad times, and thus lessened pressure on the Eastern wage scale. Third, that strikes and labor unrest did exist in the East during the 1870s and 1880s is no proof that a safety valve was not operating, for this discontent must be weighed relative to the situation in other countries with no frontier. Labor was not sublimely happy anywhere, but it was less discontented in the United States than in European countries.[45]

Finally, we must recognize that even if in the post-Civil War era more farmers went to the city than city dwellers to farms, and even if immigrants from abroad more than replaced farmers and workers who migrated westward during boom periods from the East, the operations of the safety valve did not cease as they would have if a static economy had existed in both East and West. Instead the agricultural sector was growing in the West and the industrial in the

East, so that newcomers entering either labor market were not victims of unemployment. Jobs were continually multiplying, and a key question is: Did they multiply as rapidly in both sectors as the newcomers came in, and if so was this the result—direct or indirect—of the expansion of the economy westward? Simply to look at the supply side of the market is not enough; the elasticity of the *demand* for labor as well as the supply must be evaluated. If both demand and supply showed dynamic upward shifts, and if the frontier accounted for these advances, the market position of the workers was more favorable than it would have been, and the safety valve was operating.[46]

By viewing the frontier's economic impact on workers in this light, two things become apparent. One is that any deflection of laborers to the West—whether wage earners, farmers, farm laborers, tenants, or craftsmen—would relieve pressure in the East and have a buoyant effect on wages. To say that the migration of wage earners alone would have such an impact is to obscure the true issue. All classes, both native-born and foreign, migrated to the frontier during eras of prosperity. Whatever their status in the East's economy, their departure was felt, for any movement from a relatively inelastic labor market—even of a half-dozen people—would have a slight effect on wages. To borrow the complex terminology of wage theory, "any given percentage decrease in the labor supply will exert an upward pressure on wage rates in inverse proportion to the absolute magnitude of the elasticity of the demand for labor." The frontier accentuated that upward pressure by making Westerners out of immigrants who might have become Easterners, Western farmers out of Eastern farmers, and Western wage earners out of Eastern wage earners.[47]

A second, and no less important, conclusion can be drawn from the concept of the frontier as a region whose full economic potential was not developed at once, but over the course of a number of years. We must think of the successive Wests as regions of unexploited natural resources that could be exploited sequentially; "slab" after "slab" was peeled away as the application of technological skills made ever more intensive utilization possible. In the early stages of the development of each new agricultural frontier, farmers and younger sons of farmers from adjacent Easts were lured by the promise of exceptional yields, deflecting them from factory jobs that were opening to them as the primitive industrialization of the region immediately behind the frontier went on. This deflection prevented a depressing effect on the wage level in the successive Easts. This situation can be contrasted with that in many underdeveloped countries of the twentieth century, where the centuries-long mining of the soil has reduced the marginal production of labor in agriculture to near zero, releasing farm workers to industry at subsistence wages. The frontier prohibited such a situation in the United States of the nineteenth century. At times, when industrial labor was producing more efficiently than farm labor, industry would attract workers from the agricultural sector, as it did in the late nineteenth century. But even then it was forced to pay a higher price than would have been the case had not agricultural expansion decreased the elasticity of the labor supply.[48]

While agriculture continued to contract the labor market available to Eastern employers, the subsequent economic development of successive Wests still further restricted the free market in workers. On each new frontier "slabs" of resources—drawn from the soil, vegetation, and subsurface deposits—were successively utilized as the region "grew into" the economy. This process of "sequential growth" had an extremely favorable effect on the increase of employment and per capita income, for the addition of new resources to those being exploited inevitably raises the marginal product of both capital and labor. In a near full-employment economy such as existed in the United States save during depression periods, the result was not only the bidding up of wages but the bidding down of consumer goods, to produce the highest level of real per capita income in the world of that day. The American worker, thanks to the sequential development of "slabs" of frontier resources, came nearer to realizing the standard of living to which he aspired than his fellow workers in Europe. He may have been discontented, but his discontent was less than in less-favored countries. The operation of the "resources" safety valve saw to that.[49]

Discontent was further lessened by the continued operation during the nineteenth century of a "socio-psychological" safety valve. Even those American workers who would never be able to escape to the frontier were willing to endure their plight because they *believed* that one day they would. This belief rested on some foundation, for the sequential development of successive Wests created an opportunity for upward social mobility unparalleled in other nations. Men literally "grew up with the country" as the enterprising became merchants or lawyers with all the status that went with such positions, the less fortunate enjoyed greater affluence as their lands increased in value, and the least fortunate were pushed upward on the social scale by the continued influx of newcomers even less fortunate than themselves. The fluid society of Western America bred an unquenchable hope and a faith in the rags-to-riches formula that permeated all the land. It also convinced even the most oppressed Eastern workers that their turn on the economic escalator would soon come, for in the newer Wests the traditional symbols of wealth and status were more freely distributed than in conventional societies. None among these ranked higher than ownership of private property, and this the frontier brought within the reach of the common folk. To a laborer who believed that he would someday possess land, the social system seemed worth preserving; why attack capitalism when he was destined to become a capitalist himself. Unionism and labor unrest were both retarded by the operation of this "socio-psychological" safety valve.[50]

In three ways, then, the frontier did operate as a safety valve during the nineteenth century, although its effect gradually diminished as distances to the new settlements multiplied and the dream of rags to riches faded for the Eastern laborer. That it was ever during the nineteenth century a "direct" outlet for displaced wage earners is untrue, just as it is untrue that depressions drove workers from factories to Western farms. But the frontier did convert Eastern farmers into Western farmers and Eastern city workers into Western town workers, removing both from the Eastern job market, decreasing the flexibility of the labor supply, and altering the wage structure upward. The frontier did provide jobs through the sequential development of its natural resources as the marginal product of labor was forced upward and the living standard improved. The frontier did offer solace to the oppressed by conjuring visions of limitless opportunity amidst the virgin wealth of the West, and even though few found the pot of gold, the faith that it could be found persisted. Not every gambler must win to keep the faith of gamblers alive. As an "indirect" safety valve, a "resources" safety valve, and a "socio-psychological" safety valve, the frontier played a role in shaping both the economy and the social order of the United States.

So believed the thousands and hundreds of thousands who flocked to the frontiers. They came from farm rather than factory; the majority were males below the national average in age but with a sprinkling of oldsters, and all were infected with restlessness and ambition.[51] As they moved they followed a pattern that was roughly the same in all

Wests, but varied so widely that generalizations about the settlement process are unreliable.

Contemporaries believed that they understood the pattern perfectly. Thomas Jefferson wrote in 1824 that a "philosophical observer" traveling from West to East would meet "the gradual shades of an improving man" until he found the highest type in the Atlantic seaboard towns.[52] Others designated the types to be encountered—fur trapper, pioneer farmer, equipped farmer, town dweller—all following pursuits that gradually conquered the wilderness; here, they fondly believed, was "the machinery of *world making* at work . . . , the progress of society going on under your eyes.[53]

Frederick Jackson Turner accepted their beliefs unquestioningly when he penned his essay on the frontier, for one of his most respected teachers, Richard T. Ely, made this evolutionary progression the theme of his work on political economy. All mankind, Ely taught, evolved social institutions through successive stages: hunting and fishing, pastoral, agricultural, trades, and industrial.[54] Little wonder that Turner could write in 1893: "Stand at Cumberland Gap and watch the procession of civilization, marching single file—the buffalo following the trail to the salt springs, the Indian, the fur-trader and hunter, the cattle-raiser, the pioneer farmer—and the frontier has passed by. Stand at South Pass in the Rockies a century later and see the same procession with wider intervals between."[55]

Actually man does not behave in such an orderly way. Frontiersmen did not move in neatly arranged columns, each caring for its own task in advancing civilization. Instead they scattered in all directions and mixed so completely that fur trappers and town planters sometimes operated side by side. Nor could the "frontier types" be so exactly designated, for the pioneering process required a complex variety of skills that defied any simple definition. The West was won not only by hunters and herdsmen and farmers, but by miners, explorers, soldiers, lumbermen, land speculators, missionaries, road and railroad builders, merchants, flour millers, blacksmiths, distillers, printers, lawyers, and an uncountable host of others. All played their parts, sometimes in several roles, and all showed little respect for laws of social evolution as they sought opportunity without paying heed to their proper roles in the emergence of civilization. Yet certain stages in the advance of settlement can be identified.

Usually the first newcomers on a previously undeveloped frontier were those who came to *use* rather than *subdue:* fur trappers, explorers, missionaries, and sometimes herdsmen. Their pursuits depended on maintaining wilderness conditions, for the arrival of permanent settlers would drive out the fur-bearing animals, scatter the Indians whose souls the missionaries sought to save, and break up the open grasslands needed by cattlemen and sheep drovers. So these pioneers were driven relentlessly westward, to make the first reluctant assault on nature and to pave the way for those who were soon to come.

This they did, from the Atlantic to the Pacific. Fur trappers from Plymouth and Boston blazed the trails into the Connecticut River Valley during the early seventeenth century, while their counterparts to the south were leading the way into the unknown Piedmont behind Virginia's fall line. Hunters discovered the passes through the Appalachians and advertised the riches of Kentucky's bluegrass country. Caravans of pack horses carried the goods of Pennsylvania traders into the Ohio Valley as the vanguards of the assault on French ownership of that region. Beyond the Mississippi the rugged mountain men investigated every nook and cranny of the Far West in their search for beaver pelts. Wherever they went, fur trappers destroyed Indian self-sufficiency, spied out the routes of travel, and publicized the riches that awaited later comers. Where conditions were ripe, miners also leaped far ahead of the frontier of settlement, to build the shanty town camps that served as lodestones to farmers and suppliers eager to capitalize on the abundant wealth that lined prospectors' pockets.

Missionaries were seldom far behind. From the days when John Eliot carried the Gospel to the red men who fringed the Massachusetts Bay settlements, they moved along the most advanced frontiers in their search for souls. They, too, advertised the West and pointed out its most attractive features; the Methodist exhorters who brought the white man's Book of Heaven to the Oregon country played an essential role in peopling that land. Soldiers sometimes accompanied the missionaries and regularly appeared on remote frontiers; the "warlike Christian men" recruited by Virginia to defend its borders in 1701 were the direct ancestors of the dragoons whose Colts and Winchesters subdued the Sioux of the Great Plains a century and a half later. Herdsmen were similarly omnipresent in the successive Wests; Boston had its "cattle frontier" along the Charles River in the 1630s, and long before the Revolution, travelers noted ranchers along the Virginia borderlands who "go in ganges . . . which move (like unto the ancient patriarchs or the modern Bodewins in Arabia) from forest to forest in a measure as the grass wears out or the planters approach them." From those days until the triumph of the cattle kingdom on the Great Plains herdsmen roamed ahead of the line of settlements, unwittingly leading on the farmers who would drive them from their lands.

These farmers made no compromise with nature; their livelihood depended on clearing the forests or breaking the prairie sod, not on preserving the wilderness. They came to *subdue*, not to preserve. Yet even along the farming frontiers this process was relatively slow, for the three types of farmers distinguishable in the pioneering process enjoyed varying degrees of success. On the outer fringe of the agricultural zone could normally be found the "squatters" or "backwoodsmen" or "hunters" as they were variously known to contemporaries. Behind them lived the "small-propertied farmers" with little capital but an ambition to stay and grow up with the country. The third group comprised the "propertied farmers" who completed the frontiering process. These seldom followed each other in orderly sequence; squatters lived side by side with propertied farmers on occasion, and on others small-propertied farmers led the advance into virgin regions. Yet visitors to the eighteenth- and nineteenth-century frontiers consistently noticed these three agricultural types.[56]

The backwoodsmen fascinated travelers from abroad who lavished on them their best descriptive efforts. Some were psychological or social misfits of the sort inhabiting the urban jungles of today; most were poverty-stricken, perennially restless, drifters by inclination, and hopelessly sunk in indolence. They sought the outer fringes of the settlements partly to escape the company of their fellows whose superiority accentuated their own sense of inadequacy, partly because there nature's abundance allowed them to live with a minimum of effort. Few owned land and fewer still made an honest effort to bring that land into production; they made a pretense of planting crops but lived largely by hunting as they lazed away their days dreaming of the later comer who would buy their "improvements." "The great abundance of wild game allures them to the forest," wrote a traveler, "and from it they obtain the greater part of their miserable subsistence. In consequence of this, they neglect the cultivation of their lands; their buildings go to decay, their fences generally made of brush, are levelled to the earth by the passing wind, and are never rebuilt unless imperious necessity requires it."[57]

One distinguishing mark of the backwoodsmen was their indolence; they were, Timothy Dwight observed, "too idle, too talkative, too passionate, too prodigal, and too shiftless to acquire either property or character." This was partly a product of nature's abundance, which made subsistence possible with scarcely an effort, partly a result of bodies starved for healthful foods and vitamins. Squatters in the forested East lived in the shade until they became wan and pale "like vegetables that grow in a vault, pining for light."[58] Work was studiously avoided. Travelers noted that backwoodsmen usually lived near streams to avoid drawing water from a well, let their crops rot in the field because they were too shiftless to harvest, and preferred to hover over dying embers rather than gather more wood.[59] Hard work, usually noted by both contemporary travelers and late historians as a frontier trait, was no besetting sin of these frontiersmen.

Restlessness characterized them no less than indolence. Moving on was a habit with the backwoodsmen. Usually they migrated eight or ten times during their adult years, vainly seeking the prosperity that they were predestined never to achieve. "These people," observed a traveler, "retire, with the wolves, from the regular colonists, keeping always to the outside of the civilized settlements." Often a backwoodsman would resume his wanderings even when he had no place to go, for they shrank from the signs of civilization and were, as one put it who knew them well, "never satisfied if there is any white man between them and sundown."[60] Occasionally a squatter conquered his impulses and remained to grow up with the country, but those who did so were few. Most moved, pursued by the neighbors whom he abhorred, through the forested Wests east of the Mississippi, across the prairies of the Great Valley, out onto the plains. Horace Greeley found them squatting in isolated desolation along the stagecoach routes, living in hovels that would make fair hog pens, waiting for someone to buy out their "claims" so that they could drift onward again.[61] Only the closing of the frontier ended their fruitless quest for the undefinable "something" that they could never find and drove them to the marginal farm lands and skid rows that they frequent today.

Both the laziness of the backwoodsmen and their urge to move marked them as victims of what modern sociologists call "anomie." This is a state of mind in which the individual's sense of social cohesion is weakened or broken, and arises when he leaves a familiar environment with a corresponding disruption of connections, social status, and economic security. Those afflicted feel rejected and are burdened by a crushing sense of defeat and injustice. Their urge is to

rebel against society, by moving away from their fellows, and by re-
fusing to bear their proper burdens. Thus laziness is a symptom of
anomie no less than mobility.[62] The backwoodsmen, oppressed by a
sense of hopeless displacement and rejection, rebelled against the
strange tasks that confronted them on the frontier, and developed hos-
tilities that were characterized by indolence and aggression. Travelers
noticed that they were often arrogant and abusive, demanding to be
treated as kings rather than as outcasts. "These much-isolated people,"
wrote one, "look upon themselves as Nature's aristocracy."[63]

To the uninitiated, the small-propertied farmers who displaced the
backwoodsmen could scarcely be distinguished from their predecessors. Most had little capital and lived in near poverty; many were
wanderers by instinct, destined to move several times before settling
down. Few showed the gloss of culture or education. Yet they differed
from squatters in their basic attitudes. They were hard working and
determined, relieved of any sense of anomie by the neighbors who
moved in with them, conscious of belonging to a social group, and
viewing themselves as harbingers of civilization rather than as seceders
from society. They came west not as wanderers but to clear the land,
plant crops, improve their properties, and grow up with the country.
They might move again, but only when the move seemed a good speculation, and not simply to escape neighbors. Small-propertied farmers
also differed from backwoodsmen in their ability to borrow money,
thus assuring the capital needed to begin to improve their status in the
community.[64] These were the men and women who were to make the
first telling assault on nature that forecast the passing of the frontier.

So their pattern of life differed from that of the backwoodsmen.
Hunting still provided many of life's staples, but each year the farmer
widened his clearing or turned under more prairie sod, not to create
salable surpluses, but to care for the needs of his ever-growing family.
A substantial log cabin or sod house, usually built with the aid of
neighbors, soon replaced his rough hut or lean-to. Fences closed his
fields against animals. Orchards were planted. A few cows were purchased to supplement the hogs that were commonplace on all frontiers. Self-sufficiency was eventually realized; then surpluses began to
multiply that could be sold to newcomers and eventually on a wider
market.[65]

The small-propertied farmers performed one essential service: they
demonstrated the productivity of each new region and thus opened the

door to later comers with sufficient capital to require security before migrating. Once an area had been proved, the capitalists came in droves to harvest the large returns on investment possible in new lands. Some were propertied farmers or planters who bought out their small-propertied predecessors, expanded the clearings, built barns and outbuildings, replaced the log cabin with a frame house, enlarged the herds by providing winter feeding, and developed the social activities of a matured social order. Others were land speculators who recognized that the thickening population in an area of proved fertility was certain to spell profits for those who held property. Still others were town planters and the dozens of tradesmen needed to perform the service and marketing functions of an expanding society. These three frontier types did not arrive simultaneously or in any set order; on some frontiers town planters might lead the way; on others speculators might reach the scene even before the propertied farmers. On the Great Plains printers sometimes set up shop in the midst of a treeless wasteland, confident that the site would attract town dwellers. No orderly frontier pattern existed, but the various Wests were settled.[66]

In this process, speculators and town planters played a role unrecognized by early historians of the frontier. Speculators were everywhere along the fringes of settlement, from earliest times to the closing of the West, for to most pioneers the principal attraction of the frontier was not good soil but the chance to sell at a profit to later comers. Two types existed, the squatter or small-propertied farmer who acquired excess holdings in the hopes of resale, and the professional land jobber who absorbed the richest agricultural sites or the spots suitable for development as towns. Both slowed the process of settlement by forcing pioneers to pay heavily for lands; even after the passage of the Homestead Act in 1862, speculators managed to acquire the choicest plots near transportation routes or especially favored by nature. "The speculators in broadcloth," wrote Horace Greeley in 1859, "are not one whit more rapacious or pernicious than the speculators in rags, while the latter are forty times more numerous. Land speculation here is about the only business in which a man can embark with no other capital than an easy conscience.[67] To the frontiersman there was a difference, and his hatred was reserved for the professional who snatched away the better lands that he wanted for himself. A traveler in Arkansas saw one hundred armed men moving a whole town to another site because a court decision had awarded that area to a speculator.[68] Few land jobbers grew rich, but they were gamblers by nature and as typical of the frontier as the rancher or backwoodsman.

Town planters were just as omnipresent, even on the outer fringes, for villages sometimes sprang up before the area round about was occupied. Forts, trading posts, and mining camps often attracted clusters of town dwellers when the frontier of settlement still lay far to the east; other towns were planned by promoters who chose a favorable spot at a crossroads or mill seat, then printed colorful literature to attract purchasers for their lots. On occasion "paper towns" multiplied so rapidly that territorial legislatures reportedly considered setting aside a few acres for the farmers they hoped would arrive. "You may," noted a visitor to the West in the 1830s, "see streets of town-like residences springing up in the midst of the primeval forest,—the squirrel gamboling in the branches at a musket-shot from the 'store,' where the counter is crowded by the silks of Paris."[69] Clearly the city was not a product of a long evolutionary process on the frontier, but an agency for the advance of settlement no less important than the mine or farm.

This is important to realize if we are to visualize accurately the whole frontier process. The towns and villages of the successive Wests offered a haven for discontented urban Easterners scarcely less alluring than that provided by virgin lands for farmers. In them was exceptional opportunity for tradesmen and professional men of every hue. One Illinois hamlet advertised in 1818 that it needed artisans, carpenters, joiners, millwrights, brick layers, stone masons, blacksmiths, painters, shoemakers, hatters, tailors, merchants, lawyers, physicians, schoolmasters, and others. Lawyers were in special demand to handle the litigation growing from conflict over land titles. "In a new town," wrote a jaundiced observer, "which is brevetted a 'city' as soon as there is more than one house, the rumseller follows hard on the footsteps of the settler; then comes the lawyer, who immediately runs as a candidate for county offices, foments grievances, and shows every man how he can get the better of his neighbor."[70] Whatever their trade or profession, these town dwellers were pioneers no less than the squatter or rancher. They were restless, ambitious, and willing to risk security for the chance to grow wealthy. Many were addicted drifters, moving from frontier village to frontier village just as the backwoodsmen moved from clearing to clearing. Others found prosperity as the town they chose prospered, and stayed to become community leaders. The "urban frontier" operated very much in the manner of the farming frontier, and exhibited many of the same characteristics.

◆§◆§ THIS BRIEF SURVEY of the pattern of settlement on the successive frontiers of the United States makes one fact obvious: the process was far more complex than Frederick Jackson Turner and his followers envisaged. Pioneers, blissfully unaware that they should have been illustrating the laws of social evolution, refused to move in orderly columns, scattering instead helter-skelter wherever opportunity beckoned. Trappers, miners, explorers, and herdsmen almost rubbed elbows as they went their ways in search of the wealth that their respective skills promised. City dwellers mingled with propertyless farmers; speculators and frontier lawyers joined in transplanting civilization to lands recently snatched from nature. All had one purpose in mind: to find new opportunity in a newer land. They found that opportunity and, by doing so, settled a continent.

Clearly the frontier was not simply a line drawn exactly across a map. It was a broad zone in which men with countless skills labored to exploit virgin riches. It was, moreover, a migrating region, moving westward at a rate of from ten to forty miles each year. At times, when a natural or Indian barrier lay ahead, it might contract as it did in the eighteenth century when the shock troops of expansion were held back by the Appalachian Mountains and the French with their Indian allies. At others it might broaden, as in the 1830s and 1840s when its advance agents ranged a thousand miles beyond the frontier of farms and towns in the Mississippi Valley. Yet always this zone did migrate, and always it provided a haven for men who sought opportunity in newness.

3

The Frontier
and the
American Character

LET US INDULGE in a thoroughly unhistorical speculation. Suppose that in the year A.D. 752 the emperor Hsüan Tsung, wearying of the brilliant scholars in his Academy of Letters and moved by the plight of his overcrowded peasantry, decided to dispatch his most experienced navigator, Bo Ko Lum, to search for a route to thinly settled Europe. Assume that Bo Ko Lum, sailing eastward with three sturdy ships, made his landfall in a gentle country that he mistook for a remote outpost of the Frankish kingdom where he was welcomed by friendly natives called, by the Chinese, Red Franks. Pretend that this newly discovered continent, later called Frankland, was occupied over the next century by hundreds of thousands of settlers from China's overpopulated mainland. They would fashion rice paddies, build their pagodas to worship at the shrine of Buddha, and slowly advance their Asiatic civilization eastward, led by venturesome fur trappers in flowing silken robes. As they moved ever onward toward the rising sun until they reached the distant Atlantic they would leave behind a new Orient, transplanted across the seas, and modeled after the Orient they had left behind.[1]

But would this civilization be an exact replica of the old? It would not. Chinese pioneers would discover that silken robes were less resistant to wilderness wear than jackets and pantaloons of hides, that corn and wheat were more easily produced than rice, and that decrees of a distant emperor were easily ignored by a people whose unique problems demanded unique local solutions. They would, over the course of years, change in appearance, in dietary habits, and in social values as the wilderness of Frankland altered their customs and institutions. A future Chinese historian might write that they had been Franklandized by the New World environment. Yet would this transformation convert the colonists into replicas of the pioneers who actually settled the Wests? Certainly not. Transplanted cultural patterns would be too powerful to be completely submerged. The imaginary Frankland as an outpost of China would have borne little resemblance to the actual America as an outpost of England. But it would also show little similarity to the China from which the settlers had come.

This imagined situation brings into focus the basic question that must be answered if we are to appraise the influence of the frontier on American civilization. Can a culture be basically altered by transplantation to a different physical environment? And, if it can, how is this accomplished? To solve these problems we must weigh the relative influence of traditional cultural forces and the physical environment in shaping group cultures.

Geneticists have learned a great deal about the hereditary process. They know that traits are transmitted from parents to children through the forty-six chromosomes present in every fertilized ovum, that these chromosomes are made up of complex molecules called "genes," and that these genes are reshuffled from generation to generation, giving rise to the endless new combinations that relieve us of the unpleasant necessity of all looking alike. They also know that hereditary traits are rigidly restrained (save in the rare case of mutations) and that they are passed along by the genes from generation to generation utterly unchanged by life experiences. This means that *learned* skills or experiences cannot be inherited; we inherit only a certain physical-chemical organization observable in the form of the physical structure, intelligence, temperament, and innate drives.

Environment plays an equally important role in shaping our behavior. Actually we are influenced by two interacting environments, the "primary" or *physical* environment that comprises the world of nature about us, and the "secondary" or *social* environment provided by the human group in which we find ourselves. Of these two, the latter is more immediately important, for the social group serves as a medium through which primary environmental forces reach the individual; its influence operates within limits set by the physical environment but within these limits it plays a transcendent role. Each group has its own patterns of behavior known as a *culture*, which include the shared knowledge, beliefs, customs, and habits that have been acquired by living together over the course of generations. These "cultures" vary from group to group and account for many of the differences that distinguish peoples; they determine the nature of the skills that we acquire, the knowledge that we accumulate, the basic assumptions that we hold, and the conscious or unconscious values that govern our behavior. This means that each group has its own social environment that affects the behavior of those within the group.[2]

The culture of any people tends to change constantly as traditional practices are eliminated and adjustments made to meet new situations. In a forming social order these changes occur frequently as the group adjusts itself to its physical environment, accustoms itself to surrounding peoples, and experiments with behavior patterns. Once established, however, these patterns tend to perpetuate themselves; although change continues, the rate of change slows as each society tends to regard its culture as proper and to resist further alteration. At this point in social evolution the group is a victim of ethnocentrism.[3]

Thus man's social behavior is influenced by both heredity and environment. Inherited characteristics are passed from generation to generation and change so slowly as the evolutionary process operates that differences are not observable within historical periods; they are unaffected by experience, although modes of expression may be altered by cultural change. Environment is both physical and social, with the latter more determinative of social behavior within limits set by the former. Central to the social environment is the "culture" of each group. This emerges in the early stages of social organization and while changing constantly to adapt to changing conditions—in the physical environment, technology, ethnic variation, and the like—tends to solidify and to be increasingly resistant to change as ethnocentrism becomes a factor. Such changes as do occur after this point result from continuing alterations in the physical environment and from interaction with adjacent cultures that mutually influence each other.

Against this background of established theory, we can ask three questions essential to understanding the frontier process: Is the behavior pattern of the individual altered by changes in the physical environment? Is it changed by deviations in the social environment? And does an alteration in the social environment affect group behavior? Experiments conducted by anthropologists, sociologists, and social psychologists shed some light on these problems.

Social scientists are now unanimous in their belief that the physical environment is not solely determinative of human behavior. Two obvious examples will demonstrate this point. First, several different cultures have been shown to exist within one physical environment: the Hopi and Navajo Indians of the southwestern United States lived during the early nineteenth century in the same geographic province, yet the Hopi were monogamous, adept in ceramic arts, skilled weavers, and capable farmers, while the Navajo were polygamous, produced no ceramics, confined weaving to women, and supported themselves by herding livestock. Second, intruding cultures adapt differently to identical physical environments. Southern California was occupied successively by Indians, Spaniards, Mexicans, and Anglo-Americans. The Indians developed a culture based on food gathering, the Spanish-Mexicans one resting on herding, and the Anglo-Americans one built on farming and industry.[4] Obviously the reaction of any culture to the physical environment depends not only on the environment but on the nature of the transplanted culture.

If the geographic setting does not determine cultural patterns, are they altered by the changing social environment? Two seemingly unrelated experiments show this to be the case. In one a young ape, reared in the identical environment of a human child of his own age, learned eating and toilet habits and even the meaning of some words but could never speak, for no amount of training could offset the limitations imposed by heredity. In another a young girl who had been neglected by her parents and allowed to rear herself in a dark closet was given the best training possible when discovered, but was never able to catch up with her age group in skills, language, or mental ability. Environment blocked the mental and social growth of the girl, just as heredity blocked the mental and social growth of the ape.[5]

Further evidence indicating the ability of the social environment to alter human behavior is provided by numerous experiments with identical twins. Having the same genetic origin, and thus the same heredity influence, any differences between such twins must depend on the different social and physical environments in which they have been reared. Studies in such cases suggest that the intelligence level as measured by IQ tests is directly proportional to the amount of education; two sisters separated at the age of eighteen months and subjected to different educational experiences showed a difference of twenty-four points on the intelligence-quotient scale at the age of thirty-five years. Similar experiments indicate that in both intelligence and personality the deviation between identical twins reared apart is as great as between nonrelated persons.[6] These results are substantiated by studies of Negro children transplanted from the inferior schools of the segregated South to the better schools of the North; they reveal a steady improvement in intelligence and social behavior as the inherited abilities of the Negroes are altered by an improved environment. The child of a steelworker in Birmingham, England, suddenly shifted to the home of a steelworker in Birmingham, Alabama, would act and talk and think differently than if he had been raised at home. Yet the physical environment would be about the same in each instance; the principal change would be in the social environment.

Studies also suggest that social environment changes group behavior. Japanese living in Hawaii develop mannerisms different from those of their homeland, revealed especially by more individualistic and assertive attitudes. Similarly Chinese transplanted to Hawaii and to the mainland of the United States behave differently; those in Hawaii are more outward in their emotional expressions than those on the mainland, who feel restrained by the presence of unsympathetic Occidentals. The inscrutable Oriental of California's discriminatory past became a gay, laughing extrovert in Honolulu, where he felt accepted and free of social disapproval. That group traits can be modified is also shown by studies of ability in different classes in the United States; these reveal that children on high socioeconomic levels are more intelligent than those from lower classes. Research such as this, fragmentary though it may be, indicates that both individuals and groups respond to social-environmental forces.[7]

Yet such changes when they do occur are accomplished only by overcoming a vast inertia of tradition that varies its influence with each situation. A few examples will make this clear. New Englanders originally built two-story barns on hillsides where hay wagons could drive directly into lofts on the second floor; their descendants in the flat Middle West continued to build barns in this fashion even though they had to construct an earthen runway to the second floor. Londoners in the seventeenth century adjusted to the narrow streets by building overhanging second floors; these same Londoners built identical homes in Boston where space was no problem. Roads were laid out along sectional lines in the Midwest; pioneers in mountainous country continued to follow surveyors' range lines even though highways following hill contours would have been easier to construct. Summer vacations for schoolchildren originated in farm areas where help was needed in planting and harvesting, but persist in the schools of urban America. Clearly cultural patterns, once established, can be changed only with difficulty, despite alterations in the social environment.[8]

These conclusions can be substantiated—but by no means proved —by observations of modern groups brought face to face with conditions comparable to those that existed on the American frontier. During the 1930s the Farm Security Administration established seven communities where families from a variety of backgrounds were abruptly brought together. Their behavior in this unfamiliar situation, not unlike that of a pioneer settlement, suggests that the social environment altered behavior patterns very much as it did in the successive Wests. Social relationships tended to disintegrate, as men and women associated with others of comparable economic status or whose personalities complemented their own. The new friendships were formed with those living nearby, for a more extended time was needed to develop relations with persons of like interests living far away. Particularly marked was the tendency of families that had been most mobile in the past to leave the communities, explaining that their golden dreams had not materialized.[9] These behavior patterns were a product of the unfamiliar social environment; notable, however, is the fact that they only slightly modified established habits.

On the basis of these modern-day studies by behavioral scientists we can advance certain hypotheses that can be applied to frontier societies:

- The "primary" or physical environment did not directly determine such cultural deviations as existed on the frontier, although it laid the basis for such deviations by offering individuals a unique man-land ratio that stimulated an urge for self-advancement.
- The differing *social* environment of frontier communities fostered the growth of unique folk cultures, based on but distinguishable from those of the successive Easts. This was because:
  a. The diversity of ethnic and social types attracted to pioneer

settlements contributed to creating a fluid social order where ethnocentrism was lacking.

b. Social controls and traditionalism were diminished by isolation and the dispersion of settlement, with a corresponding impetus to innovation.

c. The absence of a solidified social order with established in-groups and out-groups allowed opportunity for greater vertical mobility.

In essence, then, the principal effect of the frontier social environment was to weaken traditional controls and values. The pioneer found himself in a fluid, ever-changing, unstabilized society, where accustomed behavior did not bring predictable results and where experimentation seemed more essential than in established cultures. Change, not tradition, was the order of life.

Just as important was the fact that the pioneers realized that in moving westward they severed their ties with tradition. The act of migration disrupted the social relationships that had assisted them in patterning their behavior in their old homes. In their new homes the sense of nonbelonging was accentuated, for most frontier communities were settled by men and women from a variety of places and social backgrounds; Yankees and Yorkers, Southerners and Northerners, natives and immigrants, all met and mingled on a common ground. Language barriers and differing social customs made cohesion difficult, for a Vermonter in Illinois might not be able to communicate with the German who lived nearby, or might feel superior to the Tennessee uplander who had taken out the next farm.[10] Distances between neighbors, growing steadily greater as the frontier moved westward across the prairies and plains of mid-America, also heightened the feeling of removal from the group, as did the economic uncertainty of life in an untested new region. The typical frontiersman was oppressed by a sense of social weightlessness (to borrow a term from the space age), which generated a feeling of not belonging fatal to cultural cohesiveness.

The result was a mild form of mass anomie everywhere on the frontier. To some degree all pioneers, even those who succeeded most rapidly, felt a sense of social deprivation, based on their failure to establish comforting social relationships with their neighbors, the absence of defined social norms, and the failure of the new land to meet their unrealistic expectations. This was reflected in the lawlessness and disorder usual in most frontier communities, by the emotional religious practices common there, and by continuing mobility. It was revealed also by the greater degree of political participation in frontier areas as individuals sought to gain status and economic benefits by assuming leadership roles in the unstructured society.[11] These attitudes and desires marked frontier communities as different from those with tightly structured cultures. Rarely had society been so disrupted, so fluid, and so susceptible to forces inviting change. Here was a new social environment, powerful enough to alter men and institutions.

Let no one, however, be misled into believing that the frontier could affect *major* changes in either the personalities or the behavioral patterns of frontiersmen. As in human behavior today, the bulk of the customs and beliefs of the pioneers were transmitted, and were only slightly modified by the changing culture in which they lived. This can be demonstrated by contrasting the civilizations that emerged in Spanish and English America. True, the physical environment of these two areas varied greatly. North America, with its well-watered woodlands, its fertile prairies, and its vast resources in forest and mineral wealth, offered far greater opportunity for the relatively propertyless individual than less-favored South America. There rugged mountains, semiarid plateaus, and dense jungles restricted the areas where small farmers or herdsmen could utilize nature. Only on the Argentine pampas and the Brazilian plains did a temperate climate, navigable rivers, and good soil beckon exploiters, and even there government largess rather than individual initiative governed the settlement process.[12] Yet men, not geography, explain the differences between the Anglo-American and Latin-American frontiers, for individuals of different backgrounds will respond in different ways to identical physical environments.

The ferment of the Anglo-American frontier was partly a product of the ferment of the democratic, commercial, and industrial societies in which it originated. These produced settlers who, by training and tradition, were capable of unleashing the energies of individual initiative to extract the frontier's natural resources. On the other hand, the Latin-American pioneers were governed by traditions that ill-equipped them to exploit the New World's riches, for they had been reared in a culture where the individual's freedom—politically, religiously, and economically—was rigidly restrained.

For this difference the chronology of settlement was partly responsible. Spain's New World frontier was founded, and its culture solidified, in the fifteenth and sixteenth centuries when Europe was entering its modern age. An absolute monarchy had just been imposed on the feudal nobles, middle-class capitalism was in its infancy, church and state were united under the dictates of the crown, and explosive nationalism prevailed in the wake of the expulsion of the Moors. The resulting combination of royal absolutism, a militant national church, and a martial spirit created a colonial society in which the small-propertied individual was allowed scant freedom to exploit frontier resources. He was restricted politically by all-powerful viceroys, commercially by an inflexible mercantile system, and economically by the operation of the semimanorial *mita* and *encomienda*. Moreover, a humane church policy that sought conversion rather than extermination for the Indians helped create a native labor force to monopolize jobs that might otherwise have attracted immigrants from Spain. The result was a transplanted European culture, administered by a centralized bureaucracy, and designed to enrich the monarch and his favorites rather than the individual pioneer.[13]

England, on the other hand, entered the race for colonies in the seventeenth century, with institutions far more modern than those Spain transplanted to America. The political theories of the Stuart monarchs were still those of divine right and royal absolutism, but both the promoters of England's colonies and the "adventurers" who peopled them were generally foes of this official theory and active proponents of parliamentary constitutionalism. Thus inclined, they were ready to accord the colonists a degree of self-rule, as they did when Virginia established its House of Burgesses and Massachusetts its General Court—steps that established a precedent for representative government. Political liberty was strengthened by the constitutional controversies that troubled England during the remainder of the seventeenth century. The Puritan rebellion and the Glorious Revolution were shattering blows against absolutism. That the colonists would have followed the path toward democracy, with or without a frontier environment, seems doubtful had the way not been pointed by these events.

Economic institutions emerging in England also favored the rise of a colonial spirit of individual initiative. The prevailing theories of commercial capitalism, combined with a lack of effective centralized authority at home, allowed the English colonies to be established as quasi-public enterprises founded in the hope of gain. This, in turn, permitted the colony planters to slough away the restrictive controls that shackled the economy of less developed nations—feudal land tenure, medieval guilds, and monopolistic trading concepts. Instead, private land ownership, individual handicraft trades, the wage system, indentured servitude, and private contracts became the hallmarks of the American economy, all offering opportunity to farmers, planters, merchants, and craftsmen to better themselves. The English pioneer came from a culture where he had been trained emotionally to exploit the resources of the frontier. He was equipped, as his Latin-American counterpart was not, to move whenever opportunity beckoned, and to profit by each move.[14]

This was demonstrated as the Anglo-American frontier crept westward, for the ethnic groups that it attracted responded in different ways to the physical environment. Most who migrated directly from Europe to the West integrated rapidly into pioneer communities, thus falling at once into the social environment of the frontier. These men and women soon learned the customs and language of those about them, and within a generation or two were almost indistinguishable from their neighbors. Other Europeans, however, settled in ethnic communities where they spoke their native language and remained isolated from the practices of American pioneers. The persistence with which Old World customs and thought patterns were retained in these pockets of settlement demonstrated that the *physical* environment of the frontier did not alter newcomers. This was the function of the *social* environment alone.

The French who occupied a number of town sites in the Mississippi Valley during the seventeenth and eighteenth centuries clearly illustrate this fact. There they remained until the nineteenth century when American pioneers engulfed the lands about them, living and working as had their ancestors and revealing few of the traits of the stereotyped pioneer. By contrast with their new neighbors, the French were indolent and lazy, lacking the bustle and energy usual among small-propertied frontiersmen. They enjoyed dancing and music, and shocked the sober Americans with their gaiety. Mobility was uncommon; they preferred to stay near their churches and families rather than seek opportunity elsewhere. Their farming habits were similarly inherited, for they tilled long fields modeled after those of manorial France, even though the landscape of the midwest was ill-suited to this division. Their farm implements were those of their ancestors rather than those developed in America.[15]

Germans who fled the Rhenish Palatinate in the seventeenth and eighteenth centuries to establish themselves in the Pennsylvania back country, and their countrymen who filled pockets of settlements in the Middle West a hundred years later, similarly remained stubbornly resistant to the process of "Americanization" that was supposed to take place on the frontier. Their dream was of a good barn and security, not speculative profits. So they showed no tendency to move about as did the usual pioneers; the "Pennsylvania Dutch" of today offer convincing proof of their willingness to stay in one place. Because they had permanence in mind, they cleared the land thoroughly, shunning the slovenly habits of their American neighbors, and preserved its fertility by manuring and by rotating crops. Knowing that well-cared-for animals ate less, they built sturdy stone barns with overhanging eaves, even though they and their families lived for a time in hovels. While Americans were inclined to plant cash crops that would bring the greatest return, the Germans used their fields for a variety of crops to protect against the disaster that might fall through blight or a glutting of the market. This same frugal spirit compelled them to consume the produce that was less in demand, and sell the choice or most expensive products. They lived, in other words, much as their peasant ancestors had lived in Germany. The speculative, exploitive, wasteful habits of frontier America affected them not.[16]

While Germans and French best illustrated the different responses of ethnic groups to the physical environment of the frontier, all nationalities responded in predictable ways. Contemporaries sometimes amused themselves by ranking newcomers according to their skills in pioneering. Germans and Scots were rated "the most industrious, prudent, and successful."[17] The Irish were labeled inadequate for wilderness tasks because of indolence and love of village life, the French because they reverted to hunting, and the English because they clung so tenaciously to British customs. Tales were told of newcomers from England whose cattle died when their owners insisted that barns were as unnecessary in Pennsylvania as in Cornwall, who laboriously dug wells when sparkling water could be dipped from streams, and who insisted on migrating with all their belongings when their needs could have been supplied from the countryside. John Bull, wrote one visitor to the West, would carry with him not only every possession "but even the fast-anchored isle itself, could he but cut it from its moorings."[18] Clearly the physical environment of the frontier did not recast newcomers into a common mold.

This was to be expected. Men instinctively resist change; traditional patterns of behavior create a comforting sense of security that is lost with innovation. Too, imitation requires far less effort than invention. Pittsburgh's founding fathers based the first municipal code of the village on the codes of other eastern cities with which they were familiar. When Louisville founded its school system a delegate was sent east to "examine the most respectable of their monitorial establishments." The first school was modeled on one in New York with modifications adapted from Philadelphia and a faculty recruited from Columbia, Yale, and London.[19] Nostalgia also played a role in perpetuating traditional practices on frontiers, for homes that had been forsaken in the East were endowed with warmth and glamor in the imagination of homesick pioneers. Even the half-savage mountain men thought longingly of the civilized life they had forsaken. One told of riding into a grove of cottonwoods where birds sang merrily. "I laied down in the shade and enjoyed their twittering for some hours," he wrote that night. "It reminded me of home & civilisation."[20] Added a traveler much among the pioneers of the Far West: "The thought of home is ever rolled, like a sweet morsel, under the tongues of their souls."[21] Resistance to the corroding influence of a frontier environment was heightened by such sentiments.

৵§৵§ NO *PHYSICAL* environment could have weakened such allegiance to traditionalism, but not even established custom could withstand the corroding impact of the frontier *social* environment. Behavioral patterns, value scales, and modes of thought that emerged in early pioneer communities and that were carried from community to community by successive waves of advancing frontiersmen proved too powerful to be resisted. Even the "ethnic pockets" that clung most doggedly to Old World habits were affected as American neighbors demonstrated the practicality of frontier-tested practices. A German traveler in the West, after noting that one of his newly arrived countrymen looked completely out of place, went on: "Visit him on his thriving farm ten years hence, and, except in the single point of language, you will find him (unless he has settled among a nest of his countrymen) at home among his neighbors, and happily conforming to their usages."[22] Even the most hidebound Englishman learned, as one of them observed, "that he has got to a place where it answers to spend land to save labour; the reverse of his experience in England; and he soon becomes as slovenly a farmer as the American, and begins immediately to grow rich."[23] Conformity to a unique social environment was easier than resistance. The frontier did alter individuals and institutions.

For the spatial frontier, to the visitor or new settler, was a different world. Those who crossed the borderline and recorded their impressions spoke of a cultural fault as observable as a geological fault. Beyond they found a people who behaved and thought and lived in a manner distinctly different from Easterners. Here was "a state of society wholly differing from any that we had seen before," wrote one traveler, and another felt that he was suddenly "a stranger among a people, whose modes of existence and ways of thinking are of a widely different character from those, in the midst of which he has been reared."[24] Americans were as conscious of the division between East and West as travelers from overseas. "Language, ideas, manners, customs—all are new," observed a pioneer newly arrived in backwoods Michigan; "yes, even language; for to the instructed person from one of our great Eastern cities, the talk of the true back-woodsman is scarcely intelligible."[25] Added another from the Ohio Valley frontier of the 1830s: "The people of the west, viewed as individuals, resemble the inhabitants of almost every clime; but taken as a whole, they are unlike every people under heaven. They have come hither from the four quarters of the globe, with manners and habits and genius and temperament, as different as the nations from which they have severally sprung. Every thing is new, just coming into existence."[26] These observers, and others like them, were acutely aware that the social environment of the frontier was distinct from that of the East.

These differences, moreover, were altering the whole national character and converting the Americans into a people strangely unlike the Europeans from whom they sprang. "If I were to draw a comparison between the English and Americans," one English traveler decided, "I should say that there is almost as much difference between the two nations . . . as there has long been between the English and the Dutch"; another judged them to be "as unlike the English as any people can well be."[27] Significantly, the features that most clearly marked the Americans as unique were frontier characteristics, and were found most deeply etched in the West. Travelers observed there the "slight, but perceptible peculiarities of national character which our peculiar circumstances and condition have imposed upon us"; those same traits were "least observable where the population is most mixed, and are scarcely perceptible in our larger commercial towns and cities."[28] Lord Bryce, one of the most penetrating observers of nineteenth-century America, believed that the West was the most distinctively American part of America, precisely because the points in which it differed from the East were the points in which America as a whole differed from Europe.[29]

Observers differed widely on the exact traits that were emerging in the American character as a result of the pioneering experience, but agreed on certain basic characteristics. One Westerner, who pondered much on the West's influence during the 1850s, believed that the frontier spawned a desire for individual self-improvement even at the expense of society, a supreme confidence that refused to recognize error, and a restlessness that led men to change their habits as often as they did their abodes.[30] Three decades later a visitor to the Far West concluded that a capacity for self-help, a willingness to aid others in distress, a dislike of hypocrisy and pretense, and a manliness exhibited in respect to women were basic frontier traits.[31] To Lord Bryce the Westerner was unique in his veneration of democracy, his unwavering nationalism, and his belief that the world could be reformed with his help; he was also unusual in his practicality, his materialistic philosophy, his aggressive optimism, and his go-getter attitude.[32]

Few observers of the Western scene were capable of such penetrating observations, but many contributed their mite to the picture of the American frontiersman. To polished travelers from London or Boston he was an uncouth savage, degraded by his wilderness environment, and a traitor to the civilization in which he was reared. "As man civilizes the wilderness," wrote a visitor from Britain, "the wilderness more or less brutalizes him. In thus elevating nature he degrades himself."[33] Indolence, profligacy, and bad manners were as truly a product of the frontier as deer hides or beaver pelts to the majority of observers. Few recognized that refinements could not flourish in a new country, and that this regression toward the primitive was only temporary.

To those who could see the true man beneath his uncouth manners, the pioneer was distinguished by a variety of traits, good and bad. He was notable for his openness, the easy manner in which he adjusted to new situations, and his attachment to freedom. Some visitors branded him as hopelessly utilitarian and dourly taciturn; nearly all marked his restless energy, his eager perseverance, and his willingness to support "every species of improvement, both public and private." Scarcely an observer but commented on his lack of attachment to place, and his tendency to roam constantly.[34] "A restless temper seems to me one of the distinctive traits of this people," noted Alexis de Tocqueville. ". . . We have been told that the same man has often tried ten estates. He has appeared successively as merchant, lawyer, doctor, minister of the gospel. He has lived in twenty different places and nowhere found ties to detain him."[35] Incomplete though this catalogue may be, it suggests that those who knew nineteenth-century America best recognized that a national character was developing, and that it was rooted in the frontiering background of the people.

⌖⌖ HOW ACCURATE were these observations? That question cannot be answered without an understanding of what a "national character" is and is not. A national character is not an absolute quality persisting unchanged through the ages any more than it is a body of characteristics shared by every single person in a country. It rests neither on geographic adjacence nor on a commonly shared historical experience. Above all, national character is not, as was so often stated in the nineteenth century, a product of ethnic grouping mirroring hereditary racial traits.[36] Historians, discouraged by the inaccuracy of these traditional concepts, have been sometimes inclined to deny that a national character has existed. This is unfortunate, for the term is definable and the concept is an essential tool in historical interpretation.

Modern social scientists view national character as a product of both group culture, and "personality." Group culture is the accepted pattern of behavior in any society. "Personality" may be defined as the body of habits, traits, and attitudes of an individual as they are shaped both by his inner motivations and goals, and by his role in the group of which he is a part. Implicit in this definition is the understanding that the group culture partly determines personality, for the individual's goals and motives are influenced by the goals and motivations of the group. A "go-ahead" society such as that of midnineteenth century America helps endow its members with the go-ahead spirit. The determinant of national character, then, is the group culture acting upon and molding the personality of individuals. This concept recognizes that the national character changes as the culture changes and is not immutable; similarly, it acknowledges that individuals respond in differing ways to group influences and hence that national character is reflected in various ways among different people. Most important of all, it equates national character with neither race nor physical environment, yet is postulated on the belief that an altered social environment affects the culture, which in turn affects the individual. The personality of the individual and the culture of the group alike respond to changes in the social environment.[37]

The interaction of group culture and personality creates within a nation a body of beliefs and behavior patterns that are widely recognized, both at home and abroad, as being more common there than elsewhere.[38] This "national character" is a historically conditioned and commonly shared system of values and practices. It is, as one social scientist has said, the kind of character that makes the members of a society *want* to act the way they *have* to act as members of that society.[39] Obviously the needs and demands of a society change constantly, and as they do the social organization changes together with the demands for conformity placed upon its members. Hence the "national character" is fluid and changes as the society and culture change. Obviously, too, all individuals within a social group do not develop personalities reflecting the national character. Rebels persist within any society, although their conduct is governed by the rules of that society governing rebels. Yet pressure for conformity is constant; all social groups reward those who follow an accepted behavior pattern and punish those who do not.

&§&§ IN APPLYING these concepts to the United States, the American national character can be defined and its characteristics identified only by separating the basic forces *creating* that shared behavior pattern which is the national character, from the *manifestations* of that character.

Social scientists have isolated four basic elements that help shape the unique attitudes and traits of the people of the United States. One is the motivation that impels Americans; their ambition is success and they measure their worth as much by the upward distance they have traveled in society as by the position they have reached. They think in terms of social mobility and movement along the social ladder rather than of compartmentalized classes or stability; as a result they are excessively concerned with conformity, which seems essential to win the support of their peers needed for each upward move.[40]

Secondly, Americans differ from other peoples in their inner direction. Their ancestors in medieval days were "tradition-directed" as they conformed to the fixed rules of a stabilized society; with the greater freedom possible in modern times, men became increasingly "inner-directed" as they followed individual bents in achieving success. This "inner direction" persisted through the nineteenth century, but in the twentieth a changed economy decreed that most individuals could no longer gain a living simply by mastering an environment; they must win the favor of those about them and shape their conduct to that expected by society. They had become "other-directed," and had replaced their gyroscope with a radar screen. This change from "inner-directed" to "other-directed" is uniquely American, and helps define the national character.[41]

A third key to understanding the people of the United States is the intense competition that serves as a stimulus to their actions. Rivalry is a part of men's lives, and with it a hostile tension that breeds distrust of others. This in turn fosters a sense of failure that stimulates a craving for love and recognition. Americans are unique in their excessive insistence on affection and glorification.[42] Finally, social scientists insist that American culture is unique in its predilection with the individual. In other cultures tradition and the group govern behavior, but in the United States these controls have diminished until the people are oppressed by a sense of social and psychological isolation. This leads to violent exhibits of emotion, expressed especially in manifestations of gladness or sorrow.[43]

Social scientists believe, then, that Americans stand apart because of the strength of their drive toward success and the resulting social mobility, their dependence on the opinions of their contemporaries, their preoccupation with the individual as opposed to the social group, and the inner tensions that result from inevitable failure in a highly competitive society. All of these observations have one thing in common: They stress the competition that governs behavior in the United States. It is this that drives men up the ladder of success, makes them dependent on the favors of their peers, stokes their inner conflicts, and impels them toward an individual-centered existence in which they seek self-elevation without regard to the welfare of society. The

American character is, in essence, a group of responses to a highly competitive culture.

The *manifestations* of these character traits substantiate the validity of these theories. Americans in the nineteenth and twentieth centuries have behaved and thought in distinguishable patterns not shared in equal degree with the peoples of other nations. Observers from overseas, from the days of Alexis de Tocqueville and Michael Chevalier to the days of Lord Bryce and Sir Denis Brogan, have sought clues to these identifiable characteristics and value scales, and have arranged an impressive catalogue of exhibits. Modern scholars have added to the list. The result is a bill of particulars that reveals the American character in a variety of facets, which may be roughly grouped into a few categories.[44]

As an economic man, these cataloguers believe, the American differed from his European contemporaries of the eighteenth and nineteenth centuries in his belief in the universal obligation of all persons to work endlessly in their eternal pursuit of material gain. No one could be excused, neither the successful merchant who had accumulated a fortune, nor the abstract thinker who preferred to spin out fine webs of learning. The progress of society demanded that all labor at top speed with no time wasted on frivolity. Travelers constantly marveled at the speed with which Americans ate and rushed away, even though they had no place to go. "The sense that there is no time to spare," observed Lord Bryce, "haunts an American even when he might find the time."[45] This nose-to-the-grindstone philosophy, linked with the "go-ahead" spirit that permeated nineteenth-century enterprise, endowed the people with certain characteristics: an acceptance of materialism with a corresponding distrust of esthetic and intellectual pursuits, a dislike of a leisure class, and an inability to enjoy recreation or luxuriate in indolence. Americans even played games with a grim determination to win rather than for pure sport.

As a political man, the American was a defender of both political and social democracy. The Constitution was his Holy Grail, to be venerated as the symbol of mankind's equality. But democracy was more than an open ballot box; democracy was the right of every individual to command the respect of his fellows, whatever his status in life. Upward social mobility was the lot of every man worth his salt; in a land where the rags-to-riches saga was daily enacted, all men should be treated as equals because all were potentially equal. The neighbor's daughter who waited on table should be called a "lady" rather than a "servant" because she might marry the village banker tomorrow; the hack driver was entitled to write "Esquire" after his name because the town lots in which he speculated might be sold for a fortune in the next real-estate boom. Even children, travelers noted with horror, were ill-behaved monsters because parents treated them as equals rather than exercising authority over them.

Americans also were endowed with a variety of beliefs and practices that struck visitors as strangely different from those of their homelands. They were an inventive, self-reliant people, who placed little trust in tradition but were inclined to experimentation and innovation even when time-tested practices were suitable. They were adept in countless skills, and were almost universally jacks-of-all-trades. They were always moving about, with no attachment to place and no respect for the ways or homes of their ancestors. They were shamefully wasteful, throwing away objects that would be used happily by a European and sacrificing nearly new houses to make way for the next "development." Americans elevated women to a pedestal, showered them with gadgets that would relieve them of their rightful duties in the home, and treated them with a respect that struck masculine visitors as disgraceful. Lawlessness was also a consistent fault in the United States, where people seemed to take malicious pleasure in flaunting authority. The American, wrote Rudyard Kipling, loves to flout the law he makes just as much as he loves to make the law he flouts.

This legal delinquency, it was noted, was one manifestation of a strong spirit of individualism that permeated the American character. From colonial days when merchants defied Britain's trade regulations to the late nineteenth century when business titans preached the gospel of "rugged American individualism," the people demanded freedom from government as well as freedom under government. At times this defiance took bloody form when vigilance committees "stretched hemp" or lynch mobs defied legal processes by executing victims who were sometimes innocent. At others it followed more placid channels as otherwise respected citizens ignored laws that they disapproved or raised the banner of private enterprise against legislative measures that would protect consumers or competitors. Whatever its direction, individualism has been earmarked as a distinctive trait.

Yet to brand the American people as materialistic, inventive, wasteful, and individualistic defiers of the law is to uncover only one side of the coin. Money conscious and hard working they might be, but they were equally idealistic and optimistic in their expectations for themselves and all humanity. No country surpassed the United States during the late nineteenth century in sums collected for philanthropic purposes, both in terms of individual and national income.[46] No nation exhibited such boundless faith in the future, manifested in extreme form by communal societies bent on hurrying the coming of utopia, and more normally by a quiet confidence in the splendid destiny of the American dream. Internationally this meant the "manifest destiny" of the nation to share its beneficial democracy and its abundance with less-favored peoples; individually it meant the Horatio Alger-like ascent of the humblest to the thrones of the great. On a more personal level, optimism encouraged the aggressiveness and boasting that were singled out as the country's most disagreeable traits. All of these manifestations suggested an immature society, uncertain of its values, and often retreating into arrogance to conceal its own uncertainties.

ONE MAJOR QUESTION must be answered before turning from this portrait of the American character sketched by observers and modern scholars: What was the source of these traits and beliefs? Some students insist that travelers exaggerated the uniqueness of the nation's culture, and that American civilization is only a carbon copy of the British civilization from which it sprang. Those preaching this view hold that migrating Englishmen left behind their feudal institutions, but brought a training in democracy and industrialization that matured rapidly in a land where the retarding influence of traditionalism was lacking. Thus the differences between Britain and the United States are of degree rather than kind, and owe nothing to the physical or social environment of the New World.[47]

Other modern scholars have traced the distinctiveness of American culture to its agrarian background. The extensive agriculture suitable to New World conditions, they argue, forced the farmers who formed the bulk of the population to develop traits now considered uniquely American the habit of hard work, materialistic attitudes distrustful of cultural achievement, individualism, wastefulness, social and physical mobility.[48] Still other investigators find the key to the national character in the cry of a twentieth century visitor from

Russia: "One must remember the age of the country to understand Americans."[49] They maintain that the absence of a feudal past allowed the United States to step into the modern world without the encumbrance of a rigid class structure, outworn economic practices, and traditions that weighed against optimism, social mobility, individualism, and other noticeable American traits. These traits were those of any modern people, appearing first among the Americans but shared by all the Western world eventually.[50]

Two other theories contribute to the total picture. One traces the national character to the abundant natural resources of the New World; as these were utilized over the course of centuries in a series of sequential steps made possible by technological improvements the United States became a "land of plenty" where unparalleled opportunity bred individualism, democracy, mobility, and optimism.[51] The other finds the mobility of the American people their most distinguishing trait, and that this "locomotive instinct" has in turn fathered their social mobility, their democratic practices, their impatience with obstacles to individual self-advancement, and their optimistic belief in a better future.[52] The "M-Factor" in American history, argue the proponents of this theory, was principally important in creating the national character.

⋙⋙ WITHOUT SPECIAL PLEADING, it must be pointed out that all of these explanations stem immediately or remotely from the "frontier hypothesis" of Frederick Jackson Turner. The agricultural practices that left their mark originated precisely because American farmers were pushing into virgin lands instead of following the traditional customs of Europe. The medieval heritage played little part in the nation's development simply because an attractive man-land ratio lured settlers across the seas, forcing them to discard cultural baggage along the way. The New World was a land of plenty solely because its resources were untapped at the time of discovery, and only partially exploited by the early developers. Mobility became a habit largely because Americans contracted the habit of moving as they advanced into unoccupied lands. Once this habit was established their attachment to place lessened; they could move from east to west, from job to job, from city to city, and from country to city. In other words, the relative vacuum of cheap lands that attracted Europeans to America and Americans to the West accounted for the agricultural practices, the newness, the resources, and the physical mobility of the people of the United States. Had the North American continent been settled by an advanced people in 1492, none of these forces could have operated exactly as they have.

4

The Frontier: Cradle of Barbarism or Civilization?

SINCE THE DAYS of Frederick Jackson Turner, uncritical historians of the frontier process have accepted a plausible explanation of the manner in which pioneering altered men and their institutions. As settlers moved westward, they said, the garments of civilization were discarded. Some were shed as superfluous during the journey. Others were cast aside as frontiersmen grappled with raw nature in their new homes; to subdue the wilderness or tame the plains they must revert to a state of near savagery, abandoning cultural pursuits while they planted the first seeds of civilization. Then—so the story goes— the influx of later comers thickened population and began a gradual ascent from primitivism. Eventually a fully matured social order emerged. This differed from its counterparts in the East, altered by the impact of a unique environment, the acculturation inevitable as pioneers from differing backgrounds met and mingled, and the accidental deviations occurring in the evolution of isolated societies. As these altered frontier communities merged into a Western social order, these differences marked it as distinct. An "Americanization" of men and institutions had occurred.

This explanation is notable for its persuasive plausibility. But can man discard his cultural heritage overnight, reverting to near savagery on contact with the wilderness? Or does he, as a product of a centuries-old culture, cling to civilization and resist the eroding influences of a primitive environment? These questions must be examined if we are to understand the frontier process.

◄§◄§ THAT SOME pioneers did secede from civilization, and that all were infected with germs of primitivism by their wilderness life, is amply documented by the observations of visitors to America's successive frontiers. Travelers who entered the new settlements were conscious of a lowered cultural level. All about them, as one observed, were men who had left the East with knowledge and refinement, but who now stood "a striking gradation nearer to the savage." To another, passing that boundary line meant that he was "quite out of society; every thing and every body . . . looks wild and half savage."[1] The frontier was a land apart because savagery was nudging civilization into the background.

Testimony on this point is abundant, and embraces successive frontiers from the earliest settlements to the last. The Dutch pioneers on the Hudson and the Swedish on the Delaware seemed wild and half civilized, guilty of debauchery, drunkenness, fighting, and lawlessness, for, as one visitor put it, "having no other people to associate with than the native Indians, they soon began to differ more and more in their actions and manners from the Europeans" until they were "not much better than savages."[2] A century later a minister on the Carolina frontier was rudely told that the settlers wanted no "D——d Black Gown Sons of Bitches among them" to interfere with their constant "Revelling Drinking Singing Dancing and Whoring." There, he sadly reported, "many hund[reds] do live in Concubinage, swapping their wives as Cattel, and living in a State of Nature, more irregularly and unchastely than the Indians."[3]

As the frontier crossed the Appalachians the thermometer of sin rose steadily. Kentucky was "Rogues' Harbor" to Easterners—a gathering place for "one-eyed savages," "semi-barbarians," and "a kind of humanized Ourang outang."[4] There fights occurred with no holds barred and each combatant seeking to maim his foe by biting off a nose or gouging out an eye. In 1798 the state legislature decreed special penalties for those guilty of slitting a nose or ear, or putting out an eye "while fighting or otherwise."[5] Tennessee courts regularly recorded the phrase "nose was bit"; a visitor to the Nashville jail in the 1830s found three prisoners, one confined for stabbing, one for gouging, and one for biting off an enemy's nose. Told on that frontier was the tale of the well-known eye gouger who, after conversion at a camp meeting, wrestled with the Devil on the mourners' bench while his friends shouted: "Gouge him, Billy! gouge him, *Billy! gouge* him."[7] Even more common were records of battles where kicking, biting, and slashing with dirks or bowie knives were the order of the day.[8]

ఆ§ఆ§ WITH THE SPREAD of settlement beyond the Mississippi, the pace of lawlessness accelerated. The bowie knife, travelers reported, was an item of attire as essential as trousers, and even more useful; it was used so often that Iowans were world-famous for their brutality and cruelty in the 1840s. "For myself," testified an Illinoisan, "I would as soon go into exile at once as to emigrate to Iowa as it is."[9] Throughout the Valley profanity, tobacco spitting, and drunkenness were the bane of all civilized travelers; Charles Dickens left there convinced that frontiersmen were so addicted to chewing that "they expectorate in dreams," while swearing was elevated to such sublime heights that no frontiersman could speak without "uttering as many oaths as . . . necessary and intelligible words."[10] Home-distilled whisky, made from corn and selling for twenty-five cents a gallon, was consumed on every social occasion from a militia muster to the ordination of a new minister. "I have rarely," observed a visitor on such an occasion, "seen so many people drunk and nowhere so many brawls and rows."[11]

Nor was there a slackening of evil as the frontier advanced across the plains and mountains of the Far West. The disorder and savagery of the mountain men's rendezvous, the mining camps, the cow towns, and the "hells on wheels" that housed the railroad construction crews has been too often chronicled to require repetition.[12] Among the more respectable inhabitants the moral standard was not significantly higher, if travelers can be believed. "Liquoring up," noted a visitor to Colorado, "seems to be the sole amusement of the Inhabitants."[13]

Whisky sellers were everywhere, even distributing themselves along the stage coach routes to cater to thirsty riders. Drunkenness was so common that the Sabbath day was commonly turned into a three-ringed carnival where gambling and carousing shocked the prudish and dismayed the pious. Ralph Waldo Emerson might have had such scenes in mind when he wrote: "The pioneers are commonly the off-scourings of civilized society."[14] There was a Wild West in those days, wild because some of the settlers had temporarily shed the garments of civilization as they adjusted to frontier life.

Despite this evidence, we must ask ourselves one significant question: Were the successive Wests occupied largely by profane, tobacco-spitting, nose-biting, eye-gouging, Sabbath-breaking, drunken, half-horse and half-alligator rip roarers? Obviously not. This distortion has been perpetuated by two misconceptions.[15]

One originated in the tendency of visitors to single out unusual frontier types for extended description, partly because they were fascinated by the lawless reprobates who contrasted so sharply with the prosaic citizens of their own social circles, partly because they sensed that the market for their books would expand in proportion to the amount of blood and thunder they could capture on their pages. So they fastened upon a few pockets of lawlessness—the Mississippi River towns, the annual rendezvous of the mountain men, the cow towns and mining camps—and pictured them as typical of all the West. Actually these backwashes were peopled by only a handful of the thousands of pioneers who advanced the frontier westward. Just as misleading was the failure of visitors to distinguish between "backwoodsmen" or "squatters" on the one hand and the small farmers who made up the bulk of the frontiersmen on the other. The squatters were maladjusted discontents who fled society to spend their lives in sloth, indolence, and ignorance, just as do their counterparts in the skid rows of today's cities. Yet they, like the river men and mountain men, captured the interest of travelers, who described them so often that both contemporaries and later historians were misled into picturing them as typical pioneers.

The opposite was true. These types existed only on the remote fringes of the settled areas where conditions were atypical rather than typical. Partly responsible for their antisocial behavior was the inclination of lawless men to concentrate in lawless regions; the sparsely peopled frontiers attracted outcasts who rebelled against authority. "It is not merely American but human nature," wrote Sidney Smith, "that the lawless will run to where there is no law—and there they will make the rule of the strongest reign. Where is an American vagabond so likely to go as to a frontier territory?"[16] Once in the West, these men responded to social forces recognizable to any student of human behavior. The normal man is self-centered with an instinctive urge to do what he pleases regardless of consequences; the great majority, however, are restrained by the habits and regulations of society, which shape conduct along lines suitable for group living. When these restraints are removed, as they were on the outer reaches of the frontier, there occurred a reversion to anti-social behavior. This happened only in the most thinly occupied regions, peopled by hunters, trappers, cattlemen, miners, and squatters. Among the mass of pioneers, living near their neighbors, no such reversion took place. "When several families settle at the same time and place," noted an observing traveler, "the colonists do not as easily become brutalized as the solitary settler."[19]

That this handful of outcasts should be pictured as typical frontiersmen was unfortunate. The true pioneers—those who subdued the West—were the small-propertied farmers, ranchers, and entrepreneurs who formed the bulk of the advancing population. They were of a different breed, in outlook, in purpose, in social philosophy, from the hunters and squatters. They came to stay, and to grow up with the country; stay they did as they transformed the wilderness into a civilization. These were America's true frontiersmen, in numbers and in impact. If we are to understand the frontier process, we must inquire whether they succumbed to barbarism or sought to perpetuate the culture they had known in the East.

∞∞∞ CARELESS GENERALIZATIONS about this point must be avoided, for individual differences within this group were numerous. Some did revert to primitivism as they were infected by the frontier fever and became perennial drifters. The great majority, however, carried to their new homes a firm desire to transfer to the West the cultural institutions of the East. They came determined to make no compromise with the environment; they would plant a civilization complete with schools, churches, literary societies, newspapers, libraries, and a thriving cultural life. Nor did this seem an unattainable dream, for nearly every pioneer settlement contained an educated minority that could serve as the medium for the transmission of Eastern culture. The determination of this cultured elite to duplicate the civilization of their homelands served as a strong deterrent to any regression that might be wrought by the social environment of the frontier.

Certainly that determination was there. Wrote Henry Ward Beecher as he watched the westward-flowing tide of the 1850s: "They drive schools along with them as shepherds drive flocks. They have herds of churches, academies, lyceums; and their religious and educational institutions go lowing along the western plains as Jacob's herds lowed along the Syrian hills."[19] So slavishly did some imitate Eastern life that their villages could scarcely be distinguished from those they left behind. "Were I," a traveler noted, "to drop, like Cyrano, from the moon, and to land, unlike Cyrano, in Painesville, Ohio, I should immediately inquire for the Boston and Albany station. There are the same drooping elms, the same pilastered houses, the same Common, the same noble churches, as in lovely Massachusetts."[20] Many in frontier communities were eager to support schools and churches as symbols of civilization, even, as a visitor to the West wryly noted, those "not especially controlled by the influences that school-houses and churches create."[21] A housewife on a Kansas homestead summed up the dreams of most pioneers when she reminisced: "I have read in books that the people of the frontier kept moving ever westward to escape civilization. But if my experience counts for anything, such people were the exceptions. So eager were we to keep in touch with civilization that even when we could not afford a shotgun and ammunition to kill rabbits, we subscribed to newspapers and periodicals and bought books."[22]

This was to be expected. The pioneers were cultural transplants who had moved to new homes not to escape the old, but only to achieve greater economic and personal self-realization. They went west in hope rather than despair, and so they looked back upon the value system of the East with nostalgia instead of bitterness. To expect them to shed cultural baggage under these circumstances would be to deny the force of habit in human nature. Alexis de Tocqueville spoke truly when he characterized the frontiersman as "a highly civilized being, who consents for a time to inhabit the backwoods, and who penetrates into the wilds of the New World with the Bible, an axe, and some newspapers."[23] As they moved, the culture that the pioneers carried with them was diluted, but their loyalty to it was strengthened. Forced to shed some elements of their civilization, they clung so tenaciously to the remainder that it assumed a new importance in their lives. Morality, education, and learning bulked larger in the consciences of the "better sort" in the West than among their counterparts in the East.[24]

◄§◄§ CAUTION MUST once more be exercised as we survey the end result of this Western dedication to Eastern cultural standards. Masses of evidence can be summoned to prove that frontiersmen read books and newspapers, founded schools and churches, patronized literary societies and subscription libraries, and generally behaved in a manner rivaling that of the elite of Boston or London. Travelers by the score, and modern scholars no less numerous, have paraded statistics to show that the pioneers varied not one whit from their Eastern cousins both in opportunity for cultural advancement and in the avidity with which they embraced that opportunity. Such evidence is impressive, and does reveal a frontier society far removed from barbarism. But before it can be completely accepted, we must ask one pertinent question: How typical of *all* frontiersmen were the men and women who served as harbingers of civilization during the frontier's advance?

No simple answer presents itself. For every contemporary document describing the eagerness with which a pioneer community supported piety or education, there exists another depicting a neighboring community as sunk in impiety or ignorance. Every traveler who describes a visit to a primitive cabin well stocked with books can be matched by another who found only indifference to learning throughout the West. Clearly such evidence is too contradictory and too unreliable to be used as a base for generalizations concerning the extent of cultural transplantation that took place. Individual differences being what they are, we can only conclude that some pioneers transported civilization westward with them, and that others did not. This platitude gives rise to two allied problems: Did the frontier's social environment diminish the proportion of the total population dedicated to cultural pursuits, and did the transplanted culture survive unchanged in its new habitat? We can seek a solution to both by first summarizing the abundant evidence substantiating the high level of frontier civilization, then by noting the extent to which that civilization failed to endure in exactly its Eastern form.

The success of some Easterners in creating patent-office models of their homeland communities can be illustrated in the hamlet of New Salem, Illinois, where Abraham Lincoln whetted his taste for learning. In 1832 New Salem was only three years old and boasted less than 150 inhabitants, yet it supported a good subscription school, a flourishing debating society, a nonsectarian Sunday School, and several respectable private libraries whose owners cheerfully loaned their books. Much has been made of the fact that young Lincoln had to borrow books, but less of the equally significant fact that books were on hand to be borrowed. The future President was able to thumb the pages of Shakespeare and Robert Burns, to study Kirkham's *Grammar* and the six books of Euclid, and to read Paine and Volney and Jefferson as well as newspapers and periodicals. Yet New Salem flourished for only six years and was a ghost town in ten.[25]

A similar story, on a grander scale, can be told of Lexington, Kentucky, which in 1810, with a population of only four thousand persons, could proclaim itself the "Athens of the West." There two bookstores dispensed learning, three academies flourished, and Transylvania University attracted students even from the East by its rich intellectual fare. This atmosphere attracted writers, editors, architects, and even painters. Within a few years Lexington boasted a theater, a natural history museum, reading rooms, a remarkably good magazine called the *Western Review,* and its own school of painting under Matthew Jouett. There in 1817 the first performance of a Beethoven symphony in the United States was conducted. Lexington's cultural supremacy was soon rivaled by Cincinnati, which was so successful in "heaving up a pile of intellectual achievement" (to quote a local editor) that a citizen, plagued by the excessive demands on his time, wrote feelingly: "twenty sermons a week—, Sunday evening Discources on Theology—Private assemblies—state Cotillion parties—Saturday Night Clubs, and chemical lectures— . . . like the fever and the ague, return every day with distressing regularity."[26]

So demanding was the urge to perpetuate Eastern civilization that some among even the most primitive frontiersmen succumbed. Daniel Boone and his fellow long hunters of early Kentucky read *Gulliver's Travels* around their campfires and were so impressed that they named a stream Lulbegrud's Creek.[27] A few of Boone's successors, the half-savage mountain men who roamed the Far West in quest of beaver, also read avidly whenever books were available; one trapper recalled a winter camp in which he and his companions sampled Byron, Shakespeare, and Scott, in addition to the Bible and Clark's commentary on the Scriptures, as well as "other small works in Geology, chemistry and philosophy." Another confessed that he had learned much from the "frequent arguments and debates held in what we termed 'Rocky Mountain College.'" Even such an illiterate old reprobate as Jim Bridger enjoyed hearing a companion read Shakespeare aloud. On one such occasion the tale of the murder of the two princes in the Tower aroused a violent denunciation of the bard who, he declared, "must have had a bad heart and been as devilish mean as a Sioux, to have written such scoundrelism as that."[28]

Cowboys, whose secession from civilization was almost as complete as that of the fur trappers, were also sometimes avid readers, even though books were virtually unattainable. Some were so starved for literary fare that they read and reread the labels on tins in the cook's shack until they could recite every one from memory, syllable by syllable. Tenderfeet who did not "know their cans" were social outcasts when a cowboy shouted a key phrase and the whole group chanted in unison the words on every label in the ranch. When mail-order catalogues appeared they were memorized just as thoroughly. One cattleman was so hungry for unfamiliar words that he reined in his horse when he saw a scrap of paper on the ground. "I got down and picked it up," he later recalled, "simply because I was hungry for something to read, if not more than two or three words." Another read a patent medicine advertisement so often that he convinced himself that he exhibited the symptoms of seven diseases, all fatal.[29]

Miners were just as determined to maintain their ties with the past, and when they had the means to do so, they did. Virginia City, Nevada, which symbolized lawlessness to a generation of Americans, within two years of its founding had schools for a thousand children, three theaters, and an opera house seating two thousand persons where "Italian and other operas by the best composers were produced."[30] Denver in 1860 was marked by its "extreme respectability"; its saloons served champagne and catawba wine as well as Tanglefoot Whisky, and schools, libraries, theaters, and literary societies flourished. Even Leadville, Colorado, one of the last "Wild West" towns, in 1879, in addition to its 110 saloons, boasted four daily newspapers, five churches, three schools, and a branch of the YMCA, all reported to be doing a land-office business. Leadville, observed a British visitor, "was like some thriving provincial town. The men would not have looked out of place in the street, say, of Reading, while the women, in their quiet and somewhat old-fashioned style of dressing, reminded me very curiously of rural England."[31]

If the impulse to perpetuate Eastern civilization touched such social rebels as trappers, cowboys, and miners, it also shaped the ambition of the small-propertied farmers and entrepreneurs who made up the bulk of the frontier population. Schools were first on their agenda, for education would bridge the gap between Eastern culture and Western primitivism, perpetuate traditional values and learning, and even (some frankly admitted) help sell real estate in pioneer communities. "There is," observed Timothy Flint, "a general and anxious consciousness, on the part of parents, that their children must be instructed"; a traveler in Ohio in 1808 underlined these remarks when he wrote: "The education of children in this country is considered and made an object of particular concern."[32] This was understandable. The principal hope of all pioneers was self-betterment, and this meant equipping children to rise in the social scale. The South Carolina Regulators mirrored the spirit of the frontier when they demanded schools that the young might "be early taught the principles of Religion and Goodness, and their Heads and Hands, be employ'd in Exercises of the Manual and Useful Arts."[33] So did the founders of the University of Nebraska a century later when they sang a special hymn proclaiming:

> Upon this wild and lone frontier
> Behold this edifice we rear;
> With yet no home to call our own,
> Man cannot live by bread alone.[34]

Schools satisfied both the idealism and the practical instincts of the pioneers.

They were established, too. "If but half a dozen families settle in a new township," observed a traveler on the Ohio frontier, "they build themselves a school-house in the center."[35] One Tennessee community built five schools within two years of its founding. Pittsburgh hired its first schoolmaster in 1761 when still a frontier fort. In Ohio more than one hundred academies were founded between 1803 and 1840. A typical Wisconsin frontier community spent appreciably more money per pupil than a similar community in Vermont. Denver's first school was opened in the autumn of 1859 when the Pike's Peak gold rush was still in its infancy, and by the end of 1860 the village had three in operation. Nevada's school law was passed in 1861 when the principal settlement at Virginia City contained only two or three children. Texas settlers listed as a principal grievance against Mexico that country's failure to provide education for their children. A group of pioneers who arrived in Buffalo County, Nebraska, in 1871 organized a school district while still living in the railroad cars that had brought them west, and levied a tax on themselves to build a schoolhouse.[36] Clearly some frontiersmen were as eager as Easterners to provide their children with educational boot-straps.

Above all, these Westerners insisted that schools dispense the educational diet then popular in the East. This meant undiluted doses of Latin and Greek, for those were the days when a classical education was the sole avenue to culture. "Should the time ever come," pontificated a Western writer in 1820, "when Latin and Greek should be banished from our universities, and the study of Cicero and Demosthenes, or Homer and Virgil, should be considered as unnecessary for the formation of a scholar, we should regard mankind as fast sinking into absolute barbarism, and the gloom of mental darkness as likely to increase until it should become universal."[37] His warning was heeded, for as schools sprang up, the ancient languages bulked large in their instructional programs. A school founded in a Kentucky hamlet in 1787 proclaimed that it would teach "the Latin and Greek languages, together with such branches of the sciences as are generally taught in public seminaries." Ohio's early schools so immersed their pupils in classical subjects that one of their products reported years later that he could repeat from memory whole books of the *Aeneid* of Virgil and the *Iliad* of Homer. Indiana's territorial legislature specified in 1804 that a new school at Vincennes should teach "the Latin, Greek, French, and English languages, mathematics, natural philosophy, logic, rhetoric, and the law of nature and of nations." Not only was this curriculum duplicated at a seminary opened at Bloomington a few years later, but the building was modeled after Nassau Hall at Princeton. Beyond the Mississippi the story was the same; when the University of Kansas was founded in 1865 instruction was available in classical subjects as well as modern literature and civil engineering.[38]

Those pioneers who interested themselves in schooling accepted no compromise with practicality, but were bent on transplanting the best of Eastern culture to their Western communities.

ـeﭻ IF SCHOOLS were necessary to inculcate the young in traditional values, newspapers and magazines must serve as a bridge between West and East for adults. So it was that newspapers were usually the first cultural transplant in each new community. Travelers expressed amazement that every "collection of houses in America which can by any stretch of courtesy be called a town" supported a printing press and a hard-working editor. Not uncommonly a journeyman printer arrived simultaneously with the pioneers, driving a cart with his fonts and hand press, and ready to accept the small subsidy that the town planters would give to advertise their community. An editor who in the fall of 1854 opened shop on the unpeopled prairie of Kansas had the satisfaction of seeing the town of Leavenworth take shape around him and the circulation of his weekly climb to three thousand copies within five months. Another used the stump of an ancient oak as his editorial chair and the top of his beaver hat as a table to bring out the first issue of the Omaha *Arrow* just twenty-eight days after that village was planted.[39] The frontiersman who wanted a newspaper seldom had long to wait.

The enterprise of these editors was explained by the fact that they were nearly always sure of finding readers, for American frontiersmen subscribed to newspapers in surprising numbers. In 1840 the West could boast one newspaper for every 12,000 persons. Indiana supported a weekly or daily paper for every 9,940 inhabitants at that time, and Ohio one for every 9,264; through the Mississippi Valley as a whole about one third of all families subscribed to one or more papers.[40] As the frontier advanced, so did the thirst for news. Texas had thirteen newspapers by 1840, Nebraska more than one hundred when a decade old, and sparsely peopled Idaho no less than twenty in 1880. San Francisco by the middle 1850s supported more newspapers than London; Denver in 1871 needed six to satisfy its ten thousand inhabitants. Travelers never ceased to marvel that backwoods hamlets with only a handful of settlers could sustain an editor; one reported three papers circulating in Little Rock when the population was only six hundred persons.[41] Westerners could appreciate the story of the stranger who asked how one small town could support four newspapers, and was told that it took four newspapers to support such a town.[42]

⋖§⋗ FOR BETTER-EDUCATED pioneers a sturdier literary fare was necessary; they must have books in quantity and variety to satisfy their cultural cravings. The demand was sizable, for every community contained a circle of well-read citizens who kept abreast of the latest publications in England and the East. "In circles where I visited," wrote a traveler from Kentucky in 1802, "literature was most commonly the topic of conversation."[43] Another recalled visiting a newcomer to pioneer Louisville who owned a copy of *Ivanhoe*, then recently published; within an hour two neighbors had called to borrow the book. Travelers time and again catalogued the extensive libraries that they found in remote log cabins, with works of Shakespeare, Scott, Burns, Sterne, Coleridge, Shelley, and Byron often in evidence.[44] "It was gratifying," wrote one, " . . . to hear Shakespeare, Scott, and Byron quoted familiarly amongst the wilds of Louisiana." Another recorded his delight at finding a housewife in New Madrid who was "perfectly acquainted with Plato, spoke of him as familiarly as a school boy does of Washington."[45] His experience was matched by a later visitor who encountered in the Far West a lady reputed to be a deadly shot, a great rider, a horse tamer, and the conqueror of a grizzly bear but was never happier than when reading Herbert Spencer.[46] The boy in backwoods Indiana who gathered nuts each fall to sell at six cents a bushel so that he could buy copies of Plato, Dante, and Milton may not have typified frontier youth, but he was not entirely unique. "In travelling through the country," noted a New Englander after visiting backwoods Illinois, "one will meet with a well thumbed and select library in the log cabin, and listen to discourse on any topic in that rude home which would give spirit and life to an assemblage in a Boston drawing-room."[47]

That Westerners with literary appetites were relatively numerous was demonstrated by the sales of publishers, for in the pre-Civil War period they agreed that the Western market made the difference between profits and bankruptcy. During the winter, when frozen rivers ended contact with the frontier, a number closed their doors while others operated on a reduced scale. "The publishing season," wrote a

New York author in mid-November 1845, "is now nearly closed, [and when] the rivers are frozen . . . it will be over." James Fenimore Cooper was told by his Philadelphia publisher in 1832 that an unexpectedly early freeze had hurt the sales of his latest book, *The Bravo*. Reputations of authors were made or broken beyond the Appalachians; an editor explained to Henry Wadsworth Longfellow that top royalties could not be paid to James Russell Lowell because he enjoyed no reputation in the West. "I know the test of *general* popularity as well as any man," he said, "—and he has it not. He is well known in New England and appreciated there but has not a tythe of the reputation *South and West* possessed by yourself and Bryant."[48]

The demand for books in the West attracted publishers to frontier villages, especially in the prerailroad days when transportation problems plagued those who operated in the East. Most were newspaper publishers who used their presses during slack periods to print broadsides, pamphlets, and occasional volumes of verse or prose; the first book published west of the Appalachians was produced in 1793 by the editor of the Pittsburgh *Gazette*. Haphazard though their operations may have been, their output was not inconsiderable. By 1815 printers in Kentucky had produced 647 titles, by 1820 Ohio's output approached 600, by 1835 Indiana's presses were responsible for 601, and by 1840, 474 had been published in Illinois.[49] Here was testimony to the market for reading material in the West, for the pioneer printers would produce only what their customers would buy.

This same appetite for books was demonstrated by the multiplication of bookstores in pioneer communities. One dealer had this forcefully brought home when, in 1804, he crossed upper New York state to open a shop in Toronto. At Canandaigua, then a hamlet on a raw frontier, he was physically detained until he agreed to open his store in that village.[50] Elsewhere the story was not far different; travelers often expressed surprise that frontier outposts could support booksellers as they did. Lexington, Kentucky, contained less than seven hundred inhabitants in 1788, yet six dealers advertised books for sale. Eight years later Cincinnati's five hundred settlers could choose between two bookstores, one of which advertised "books of divinity, law and physic, several entertaining histories; some English and Latin school books; a variety of books for the instruction and entertainment of children; American magazines and museums of the latest date."[51] Davenport, Iowa, opened its first bookstore when the town was less than three years old and the population under five hundred. Even the boisterous mining camps of the forty-niners supported an itinerant peddler who advertised "the works of Shakespeare, Byron, Milton, Gray, Campbell and other distinguished poets."[52] Either the book dealers of the West were incorrigible optimists, or they recognized a profitable market for their wares.

With this demand, subscription libraries were certain to mushroom in the West, distributing as they did the cost of books among many specie-poor pioneers.[53] Dayton, Ohio, began its first library in 1805, when the town was less than ten years old and the population below one hundred; so eager were the subscribers that they drew lots to determine who would see the volumes when the first shipment arrived. Even earlier the citizens of Lexington had raised $500 to purchase books from the East; by 1800 a dozen communities in Kentucky, all with fewer than eight hundred inhabitants, followed their example. Cleveland's first library was established in 1811 when sixteen of the sixty-four settlers pooled their resources. In Madison, Indiana, all twenty-four male inhabitants contributed $5.00 each to finance the initial purchases. Davenport, Iowa, found fifteen of its three hundred inhabitants ready to support a circulating library. Three flourished in San Francisco in the early 1850s.[54] So went the story on each successive frontier. What these libraries meant to the pioneers is suggested by the reminiscences of an Ohio settler who recalled his thrill when the first books reached his community: "I had no candles; however, the woods afforded plenty of pine knots—and with these I made torches by which I could read, though I nearly spoiled my eyes. Many a night I passed in this manner till 12 or 1 o'clock reading to my wife, while she was hatchelling, carding or spinning."[55]

The best publicized of these frontier institutions was the "Coonskin Library" of Ohio. This began in 1803, when the farmers of Ames Township, plagued by the usual shortage of cash, pledged the proceeds of a winter's trapping and hunting to a "Western Library Association," founded on the spot to provide "the many beneficial effects which social libraries are calculated to produce in societies." With furs gathered by twenty-four persons, Samuel Brown took off for Boston that spring, there to sell the pelts for $70. He returned with fifty-one volumes, including Goldsmith's works, Ramsay's *History of the American Revolution*, Playfair's *History of Jacobism*, Harris' *Minor Encyclopedia*, Morse's *Geography*, and a sampling of biography and history. When these treasures were dumped from saddlebags to a cabin floor the awestruck members felt, as one wrote, that "the library of the Vatican seemed a mere trifle by comparison."[56]

If subscription libraries distributed the cost of books, literary and debating societies spread their learning through frontier areas. These multiplied almost as fast as pioneer towns, especially in the trans-Mississippi West where many a community boasted a dedicated group of culture worshippers who met weekly to discuss literature or dispute among themselves. By the autumn of 1854 a periodical could announce that not more than a handful of towns in the West would be lacking a course of lectures or discussions that winter.[57] "The people," a passer-by noted with obvious sympathy, "are victims of oratory."[58] Yet they always asked for more, coming from miles around so faithfully that the meetings were usually well attended, and listening to interminable hours of recitation or speech making.[59] One newcomer to a brand new town in Nebraska found two rough houses, a shambles of a hotel labeled "Frontier House," and one dugout, but a literary society was already flourishing with readings and debates held weekly.[60]

~§~§ FRONTIERSMEN obviously wanted to read and listen, but what type of books and lecturers did they demand? Such data as are available suggest that they read books currently popular in the East and Europe, or volumes that had stood the test of time, rather than contemporary books designed to instruct in practical pursuits. Of the two thousand titles purchased by five libraries on the Ohio Valley frontier before 1815, about 30 percent were literary classics, 15 percent legal and political studies, 14 percent histories, and the remainder traditional encyclopedias or works on religion, travel, and science. Scott, Shakespeare, Goldsmith, and Pope were the most popular authors, although Byron was in demand and such American writers as Joel Barlow not neglected. Romantic novels by Felicia Hemans and Thomas Moore also attracted readers.[61] Western publishers catered to somewhat different interests; of the 567 books printed in the Ohio Valley before 1815, 29 percent were almanacs and gazetteers, 23 percent religious works, 17 percent instructional books, and only 12 percent novels or essays. Local printers, more aware of the practical needs of the frontiersmen than those in New York, apparently sensed the demand for do-it-yourself and religious books that would ease the lot of pioneers in this world and the next.[62]

Significantly, publishers in both East and West failed to detect any major interest in books about frontier life, at least until the late nineteenth century when cowboys developed a taste for "Western" dime novels. Scott and Goldsmith were far more popular among the pioneers than James Fenimore Cooper, perhaps because Westerners were repelled by the unrealistic pictures of frontiersmen that he inflicted on his readers. Nor were books by Western authors any more popular, since these misguided penmen closed their eyes to the pulsating world about them and wrote instead of Eastern scenes and Eastern events in what they took to be an Eastern style. To them a sky was a "blue canopy," valleys were "vales," forests "edens," and winds "zephyrs." They, like their readers, were so eager to maintain cultural ties with the East that they failed to recognize the robust new world in which they lived. One Western writer who inflicted on the world a *Washingtonii Vita* written in Latin, and another guilty of a four-volume effusion called *Fredoniad: or, Independence Preserved, an Epic Poem on the Late War of 1812* testify to the dreadful impact that the cult of Eastern worship had on literary-minded pioneers.[63]

&§&§ NO LESS than books, the theater thrived on the frontier, and revealed the same insistence on perpetuating traditional forms. Dramatic performances began surprisingly early in nearly all pioneer communities, as Thespian societies sprang up to decorate a barn or saloon, train a group of amateurs, and invite the townsfolk in. Cincinnati's citizens saw their first theatricals in 1801 with the playing of "The Poor Soldier" and "Peeping Tom of Coventry"; Vincennes followed five years later, and from then on amateur troupes multiplied as though by magic in almost every pioneer community.[64]

Where amateurs dared tread, professionals soon followed. Theatrical companies necessarily depended on a population numerous enough to support their efforts, but only a few people were needed when enthusiasm was great enough and pockets well-enough lined. Pittsburgh opened its first theater in 1813; Cincinnati and Nashville fell into line six years later; and as the frontier swept westward others followed with remarkable regularity. By midcentury every embryo city in the Mississippi Valley supported at least one theater that attracted traveling actors from the East and even from England. From these major centers they branched out to play in any village that could provide a rough stage and benches for an audience.[65]

In the Far West the pace of theater building accelerated. Omaha staged its first performance only three years after "the streets of our city were trodden by the deer and the timid prairie wolf," as the local editor pridefully noted. Cheyenne, which sprang into existence in 1867 when the Union Pacific tracks reached Crow Creek and which boasted of being "the richest and toughest town in the West," entertained two traveling companies that fall in a ramshackle theater hurriedly built to receive them. In the mining camps of California and throughout the Far West the story was the same, with Sacramento opening its first theater in 1849 and San Francisco a year later. In these outposts such attractions as "The Bandit Chief" proved so popular that actors were paid $200 weekly and miners cheerfully surrendered two or three dollars in dust for a seat. Denver's theatrical history began in 1860 when a company that arrived in mule-drawn wagons played for six months before moving on to Central City and other mining camps. Deadwood in the Black Hills built its first theater when the camp was only a cluster of shacks and tents.[66] These scattered records tell an impressive story. Even the most culturally deprived frontiersmen were willing to pay handsome sums to capture for an evening a taste of Eastern civilization.

That the rough-hewn pioneers or miners were not content with shoddy literary fare was repeatedly demonstrated, for the playwright who dwarfed all others in popularity was William Shakespeare. The Bard's declamatory style explained this; no other author was so attuned to the Westerners' own extravagances of speech. So they demanded his plays over and over again, with *Richard III*, *Hamlet*, *Othello*, and *Julius Caesar* winning widest acclaim. Of more than seven thousand plays presented in five western centers between 1794 and 1840, over four hundred—or about one in eighteen—were by Shakespeare, a record approached by no other author.[67] On later frontiers the pattern varied but little. Twenty-two of the Bard's plays were given in California theaters within a decade of the arrival of the forty-niners, with *Richard III* leading the list. In the same period the theaters of San Francisco offered 907 plays, 48 operas, and 84 ballets and pantomimes. There was a justified tone of self-assurance as well as provincialism in the words of a San Francisco editor who wrote in 1854: "The Californians are as good judges of acting as can be found anywhere; and they care not a fig for the opinion of New York or London. When we pronounce a favorable verdict, we are able to back it up with a fortune, and snap our fingers in the face of the world."[68] That frontier was growing up.

THE BILL of particulars that has been summoned to demonstrate the unwillingness of the pioneer to discard the garments of civilization is impressive, and might by some be considered convincing. Many frontiersmen did prize schools, thirst for traditional literature, and patronize theatrical performances on a scale rivaling that of the East. They were, apparently, determined to transplant their cultural heritage intact, unchanged by contact with the wilderness environment that they had temporarily adopted.

Impressive though this evidence may be, it fails to substantiate the conclusion that the successive Wests were merely transplanted replicas of the Easts from which they emerged. Nor does it prove that every Westerner, or even a substantial number of pioneers, resisted the erosive effect of the primitive social environment. Analysis of the writings of travelers who described urbane frontiersmen addicted to novel reading, theater going, and cultural pursuits makes clear that these visitors were mingling only with men and women whose tastes paralleled their own. This was natural; the well-read Englishman visiting a pioneer community would be little inclined to seek out illiterates and others of the culturally deprived. Similarly most Westerners who wrote glowingly of the dawning civilization of the frontier belonged to an educated minority and were, perhaps, prone to exaggerate the maturity of their communities to attract newcomers whose interests would be like their own. Neither travelers nor the frontiersmen themselves who wrote of the frontier were typical of the frontier.

If the record keepers were not representative of the society that they described, the problem of determining the degree of popular concern with culture becomes almost insoluble. Such scant evidence as does exist, however, indicates that a majority of the pioneers were almost certainly uninterested in reading, distrustful of schools that took their children from the fields, and unfamiliar with either theaters or circulating libraries. The majority seldom visited the towns and cities where visitors found cultural interests most strongly expressed; nearly all were isolated on farms where they had access to neither libraries nor bookstores nor literary societies. Their consuming ambition was material self-advancement, and this task absorbed their waking hours. For every frontiersman who rhapsodized on the virtues of Latin or spiced his speech with quotations from Homer, hundreds remained not only indifferent but hostile to culture.

On this point testimony is not abundant, but is still meaningful. Writers anxious to prove the transit of culture westward have made much of the fact that in 1812 Kentucky had eleven subscription libraries, Ohio ten, and Indiana two. Yet this was only one library for every 37,000 persons in Kentucky, one for every 23,760 in Ohio, and one for every 12,260 in Indiana. In thinly settled areas, these figures meant that only a handful of the pioneers had access to books. Men of lofty ambition might establish fine magazines such as Timothy Flint's *Western Monthly Review,* or James Hall's *Western Monthly Magazine,* but not one of these publications survived public apathy for more than a few years.

The educational record tells the same story. Frontiersmen believed that schools were the salvation of democracy and ladders to personal advancement, but mouthing theories was one thing and paying hard money to support education quite another. In 1840 only one eleventh of the total Ohio Valley population was attending school, only one twenty-third in Missouri, and one thirty-second in Kentucky. Yet at that time in the thickly settled states of New York, Massachusetts, and Pennsylvania, one sixth of the people were receiving education.[69] Beyond the Mississippi there was no improvement; one third of the children of school age in Texas and far less than one half in Oregon were enrolled in schools thirty years after Americans occupied these frontiers. Even those who attended learned but little, for classroom facilities were less adequate than in the East, books and instructional materials difficult to obtain, vacations long to allow pupils to work on farms, and teachers often incompetent. One prospective instructor who expressed doubts of his own abilities when being interviewed for a post in a mining town was assured: "Do you retain a clear recollection of the twenty-six letters of the alphabet? For if you do, you are the equal of any educational demand this camp will make on you."[70]

Testimony such as this suggests that among the ordinary small-propertied farmers who formed the bulk of the westward-moving tide cultural progress was retarded by life along the frontiers. Particularly was this the case when the second generation that had been reared without an Eastern experience took over. The traveler who reported from Ohio: "I have not seen a book in the hands of any person since I left Philadelphia," was no less accurate than his contemporaries who described the bookstores of Lexington or Cincinnati; he had mingled with a different class of people than those comprising the urban elite, and one probably far more typical of the frontier as a whole. Similarly, the Westerner who wrote sadly that "The people here are not yet a reading people. Few good books are brought into the country," was recording his impressions of the bulk of the farm folk who were grappling to subdue nature, not of the cultured leaders who so deeply impressed upper-class visitors from the East or Europe.[71]

The prevalence of these anticultural prejudices is attested particularly by those who dealt with the common people on the more primitive agricultural frontiers. There, they reported, lack of learning bred hostility to learning, until men of above-average educational backgrounds found life unpleasant. "Here the people despise knowledge," observed a minister from the backcountry. One Tennessee promoter, seeking to attract settlers by assuring them that they would soon achieve "civilization, intelligence, comfort, and health" if they settled on his lands, was rudely told that they had come west to escape civilization, and that if it caught up with them they would move on.[72]

The temporary eclipse of learning on the frontier was to be expected, for the social environment decreed failure to the most heroic efforts to transplant immediately Eastern civilization. The West naturally attracted men of action and material ambition, rather than the studious and the contemplative. In the sifting that occurred as the westward movement went on, those with the greatest sensitivity to learning, those with the most developed intellectual interests, were left behind. Cultural baggage may not have been shed along the trails, but cultural people were; "In traveling from the coast to the interior," observed an English visitor, "the proportion of uneducated persons appears to be the greater the farther to the westward."[73] Those who reached their new homes with the lamp of learning still lighted found that the flame soon flickered. They were victims of the atomization of society that occurred on all frontiers; cultural progress is always greatest where men of like interests live elbow to elbow and can profit from cooperation and mutual encouragement. In the West they were isolated or transitory. "Those who are here to-day are gone tomorrow," wrote an observer, "and their places in society filled by others who ten years back had no prospect of ever being admitted.

All is transition, waves follow one another to the far west, the froth and scum boiling in advance."[74]

If these conditions doomed transplanted culture on the frontiers, so did the social climate that prevailed there. The people were different—in values, purpose, and prejudices—from those of the more compact societies in the East. These differences mirrored the physical environment: the changed man-land ratio and abundant natural resources that spelled opportunity for the gifted, the chance to practice social democracy, the relative isolation from traditional living patterns. The opportunity for self-improvement created by this frontier world placed a premium on tasks and values that fostered material progress, rather than cultural. Specifically, the social environment engendered in newcomers a materialistic philosophy, faith in hard work as a panacea for all problems, and dependence on emotionalism, all of which slowed the transit of civilization westward.

Hard work was a way of life with the small-propertied farmers and entrepreneurs who made up the bulk of the westward-flowing population tide. So long as fields must be cleared, prairie sod broken, homes built, fences constructed, and the earth made to yield up its fruits, there was no time for abstract thought or artistic creation. "We have as yet," recorded a pioneer on a new frontier, "had but little leisure to think of any thing, beyond the calls of necessity," and this was the fate of his fellows everywhere. As an observing French commentator noted, "He has been obliged to occupy himself much more with the cultivation of the earth, than of himself."[75] Back breaking tasks must occupy the pioneer's time from morning until night if he was to fulfill his obligation to society and start himself along the road to affluence.

The hard work that was necessary on the frontier soon appeared as a virtue to frontiersmen. This was understandable. Men through the history of civilization have progressed in well-defined stages, fulfilling first their need for food and drink, then for security, next their desire for social acceptance and affection, and finally the urge for prestige. Each of these needs must be satisfied in turn. When in any social group this sequential order is upset, the next highest level cannot be achieved.[76] So the average frontiersman was conforming to established patterns when he concentrated on his physical wants; until those had been satisfied, he had but slight urge to express himself culturally. He was, moreover, true to the evolutionary pattern when he manifested hostility toward education and the arts, for men are normally antagonistic toward achievements that are unattainable.

To the pioneer, any man who wasted his time in abstract thought or by creating beauty was a traitor to society; utilitarianism was the test of any activity. The folk heroes elevated by the West were men of accomplishment rather than contemplation; Davy Crockett and Daniel Boone were venerated there, not Dr. Daniel Drake nor Timothy Flint. Andrew Jackson was the idol of the pioneers not because he was a capable lawyer and a successful diplomat, but because he was an Indian fighter and a champion of the "true-grit West" against the effete East. Wrote an observer who knew the pioneers well: "A wheat field is more pleasing to their taste than a flower garden. A well-ploughed lot is more satisfactory to their eye than the most exquisite painting of a Raphael or a Claude. They would prefer seeing a gristmill working on their own stream, to the sight of the sculptured marble of the Venus or the Apollo." These same views were voiced less elegantly by a Michigan housewife who, when she saw a newcomer planting flowers, sniffed that "she'd never know'd nobody to make nothin' by raisin' sich things."[77]

The frontiersman's craving for emotionalism also hindered the growth of a social climate in which creativity could thrive. This found expression in his acceptance of revivalism as a religious creed as well as a religious practice. From the Great Awakening of the eighteenth century through the Great Revival of 1800, revivalism was associated with anti-intellectualism; camp-meeting exhorters stressed the evil that had fallen on the world since Adam and Eve sought knowledge and urged men to seek salvation through faith rather than study. Opposition to learning was part of the dogma of frontier churches through most of the nineteenth century. The ideal clergyman, to the pioneer, was an illiterate spellbinder who could speak his language and fire his enthusiasms. "When I hear a man preach," Abraham Lincoln once said, "I like to see him act as if he were fighting bees."[78] A clergyman in backwoods Indiana characterized the successful frontier preacher when he described himself: "Yes, bless the Lord, I am a poor, humble man—and I doesn't know a single letter in the ABC's, and couldn't read a chapter in the Bible no how you could fix it, bless the Lord! I jist preach like Old Peter and Poll, by the Sperit."[79] Preaching "by the Sperit" may have saved souls, but it hardly fostered intellectualism along the frontiers.[80]

◄§◄§ A SOCIAL ENVIRONMENT in which people were governed by a cult of materialism, driven by popular pressures to engage in utilitarian tasks, and taught the evils of learning by the one group that might be counted on for intellectual guidance, would hardly provide fertile soil for transplanting Eastern culture. Even among the small minority eager for the transit of civilization mercantile matters soon bulked so large in importance that learning was neglected. An ambitious Tennessee pioneer found "every effort to create a thirst for science and a taste for general improvement paralyzed by the cold indifference of the better informed and by popular jealousy and suspicion."[81] His plaint could be voiced with justice on each succeeding frontier. Strive though they did, cultivated Easterners failed to duplicate in the West the civilization of their homelands.

Those who voiced such complaints or expressed discouragement as they watched their imported cultures wither away, could take solace, for the frontier was destined for neither barbarism nor the re-creation of an unchanged Eastern culture. Civilization and learning were to take root there, but only after they had been remolded to appeal to the pioneer. This meant no drastic changes; nearly all frontiersmen wanted to re-create the pattern of life and thought that they had known in earlier homes and moved far in this direction. But those patterns must be subtly altered to thrive in the social environment bred of frontier living. Later this book will trace this alteration in social and economic institutions. Here let us only suggest the changes that occurred in two cultural forms: literature and education.

The banner of rebellion against literary traditionalism was raised on the southern Mississippi Valley frontier. To the pioneer in that raw new country, the romantic effusions of popular writers, both local and imported, seemed thoroughly anachronistic. Romantic writers singing the beauties of nature seemed outmoded in a land where the tree was an enemy to be removed as soon as possible; fictional characters who spoke in the language of medieval England appeared out of place to readers whose ears were tuned to the colorful idiom of the backwoods. "We confess," wrote a Westerner in the 1830s, "we are heartily tired of the endless imitations of Scott, Byron, and Moore, and the rest of them, and stand ready to welcome something new, even though it should smack a little of the 'Horse,' contain a touch of the 'Alligator,' and betray a small sprinkling of the 'Steamboat.'"[82] Something more realistic than James Fenimore Cooper, something mirroring the unique life of the West, something glorifying the new moral values—democracy, individualism, perseverance, generosity, heroism—that Westerners rightly or wrongly believed they possessed, was needed to please them.

These stirrings of protest carried the frontier—and led America—into the mainstream of the nineteenth-century revolt against romanticism. Its prophets were a number of transplanted men of letters who had been educated in the East but succumbed to the spirit of the West. Augustus Baldwin Longstreet, with his *Georgia Scenes* of cockfights, horse swappings, and gander pullings; Johnson J. Hooper, whose hawk-nosed hero Simon Suggs admirably lived up to his motto "It's good to be shifty in a new country;" and Joseph G. Baldwin, with his *Flush Times in Alabama and Mississippi,* were heralds of realism in literature precisely because they found in the West scenes and characters so unique that they defied traditional description. "It would seem," wrote one of their contemporaries, "that the nearer sundown, the more original the character and odd the expression."[83] When this literary form flowered a generation later in the works of Bret Harte and Mark Twain, American writing had won its independence from Europe.

Educational reform was less dramatic, but equally significant. One Indiana pioneer summed up the problem when he pointed out that he and his neighbors lived "not as folks at Boston, or New-York; and did not, hence, need the same kind of education."[84] The average frontiersman, beset by the practical tasks of creating a civilization, wanted practical instruction, not immersion in subjects totally unrelated to his new life. Why learn rules of grammar that would never be applied, dead languages that would never be spoken, or the geography of places that would never be visited? "Daddy says he doesn't see no sort of use in the high larn'd things," a frontier schoolboy told his teacher, "—and he wants me to larn Inglish only, and book keepin, and surveyin, so as to tend store and run a line."[85] These were the things that mattered in the West, and time was too pressing to squander on subjects with no practical application.

These pressures sparked no revolution, but they did nudge the American educational system slowly away from its absorption in classical subjects and toward the utilitarian emphasis that has marked it ever since. A few straws will suggest the direction of the wind. An Easterner who assumed the presidency of Miami University in Ohio in 1824 determined to emphasize the classics and good literature five years later was boasting of the school as a "Farmer's College" where boys could be trained to the tasks of life. Traditionalists who tried to establish Wabash College in Indiana with a classical curriculum were told by the legislature that they would be granted no charter until the name was changed to Wabash Manual Labor and Teachers' Seminary. The Wisconsin legislature was firmly reminded by a county board of education that teachers should be trained to teach the "principles of agriculture" in all common schools.[86] Teachers on the early frontiers who arrived from the East freighted with missionary zeal for the classics were soon disillusioned in this atmosphere. "I have," wrote one sadly from the Indiana backwoods, "only three pupils professedly studying even Latin! and that only to understand *law-terms*. The rest are literally in the R.R.R. and Jogerfree!"[87] The rebellion that was to transform American education into a practical tool was already under way.

❧❧ SUCH EVIDENCE as may be summoned, then, suggests that the frontier was neither a patent-office model of the East nor a land sunk in barbarism. Those who abandoned civilization were few and uninfluential save in latter-day folklore. Those who sought to transplant to the West the unchanged culture of the East far outnumbered them, but they too were not typical. Their efforts were doomed to fail, for the social environment of successive frontiers offered scant substance to modes of thought rooted in a different social order. The opportunity for individual self-advancement, the blurring of class distinctions, the materialism and attitudes toward hard work, all contributed to the rejection of familiar patterns of culture. The result was a partial decay of imported civilizations, particularly during the first and second generations, but not a total negation. The frontier clung to tradition as tenaciously as it rejected complete dependence on that tradition.

From this merging of Eastern cultural and frontier social environment stemmed lasting changes in American life and institutions. Creative activities tended toward greater realism as culture readjusted itself to a world that little resembled the blissful one pictured by romanticists. Education was diverted toward more practical ends, with a corresponding decline in classical studies. Religion adapted to the needs of lonely pioneers who craved the excitement of salvation.

These changes—all reflecting a swing from theoretical to utilitarian approaches to life's problems—helped fasten on the United States a new respect for the practical man, and a corresponding decline in the importance of the abstract thinker. Anti-intellectualism, which still prevails to the degree that "eggheads" are scorned because the business of the nation is business, was not solely a product of the frontier, of course. Yet it remains one of the lasting, and least attractive, relics of the frontier heritage.

5

The Structure of Frontier Society

OF THE MANY MYTHS associated with the frontier, none has been more persistent than the belief that class divisions vanished there. Equality of opportunity, ran the argument of those who held this view, and the leveling impact of pioneer democracy elevated the lowly and depressed the gentry to create a classless society where each individual was judged solely on his own merits. "A pleasing feature of Western life," wrote a Westerner in 1850, "is the perfect social equality. From far and wide over-laden men here seek refuge. Strong arms and stout hearts their only wealth, all classes at last salute each other as brothers."[1] A century later the illusion persisted. "Pioneer conditions," a leading historian concluded, "were inevitable levelers of rank and station."[2]

Appealing though this folktale might be to freedom-loving Americans, it distorted the truth. Class divisions occurred in the most primitive communities, and deepened as the social order matured. The New Englander who sniffed that the people of backwoods Indiana were divided into two classes—"the superior and the inferior; the former *shaved* once a week, the latter once in *two* weeks"[3]—was caricaturing a complex problem, but there was truth in what he said. Yet the cleavages in the frontier social orders differed in depth, nature, and duration from those in older societies. These differences were to be grafted on to American society as a whole, and to persist down to the present as part of the frontier heritage.

That class divisions did exist on all frontiers, from those of Puritan Massachusetts and Cavalier Virginia to those of the Great Plains and the Far West, was recognized by both the pioneers and those who visited their settlements. In colonial America the rigid lines separating classes in Britain were scarcely slackened, for the first settlers were recruited largely from the yeoman-farmer, skilled-worker, and mercantile groups who clung most tenaciously to the belief that mankind could be categorized according to status.[4] These "middling sort" and minor "gentry" brought with them preconceived notions against egalitarianism, and did their utmost to create a highly stratified society on America's first frontier. The gentry, in the maturing back country no less than in Williamsburg or Boston, lived in great houses; dressed in ruffled shirts, ornamented frock coats, knee breeches of fine texture, and pumps with gold or silver buckles; and expected to be greeted as "Sir" or "Mister." Thomas Jefferson, at the very end of the colonial era, could note accurately that society was exactly graded, from the large landholders at the top through the "younger sons and daughters of the aristocrats" and the "solid independent yeomanry, looking askance at those above, yet not venturing to jostle them," to the laborers and servants at the bottom.[5] Society was structured, despite a century and a half of frontiering.

When settlement crossed the Appalachians in the late eighteenth century the situation changed somewhat, due largely to the waning of Britain's direct influence. The older designations of "gentry," "middling," and "common sort" began to lose their meaning as self-made men forged to the forefront as business and political leaders. With the recasting of the social order under pioneer conditions, three new classes emerged. At the summit were the "better sort," comprising the business and governmental elite, and the professional classes whose superior education elevated them above the ordinary people. Next were the "common sort,"—farmers, laborers, innkeepers, herdsmen, wagoners, river men, miners—whose inferior social status was clearly recognized. Still lower on the social scale were those branded by racial or ethnic differences; the Negroes in the South, recent immigrants from Germany or Ireland in the Mississippi Valley, Chinese in the Far West. These divisions were clearly marked in every new community, whether urban or rural. The gulf separating the pioneer aristocrat with his speculative land holdings from the newly arrived German peasant who had squatted on a quarter section of government land was as recognizable although not as great as that between an English country gentleman and the peasants who worked his estate.[6]

Divisions became even more marked as frontier communities grew to maturity. The sons of the "better sort" felt less affinity with the "common people" than had their parents, largely because they had inherited from their self-made fathers a sense of social distinction. This was sharpened by conflicts over positions of leadership. With increasing specialization the need for skilled practitioners elevated the professional classes and allowed them to challenge the established mercantile group for a place at the top of the pinnacle. At the same time both merchants and professionals felt pressure from below, for in frontier communities the laboring class increased rapidly in powers and numbers with the multiplication of economic activities. These changes tightened class lines, as the merchant class solidified against its competitors, and the upper group as a whole united to combat the rising laboring class.[7]

Travelers noted the changes often. By 1807 newly rich matrons of Pittsburgh were styling themselves and their families "the well born, to distinguish them from those not quite so wealthy"; indeed one visitor believed that frontier city had "castes of society, graduated and divided with as much regard to rank and dignity as the most scrupulous Hindoos maintain."[8] Lexington, Kentucky, at that same time contained "a small party of rich citizens . . . who live in a handsome manner, keep livery servants, and admit no persons to their table of vulgar manners or suspicious character." There, lines between classes were drawn with absurd precision. The wife of a dry-goods storekeeper looked down contemptuously on the wife of another merchant in the same trade, but operating on a smaller scale; the handsome daughter of a storekeeper was ostracized by the families of other storekeepers because her father helped make the goods he sold. "You do not understand our aristocracy," explained a native. ". . . He is a mechanic; he assists in making the articles he sells; the others call themselves merchants."[9] Little wonder that a traveler could write, after completing a circuit in frontier Ohio, that "grades and degrees of conventional *rank* (though, happily, not quite so distinctly marked) exist in the United States as decidedly as in any other country of the world."[10]

An analysis in depth of a typical frontier county in the Midwest substantiates these generalizations. There a social elite emerged within a decade of the first settlement, and continued to define and sharpen itself over the next years. While by no means closed to newcomers, the ranks of the self-appointed "better sort" were carefully guarded; the common folk were excluded from all social gatherings within the tightly knit circle. Common interests and tastes provided the principal cohesive factor, but an elevated economic status underlay the generally shared feeling of superiority. From this group were recruited nearly all political leaders for the community.[11]

Here, and on all frontiers, the elite sought to distinguish themselves from the masses by two devices commonly employed by aristocrats throughout history: the use of titles, and ostentatious display. Titled visitors from abroad were treated with fawning respect, often to their own embarrassment; one English traveler wrote that the respect shown them surpassed that accorded anywhere else in the world.[12] Two newcomers to a Kansas community agreed to address each other as "General" and "Colonel"; no one questioned their self-assumed ranks, but instead paid them such tribute that one became a senator and the other a social leader.[13] Even more indicative of the desire of frontiersmen to set themselves apart from their fellows was their tendency to bestow titles on all who stood slightly above the mass. During most of the nineteenth century anyone who had served a few weeks in the militia was forever after addressed as "General" or "Captain," even though engaged in the most menial occupation. "In this remote part of America," wrote a traveler in the 1820s, "judges, generals of militia, colonels, captains, and squires, are not generally men of property or education; and it is usual to see them employed in any common kind of labour."[14]

Ostentatious display also distinguished the frontier elite, as they sought to demonstrate their superiority over their fellows. Palatial houses, armies of livery-clad servants, decorated carriages, strings of horses and hunting dogs—all were noted in Western communities as the well-to-do slavishly copied what they imagined to be the lives of the English gentry. "The elegance of the houses," wrote a Cincinnati aristocrat with obvious pride, "the parade of servants, the display of furniture, and more than all, the luxury of their overloaded tables, would compare with the better houses in the Atlantic cities."[15] These were the people who rode to the hounds in fashionable fox hunts, arranged social seasons so studded with balls that dancing masters were more sought after than school teachers, and patronized the hotels that sprang up at such watering places as Kentucky's Olympian Springs, Ohio's Yellow Springs, and Indiana's Jeffersonville.[16] Pridefully a local resident of one new Western city recorded that in his town "the 'red heel' of Versailles may imagine himself in the emporium of fashion, and whilst leading a beauty through the maze of the dance, forget that he is in the wilds of America."[17] There was little in such boasting, or in the behavior of the Westerners, to suggest that they believed in frontier democracy.

This, indeed, was a word that they forgot as they arranged their social gatherings. The daughters of wholesale merchants were admitted to one fashionable cotillion, but the daughters of retail merchants were excluded; at another the women who took in sewing were considered acceptable while those who went out to sew were not. In theaters on the Mississippi Valley frontier seating was arranged to separate the audience into three groups: the "better sort," the common people, and lower-class Indians and Negroes. *Nouveau riche* in Vandalia, Illinois, wore metal eagles on their threadbare clothes to set them apart; their counterparts in Denver used heraldic crests patterned after those of Europe's nobility. "People nowadays," wryly observed a traveler, "use coats of arms who wore coats without arms a few years ago."[18] Ludicrous as this ostentation was, it revealed the frontiersman as an enemy of complete egalitarianism. The leveling influence of the frontier was matched—or almost matched—by the natural urge of men to achieve a higher status than their fellows.

❧❧ IN THIS THEY were responding to a universal impulse. Division into classes is inevitable in any social group, no matter how primitive; societies are "stratified" as naturally as animals form "pecking orders."[19] Stratification sharpens proportionately as the complexity of the social order increases, for within advanced societies, problems of living together are so magnified that the efforts of talented members must be directed toward their solution—in government, in economic activity, and in cultural affairs. The tasks of these leaders increase with the division of labor and the multiplication of social units, burdening them with ever greater responsibility. To attract men to leadership roles under these conditions, society must reward them for the self-denial and personal sacrifices that they endure, as well as for the unusual talents that equip them to serve as leaders. These rewards are given in the form of prestige, higher incomes, and popular acclaim. Thus society is assured the guidance that it needs, but the rewards create an elite group and the subordinate groups below it, all tending to perpetuate themselves.[20]

Various forms of social stratification have emerged, ranging from the religiously based *caste* system of India, through the *estate* system of medieval Europe, to the *class* system of today's Western world. Class systems, in turn, are "closed" or "open"; those in countries such as the United States with guaranteed equality before the law, free access to opportunity, and minimal political restrictions are designated "open" systems. These allow individuals to move from class to class, and sort themselves out on the basis of their abilities; the long-term result is a concentration of those with the greatest skills and energy in the upper class, and of those with less intelligence and education in the lower. Yet "achieved status,"[21] based on the ability and opportunity of the individual, is not solely determinative of the social gradation even in a completely open society, for there is a tendency among humans to assign a higher ranking to family groups that have retained wealth, political power, and leadership over the course of more than one generation. In other words, social status is hereditary as well as achievable; a transmission of a father's status to his children takes place in every stratified social order. Usually the children are able to live up to this position, for their educational level, their economic position, and their behavior patterns are those of the class into which they are born. The son of a bank clerk feels more at home in a white shirt than the son of a plumber, even though the salary of the latter may be larger.[22]

◆§◆§ AGAINST this background of sociological theory, one conclusion can be stated and several pertinent questions can be asked concerning the impact of frontiering on the class structure. The conclusion is obvious: the divisions that developed in frontier communities were inevitable, and do not indicate that the pioneers were either unusually pro- or anti-democratic. They were behaving as they had to behave in any social group. Moreover, conditions there stimulated stratification. The competition for lands as population thickened, the chance for speculative profits through the accumulation of excess holdings, and the opportunity for leadership provided by the democratic governmental structure and the recurring Indian wars provided ideal conditions for the emergence of elite groups.

The questions are equally obvious but to reach their answers requires a more extended analysis: Do classes exist in America, do they differ from those of Europe, are they recognized to exist by the average citizen, and has their structure been influenced by the frontier background? In seeking a solution to these allied problems, social scientists have conducted a number of in-depth investigations of class structure and consciousness in communities of various size. In these, trained investigators have sought to establish "class rating" in two ways: by self-evaluation in which people were asked to name the class in which they placed themselves and their neighbors, and by group evaluation in which the class divisions were designated by the investigators. In general they have used four criteria to establish social classes: how a person lives, what others think of him, what he thinks of himself, and what he does. They have found that Americans think not in terms of *class*, but of *status;* individuals refuse to assign themselves or their neighbors a place in the "lower class," but they will admit lower status than the elite of a community. Using this more respectable word in interviews, investigators have reached convincing conclusions on the nature of social stratification in the United States.[23]

The pioneer study of community class structure was conducted over a ten-year period by a team of social scientists who in 1941 published the first of four volumes on "Yankee City," a New England community of 17,000 persons.[24] They found that six classes could be identified: upper-upper, upper, upper-middle, lower-middle, lower, and lower-lower. An individual's class rating, they discovered, could not be determined by his economic position alone, but by how he lived, his family background, and above all by how he was ranked by other persons in the community. These were startling conclusions in a nation that had thought of itself as relatively classless, and inspired a rash of similar investigations. Two of these are especially pertinent, for they center on rural villages not far removed from the frontier era.

A study of "Prairietown," a South Dakota community of 3,500 inhabitants only two generations away from the pioneer settlers, showed that three sharply defined classes existed: an elite group of successful entrepreneurs and large landholders; a middle group of shopkeepers, craftsmen, retired farmers, and professional people; and a low-status group of ex-farmers, farmhands, and unskilled laborers. Membership in the elite group was based partly on wealth and education, but more on membership in a family that had lived and enjoyed wealth in the community for more than one generation.[25]

A similar study of "Plainville," a village of only a thousand persons in the southern midwest farm belt, promised few results at first; investigators were told: "This is *one* place where ever'body is equal. You won't find no classes here." Yet those who voiced this belief, when questioned, agreed that four classes were identifiable: the "upper crust," the "good lower-class people," the "lower element," and "the people who live like animals." They assigned a higher status to farmers who lived on the prairie instead of the hills, to those who used machinery, and to those of proper lineage. They admitted that these divisions affected every social activity; membership in the Boosters' Club and the Masons reflected higher social status than in the Odd Fellows or the Woodmen; the Christian Church attracted such a concentration of the elite that the lower classes "just don't feel comfortable there." These divisions had developed, it should be emphasized, among people who shared the same rural experience and most of whom were farmers. Yet some farmers were rated near the top of society by their fellow townsmen, and others near the bottom. In Plainville a man was judged by *how* he did something, not *what* he did. But judged he was, and assigned a place in a well-formed class structure.[26]

These investigations suggest important conclusions concerning the nature of the American class structure. They were based, it must be remembered, on the opinions of individuals who were judging their neighbors, and they make clear that even in small towns the people are acutely class conscious, or at least status conscious. They judge a man to be superior or inferior because he is a "real joiner," belongs to the proper church or the Rotary Club, is "part of the Garden Club crowd," supposedly has a good income, lives in a fine house in a certain section of town, and comes from a "proper" family that has managed to hold onto its wealth for at least two generations. Or, if these bases for division are absent, Americans will sort out their fellows as good or bad farmers, prairie dwellers or hill dwellers, machinery users or those who cannot afford implements. Consciousness of status has been and is a part of the American social order.

But is this consciousness greater or less than in other, nonfrontier nations? Students of the subject agree that both the extent and awareness of stratification are less in the United States than in Europe, and that birth and lineage are far less important in determining a man's status. This does not mean that distinctions have disappeared; it means only that the lines between classes are less clearly drawn than in older societies. Differences in wealth, privilege, and occupation divide Americans into status groups, but the ease of access from group to group, and the blurring of boundaries between them mark the American system as different from the European. Some social scientists feel that American society can be pictured not as a hierarchy of distinct classes, but as ranging along a continuum with imperceptible gradations from the lowest to the highest member and with no definable lines drawn between the haves and the have-nots.[27] Even the term "class" is so unacceptable to Americans that the word "status" must be substituted. Clearly the United States refuses to brand itself a stratified nation, whatever the actuality.

For this attitude, and for the variations that do exist, many things are responsible. The lack of a titled aristocracy, of a military tradition with its exacting gradations, and of a large landholding class (save in the South) during the Republic's formative period, have all played their part in retarding the division of the classes. So also has the persistence of Puritan ideals with their emphasis on frugality and simplicity, and the continuing strength of the Protestant ethic with its glorification of hard work and its condemnation of idleness. No less important is the anti-aristocratic prejudice bred into the social environment by the absence of a feudal tradition and the continuing impact of a Revolution that rejected the concept that a nobility was essential to society.

No single influence did more to downgrade the concept of class in the United States than the presence of an open frontier. For three hundred years men could move westward in search of fresh opportunity, and so long as this was possible no hereditary aristocracy could emerge. Stratification occurred, of course, but the *form* of the class system remained open rather than restricted; it differed from that of the Old World because a declassed person could always remove to the frontier rather than remain in a subservient position in his older community. Whether or not many made this move was unimportant; what mattered was that people believed this opportunity to be always open and that a rags-to-riches leap from the bottom to the top of the social scale was possible. As long as they clung to this belief, the man at the top would be less venerated than in Europe, for his neighbors knew that he had been at the bottom a short time before. No rigid class lines could be drawn while people believed that the social system was completely fluid, and that the lower-lowers of today would be the elite of tomorrow. The frontier was one of the most important forces creating the uniquely American class structure.[28]

◆§◆§ THE FRONTIER also played an essential role in shaping a distinct class system by allowing more individuals to move upward in the social scale more rapidly than in older societies. "Vertical mobility"—the rise of persons from class to class and their acceptance in their new status—has always been possible in any "open" society and especially in democratic societies where positions at the top are relatively more available, legal obstacles to advancement fewer, and lineage not solely determinative of social status.[29] Yet in no country has ascent from class to class been easier, or thought to be so common, as in the United States. The part played by the frontiering experience in explaining this phenomenon must now be appraised.

Today the rate of vertical mobility is approximately the same in America as in western Europe. This may be explained by industrialization, which has speeded the movement from class to class in older countries, and slowed the change in the United States. In England and on the Continent factories created ever more jobs during the nineteenth century, and with each an opportunity for a peasant farmer to improve himself; in the twentieth century the trend has accelerated with the multiplication of trade and service industries and the spread of bureaucracy in business and government. Men recruited to fill these posts usually rose above the class of their fathers; since World War II about one third of the labor force in western Europe has moved from manual to nonmanual posts, or from the working class to the middle class. Comparative studies of social mobility in American and European cities during recent years indicate that the rate is about the same.[30] New opportunities, all the product of the machine age, are diffusing class lines in the Old World as they radically alter the social structure there.

In the United States, on the other hand, the rate of social mobility is steadily declining as industry becomes stabilized and the job pattern more rigid. More and more men in managerial posts tend to direct members of their own family or social group into those posts; at certain elite levels a social cohesiveness develops that tends to exclude outsiders. While this operates most frequently at the higher status levels, it is apparent among all classes; truck drivers will recommend others of their own class when a job develops. This solidification means that greater energy is required to ascend the social scale; it means also that those without educational advantages find the ascent increasingly impossible.[31] Evidence to support these generalizations is scattered but suggestive; thus a study of business elites shows that in 1928 only 50 percent were recruited from upper-class backgrounds, while by 1952 the number had risen to 66 percent. Occupational and class ranks seem to be closing in the United States, and the dream of rags to riches to have run its course.[31]

Yet even today, and certainly in the past, social mobility has been a prominent fact of American life. To say that in 1952 66 percent of the business leaders came from socially elite families is to obscure the fact that 34 percent did not, and hence must have risen from the lower ranks. Every college commencement poignantly demonstrates that the sons of workers are being equipped to rise above their stations, and a major portion will do so. The rate of mobility may be slowing in the twentieth century, but the habit of mobility is too strong to be checked. No amount of evidence can conceal the fact that in the eighteenth and nineteenth centuries vertical mobility was more common in the United States than in other countries, and that even today the *belief* in vertical mobility distinguishes Americans from their European cousins. Art Buchwald, of the New York *Herald Tribune,* only exaggerated these differences when he explained to Abe Burrows why his play, "How to Succeed in Business without Really Trying," would never be popular in France. The Frenchman, he pointed out, would never believe that a dishwasher could read a book on business and then rise to the chairmanship of the board. "The chairman of the board [in France] is an eighty-seven-year-old man who took over two years ago from his father. His son is sixty-five years old and is still being trained in one of the various departments so he'll learn the business. And his grandson is thirty-seven years old, so he's considered too young to have any responsibility and is only allowed to work in the summertime. Therefore, how can a complete stranger, such as your hero, ever hope to rise in such an organization?"[33] American stratification has been less rigid than that in older societies.

Numerous factors contributed to the fact of social mobility during the nation's brief history. One was the impact of the thirty-six million immigrants who reached the United States after 1815, continuously sliding into the job structure at the lowest levels to force those above them into still higher ranks.[34] Another was the absence of a titled or hereditary aristocracy to monopolize the upper pinnacle of the social order and to guard it jealously against encroachers; as early as 1816 a writer noted that the lack of a privileged class opened the "highest honors of society and of the country" to the merchant or "any other denomination of his fellow citizens."[35] Still another was the newness of the country and the rapidity with which economic change occurred; the transition from subsistence to export agriculture, the shift to industrialism, the growth of new industries, and the multiplication of service functions have all been crammed into little more than a century. Each change meant a decrease in some types of jobs and an increase in others, disrupting the social structure and creating opportunity in the form of better positions for those energetic enough to seek them.[36]

Of the forces encouraging social mobility, however, none was more important than the existence for three centuries of a frontier of cheap land. Expansion was the key that opened the door to higher social status for millions of Americans, for the mere act of physical mobility assured opportunity for the individual to rise above his station and guaranteed that those who had thought themselves his betters would welcome him into their ranks.

For the average American the move to the frontier meant a chance to acquire lands of his own and with them a higher rung on the social ladder. For the nonfarmer, economic opportunities were also greater near the edge of settlement, for there processes of production were in more of a state of flux than in the East; between 1840 and 1880 the number of persons engaged in primary occupations (farming) in the new territories declined from 73.8 percent of the population to 44.6 percent, the number in secondary occupations (manufacturing and mining) rose from 18.8 percent to 20 percent, and the number in tertiary (trade, communications, and professional) increased from 7.5 percent to 35.5 percent.[37] Each shift opened doors to the ambitious who wished to escape from farming to business or professional careers.

The social structure in the newer settlements was in a fluid state, and this also encouraged vertical mobility. In older societies an individual moving from one class to another was forced to find new friends, join new organizations, learn new manners, and perhaps alter his political views. In pioneer communities outside the plantation South these painful adjustments were not necessary, for class affinities had not yet been established. Nor had those communities developed elite groups that barred their doors to outsiders, for time is needed for cohesiveness to close the ranks of the upper strata in any society. The children of pioneers were more inclined than others to scale these heights, for the routine of their lives had been disrupted by the move westward, and their taste for adventure whetted by the uncertainties of life in a new land. Today the children of upper-class families are more inclined to risk insecurity than those of the lower classes who shy from the hazards that await them in the climb to a higher social level. In pioneer days hazards were so much a part of life that the risks involved were no deterrent.[38]

Finally, any expanding society offered unusual opportunity to gain "achieved status," for the numbers with "ascribed status" were necessarily far fewer than in older groups. In such a social order new professions were in constant demand, and the road to the top open to all capable of filling them. Frontier communities usually needed doctors, lawyers, merchants, editors, and a host of other professional men. Nor were too many questions asked about the background of a newcomer; a glib young man could hang out his shingle as a lawyer after a few weeks of study and automatically become a member of the leadership elite. The professional standards and rigid examinations that today restrict entrance into the professions were nonexistent in frontier America.[39]

The result was a unique degree of social mobility in the successive wests. In colonial days men found that they could rise a notch in the social scale by merely crossing the Atlantic; of 275 immigrants designated as "Gentlemen" on arrival in Maryland between 1637 and 1676, only fifty bore that title on departure from England. Within the colony no one was able to inquire into their antecedents, allowing them to assume their new titles without question.[40] Within the New World, conditions allowed others to rise just as rapidly and somewhat more honestly. No nearby king, no noble class, no landed gentry, no strong military tradition, stood jealous guard over rigid class demarcations. Instead the bulk of the settlers were from middle or lower-middle class backgrounds, most were farmers or merchants, and all were concerned with the future rather than the past. Success was measured not by lineage but by the acquisition of wealth or the exhibition of leadership qualities. "In Virginia," quoth Captain John Smith, "a plaine Souldier that can use a Pickaxe and spade, is better than five Knights." The expanding economy, the continuing exploitation of natural resources, the democratic tradition in office holding, created a society in which the most humble could rise to the level of their own abilities. "But what hinders that we are not Equals in ev'ry Respect?" an upcountry pioneer asked a Virginia planter. ". . . Will you pronounce that in 50 Years, our Posterity may not ride in their Chariots, while yours walk on foot?"[41]

This bold attitude meant that the symbols of status would decline in popular esteem, and resulted in the success stories that studded the records of colonial America. Titles continued to be used and even venerated; court records and militia lists were sprinkled with "Gent.," "Master," "Mister," and "Esq.," as from 3 percent to 13 percent of seventeenth century New Englanders were accorded some title. But these terms were so casually used that they mirrored only the clerk's opinion of the person, and not his actual status. "Gentlemen" and "Esquires" worth less than a hundred pounds appeared side by side on voting lists with farmers or artisans whose fortunes were far greater. Clearly opportunity for economic advancement was creating new elites so rapidly that the older designations lost all meaning.[42] Other symbols suffered just as badly; as early as 1651 the Massachusetts General Court was alarmed that "persons of meane condition, education and callings should take upon them the garbe of gentlemen by the wearinge of gold or silver lace" and that women of low rank should appear in "silke or tiffany hoodes or scarves."[43] From Jamestown came a complaint that "our cowekeeper here of James Citty on Sundays goes accowtered all in freshe faming silke," and that the wife of a former coal miner "weares her rough bever hatt with a faire perle hatband, and a silken suite thereto correspondent."[44] These were physical manifestations of a social upheaval sparked by the economic opportunity afforded by frontier America. By the time of the Revolution the wife of a British customs agent revealed some truth as well as her own prejudices when she complained that "no distinctions, scarsly" remained in American society.[45]

With the transit of civilization across the Appalachians and the strengthening of the egalitarian tradition by the spread of the Revolutionary philosophy, social mobility became even more commonplace on the Mississippi Valley frontier. Travelers reported time and time again talking with men of humble origin who had risen to the apex of the political and economic structure. "At home," wrote a German visitor as he surveyed the lot of his former countrymen, "they were dependent laborers. Here they are independent landowners, living better than most of the better class of settlers, who look upon them with envy."[46] With their new status went a sympathy for others climbing the ladder of success and a willingness to welcome them when they arrived. Often a member of the Western elite would shrug away criticisms of unpolished newcomers by saying: "Every man stands on his own feet here," or "We all come from some place or other."[47] Abraham Lincoln spoke for thousands of frontiersmen when he recalled: "Twenty-five years ago I was a hired laborer. The hired laborer of yesterday labors on his own account today; and will hire others to labor for him tomorrow. Advancement—improvement in condition—is the order of things in a society of equals."[48] So did the ill-mannered Cincinnatian who informed Mrs. Trollope that they would not be friends in England for "I would not think of associating with anything but lords" as "I have always been among the first here, and if I travelled I should like to do the same."[49]

Westerners not only noted with pleasure the social mobility that characterized their society, but speculated on its causes. The editor of the *Cincinnati Literary Gazette* ascribed lack of class distinctions to the willingness of the people to "make experiments respecting social relations"; no others, he believed, "were less disposed to consider hereditary prejudices and heirlooms which cannot be parted with." Daniel Drake laid the social fluidity of the West to the wide range of economic activity where "the same person is compelled to do many different things, and often tempted to change his pursuits." There a young man stood a better chance of success than in the East "because not only is his field larger and competition less, but new sources of wealth and power are developed every day, and more and more." He could capitalize upon such opportunities because, in the words of James Flint, "every man is allowed to exert his talents, in the pursuit of any honest scheme, and in any part of the country, without being prevented by intolerant restrictions or internal taxes."[50] This combination of a rapidly changing social order, lack of respect for tradition, the variety of economic activity, and the absence of hereditary restrictions on freedom of enterprise all spelled opportunity to the ambitious. They also infected the frontiersman with driving ambition that sometimes knew no end. "If he possessed a 'million a minute,'" noted one observer, "he would cast about for some profitable employment, in which he might engage, 'to pay expenses.' "[51]

One in-depth case study of a Wisconsin county, based on empirical data, suggests that the rags-to-riches faith of the frontiersmen was not misplaced. There three groups vied for status positions: native-born Americans, English-speaking immigrants from England and Ireland, and non–English-speaking Europeans. The latter were at the bottom of the social scale when they arrived and were assigned the lowest tasks, usually as farm laborers, while the highest status occupations in the business and professional world were monopolized by natives. Serving as farm laborers, and supplementing their income by splitting rails or swinging a cradle scythe at seventy-five cents a day, the non–English-speaking foreigners could within two years amass the $50 needed to buy 40 acres, then mortgage their land to purchase implements and seed. Within a decade the members of this low-status group owned as many medium-sized farms as the native-born or the English-speaking immigrants; twenty years later the average size of their farms surpassed that of their neighbors. During those years the acreage of the native-born increased 153 percent and of the foreign-born 233 percent; in one decade the smallest holders expanded by 177 percent and the largest by only 35 percent. Within thirty years the lowest-status newcomers had risen to the upper rungs of the social pyramid as substantial landowners and were entering the ranks of the professions and other elite groups. These data offer no final proof for they pertain only to one county, but they strongly suggest that the frontier was a region of extremely rapid upward mobility, and that the existence of cheap land provided an escalator to the top of the social ladder that could not be duplicated in the East or Europe.[52]

Even on the Southern frontiers, where the plantation system solidified society and tightened class lines, the movement from class to class went on with surprising ease. Thus in Alabama during the 1850s, marital statistics for five counties reveal that of 361 marriages, 125 were between slaveholding and nonslaveholding families, and 31 between large holders and small holders. Thus about one third of the persons married crossed the class line between slaveholding and nonslaveholding families. Perhaps even more significant was the fact that within the upper class of large slaveholders, only 15 marriages took place. The poor were marrying the rich far more often than the rich were marrying among themselves.[53]

These data are too few to be conclusive, but when they are

bolstered by the unanimous opinion of Westerners and travelers that the frontier was a region of unique opportunity for upward mobility, they become convincing. A pioneer who observed that "here, a gentleman can be made out of the coarsest stuff in half a lifetime" was less than accurate—emigrants were warned that a fifth-rate lawyer in Massachusetts would remain a fifth-rate lawyer in Illinois—but there seems no question that the West did offer a social environment where newcomers could sink or rise to their own natural levels.[54] A man's capacities, not his ancestry, determined his eventual place in the hierarchy, to a greater degree than in older societies. There a man was asked "What can you do?" not "Who are you; who was your father?"[55] Life was too demanding in pioneer communities to afford the luxury of a dronelike aristocracy or to allow the veneration of a man simply because his great-grandfather had exhibited superior talents. Class lines were formed there but they were built on standards imposed by the community, not by history. Until they solidified, the ranks of the elite were open.

◄§◄§ ACCEPTING for the moment the concept of the frontier as a positive influence in weakening class distinctions and stimulating vertical mobility, we must still ask: how does this fragment of the pioneer heritage influence our lives today? Mobility continues as a fact of American life, but only at about the same rate as in any industrialized twentieth-century country, and is apparently a by-product of prosperity and a changing economic order rather than of any frontier contribution to the social environment of the United States. Yet there is one all-important difference. In America the people *believe* in vertical mobility as inevitable; in other nations they do not. This faith is rooted in the frontier past.

Acceptance of the rags-to-riches myth was almost universal in the United States long before it found literary expression in the pious stories of Horatio Alger and Oliver Optic. Thanks to an abundance of cheap land, limitless natural resources, and a benevolent political system that assured freedom to the individual, people believed, no one needed to stay poor. Any man with gumption, with ability, and with a go-ahead spirit could climb to the pinnacle of society. This was not a dream, but a sober fact. So why even talk of class lines? They were meaningless in a land when everyone moved from one class to another—always upward—so rapidly that they could never solidify.

These beliefs persist today, despite the contraction of individual opportunity in the twentieth-century world. To pollsters who have asked a sizable segment of the population "To what class do you belong, upper, middle, or lower?" the overwhelming answer has been "middle," whether the person answering was a corporation executive or a janitor.[56] Significantly, when asked whether they belonged to the "upper," "middle," "working," or "lower" class, the majority chose "working" rather than "lower," suggesting that even those on the bottom rung of the ladder refuse to admit their low status.[57]

These self-evaluations show that the people of the United States today, when the rates of social mobility are comparable in all industrialized countries, still cling to the belief that theirs is a land of unusual opportunity. This is the basic fabric of the "American dream," the substance of the drive that motivates a considerable portion of the population. The persistence of this belief has had, and has, a powerful impact on society, for Americans assign different values to vertical mobility than Europeans. Belief in the inevitability of progress has set their goals, motivated their drives for success, and kept society on an even keel. Faith in opportunity has helped persuade the lower classes to sustain the political order rather than to distrust its leaders as so often in other nations. Thus in France, where a closed society is believed to exist even though it does not, the dominant image held by workers is one of the unfair distribution of wealth and opportunity. Americans may complain of the inequitable distribution of wealth, but they are sustained by the belief that opportunity is still theirs. They feel that every person not only has "a right to succeed" but that it is his duty to do so.[58]

The persistence of the Horatio Alger dream in the United States can be explained variously. Basic is the tradition of the self-made man, reaching back at least to the Jacksonian era when birth in a log cabin became virtually a requirement for political success. The United States has glamorized the process of achieving success; American leaders boast of humble origins, while those of more tradition-governed nations take pains to hide their lower-class backgrounds. Their example inspires others, as does the record of immigrants who have achieved status after rising from society's most menial posts. Universal education has also strengthened faith in vertical mobility, for scarcely an American but is sure that the classroom is the threshold to self-betterment. Reassured by the knowledge that the number of students in colleges and universities increased seventeenfold during the first half of the twentieth century while population increased less than three-fold, they are certain that the breakthrough of the lower into the upper classes will continue at an ever-accelerating pace.

Belief in the persistence of vertical mobility among modern Americans has been bolstered by the favorable economic climate. The rapid shifts from primary through secondary to tertiary functions that have characterized the growth of the economy have continually created better-paying and higher-status jobs to be filled from the lower ranks. This steady upward movement has fostered the impression of a completely open society, especially as it has deterred downward mobility. No less significant is the role played by the wealth of the United States, far surpassing that of any other country. This has allowed the most equitable distribution of consumer goods that the world has known; even persons in the lowest classes have been able to buy automobiles, television sets, washing machines, and other prestige symbols. In Europe different classes have traditionally lived different lives; in the United States they share so many gadgets and luxuries that the division between classes is less apparent. All of these forces strengthen the American *belief* that theirs is a classless society offering unusual opportunity for the most humble to rise to the very top.

᪥᪥ THE COMFORTING faith in vertical mobility that characterizes the nation's dream offers an example of the continuing impact of the frontier on twentieth-century America. Since the days when "free" land beckoned the downtrodden, the people have believed that any man could shape his own destiny, and have respected those who succeeded. This faith has been sustained by forces rooted in the frontier experience, for the immigrants whose success stories inspired imitation, the economic changes that created better jobs, and the wealth that financed high living standards for the lowly, all were products of the occupation of a virgin continent. Convinced by the example of the past that life was an unswerving path into a better future, the American people have refused to admit a stratified society or inequality of opportunity, even though the tightening of class lines in the United States and the slackening of those abroad has created a comparable rate of social mobility on both sides of the Atlantic. Generations of life in a frontier-conscious land, where migration ordained a fluid social order and economic change multiplied opportunity, have enshrined faith in progress as the American dream.

6

Frontier

Democracy:

Political Aspects

"AMERICAN DEMOCRACY," wrote Frederick Jackson Turner, "was born of no theorist's dream; it was not carried in the *Sarah Constant* [*sic*] to Virginia, nor in the *Mayflower* to Plymouth. It came out of the American forest, and it gained new strength each time it touched a new frontier."[1] This simple statement has been more vigorously attacked than any other penned by Turner. Nonsense, cried the critics. Well-developed democratic theories and institutions *were* carried to America by the colonists. Within the New World the settled Easts contributed more to democratic practices—manhood suffrage, the secret ballot, equal representation—than the retreating Wests. Here was Turner at his worst, guilty not only of distortion but of positive untruth.[2]

Were those critics right? Perhaps an answer to that question can be found by examining their arguments. These may be grouped into four general propositions: the frontier failed to alter the antidemocratic behavior of those who fell under its influence; it was a region of conservatism rather than of liberalism; political and social reforms originated in the East rather than the West; and the pioneers were imitative rather than creative in their political behavior, copying Eastern constitutions when they formed their states, and lagging rather than leading in the introduction of manhood suffrage.

Personal attitudes, the critics insisted, were too deeply ingrained to be altered by a few years of pioneering. To believe that a royalist could be converted into a democrat by a brief residence in the forest was to dispute the laws of human behavior. Instead the degree of physical freedom attained by the frontiersman did not mean that he would act differently from his ancestors; if he changed at all it was in the direction of conformity as pioneer conditions reduced all to a common level and encouraged a uniform mass behavior. This often found expression in the mistreatment of ethnic minorities, with the persecution of Mexicans and Chinese serving as a glaring example. Here was evidence that the frontier fostered belief in the inequality of man, not the opposite.[3]

Nor were the successive Wests cradles of liberal thought, fostering democracy and egalitarianism. Had they played this role, how account for the stratified society and restricted suffrage of the Revolutionary era, after a century and a half of pioneering? How explain the fact that during the war Westerners were as likely as Easterners to be found among the Tories, fighting for royalty? In the new Republic, Jeffersonianism was really a protest of agriculturalists against capitalists, not of frontier democrats against Eastern aristocrats; even "Jacksonian democracy" originated among Eastern workers and was nurtured by the support of planters, farmers, working men, and small entrepreneurs. After the Civil War the outbursts of frontier "radicalism" that manifested agrarian discontent were actually conservative movements, designed to check the advance of industrialism and maintain the *status quo*. Rather than fostering democratic change, the West served as a brake on progress.[4]

This was shown when the frontier lagged rather than led in urging the acceptance of political devices that would assure equality to all men. The landmarks of reform—tax-supported schools, direct legislation, civil service, primary nomination, the initiative and referendum —were the products of agitation nurtured in the thickly settled East. This was demonstrated by comparison with nonfrontier countries; among the industrialized nations of Europe the lower classes achieved political power and outlawed privilege more rapidly than in the United

States. The frontier, by absorbing discontented elements from the East, retarded rather than stimulated political reform.[5]

Finally, critics insisted that the transit of democracy was from East to West, from Europe to the forests of America, rather than vice versa. Representative institutions had been developing in England for some three centuries before Jamestown and Plymouth were settled, as the rising middle class assumed control first of the economic and then of the political structure of the realm. By the time the colonists sailed for America they could carry with them a belief in representative government and acceptance of the right of dissent. Settlers from Spain, France, and Holland, by contrast, lacking such a heritage, planted the seeds of aristocracy in their segments of the New World, dooming democracy outside of the United States.[6] The principles of self-rule *were* carried in the *Susan Constant* and the *Mayflower.*

Within the new nation, the tide of political reform still swept from East to West. Instead of innovating democratic practices—manhood suffrage, a shift in power from executive to legislative branches, rapid rotation in office, devices to assure popular access to officials—the frontier states borrowed wholesale from the settled states as they formed their constitutions. All used Eastern techniques when drafting their frames of government. All accepted judicial review, even though this device to negate the will of the majority was under bitter attack at the time. Many protected property rights from popular control by denying legislatures the right to violate the sanctity of contracts. Few Western constitutions made concessions to the current demand that officials be popularly elected, adopting instead time-tested Eastern techniques for choosing governors and allowing those administrators to appoint most other officials. Some even adopted antidemocratic practices unacceptable in the East; thus Kentucky's first constitution provided that the governor and senators be elected by an electoral college far removed from the people, while in Tennessee justices of the peace were chosen for life by the legislature.[7]

The democratic lag on the frontier was shown especially in the failure of Western states to liberalize their franchise. This reform began in the East during the Revolution, when five of the older states lessened property requirements of voters and one, Pennsylvania, opened the ballot box to all who paid any public tax. By 1792 four other states, all in the East, had followed Pennsylvania's example and two of these—New Hampshire and Georgia—abandoned even the tax qualification in 1798. Yet when Ohio entered the Union in 1803 her constitution restricted voting to property holders; not until Indiana became a state in 1816 was Pennsylvania's example of 1776 copied beyond the mountains.[8] Here was evidence that the frontier was a land of imitation rather than innovation, and that the emerging democracy of the Western world was a product of pressures applied by emerging lower classes rather than by pioneers.

ఆইఆই HOW VALID were these arguments? We can grapple with that question only after making clear that we are discussing not democracy but *American* democracy, as was Frederick Jackson Turner when he made his oft-disputed statement.[9] Our discussion is based on the premise that there is a slight distinction between both the theory and the practice of democracy in the United States and Europe. This does not imply that America's debt to the Old World was insignificant; from England it borrowed the common law, a system of local government, a belief in a government of laws and not of men, and a variety of practices in representative government; from France it accepted the philosophy and example of a revolution that provided constitution makers with ringing phrases for generations to come. Europe also contributed the concept of man's right to choose his own means of salvation, a product of the Protestant Reformation and an essential plank in any democratic platform. That democracy did thrive in the Anglo-American portions of the New World was due primarily to this inheritance, which Spanish-America and French-America lacked.

American democracy differs from European in several ways. One is the relative lack of acknowledged class lines and the acceptance of each individual on his own merits. The freedom of every person to shape his own destiny, whatever his lineage, has been translated politically into an enduring faith in the "common man"—into the belief that the plain people are worthy of equality, freedom, and a share in the government. Sure of himself and his destiny, the American more than the European views the government as *his* property, to be used or changed as he sees fit. He has, to an unusual degree, a manipulative attitude toward both his constitution and elected officials; leadership must come not from the elite few but from the ordinary many. A nation in which the taxi driver addresses the governor of his state as "Mac" may be no more democratic than England or France, but the nature of the democracy is different.

American political faith deviates from the European in its emphasis on the inevitability of change. People in the Old World, burdened by their medieval heritage and shackled by traditionalism, are less inclined to look upon progress as the normal state of affairs. They view governmental institutions as solidified, changeable only by violence. Americans are calmly confident that peaceful means will be found to solve the most complex problems, and certain that democratic practices will eventually bring peace and prosperity to all. Their abhorrence of violence is shared by the English, but not their faith in progress.[10] This belief has allowed political institutions to evolve without the disorders that have marked change in many European nations.

Finally, there is a freshness in the American political atmosphere that has struck visitors to the nation's shores from the eighteenth century to the present. Observers have found in the lifted head of the American woman, the persistent ability of chance acquaintances to pry into the personal details of one's life, the universal faith in the infallibility of the majority, the dislike of privilege and the privileged, the aloof indifference of waiters to the needs of their customers, the surly independence of taxicab drivers, the eagerness of parents to cater to the whims of their children, the annoying habit of engaging strangers in conversation, the tendency to fasten nicknames on governmental officials, and the insistence on equal opportunity for all, evidence that the American environment did add something to democratic theories and practices imported from abroad. This "something" is not measurable by empirical techniques, nor capable of reduction to statistical tables, but too many generations of Europeans visiting America and Americans visiting Europe have testified to its existence to dispute its reality.

⋅§⋅§ THE DIFFERENCES that distinguish American from European democracy are traceable to a complex of forces, but our concern is with only one of these: the influence of three centuries of frontiering. Over the course of many years both visitors from abroad and students of the local scene have suggested a variety of means whereby the pioneering experience altered democratic theories and practices in the United States. The frontier, they argue, affected these changes by providing opportunity for individual betterment and a corresponding dislike of external rule, by serving as a leveling force that lessened the economic gulf between peoples, by altering the power structure and opening the door for new leadership, by creating a social atmosphere scornful of tradition where experimentation in institutional forms was acceptable, and by allowing repeated experiments as frontiersmen rebuilt their governments on successive frontiers. These five arguments must be examined before we test their validity against the actual history of democratic change on the frontier.

The opportunity for individual self-betterment provided by abundant natural resources in successive wests, and the even more important belief that opportunity was open to all, radically altered the pioneers' attitude toward government. In America all men could acquire the possessions that stood for privilege in older countries; why then should not all men share equally in control of the state? "The price of land," wrote a Westerner, "is the thermometer of liberty—men are freest where lands are cheapest."[11] Alexis de Tocqueville, one of the shrewdest of all European observers, believed that God had assured freedom for the Americans by placing them in a boundless continent where they needed only to shift to the frontiers to secure the material basis for equality.[12] No man, no matter how poor, would bow before a landed gentry when he was confident that he would one day possess estates of his own. The frontier elite might think of themselves as the "better sort," but their less fortunate neighbors refused to admit that "betters" existed. So long as economic equality was within reach, political equality was its inevitable by-product.

The frontier also fostered a unique type of American democracy by serving as a leveling force that minimized traditional differences between men. This occurred partly as a result of the sifting process that kept the very rich and the very poor from migrating; the wealthy, an Englishman on the Ohio frontier noted, "were deterred by the difficulties attending a new settlement; the indigent by the impossibility of getting vacant lands."[13] In the West equality of opportunity continued to lessen class distinctions, and to depreciate the importance of inherited status, social prestige, or correct lineage. Tocqueville insisted that belief in equality was the key to understanding the people of the United States, the "fundamental fact from which all others seem to be derived."[14] He recognized also that this attitude had been nurtured by the social environment of the frontier, where the principle of egalitarianism was so enshrined that a candidate could succeed politically only by pretending to be of, not above, the common people. William Henry Harrison's "Log Cabin campaign" of 1840, the Republicans' stress on "Honest Abe the rail-splitter" in 1860, the popularity of "Sockless Jerry" Simpson among the Populists, all testified to antiaristocratic prejudices. Wrote an observer from the Indiana frontier: "Would a candidate cough?—he puts no hand up, nor turns aside his head. Must the nose be blown?—he draws out no handkerchief. Would he spit?—he neither goes to the door, nor uses a perfumed cambric, like a first rate clergyman. Why?—because all such observances are regarded as signs of pride, and if you despise them not, your election is hopeless."[15] This was a different breed of democracy than that known in nineteenth-century England.

Even more important was the frontier's role as a catalyst in altering the leadership structure within pioneer communities. In established societies with long-functioning power structures, apathy and a tendency to trust those in control tended to concentrate governmental functions in the hands of certain classes, groups, or families, thus closing the door to outsiders.[16] No such structure existed in the new communities of the West. Those who could convince their neighbors that they possessed certain qualities—energy and ability, identification with the interests of the people, readiness to follow instructions from below—were able to achieve political power, whatever their backgrounds. Leadership is normally entrusted to those who best live up to the standard of behavior valued by the group.[17] On new frontiers, there was every opportunity for those persons to sort themselves out, even though they had played no similar roles before. This was a powerful democratizing influence.

As this sifting went on, certain qualities emerged as valuable in pioneer communities. The frontiersmen wanted leaders who lived as they lived, and thought as they thought. "The successful politician," wrote one of the most observing visitors to the frontier, "in a new country, where deference for experience or culture has not yet grown up, is, after all, the man who has most facility in expressing the ideas which are filling the heads of his neighbors."[18] He must be a man abundantly possessed of the attributes essential in pioneer life, and above all he must appeal to the voters as an equal rather than as a superior. They wanted a candidate who (as one put it) "ain't too darn'd proud to shake hands with a poor man."[19] A prospective office holder who campaigned by singing songs, winking at the spectators, and eating an onion in one hand and corn pone with the other; or one who (in the words of one grateful voter) invited a whole militia company into the local groggery "not to take a *little* of something to drink, but by J———s to drink as much as they had a mind to,"[20] might not be setting high standards of political morality, but he was proving himself a real representative of the people. The willingness of Westerners to elect such men opened wide the door of opportunity to many who would have been barred from office in the East.

Such extreme political demagoguery was far from typical, for while the power structure was altered by the social environment of the frontier, the pioneers instinctively elevated men of proved ability and usually of affluence to posts of command. This had been their political habit for generations, and it was too strong to be broken. Yet in doing so, they transferred power from the well-born to the men "who are in fact the generals of the great migration," as an able observer noted. They shifted authority from the territorial governor inflicted on them from the East, and gave it to the local magistrate who might have been a teamster or a steamboat captain or a lawyer before his elevation to office.[21] They normally chose as their leaders merchants and professional men who had proved themselves by achieving economic and social success in their new homes; very often in pioneer communities they entrusted authority to the little band of Freemasons who formed a cohesive elite group among the first settlers.[22] But these were merchants and professional men attuned to the Western scene and fitted to grapple with the problems of Western life. Such changes in leadership certainly altered the nature of democracy.

This new type of leader was acceptable because in the West the dead hand of political tradition weighed less strongly on the people. Lacking a feudal heritage, and disdainful of even the recent past as a proper guide to life in a new land, the pioneers lacked the sense of political continuity that tended to perpetuate practices or group controls in older societies. They were freer to experiment, and bolder in their experimentation. In the Western states, Alexis de Tocqueville observed, "the inhabitants are but of yesterday," and so have "escaped the influence not only of great names and great wealth, but even of the natural aristocracy of knowledge and virtue."[23] This rebellion against traditionalism was intensified by resentment against the immediate past; frontiersmen were certain that the East—whether symbolized by England's parliament in the case of the Virginia Company or by Washington's congress to the Californians—was too stultified to comprehend or solve their unique problems. The recurring demands for self-determination sharpened the Westerners' interest in government, and deepened their faith in democracy as an instrument for man's use.

Finally, an American brand of democracy was fostered by the recurring rebirth of government as the frontier advanced westward. "The western states of America," wrote a visitor, "are each a nursery of freedom: every new settlement is already a republic *in embryo*."[24] From the seventeenth century on, new governments were continuously born along the fringes of settlement, whether a Virginia House of Burgesses, or an assembly of the Watauga Association, or a new state in the Rocky Mountain country. Each meant an opportunity for experimentation, for adjustment to new conditions, for the introduction of democratic practices. Insomuch as most of these governments were formed in the late eighteenth and nineteenth centuries when the area of self-rule was expanding throughout the whole western world, Westerners were able to adopt reforms being tried elsewhere and adapt them to their own needs. This was important, for the frontier was not an area of political innovation; its contribution was to imitate and apply the democratic theories emerging in Europe and the East.[25] In this fashion, no less than in others, it gave its stamp to a uniquely American form of democracy.

These explanations of the frontier's role in fostering an *American* democracy have the ring of truth about them, but it must be noted that they rest only on the observations of a few travelers and the theorizing of even fewer scholars. They can be substantiated only if put to the test of historical application. Was the frontier a catalyst inducing democratic change? Did it operate as a laboratory where liberal theories were tested, sorted, and utilized? Before seeking to answer these questions, we must establish a theoretical base by making a few observations on modern group political behavior that seem pertinent to an understanding of similar behavior in the past.

This is possible because in recent years the demands of the Great Depression, World War II, and the dramatic shifts accompanying the population explosion have forced the creation of several new communities, many in the form of federal housing projects. These have been peopled by diverse groups, drawn together without any prior mingling, under conditions vaguely comparable to those in frontier settlements. One such unit was so poorly constructed that the inhabitants faced numerous problems; another was well-planned and built, assuring the newcomers a comparatively trouble-free existence. The behavior of the two groups under these opposite conditions was revealing. Those in the poorly designed unit were forced to grapple with their problems; to meet these they organized, established committees, and within a few months evolved a whole leadership structure that effected the reforms they sought. Those in the well-built housing project tried to form a similar organization, but public interest was so slight and candidates so few that their efforts soon collapsed. Because widespread community participation was not essential, no governmental structure emerged; because adversity had not created major needs, leadership roles carried no special status and could not be filled.[26]

In frontier communities, the pattern was comparable to that in the poorly equipped housing unit. There adversity created numerous problems that could be solved only by cooperative action under effective leadership. There the settlers, recruited from scattered areas but sharing a common economic and social status, found such cooperation easy. In any unstructured social group the establishment of some government is a brutal necessity; in pioneer groups the lack of traditional elites opened the door to any person to assume leadership whatever his prior training. Frontier communities, in other words, provided a near-perfect laboratory for democratic experimentation. If political theory and modern examples have any validity, we would expect to find certain trends noticeable there: a broadening of the franchise, wider participation in elections, restriction of executive and increase in legislative power, a rapid turnover of officeholders to provide greater popular control. Does the political history of the United States substantiate these hypotheses?

∾§∾§ AMERICA'S FIRST frontiers seemed unlikely places for democratic gains, and those of New Amsterdam and New Sweden especially so. Both were governed by autocratic companies concerned only with profits; both were peopled by colonists bred in a tradition of kingship and with no prior experience in self-government. Yet opportunity stemming from abundant land soon undermined company control; within a few years officials reported that the settlers were defying their rulers and scattering widely to find the best trading or farming spots. "Here are as many who will scatter," complained an agent of the New Sweden Company from the Delaware Valley, "as there are who will hold things together." When authorities tried to curb this trend, the people were driven to near-rebellion, drafting petitions, and voicing such threats that in New Sweden the governor was forced to call together the "best men" to draft an ordinance that would allow some popular control of the government. The Ordinance of 1655, adopted with "the consent of most of the men," was hardly democratic by modern standards, but this is unimportant.[27] What is important is the fact that the frontier's cheap land had encouraged a small step toward democracy. Its significance can be judged by the length of the step, not by the attainment of any goal.

The Anglo-American frontiers offered more fertile soil for democratic growth; the settlers came from a land soon to accept parliamentary supremacy, and in the New World lived in an atmosphere of permanent settlement rather than temporary trade. The result was no sudden surge of democracy, but instead an eroding away of aristocratic restrictions on land holding and commerce, which paved the way for democratic reform. This could not be fully realized until the frontier crossed the Appalachians, removing Americans from the direct influence of European tradition and rulers.

These generalizations can be illustrated in the early history of Virginia. The establishment of a House of Burgesses in 1619 was a step toward self-rule, but its importance can be exaggerated; the liberalism of some Virginia Company officials had more to do with its establishment than the insistence of the settlers on representation. Nor did the Burgesses ordain democracy as Virginia's wave of the future, for their powers were rigidly restricted after the Restoration and again after Bacon's Rebellion.[28] Yet during those years the social structure was recast in Virginia. The passing of English-born leaders after 1630 opened the way for the emergence of a new leadership structure, its members still drafted from the ranks of the well-to-do, but now largely self-made men who better represented the interests of the people than the gentry they displaced. More significant was a change in land holding, to displace the imported "strict settlement" pattern that allowed property to be entailed to the eldest son for generations. In America land was so cheap that there was no need to penalize younger sons to preserve estates, especially as those estates wore out under wasteful farming methods and were less valuable than newer plantations in the interior. In practice the laws of entail and primogeniture had ceased to operate in Virginia by the end of the seventeenth century, allowing a dispersal of land holdings that served as a base for political democracy.[29] Without a frontier, such a scattering of estates would have been impossible.

In Massachusetts a comparable change in the social structure occurred, with even more meaningful results. As in Virginia, colonial government in the early years was vested in an elite; men of substance were re-elected to the Court of Assistants so regularly that only thirty-five new members were chosen in the first half century. Yet pressures from below forced democratic changes: the franchise was liberalized, the Assistants' right to levy taxes challenged, and in the 1680s property holding substituted for church membership as a requirement for electors. More significant were the changes in local government. As cheap lands encouraged a dispersal of settlement, small communities multiplied in the interior. Needing orderly administration, and with neither dictation from above nor familiar English precedents on which to build, they developed town meetings as functional agencies to solve their many problems. By 1636, only eight years after the first settlement on Massachusetts Bay, these were so common that the General Court gave towns the right to choose their own officers, and five years later town meetings were opened to all freemen, regardless of church membership. Gradually their powers were expanded to include all local functions. This development was the more remarkable in that there was no similar evolution in England, where vestrymen chose the "most substantial" of their numbers as parish officials and county officers were named by royally appointed justices of the peace.[30] Abundant lands in America had, in a remarkably short time, triggered the emergence of significant democratic institutions.

These local gains were to bear fruit throughout New England by the time of the Revolution, in the emergence of a surprisingly democratic governmental structure at all levels. Massachusetts, true, limited the franchise to holders of forty-shilling freeholds or owners of property worth forty pounds. Aristocratic as this might appear on the statute books, it eliminated few voters, for the average eighteenth-century farm ranged from 80 to 150 acres, while one of only 12 acres qualified its owner as a voter. Insomuch as 90 percent of the people were farmers, something more than 85 percent of the adult males were eligible to cast their ballots. Even in the cities and towns the majority of the inhabitants were skilled artisans or shopkeepers whose property was worth at least forty pounds.[31] Cheap lands had allowed so many people to acquire property that the inherited legal restrictions on voting were rendered meaningless.

This was not a local phenomenon; in all colonies by the time of the Revolution, imported gentry had been replaced in authority by home-grown gentry whose interests in large part mirrored those of the people they governed. Within this elite group, changes occurred frequently, especially as the creation of new governments along the frontiers forced the elevation of new officials to power. This pattern of constant change rendered the social basis of public life insecure, its stability delicate and responsive to pressures from below. These pressures were multiplying, for the franchise was steadily broadening as men capitalized on the abundance of frontier land to acquire the property that would qualify them as voters. Despite property qualifications and the disenfranchisement of minority groups, perhaps 50 percent to 75 percent of all adult males were free to vote on a freehold basis by the time of the Revolution. This was a number unapproached in England or any other nation.[32]

When the thirteen new states adopted their constitutions, six moved slightly in a democratic direction, but in all much remained to be done before qualifications for suffrage could be said to be democratic. Property requirements for voting and office holding, religious tests, and the removal of many offices from popular control all interfered with popular self-rule. During the next few years as the liberal atmosphere of the Revolution waved them on, a number of states substituted tax paying for property holding as a qualification for voting. In three, New Hampshire, Delaware, and Georgia, payment of a poll tax sufficed, opening the ballot box to virtually all adult males.[33] The older Eastern states were clearly moving toward greater democracy. This was the situation when the first Western states entered the Union.

One, Tennessee, made but few concessions to democratic reform. The framers of its constitution, dominated by Eastern planters who had migrated from North Carolina, borrowed all but 25 of the 116 sections from constitutions of the older states, and retained such conservative features as property qualifications for voting and office holding, a religious test, and life tenure for the powerful justices of the peace.[34] In the other new Western state, Kentucky, the state-making process more nearly typified future trends. There three factions vied for control of the constitutional convention: property-conscious planters who had recently migrated from Virginia, lived in the rich bluegrass country, and wanted an undemocratic government modeled on that of the Old Dominion; small-farmer radicals longer resident on the frontier who sought a unicameral legislature, manhood suffrage, representation based on population, and the elimination of slavery; and a sizable body of moderates who were ready to swing as the tide turned. Here, in other words, were the factions who would debate democracy in nearly all future states, one rooted in the East and determined to perpetuate aristocratic controls, another oriented to the West and pledged to secure complete self-rule, and a third holding the balance of power between the two.[35]

The result was predictable, for only compromise could produce any frame of government. The Kentucky Constitution of 1792 was based on that of an Eastern state, but the choice of Pennsylvania rather than Virginia as a model represented a minor triumph for the Westerners. Radicals also wrote into the document clauses granting manhood suffrage, abolishing religious tests for office holding, and guaranteeing a secret ballot; conservatives contributed sections setting up a cumbersome electoral-college system for the selection of the governor and state senate, and providing for the appointment by the governor of judges and justices of the peace. In essence, the constitution was aristocratic, for the absence of property qualifications for voting meant little in a frontier state where land titles so overlapped that listing of freeholders was impossible.[36]

This cannot be interpreted to mean that the Kentucky frontier was antidemocratic. The framers of the constitution of 1792 were not typical pioneers; that document was foisted on the small farmers by a closely knit group of Easterners. This negation of the popular will aroused a storm of protest from democratic elements that gained so much momentum that a second convention met at Frankfort in 1799. Again conservative and radical elements vied for control, and again compromise was necessary. Radicals won an important victory when they obtained a direct vote to elect the governor and senate, but they paid for this victory with a return to a voice vote rather than a secret ballot in elections. The convention also assured continuation of slavery, which had been a prime target of the frontier forces.[37]

Government making in Kentucky demonstrated that there could be no clear-cut division between a conservative "East" and a democratic "West," and the subsequent history of the formation of states substantiates this conclusion. The importance assigned to local issues having nothing to do with democracy, the influence of political parties, the class divisions emerging as social stratification went on, and conflicts over land and property all created pressures on every delegate and helped decide every issue. Yet Kentucky made some progress, within ten years abandoning three of the five devices used in Virginia to maintain aristocratic control: property qualifications for voting, inequality of representation, and an established Church. Only slavery and the plantation system remained. These gains were made over the opposition of an entrenched group of newly arrived planters who had brought with them from the East the values of an established society and a firm determination to perpetuate property rights in land and slaves. Pressure from small-farmer pioneers longer oriented to Western values weakened, but did not end, the strength of this group.

Both Kentucky and Tennessee drafted their first constitutions while dominated by a planter leadership imported from their mother states, Virginia and North Carolina, but government making in the Old Northwest suffered no such handicap. There existed an unusual opportunity for pioneer democracy to thrive uncontested. The population was remarkably homogeneous in economic and social status, yet recruited from such a variety of backgrounds that no built-in leadership group existed. Within the Old Northwest few farms surpassed 250 acres, which meant that no land holding elite had developed and the governing group must be drafted from the mass of the people. Those who gained power were men sufficiently able, and sufficiently glib of tongue, to convince the voters that they represented the popular will. Even more important was the widespread interest in politics, for the region was acutely conscious of its needs and aware that only vigorous leaders could supply them. Prosperity and future growth depended on more liberal land laws, better roads, protection against Indians, and a dozen other things needed on most frontiers. Officeholders who could work toward these ends, on both local and national levels, were essential.

This atmosphere endowed leadership posts with a status that made them eagerly sought after by capable and ambitious young men; it also led to an extraordinarily high level of political participation. "Every body," wrote an Indiana settler, "expected at some time to be a candidate for something; or that his uncle would be; or his cousin, or his cousin's wife's cousin's friend would be; so that every body and every body's relations's friends were for ever electioneering."[38] One Ohio county produced no less than ninety-four candidates for the ten posts allotted it in the constitutional convention of 1802.[39] With this vying for office, and with the lively public interest in seeing that the right men were chosen, politics electrified the atmosphere months before each election. Every militia muster, every cabin raising or shooting match or log rolling, every Fourth of July celebration, was converted into a political convention as rival candidates stated their claims, bought drinks, and kissed babies. These pioneers were determined to select capable leaders who understood their wishes. Any politician who could demonstrate his ability to represent them would win their favor, whatever his prior status or lineage. Here was an ideal breeding ground for democratic practices.[40]

Yet such is human nature that the restraints on self-rule normal in established societies appeared in the Old Northwest, although in modified form. While no planter class served as a brake on the popular will, a new elite of land speculators, merchants, and professional men in every new community arrayed themselves against mass control of the government. Human lethargy also played its part, especially in the constitution-drafting process, for mankind instinctively trusts the tested rather than the untested; delegates to conventions often adopted accepted devices used in Eastern states rather than more democratic practices of their own invention. These dual pressures—of propertied interests distrustful of popular control and of tradition-minded men apprehensive of experimentation—meant that the state constitutions drafted in the Ohio Valley would be imitative rather than creative, that they would reflect compromises essential in reconciling conflicts between contending factions, and that they would not automatically enshrine the democracy that was the faith of a majority of the people.

Given these conditions, the results were predictable. Only 11 of the 106 clauses of the Ohio Constitution of 1802 were original, only 21 of the 129 in the Indiana constitution of 1816, and only 15 of the 98 in the Illinois constitution of 1818. The remainder were copied from constitutions of Eastern or neighboring states, with an increasing tendency to rely on examples from near at hand. This practice meant that democratic innovation was slight on the Ohio Valley frontier, but it emphatically did *not* mean that democratic gains were not registered there. The tendency of constitution makers was to copy sections of other documents that mirrored their own philosophy, and to write new ones only when a satisfactory example could not be found. They selected from older frames of government the most democratic features, and welded them into documents that were surprisingly liberal for that day. Ohio opened its ballot box to all who paid any tax or had contributed work on the roads; Indiana and Illinois adopted manhood suffrage. Supreme power in all states was vested in a popularly elected legislature, whose members were rotated frequently, and in Ohio and Illinois the legislatures were unrestrained by any veto power on the part of the governor. Even judges were elected in Ohio for short terms, so that the courts would reflect the popular will.[41] So insistent was the demand for election of officials, reported a cynical New Englander from Indiana, that every office was in control of the people from the governor's down to fence-viewer's clerk's assistants, and some wanted to let the electorate choose schoolteachers and professors at the state university.[42]

In the other states of the Old Northwest and beyond the Mississippi the story was the same, for the pattern of state making was established in the Ohio Valley and varied little thereafter. Manhood suffrage was the universal rule, usually granted after residence in the state of six months or a year. Legislative powers were broad at first, then temporarily restricted in constitutions adopted immediately after the Panic of 1819, for the misrule that helped precipitate that financial debacle made the people distrustful of unrestrained popular control over property rights. They responded by writing longer and longer constitutions that themselves served as laws, or by limiting the functions and authority of assemblies while increasing those of governors. This setback was short lived; in 1844 Iowans rejected a constitution judged insufficiently republican and accepted another two years later when convinced that it gave adequate powers to the legislature. In general, constitution making throughout the West revealed faith in democracy and in the relatively unrestrained right of the peoples' elected representatives to govern.[43]

On the level of local government the trend toward democratic practices was equally apparent. In the Old Northwest, the first charters inflicted on towns were patent-office models of those used in the East, for the rural-dominated legislatures had little concern with urban affairs. These undemocratic instruments, most of them restricting the suffrage and entrusting the mayor with excessive power, were short lived. During the 1830s and 1840s they were revolutionized to abolish property qualifications for voting and office holding, and to shift authority to elected councils. In Milwaukee a suggestion that aldermen hold office for three years was shouted down as "placing them beyond the reach of public opinion for a time almost equal to an age in older communities." Rotation in office was adopted with such enthusiasm that the mayors became mere figureheads, drawing no salary in Buffalo or Detroit, and but a pittance elsewhere. So persistent was the democratic trend that local government in much of the Old Northwest was placed in the hands of unpaid merchants and professional men during the post-frontier era, on the theory that they would remain closer to the people than politicians.[44]

In the rural counties of the Old Northwest the story was the same. A case study of grass-roots democracy in Trempeleau County, Wisconsin, during its pioneer period, is revealing in this respect. There county affairs were entrusted to a board of supervisors; township affairs to an annual town meeting. Although both institutions were imported, with their authority and delineation of functions prescribed by the state legislature, their operations showed marked differences from their counterparts in the East. Popular participation in town meetings was unusually high, ranging between 62 percent and 73 percent of all adult males; these meetings were also notable for spirited debates that revealed a lively interest in democratic processes. This same interest produced an exceptionally large number of candidates for county and township offices, many of them young recent arrivals who felt themselves better able to represent the people than older leaders. Members of the status group in control were so seriously threatened by these upstarts that they had to choose between defeat and welcoming their challengers into party councils where they were allowed a minor share of patronage. These pressures kept politics in a constant state of flux, with frequent elections, abundant candidates, and an unusual opportunity for all to participate in political decision making.[45] Here, in other words, was a community practicing a vigorous brand of democracy.

The result was not anarchy, for voters showed an instinctive preference for experienced candidates whose wealth was above the average. Trempeleau County during its pioneer period elevated thirty-two men to major political responsibility and 169 to minor posts. All were well-to-do, but some of the richest men were passed by, suggesting that wealth alone did not make a man a leader. Nearly all were American-born, most in the Northeastern states, although the number of foreign-born in minor leadership roles grew from 26 percent to 56 percent as the immigrant population of the county increased from 40 percent to 63 percent of the whole. During the earliest years, 83 percent of the leadership group were farmers, a figure that later fell to 67 percent as government functions were assumed by professional and businessmen. If Trempeleau County is typical of the West, pioneers chose political leaders who had some experience in the democratic United States, who were above the average in wealth, and who shared their own problems and beliefs; farmers seemed inclined to elect farmers as local officials, whatever their educational or military backgrounds. Most significant of all was the fact that in Trempeleau County twenty-six of the thirty-two major leaders assumed their roles in the first decade of the community, and only six in the next decade. Clearly in that fluid pioneer society the opportunity for political advancement—and hence the achievement of status—was greatest on the raw frontier and diminished with the thickening of population. Here again is a suggestion that pioneering did stimulate democratic tendencies.[46]

This becomes increasingly apparent if we contrast Wisconsin with the South of that same day. There, even on the frontiers, an atypical process of settlement created a social setting quite different from that in Northern pioneer communities. In the better-soil regions of Alabama and Mississippi or of Arkansas and Texas large planters usually began arriving only two or three years after the first settlement, with money to buy up several farms for consolidation into a plantation. Their coming introduced an elite class accustomed to leadership and helped expel a poorer class of small farmers who would provide a bulwark for democracy. These planters, with the support of a community whose respect they expected and achieved, simply perpetuated the tested forms of local government they had known in the East. Undemocratic county courts, monopolizing all executive and legislative as well as judicial functions, became the typical governing units of the Old Southwest. Yet their authority did not go untested, for the democratic impulse was powerful enough to secure the election rather than appointment of a few county-court members in Alabama, and the separation of judicial and legislative functions on the local level. The Southwest lagged behind the Northwest in democratic reform, but the frontier did loosen the bonds of custom even there.[47]

AGAINST this background of historical evidence, the question can now be asked: Did America's pioneering experience create or alter its democracy? In answering, one fact emerges at once. The West was not a breeding ground but a spawning ground for democratic theory and practice. Whether framing a constitution or drafting a town charter, frontiersmen were imitative rather than creative; they preferred to copy tested clauses from frames of government proved in the East to experimenting with more democratic new provisions. This was true even during the Populist period when the West flamed with dissent; the constitutions of the Omnibus States admitted in 1889 and 1890 were borrowed from those of older states no less than that of Ohio.[48] Happily, however, the democracy so dear to the Westerner was universally popular at that time; manhood suffrage and devices extending popular control were demanded in the East as fervently as in the West. The abolition of property qualifications for voting inspired a crusade that swept Massachusetts and New York into line in the 1820s, and in the 1840s touched off a minor war in Rhode Island. When Westerners drafted their frames of government they had only to sort out the most suitable from the old, with many examples from which to choose. Thus, though imitative, they tended to copy the more democratic features of Eastern constitutions to create Western constitutions that were more democratic than their models. "The departures from long established usages," noted a Westerner, "have tended gradually, and almost uniformly, to democracy."[49]

In still other ways the existence of a frontier served as a democratizing influence during the nineteenth century. As long as the nation believed that cheap lands would lure workmen westward, Eastern conservatives would be inclined to accept democratic reforms, for the liberalization of the franchise seemed a cheap price to pay for checking a migration that would deplete tax and labor rolls. The equality of opportunity usual on frontiers also played a role; in the West the rich became richer but the poor a good deal less poor and so more determined to share in the government to which they looked for future economic gains. Unusual opportunities for self-advancement in the West similarly released new talents and energies, many of which found expression in political activity, just as they would in any area undergoing change. Equally important was the fact that frontier mobility subjected imported institutions to heavy strains; every county that gained population demanded a greater voice in governmental affairs, and every one that failed to gain struggled to retain its power. This meant a wider range of discussion than in stabilized communities, and more frequent voting. The democratic processes were given an opportunity to operate more often on the frontiers, and strengthened accordingly.[50]

The sum total of these changes was to vest greater control of the government in *all* the people, and to remove it from the hands of any elite, whether hereditary or economic. This seemed fair in a land where class lines were disappearing; who would dare deny a voice in governmental decision making to a humble newcomer who might make a fortune before nightfall or charm his fellow citizens into a place among the political elite at the next election? Men should not be treated as equals only because the Declaration of Independence *decreed* them equal, but because they could actually *be* equal amidst the opportunities of a new land. These democratic attitudes were not carried to the New World on the *Susan Constant* and the *Mayflower*. They were a product of the turbulent social scene created by the westering urge of the pioneers.

7

Frontier Democracy: Social Aspects

To UNDERSTAND the uniqueness of *American* democracy we must consider not only the form of government and the extent of popular participation, but the way in which the people of the United States view government and society as a whole. Do they regard the state as the master or servant of its citizens? Do they consider their fellow men as equals, or as inferiors and superiors? In seeking answers to these questions, our concern is not with what *is*, but with what is *thought* to be. If the image of the social order common among Americans differs from that usual among Europeans, and if the differences can be explained by the pioneering experience, we can conclude that the frontier has altered the national character as well as institutions.

In this quest, two concepts are especially important: that of "individualism" and that of "equality." Visitors from abroad feel that the people of the United States have endowed these words with distinctive meanings. In no other nation is the equality of all men so loudly proclaimed; in no other country is the right of individual self-assertion (within certain areas) so stoutly defended. Travelers have also noted the relationship between the two concepts. Because all men are judged to be equal, all are assured the same freedom of individual expression. "They are apt to imagine," wrote Alexis de Tocqueville in the early nineteenth century, "that their whole destiny is in their own hands."[1] Tocqueville believed that this attitude was dangerous, threatening as it did the atomization of society.

&§&§ HIS FEARS were groundless, for even as he wrote conformity was displacing individualism as a national cult, save in one important aspect.[2] To Ralph Waldo Emerson and Henry David Thoreau society may have been the sum of atomized individuals, but to the generations that followed the emergence of an industrial-urban complex that made social interdependence essential to survival was one of the stark realities of life. In this integrated society, the fact of individualism, if not the *theory* of individualism, was gradually altered. In theory individualism meant the right of every person to make his own decisions and choices without regard to their effect on the social group. In practice, this was acceptable only in the sphere of economic activity. In that realm, a sink-or-swim philosophy gained acceptance and still prevails. If a man makes a wrong decision, and a business fails or a job is lost, no one is to blame but the person himself. If his decision is correct and he does well, we believe that he should be rewarded by advancement to positions of ever higher prestige. The direction in which he moves is his responsibility alone; the successful person enjoys a sense of his own greatness quite unrelated to those around him.[3] Individualism in the economic world seems fair to Americans as long as equal and plentiful opportunity exists for all, and who can doubt its existence in a land of abundance? Social-security systems, unemployment benefits, Medicare, and a host of other security measures today challenge the fact of economic individualism, but the theory is still vigorously defended.

Individualism in its distinctly American usage does not apply to the noneconomic world. It grants no license for freedom of personal expression; no respectable citizen would dream of exhibiting a unique personality in the clothes that he wears, the manners he adopts, or the behavior that he exhibits in public. The Frenchman instinctively distrusts the outsider and shuns cooperation; the American instinctively follows the herd. "Americans," observed Peter Ustinov, "are always attempting to run away from conformity, but unfortunately they always start running in the same direction."[4] Twentieth-century travelers have pointed out the monotonous uniformity of the streets, the towns, the cities, of the United States. "Not a single American," wrote one, "can distinguish Main Street in one town from Main Street in one of hundreds of others."[5] Let a Hollywood actress or a spotlighted pop singer adopt a new hair style and women rush to their hairdressers to imitate her. Let a public figure appear in a novel hat, or trousers, or haircut, and men fall into line. Even political behavior is regimented, as Americans dutifully cast their ballots for Democratic or Republican candidates rather than for the dozens of parties that range across the political spectrum in Europe. And woe unto the American who defends a belief that is currently unpopular, either of the extreme left or the extreme right.

The oft-defended individualism of the United States is no guarantee of the individual's freedom of expression, but is manifested in two ways, each related to the other. One is a relative lack of respect for the law; the typical American is more inclined to flaunt regulations, or to whittle a few illegal dollars from his income tax, than his British cousins. The other is a resentment of governmental meddling in private affairs. Some Americans preached individual freedom when the Eighteenth Amendment told them what not to drink, and the bootleggers' paradise of the 1920s was the result. Some raised an umbrella of "rugged American individualism" over their heads when the regulatory measures of Progressivism or the New Deal threatened to interfere with their free use of property. Some, living in the Southern states, hoisted the banner of states' rights when federal agencies told them to integrate their schools, but what they really defended was the right of every individual to like or dislike persons of his own choice, whatever the effect on society. All were proclaiming their defiance of the government, and demanding that it cease telling them how to live or manage their affairs. The American is willing to conform if he personally decides to conform, as he does in adopting the style of his clothes or the brand of popular music that he will enjoy. But the American is not willing to allow his elected representatives to decide that conformity is for him. This is the essential difference between the individualism of the United States and that of Europe.

◆§◆§ AS LONG AS we dwell in the realm of theory, nothing could be easier than to link this distinctly American faith with the frontier experience. The modern American believes that each person shall be allowed to rise or fall in the workaday world as his own grit and ability decrees; he also clings to the belief that the government should not interfere. Such a system could operate only in a land of equal opportunity, where the dispossessed could begin life anew without too much difficulty, where new jobs were being created to absorb an expanding population, and where resources were so abundant that all could share in their wealth without governmental intervention in the role of umpire. Only in frontier America did this combination of beatitudes exist. Hence American individualism is the product of the frontiering experience. So men reasoned in the nineteenth century, and so many believe today.

This myth has been fastened on the public mind by the plausibility of logic. Nothing is more obvious than that the pioneer would resent social controls, or that he would be able to escape dependence on society. He had, after all, fled his fellows to battle the wilderness alone. In his new home the solitude in which he lived, the vastness of the world about him, and the assurance that he acquired as he combatted nature, contributed to a spirit of self-reliance that was universal among pioneers. This was accentuated by the richness of the land, and the equally shared opportunity to exploit those riches. Where all were potential millionaires, property assumed a new importance, even to the propertyless. Men on the frontier, Americans of the nineteenth century believed, were so confident of affluence that they needed no help from society and wanted no meddling by society. "Here," wrote a visitor to the Colorado mines, "a man looks upon the wealth of others as held in trust for himself, and will suffer no diminution of its sanctity."[6] This attitude fostered rugged American individualism in its truly American sense.

Just as persuasive was the frequent testimony of travelers and Westerners that the West actually was a land of unbridled liberty where men behaved according to the dictates of their consciences, and devil take their neighbors. "Liberty here," wrote an Englishman from the Kentucky backwoods, "means to do each as he pleases, to care for nothing and nobody."[7] This was natural in the borderlands, where men were free to shape the course of their lives without nearby neighbors inflicting their wills or watchful officials meddling in their affairs.

There every man was king, and kings could rule themselves. When passengers on a keelboat tried to stop a frontiersman from singing on the Sabbath they were heatedly informed that they were in a "land of liberty" and had no right to interfere. A recruit among the fur trappers of the Rocky Mountain country was told by an old-timer that he had only to mind his own affairs to get along. "If you see a man's mule running off," the newcomer was advised, "don't stop it—let it go to the devil; it isn't yourn. If his possibles sack falls off, don't tell him of it; He'll find it out." A pioneer who told a visitor that he was moving from Arkansas to Texas because he "had heern there was no sich thing as a government there, and not one varmint of a lawyer in the *hull* place" only personified what the United States believed to be the spirit of the whole frontier.[8]

This nineteenth-century image of the West perpetuated the belief that the pioneer was opposed to all governmental regulation of economic activity. If steamboats had accidents that killed hundreds of persons yearly, nothing should be done, for steamboats were the life-blood of the Mississippi Valley, and a few lives were a cheap price to pay for the economic activity that they fostered.[9] If speculators absorbed the best lands, or miners appropriated mineral wealth, or lumbermen stripped away the forests, or "Sooners" illegally usurped the prime acreage in land openings, the social losses were insignificant compared to the benefits that accrued when the free-enterprise spirit was unleashed amidst the West's resources. These were the tales spread across the nation by the frontiersmen and their visitors, until they became a part of the nation's folklore. The frontier was a land of individualism, and American individualism was its natural offspring. This was a myth accepted throughout the nineteenth century and beyond.

ACTUALLY, the legend of frontier individualism rested on what people thought should be true, rather than what was true. The West was in truth an area where cooperation was just as essential as in the more thickly settled East. The danger of Indian attack, the joint efforts needed to clear the forests or break the prairie sod, the community of labor required for the variety of enterprises necessary in establishing a settlement, all decreed that new communities be occupied by groups, and never by solitary individuals. "In a young country," noted a visiting Englishman, "they must assist each other, if they wish to be assisted themselves—and there always will be a mutual dependence." Alexis de Tocqueville expressed nothing less than the truth when he observed that "In no country in the world has the principle of association been more successfully used, or applied to a greater multitude of objects, than in America."[10]

This "principle of association" was more essential on the frontier than in the East. Cooperative enterprise is instinctive among all groups, even of the most primitive tribesmen, for habits of mutual dependence developed by family life during infancy are extended as people realize that the benefits of joint activity compensate for the work involved. Cooperation is normal within every in-group, but accentuates when the in-group is in conflict with an out-group and group solidarity is strengthened. This was the situation in frontier communities, where conflicts with Indians, with raw nature, and with dominating Easterners heightened the spirit of interdependence. In the West social cohesiveness, standardized behavior, and restrictive limitations on individual freedom were more acceptable than in the East.

So closely knit were pioneer groups that privacy of person or mind was virtually unattainable. Where neighbors were relatively few and newcomers a treasured rarity, every stranger was of rapt interest and a heaven-sent opportunity to relieve the tedium of existence. "You are in a house of glass," complained one annoyed traveler as he endured the probing of the frontiersmen; another added that "privacy, either in eating, sleeping, conversation, or government, seems quite unknown, and unknowable."[11] So prevailing was the community spirit that no one dared express individuality; people lived and dressed and thought exactly alike. "Whoever ventures to differ essentially from the mass," recorded a newcomer to the Michigan frontier, "is sure to become the object of unkind feeling, even without supposing any bitter personal animosity." And Charles Dickens, vitriolic as usual in his impressions of the Mississippi Valley pioneers, complained of "such a deadly, leaden people; such systematic plodding weary insupportable heaviness."[12] These may have been exaggerations, but they were accurate in the over-all estimate of the spirit of cohesiveness existing in pioneer communities. Amidst the anonymity of a city, a person might dare to be different; amidst the intimacy of the frontier, he did not.

Much of this spirit was rooted in the stark realities of backwoods life, for cooperation was as essential to survival as a "Kentucky" rifle or a Colt revolver. Men went west in groups to minimize the

Indian danger and the hardships of travel. When the journey was long and difficult, they organized a walking republic, complete with administrative and judicial officials to whom they delegated needed authority. As soon as they reached their destination they provided for the common defense by building a blockhouse or forming a militia company. These log or adobe forts became the centers of neighborhood life, especially in time of danger when the whole community "forted up" and shared guard duty until the threat passed. "Their common security," a pioneer told a traveler, "locked them in amity." Years after the times of danger a frontiersman remembered the pleasure they had provided because "we were so kind and friendly to one another."[13] Commonly shared perils were a cohesive force among the homesteaders of the Great Plains no less than among earlier pioneers, for there grass fires, grasshopper invasions, and cattle wars banded the people together to combat mutual enemies.[14] Any who refused to share were banished as traitors to society; there was no place for the uncooperative eccentric in a land where joint effort was the key to survival.

Cooperation was just as essential in times of peace as in times of war. Needed goods were imported by mutually owned caravans. Neighbors assisted in the "cabin raisings" and "barn raisings" that provided every newcomer with a home, and in the "logrollings" that helped him clear his fields. They joined in "corn huskings" and "quilting bees" and "fulling parties" where newly woven cloth was prepared for the housewife's needle. Scarce an activity in a frontier community that did not lend itself to neighborhood enterprise; records of pioneer settlements bristle with accounts of spinning parties, goose pickings, apple parings, rag cuttings, carpet tackings, wool pickings, and a dozen more. "A life in the woods," observed a visitor from Britain, "teaches many lessons, and this among the rest, that you must both give assistance to your neighbor, and receive it in return, without either grudging or pouting."[15] Little wonder that students of the frontier refer to the "principle of mutuality" when speaking of life in the West.

The community benefited no less than individuals from mutual enterprise, because the necessity of common labor for society's good was cheerfully accepted as a part of pioneer life. Was a new church required, or a new school to be built, all hands turned out with axes and adzes to buckle to the task. "The neighbors divided themselves into choppers, hewers, carpenters, and masons," recalled an Indiana settler. "Those who found it impossible to report for duty might pay an equivalent in nails, boards, or other materials."[16] When a road was to be constructed, or a bridge thrown across a stream, all were expected to help, since on the frontier division of labor was little known. Communities organized "Claim Clubs" to guard land from or for speculators, and in the Great Plains country recruited members to drive cattle from planted fields. Pioneer farmers, wherever they lived, were not so wedded to individualism that they would scorn help when help was needed.[17]

Even those crown princes of individualism, the ranchers and miners, depended far more on joint effort than on self-prowess. Cattlemen on the Great Plains lost no time in forming associations that not only supervised the semiannual roundups, but that seriously restricted private enterprise by regulating pasturage on the open range. Community activity also quickened in time of emergency, furnishing men and horses to hunt down herds scattered by fire or drought. Cowboys as well as ranchers recognized the value of group activity; in 1883 some 325 in Texas organized to demand a $20 monthly raise, which they won after striking five ranches at roundup time.[18] So did miners. The lone prospector is a figure from fiction rather than reality, for no single man could live long in the rugged mountain country of the early West. Most prospecting was done in groups of five to twenty men, usually well-mounted and provisioned, and led by a miner sufficiently versed in geology that no time was wasted on unlikely spots. Mining was never an individual enterprise, but was conducted by partners or teams who divided the labor and shared the profits. The rugged individualist, defending his claim with a six-shooter, had no place in the real Far West. "The Americans," wrote a Scottish visitor to the California gold fields, "have a very great advantage, for . . . they are certainly of all people in the world the most prompt to organize and combine to carry out a common object."[19]

On all frontiers community effort found particular expression in law enforcement. Renegades from society posed a problem in new settlements, attracted as they were by the hope of quick wealth and the absence of machinery to administer justice, but when they became sufficiently numerous to threaten life and property, the sober citizens banded together to meet the situation head on. Known variously as Regulators or the Regulation in the forested regions, as Anti-Horse-Thief Associations on the Great Plains, and as Vigilantes in the Far West, they served as law officers, courts, and executioners, rounding up the worst offenders, subjecting them to a summary trial, and either hanging them to the nearest tree or banishing them from the community. So effective were they that in one California mining district 500 miles long, occupied by a hundred thousand turbulent men who had riches to tempt the outlaw but neither government nor locks as protection, "there was," noted a visitor in 1850, "as much security of life and property as in any part of the Union."[20] This security was won at a grim price; vigilantes sometimes degenerated into lynching mobs that took the life of many an innocent man. Yet the readiness of frontiersmen to cooperate for protection, and their instinctive skill in organizing, underlines the myth of frontier individualism.

This was made even more obvious by the willingness of pioneers to accept governmental regulations that might have aroused protests in eastern cities. Blue laws were commonplace in many areas, restricting private behavior in a manner reminiscent of seventeenth-century Boston. Ohio in 1816 levied heavy fines for swearing by God, Christ, or the Holy Ghost; shooting bullets across a stream; and running horses in towns. Still heavier penalties awaited anyone guilty of arranging a puppet show, wire dancing, or tumbling. Illinois decreed a fine of $25 for any person selling cards, dice, or billiard balls. Towns studded their statute books with laws forbidding the playing of ninepins, serenading, or making a noise with "drums, fifes, horns, pans, kettles or with anything whatsoever."[21] Frontiersmen accepted infringements on individual freedom needed to protect the community against gambling, time-wasting entertainment, or sleep-disturbing noise, just as had the Puritans.

Less well known was the willingness of the pioneers to adopt laws governing economic behavior, at least in the infant urban communities of the Midwest. Citizens were required to sweep the streets before their doors, and to conform to certain standards in advertising their products. Trade was regulated more exactingly than in the East, because firm measures were necessary in near-monopoly situations to protect the uncertain food supply, prevent speculative pricing in times of shortage, and force licensed merchants to compete honestly with each other. Chicago confined the sale of meats and vegetables to certain times and places where they could be inspected to protect the public health. Other pioneer cities fixed the price of bread, regulated fees of hackmen and carters, and regularly checked the accuracy of weights and measures.[22] Not even private property was too sanctified to escape controls designed for the public good.

Regulation by state and national agencies was equally acceptable to the pioneer—when he judged the laws to be in his own interest. Texas in 1883 set up machinery to control railroad rates and force roads to haul cars of their competitors, although such a measure invaded property rights that had been held sacred. Texan cattlemen welcomed laws governing the conduct of drovers on the "long drives" to the Kansas railroads, even though their own liberties were threatened.[23] A few years later the embattled farmers of the Great Plains raised the banner of Populism to demand governmental regulation of the railroads, a "socialistic" parcel post service, and the curbing of monopolies. To the frontier-oriented Westerner, the government could be a valuable ally as readily as a dangerous enemy, and should be viewed in either light as the immediate situation dictated.

ON THE BASIS of this analysis of Western opinion, we can now seek answers to two questions: Was frontier individualism a myth, and if not, how did it differ from traditional individualism? One conclusion is obvious: in the social realm the pioneer was a complete traditionalist, leaning on the community no less than his city cousins. Cooperation with his neighbors was commonplace for defense, the accomplishment of essential pioneering tasks, law enforcement, and a host of other necessities. In the economic realm the frontiersman's attitudes were less sharply defined. Consistency was not one of his sins; he favored regulation that seemed beneficial to his interests, and opposed regulation that threatened immediate or potential profits. His views were, in other words, comparable to those of Eastern business leaders who demanded from the government protective tariffs, railroad land grants, and federal subsidies, while mouthing the virtues of "rugged individualism."

Yet in one sense, the frontiersman moved somewhat beyond his counterparts in the East. He was, to a unique degree, living in a land where everyone was a real or potential capitalist. Nowhere could a stake in society be more easily obtained, and nowhere was the belief that this was possible more strongly entrenched. Moreover the frontier was developed largely by capital imported from the seaboard or from Europe. The fur trade, mining, and cattle raising prospered only because a flow of money from the East and abroad made prosperity possible. "The real peculiarity of our present Pacific civilization," wrote the editor of the *Overland Monthly* in 1883, "is that it is, perhaps, the most completely realized embodiment of the purely commercial civilization on the face of the earth."[24] Dependent as they were on this flow of capital, and certain as they were that the humblest tenant farmers would someday enjoy wealth, Westerners were even more acutely conscious of the value of private property than Easterners, and more grimly determined to defend their right to use property as they wished. They would favor regulatory measures needed to attract capital or assure a healthy return on investments, but they would oppose laws that threatened profits even more vigorously than Easterners.[25]

The frontiersmen, then, were opportunists rather than consistent theorists, but to an even greater degree than the capitalists of the seaboard. They had to be. Gambling against an unpredictable nature, they were willing to follow any path that promised success. If their ends could be achieved by individualistic effort, they preached individualism. If, more commonly, cooperative labor was necessary, or the use of governmental controls, they showed no reluctance in approving these devices. Their purpose was to make a profit, not prove a political theory, and their views swung with the circumstances. Yet the widespread property holdings in the West, and the belief that every man would achieve affluence, inclined the Westerner to insist on his right to profits somewhat more stridently than others. His voice spoke for individualism louder than that of his fellows, even though he was equally willing to find haven in cooperation when danger threatened or need decreed.

The rural Westerner's inclination toward individualism was strengthened by the fact that except in periods of danger or disaster he was somewhat less integrated into society than a city dweller, especially after the frontier on which he lived had passed its pioneer stage. The Easterner, living in a land where the economy was based on division of labor, was only a cog in a machine that must keep on operating if he were to survive. The Westerner, even though he leaned on his neighbors for defense and cabin raisings and husking parties, was relatively more self-sufficient. He harbored the belief that his self-sufficiency would increase, knowing that his own abilities would assure him a prosperous future as he exploited the natural resources about him. He might need government help to regulate rates of railroads that carried his grain to market or prices of manufacturers who sold him his implements, but he wanted no government interference with his freedom as he followed the road to riches.

To this extent, the frontiersman was an individualist, and his brand of individualism was remarkably like that which has persisted in the United States as a whole. The American follows the herd in his social habits, and he is eager to accept government aid that promises benefits to his business. But he is loudest in protest when regulatory measures threaten his profits or his economic freedom. Individualism, in the uniquely American sense, does seem to duplicate the individualism of the pioneer.

᚛§᚛§ BASICALLY, frontier individualism stemmed from the belief that all men were equal (excluding Negroes, Indians, Orientals, and other minority groups), and that all should have a chance to prove their personal capabilities without restraint from society. This seemed fair in a land of plenty, where superabundant opportunity allowed each to rise or fall to his proper level as long as governments did not meddle. Faith in the equality of men was the great common creed of the West. Only an understanding of the depth of this belief can reveal the true nature of social democracy on successive frontiers.

To European visitors, this was the most unique feature of Western life and thought: the attitude that set that region apart from Europe or the East. "There is nothing in America," wrote one, "that strikes a foreigner so much as the real republican equality existing in the Western States, which border on the wilderness."[26] The whole attitude of the people was different; calmly confident of their own future, they looked on all men as their peers and acted accordingly. One Westerner who defined the frontier as a region where a poor man could enter a rich man's house without feeling uneasy or unequal was not far astray. Menial subservience was just as unpopular there as haughty superiority. Dame Shirley, writing from the California gold fields, felt the "I'm as good as you are" spirit all about her, and believed that only an American frontiersman could

> Enter a palace with his old felt hat on—
> To address the King with the title of Mister,
> And ask the price of the throne he sat on.[27]

Everywhere men of all ranks exuded that easy air of confidence that went with complete self-assurance, meeting travelers on terms of equality that charmed those democratically inclined and shocked those of opposite prejudice. "The wealthy man assumes nothing to himself on account of his wealth," marveled one, "and the poor man feels no debasement on account of his poverty, and every man stands on his own individual merits."[28] The spirit of Western democracy was captured by a cowboy addressing a disagreeable scion of British nobility: "You may be a son of a lord back in England, but that ain't what you are out here."[29]

In the give and take of daily life, Western egalitarianism was expressed in the general refusal to recognize the class lines that were forming in every community. Some of the self-proclaimed "better sort" might hold themselves aloof and put on aristocratic airs, but they were atypical of the great mass of the people. The majority, in evaluating those about them, applied value judgments that differed from those in communities where tradition played a stronger role. Men were weighed on their present and future contributions to society, with total disregard for their background. Each played a role in the developing social order, and as long as he played it well he was respected. "To be useful is here the ruling principle," wrote a Swedish visitor to the West; "it is immaterial what one does so long as he is respected and does his work efficiently."[30] Drones and aristocratic idlers were not bearing their fair share and were outcasts; men of menial rank were contributing to the community welfare and were respected. "There is in the West," noted an unusually acute observer during the 1830s, "a real equality, not merely an equality to talk about, an equality on paper; everybody that has on a decent coat is a gentleman."[31]

Contemporaries speculated often on the reasons for frontier social democracy. Most agreed that the burgeoning Western economy was basically responsible, offering as it did a chance for the lowliest to acquire prestige through accumulated wealth. All had an equal chance to improve themselves, and so all should be treated as equals; conversely, the servant who believed that he would someday be a millionaire saw no reason to be servile to his temporary betters. This was common sense, since every new community boasted dozens of living examples of rags-to-riches success: the tenant farmer who was now a county judge, the mechanic newly elected to the legislature, the farmer grown rich by the sale of lands.[32] As a British traveler saw, "the means of subsistence being so easy in the country, and their dependence on each other consequently so trifling, that spirit of servility to those about them so prevalent in European manners, is wholly unknown to them."[33] Why be servile when the man above today might be the man below tomorrow? Why cling to traditional views of rank when the heir apparent to a British earldom could be seen mowing hay, assisted by two sons of a viscount, while nearby the brother of an earl was feeding grain into a threshing machine?[34] Clearly standards on the frontier were different, and equality more nearly a fact of life.

The common level of wealth encouraged this spirit, for while differences did exist, the gulf between rich and poor was relatively less in frontier regions than in older societies. Poverty was rare in pioneer communities that had graduated from the backwoods stage; one governor complained that the number of dependent paupers in his state was "scarcely sufficient to give exercise to the virtue of charity in individuals."[35] Wealth might and did exist on rural frontiers, but its presence was less obvious than in the East, for money would buy little but land and land was available to all. Ostentatious spending existed but was uncommon, partly because luxuries and leisure were largely unavailable, partly because it would breed hostility in neighbors who resented display. "Their wealth," it was observed, "does very little in the way of purchasing even the outward signs of respect; and as to *adulation,* it is not to be purchased with love or money."[36] This leveling process underlined the sense of equality that was so typical of the frontier.

It was further emphasized by the fact that on the newer frontiers rich and poor lived, dressed, and acted much more alike than in the East. Most owned their own houses, though some might be of logs and some of bricks. Most dressed in homespun clothes and shunned the powdered wigs and knee breeches that were the badge of the gentry in the early nineteenth century; travelers frequently complained that it was impossible to distinguish the well-born from the lowly by the garments they wore.[37] Most bore themselves proudly, scorning the humble mien that marked the lower classes in Europe. "The clumsy gait and bent body of our peasant is hardly ever seen here," wrote an Englishman from Kentucky in 1819; "every one walks erect and easy."[38] When people looked and acted alike, as they did along the frontiers, treating them alike came naturally.

No less important in fanning the spirit of egalitarianism was the newness of the West, and the lack of traditional aristocratic standards there. No entrenched gentry governed social intercourse, setting the practices of those below them and closing their ranks against newcomers. Those who rose in station did not have to surmount the barrier of learning new customs as do those achieving higher status today, for conventions, deferences, and distinctions were rare among the "tree-destroying sovereigns" of the West.[39] A man's ancestry and prior history were less important than the contribution that he could make to a new society badly in need of manpower. One Westerner who remarked: "It's what's above ground, not what's under, that we think on," and another who added: "Not 'What has he done in the East?' but 'What does he intend to do in Kansas and for Kansas?' " summed up the reasons for much of the social democracy that thrived along the frontiers.[40]

This combination of causal forces—economic equality, commonly shared living standards, and the absence of traditional aristocratic values—enshrined belief in equality as the common faith of Western society. Class distinctions did exist, of course; innate differences in talent, ambition, and skill divided the various strata at an early stage in the evolution of every Western community. But relatively, these distinctions played a lesser role in the West than in the East. Instead belief in equality compelled frontiersmen to uplift the lowly and degrade the superior as they sought a common democratic level.

Elevation of the lowly was most commonly expressed by refusal to use terms designating class distinctions. Every man on the frontier, whatever his status in life, was a "gentleman," and every woman a "lady." Travelers from older societies were frequently amused to find the ragged wagoner or the ill-kempt seller of old bones addressed in this fashion; one who asked a tavern keeper in an infant settlement in New York to find his coachman was delighted when that worthy called out: "Where is the gentleman that brought this man here?"[41] "Ladies" were as carelessly designated; one traveling in the West might hear, as did Mrs. Trollope, references to "the lady over the way that takes in washing," or "that there lady, out by the Gulley, what is making dip-candles."[42] If titles could serve as social escalators, no one on the frontiers need stay long in menial ranks.

The leveling spirit of Western democracy sought not only to elevate the lowly but also to dethrone the elite. Any attempt at "putting on airs," was certain to be met with rude reminders of the equality of all men. New settlers were warned by guidebooks to mingle freely and familiarly with neighbors, and above all to pretend no superiority, if they wished to be accepted. They were told that nothing ruined a man's chances on the frontier so fatally as a suspicion of pride, which, once established, would ruin his reputation. "The cry of 'Mad Dog,' " wrote a Michigan pioneer, "is not more surely destructive."[43] Travelers were also instructed to dress in simple fashion, and to avoid display in their clothes or their speech; those garbed as mechanics risked insults far less than those dressed as gentlemen. Those who failed to heed these warnings might be greeted with such remarks as: "Hold on, tha'r, stranger! When ye go through this yer town, go slow, so folks kin take you in," or in dry tones: "Mister, how much do you ask for it?" "For what, sir?" "Well, for the town; you look as though you owned it."[44] One English newcomer who asked to be addressed as "Esquire" found that within a few days not only his host but the hired hands were calling him "Charlie"; another had the brass buttons unceremoniously ripped from his coat by a frontiersman who objected to such display. Texas rangers gambled or gave away the fancy uniforms issued to them, and stole the gold-braided suits of officers so that these aristocratic evidences of rank would not be seen.[45] "Superiority," observed an English visitor, "is yielded to men of acknowledged talent alone."[46]

Outward signs of social snobbery might arouse resentment in the West, but so did any conduct that seemed to suggest superiority. Families with sizable incomes found themselves better accepted if they lived and dressed as simply as their poorest neighbors; politicians soon realized that for success they must insist on being addressed as "Mister" or "Governor," and not as "Excellency." Even such a born-to-the-purple native aristocrat as Theodore Roosevelt took pains to understate his wealth and ancestry when on his Dakota ranch.[47] When Colonel Thomas Dabney appeared at a frontier cabin raising in the Southwest with twenty slaves to do his work he was ostracized by the community; when a traveler had the good sense to dispose of expensive luggage, he was at last accepted on friendly terms.[48] Natives and visitors alike learned that in the West refusal to drink with a stranger was interpreted as a sign of social superiority; unless they could convince their would-be hosts that they had "sworn off," even redeye whisky was preferable to the trouble that followed if word spread that they were "too good" for the community.[49]

So strong was the spirit of equality along the frontiers that any deviation was met with resentment that was sometimes carried to ludicrous ends. Frontier housewives found themselves in disfavor if they kept their homes neater or cleaner than those of their neighbors; one who had waited three years for her first caller was told: "I woulda come before but I heard you had Brussels carpet on the floor." Another who offered to lend teaspoons for a party was rudely informed that no such luxuries were wanted, for the guests would not be used to them. Even those with a few choice possessions apologized; carpets were excused as *"one* way to hide the dirt," a mahogany table as "dreadful plaguy to scour," and kitchen conveniences as "lumberin' up the house for nothin'."[50] When an Englishman remonstrated about the lack of ceremony in Western life he was told: "Yes, that may be quite necessary in England, in order to overawe a parcel of ignorant creatures, who have no share in making the laws; but with us a man's a man, whether he have a silk gown on him or not."[51] The spirit of Western social democracy could have found no more eloquent expression than that.

In practice this spirit found its most outspoken expression in the attitude of hired workers. A "servant" in the traditional sense was impossible to find in the West because any form of servility was demeaning and hence intolerable; some of the most wealthy hosts and hostesses interrupted their dinner parties to wait on table or busy themselves in the kitchen.[52] When servants could be drafted from the ranks of newly arrived immigrants or the families of less well-to-do pioneers they refused to accept that designation, but insisted on being called "helps," or "hired hands," or "ladies." The term "waiter" was equally unpopular, and was likely to call forth a spirited rejoinder from the person so addressed. Still more insulting was the word "master." A misguided traveler asking "Is your master at home?" would probably be told "I have no master"; one in the Wyoming cattle country was heatedly informed that "the son of Baliel ain't been born yet."[53] So deep was the resentment against any implication of servility that young men and women preferred to labor at poor pay under bad conditions rather than accept a post as servant.

Those who did so guarded their respectability by abolishing all traditional symbols of servitude. Livery was never used; bells to summon servants in Western inns were unknown because the "helpers" refused to respond.[54] All insisted on being treated as equals, dining with the family, meeting guests, and joining in all social functions under threat of immediate departure. One who had been told she must eat in the kitchen turned up her lip, announced "I guess that's cause you don't think I'm good enough to eat with you," and flounced from the house.[55] Nor was this rebellious spirit peculiar to household help. The oft-heard remark: "If a man is good enough to work for me, he is good enough to eat with me" was literally applied. A family who had hired several carpenters to build a barn made the mistake of an early breakfast without them one day; the next day they left. A honeymooning couple were abandoned by their hired driver when they tried to eat alone just once.[56] In public houses or conveyances the story was the same; travel accounts abound with tales of stewards who joined the card game after serving drinks, of waitresses who leaned over chairs to join in the conversation or borrow a guest's fan, of messengers who seated themselves and demanded a drink while serving their messages, of waiters in inns who joined their patrons when their tasks were done.[57] In the West men felt equal, and acted the part.

Menial tasks were as resented by servants as were menial titles. Travelers were often forced to clean their own boots in frontier inns, or to rub down their own horses while "helpers" looked on disdainfully. One who asked to be awakened in the morning was answered "call yourself and be damned."[58] On another occasion a titled Englishman in the Wyoming wilds was told to take a swim instead of a bath when he asked his hired helper to fill a tub; when he refused the angry helper shot the tub full of holes, shouting: "You ain't quite the top-shelfer you think you is, you ain't even got a shower-bath for cooling your swelled head, but I'll make you a present of one, boss!"[59] Nor did servants alone resent the suggestion of servility. A pioneer Michigan housewife who tired of seeing a guest attack the roast with his own knife and offered to carve was rudely informed: "I'll help myself, I thankye. I never want no waitin' on."[60]

Travelers who were shocked by these evidences of social democracy in the West were equally appalled by the democratic spirit which prevailed in frontier inns. There no "First Class" or "Second Class" accommodations separated patrons; tradesmen, slave dealers, farmers, congressmen, generals, fur trappers, and roustabouts ate side by side at the long tables, and all were treated the same.[61] Sleeping accommodations were allotted on a first-come-first-serve basis, with governors and herdsmen, senators and farmers, rich and poor, clean and unclean, all crowded three or four to a bed. "It has been my lot," recorded an experienced traveler, "to sleep with a diversity of personages; I do believe from the driver of the stage coach, to men of considerable name."[62] Complaints against these arrangements were summarily rejected by pioneer landlords; one visitor from overseas who objected to using a dirt-encrusted washbowl with a dozen other guests was told that "one rain bathes the just and the unjust, why not one wash-bowl"; another's protest that the sheets were dirty was answered with: "since *Gentlemen* are all alike, people do not see why they should not sleep in the same sheets."[63] The frontier inn was, as one traveler put it, "a most almighty beautiful democratic amalgam."[64]

THE SOCIAL DEMOCRACY and frontier-type individualism that characterized America's growing period have not persisted unchanged into the twentieth century. Individualism has retreated before the advance of social cohesiveness essential in an urban-industrial society. The nation's folk hero may still be the rugged individualist, but the lone wolves of the past have found that they cannot fight the pack and that in cut-throat competition all throats are cut. At least since the 1890s the economic community had grudgingly accepted the regulation that the pioneer resisted save when it was to his advantage, and today cooperation and reliance on government are almost as commonplace in the United States as in the older countries of Europe. Yet American individualism differs from that of France or England in its continued insistence on a degree of economic freedom that has long since vanished in those countries, and in a glorification of the individual's ability to care for himself despite daily proof that joint effort alone will succeed in a society increasingly enmeshed.

Just as vestiges of frontier individualism remain to distinguish the social attitudes of modern America from those of modern Europe, so do remnants of pioneer democracy. The United States is no longer a country free of class distinctions and so wedded to egalitarianism that manifestations of wealth arouse public resentment. But its social democracy does differ from that of older nations, marked by its relative lack of class awareness, and by the brash assurance of the humble that they are as worthy of respect as the elite. The house painter who addresses a client by his first name, the elevator operator who enters into casual conversation with his passengers, the garage mechanic who condescendingly compares his expensive car with your aging model, could exist only in the United States. Their counterparts are unknown in England or on the Continent partly because America's frontiering experience bred into the people attitudes toward democracy that have persisted down to the present.

8

The Economic
Impact
of the Frontier

J UST AS THE political and social behavior of the American people
was slightly altered by their frontiering experience, so were their
habits as breadwinners. This is not to suggest that either today's industrial complexes or the country's economic might are the product
of the pioneering past; the economy of the modern United States is
primarily based upon the marketing and production revolutions that
reshaped the entire Western world in the eighteenth and nineteenth
centuries. Techniques utilizing machines rather than men originated
largely in Europe, and on these the nation's production system rests.
Yet three centuries of expansion gave the economy a new direction,
endowed it with unusual vitality, and helped create a social environment in which it could thrive. Without a frontier the courses of the
country's economic evolution would have been different; without an
industrial revolution in Europe the differences would have been far
greater.

ఆర్రెఆర్రె THESE DIFFERENCES can be understood only if we think in terms of a major area of economic change lying adjacent to and immediately behind the spatial frontier, and steadily advancing westward with it. On the spatial frontier itself, unusually abundant natural resources were exploited without substantially changing the national technology or marketing procedures. The merchants, speculators, millers, artisans, railroad builders, and others who catered to the needs of pioneer farmers or ranchers followed business customs perfected in the East with relatively few innovations. Nor did the frontier zone contribute markedly to the nation's economic growth, save during periods of spectacular mineral production such as that occurring between 1849 and 1876. During the pioneering period, speculative wealth flowed westward, in the pockets of frontiersmen who purchased excess lands against resale or from the pockets of Eastern and European investors who were willing to gamble for the high returns in an undeveloped region. The capital generated in the West by this flow was often plowed back into local business enterprises, for as long as a community was growing, merchants and shopkeepers wanted to grow with it. While the national economy benefited from the expansion of credit needed to sustain a pioneer economy—the proprietor of a frontier trading post or store usually obtained goods on credit from a wholesaler in a nearby city, who in turn purchased from an Eastern supplier, who often was financed by a New York or London bank—the volume of capital flow was too small to have a major influence on the pattern of economic growth nationally.

The area lying immediately behind the spatial frontier contributed far more substantially to the growth of the country's economy. There production could be stimulated only by technological improvements and expansion of markets, as abundant resources scarcely scratched by the pioneering generation were gradually brought into full use. There a concentration of capital attracted by the prospect of large return, a thickening population promising expanding markets, a more abundant labor pool than that provided on the frontier where cheaper lands were available, and improved transportation outlets connecting with both the populated East and the growing West, attracted business enterprise and men with inventive skills. Within this post-frontier zone occurred the full exploitation of natural resources that had been discovered on the spatial frontier.[1]

The exploitation that went on within this area must be conceived as constantly recurring; the process can best be visualized as the gradual peeling away of successive layers of resources, with each layer thicker than the last as techniques for its removal were more highly refined and manpower made available.[2] The rate of exploitation was determined by conditions behind this zone, where shifts or changes in population, improvements in technology, and fluctuations in demand made certain resources valuable and so worth producing in quantity. The spatial frontier also played a part, for expansion into areas of new resources allowed their "extensive" rather than "intensive" development. Had no such frontier existed, demands of the Eastern market would have required digging deeper and deeper into known resources; this would tend to force production into enterprises in which these raw materials could be used. Instead, production in the United States could respond more exactly to demands of the market and of the population's needs. Producers could select from a variety of resources as demand dictated, creating a more diversified economy and one better able to profit from changing demands in world markets. The result benefited both the economy and the spatial frontier, the former by allowing producers to shift their output to meet demands of the market more readily than in less-favored nations, the latter by stimulating the technological innovation needed to hurry economic development.[3]

The interplay of these forces accelerated the rate of national economic growth and helped shape America's affluent society of the twentieth century. They played this role by creating new opportunities for investment that in turn encouraged capital formation.[4] Through the history of the frontier, the growth and spread of population provided opportunities for investors, both in the West and throughout the nation where belief in the opportunity of pioneering encouraged a high birth rate and a steady flow of immigration from abroad. Growth of population, expansion westward, and the influx from Europe in turn accounted for a steady expansion of the economy that was irresistible to investors. As capital flowed westward, it continually opened new areas for investment that lured still more capital. Thus each new transportation route linking East and West encouraged investment in adjacent areas where shipping facilities spelled opportunity for the shrewd producer.[5] This investment stimulated the economy, attracted workers, and created conditions inducing more investment.

These investments, in turn, developed even more capital by stimulating savings. These were possible on frontiers because per capita income was nearly always above the subsistence level, allowing even slight surpluses to be saved, a condition lacking in the underdeveloped countries of the twentieth century. They were encouraged by the predominance of individually owned farms where income was more variable than in most enterprises. The constant threat of crop failures or falling prices encouraged pioneer farmers to put surpluses aside against a rainy day. These funds contributed to the massive accumulation of capital taking place nationally. They were supplemented by a flow of money from abroad to take advantage of the high interest rates paid in new and unstable areas. A no less important source of capital was the savings effected by the sequtenial exploitation of frontier resources; without these to draw upon more capital would have been sunk in the intensive use of resources already known.[6] All of these conditions released funds for investment and reinvestment, which spurred the economy to a rate of growth unknown elsewhere. From this stemmed a per capita income higher than that of any other nation in the nineteenth century.[7]

This affluence spread slowly, for the "natural wealth" of the frontier had no effect on society until it was translated into "social wealth." Riches buried in the ground were useless until extracted by man; man could make them usable only if he had the technological know-how, suitable transportation outlets, and a political system geared to the equitable distribution of resources among the people. Had frontier America been settled by men unversed in the use of machines or lacking the incentive values of capitalism, the "natural wealth" would have remained untapped. Instead the West was occupied by pioneers capable of developing technical processes and carrying with them the seeds of democracy.[8] Inherited traits equipped the Americans to become a "people of plenty," but they could not have become a "people of plenty" if nature had not spread a frontier of undeveloped natural resources before them.

They developed these resources at a steadily accelerating rate, determined largely by their emerging technological abilities and incentives. As skills and capital multiplied, generation after generation peeled off successive layers of resources to be fed into the national economy. The first generation removed a very thin slice using primitive techniques; the next a deeper layer employing mechanical processes that were still in their infancy; the third dug still deeper with improved technological means; and so exploitation went on. The process was illustrated in simple form on the mining frontiers; there placer miners with their cradles and sluice boxes skimmed off a bit of surface wealth, quartz miners and river miners dug into the earth or dammed streams to extract a little more, and finally well-financed mining companies with drilling and rock-crushing machinery reached the hard core of precious metal deep in the earth. Sequential stages were needed to utilize nature's resources, but those sequential stages would have been impossible had not a frontier made those resources available.

The result has been relative affluence for the American people. Since the eighteenth century Europeans have marveled at the ease of livelihood in the United States and the high standard of living; they have commented on the abundance of food, the sturdy clothing, the comfortable housing. During the twentieth century real wages have far surpassed those of less-favored nations, as has the per capita income. This wealth has been used to purchase luxuries of every variety. The Bureau of Labor Statistics Consumers' Price Index, which measures the living costs of "moderate income families," has long listed as "essentials" such items as radios, electric sewing machines, refrigerators, vacuum cleaners, automobiles, and beauty-shop services. In the 1950s the list was enlarged to include television sets, electric toasters, frozen foods, and home permanents.[9] By European standards at least, the Americans are truly a people of plenty.

◄§◄§ THIS ABUNDANCE, coupled with the urge for self-improvement that was engrained in the Anglo-American character, planted traits and characteristics that have marked the American people for two centuries and that persist today. Pioneering accentuated materialistic attitudes, strengthened a go-ahead philosophy that quickened the pace of life, encouraged reckless wastefulness, and contributed to a proclivity to innovate, especially technological processes. No one of these traits is traceable solely to the frontier experience; all are rooted as much in hereditary as in environmental forces. Yet they have been identified with Americans to an unusual degree, and they have been noted particularly in frontier areas.

Materialism has been singled out by visitors as the predominant philosophy of the people of the United States. The term "Almighty Dollar" was coined by Washington Irving in 1837 and given currency by Charles Dickens in the 1840s, but long before then Americans were notorious for their determined pursuit of wealth. Thomas Moore, touring the country in 1804, could write of their love of gold

> Long has it palsied every grasping hand
> And greedy spirit through this bartered land.

Daniel Webster spoke a few years later of the "grovelling propensity" of Americans for wealth, while the caustic Mrs. Trollope found that "every bee in the hive is actively employed in search of the honey of Hybla, vulgarly called money." Another traveler of her generation observed with disapproval the universal habit of worshipping at "the shrine of Mammon."[10] A generation later, Lord Bryce believed that material progress was "the end and aim of their lives, this is their daily and nightly thought." Twentieth-century visitors saw little change in the popularity of the "cult of the dollar."[11] Evidence is overwhelming that the people of the United States were more dedicated to material advance, more worshipful of wealth, than their European counterparts.

That materialism should be a basic tenet in the philosophy of the frontiersman was logical, for his principal energies were directed toward supplying the elementary requirements of life.[12] "In the progress of society," observed a Westerner, "the physical wants are felt before the intellectual. Men appreciate the necessity of covering their backs and lining their stomachs before storing their minds."[13] As a practical individual, the pioneer realized that first tasks must come first: until his land was cleared, his buildings constructed, his drainage system laid, his family's security provided, there was neither time nor energy for expression of other facets of character. In buckling to these practical pursuits he knew that he was creating wealth—wealth that would eventually buy the comforts and culture that were his dream. Riches assumed an importance not only for themselves, but for what they would acquire. Any pioneer who despised money under these circumstances would be, as a traveler put it, a candidate for the lunatic asylum.[14]

In such an atmosphere, the frontiersman was inclined to measure accomplishment by material standards, thinking of his neighbor as worth so many dollars, or judging a building by its size and cost rather than its beauty. No American pioneer could remark, as did an Englishman when told that New York's Woolworth Building was fireproof: "What a pity." To the Westerner, material possessions were the foundation for the good life, the talisman that would flood his future with culture and comforts, and the key to an elevated social status. This did not mean that he scorned the higher aspects of civilization; we have seen that a sizable proportion of the educated elite, at least, were dedicated to transplanting Eastern culture along the frontiers. It did mean that the pioneer's immediate concern was so focused on the accumulation of wealth that material values bulked larger in his life than in the lives of persons who lived in matured societies.

Thus motivated, he was willing to make almost any sacrifices in his pursuit of gain. Leisure was a luxury that could not be afforded; in the United States in general and in the West especially the pace of life accelerated during the nineteenth century. "There is," wrote a pioneer from the Michigan frontier, "so much work to be done, and so few people to do it, that the idea of labor is apt to absorb the entire area of the mind."[15] Everywhere along the frontier travelers noted the restless energy of the people, the feverish speed with which they worked, the reluctance to rest. "Enterprise," recorded a pioneer, "is more characteristic of us than a high civilization."[16] Men were willing to live amidst discomforts and inconveniences; the travel literature is sprinkled with descriptions of miserable hovels, overcrowding, primitive furniture, and littered fields, all endured because every effort was directed into producing goods that could be translated into wealth. The frontiersman, it was observed, would sell his crop and live on unpalatable food so that he could invest surpluses in more land, or forsake a comfortable home to live in a hovel while carving a clearing on a new frontier.[17] As one observer put it: "The word money seems to stand as the representative of the word 'happiness' of other countries."[18]

Even the most sacred symbols of culture were corrupted on the frontier, if they stood in the way of material gain. "There is no Sabbath west of the Genesee"—or Missouri—or Pecos—became a byword of the West, because time was too precious to waste a whole Sunday, and work went on as usual. Ministers flattered by an invitation to visit a new community might be disappointed when they found their audience small and the invitation itself prompted by promoters who believed that a church would help sell lots.[19] Even the sanctity of the home suffered, as farmers and merchants neglected their families to spend more time at their tasks. "The exclusive pursuit of gain," sadly noted a traveler, "with the indifference to all which does not aid in its acquisition, are eating up family love and life throughout the West."[20]

Nature's beauty spots were victims of frontier acquisitiveness no less than church and home. Ugliness seemed to be sanctified by the pioneers as they littered their farms with debris, left ugly stumps standing, and neglected village improvements to use every inch of land for profit. A mill was built to utilize the water power at Niagara Falls' Goat Island, marring that stupendous spectacle for years. Mrs. Trollope, admiring a particularly lovely spot along the Erie Canal, was told by a young man that she should return five years hence for "I'll engage there will be by that time, half a score elegant factories— 'tis a shame to let such a privilege of water lie idle."[21] A conversation between a visiting Englishman and a Westerner summed up the pioneers' disinterest in aesthetic values:

> "This is really a beautiful country of yours."
>
> "Oh yes, sir; the crops are wonderfully beautiful; but you should have seen them last year. I reckon there's not a more beautiful valley in America, at least for wheat; and it's considerable of a corn country."
>
> "Yes; it seems to possess a rich soil, but I was not alluding to its fertility—I mean that it is a fine country to look at; that you have some very fine prospects."—
>
> "Oh yes, sir; I would not wish better prospects, if this weather does but hold till harvest; last year our prospects were not half so good, but we got an abundance."
>
> "I see, my friend, we do not understand one another yet; I meant it was a handsome country, as you call it, I believe; look how finely the land waves just under that mountain."
>
> "Yes, sir; the water runs off as if it was all drained; but it's mighty bad for the plough."[22]

As an Easterner wrote from California: "So the seat of empire, in its travel westward, changes its base from soul to stomach, from brains to bowels."[23] No matter where he turned, the Westerner blighted the land's beauty in his drive for wealth.

ᦂᦂ THIS PURSUIT of gain sharpened his materialistic judgments, but it also helped breed in him—and in subsequent generations of Americans—a belief that hard work was the normal lot of man. The compulsion to endless labor is diminishing in twentieth-century America, but it still distinguishes the nation. In the United States no noontime siesta eases pressures as in Latin lands, no leisurely lunch period closes shops as in Britain, no lingering conversation in a sidewalk café provides an interval of relaxation as in France. Instead the American gulps a meal at his desk or in a quick-service restaurant, flirts with speeding tickets as he rushes to business appointments, and glories in the fact that he works harder than his neighbor. True leisurely pursuits are suspect; Benjamin Franklin might have written for today when he pontificated that "Leisure is the Time for doing something useful," or James Russell Lowell when he observed that

> Pleasure does make us Yankees kind o' winch,
> Ez though 't wuz somthin' paid fur by the inch.

The American spends his spare time whacking golf balls to better his score, or slamming tennis balls to best an opponent, or climbing mountains, skiing, sailing, camping, or hunting to prove his prowess. All of this reckless expenditure of energy strikes the European as slightly mad. He treasures moments of rest that the people of the United States cannot even comprehend.

Glorification of hard work was noted as an American trait early in the nation's history. "The habits of life," recorded a sensitive observer at the beginning of the nineteenth century, "are those of an exclusively working people. From the moment he gets up, the American is at work, and he is engaged in it till the hour of sleep."[24] Travelers also noted that devotion to hard labor and distrust of leisure increased in a measurable ratio as they moved toward the frontier. "In traveling westward in this country," one wrote, "you may take your longitude by observing the decrements of the time occupied at meals."[25] In the West the pace of life accelerated; all was rush and bustle as men dashed from task to task lest one precious moment be wasted. One visitor believed that Americans lived twice as long as other people because they accomplished twice as much in a lifetime; another felt that they all wanted to perform within a year "what others do within a much longer period. Ten years in America are like a century in Spain."[26] This go-ahead spirit of the West made leisurely pursuits incomprehensible to the pioneers; travelers were frequently questioned as to their business interests because no one could understand that they journeyed for pleasure alone. One frontiersman, when finally convinced, turned to the visitor's wife with the comment: "Well, Ma'am, I wonder now if your husband, who's got nothing to do but to *spend* his money, is as happy as we Americans, who are busy *making* ours. I doubt he isn't."[27] Heard in the West was the remark that only hogs had time to live like gentlemen.

This urge to work cannot be explained solely by the frontiering experience, of course; the Anglo-American tradition, the middle-class philosophy of the early settlers, and the Puritan ethic all helped glorify the concept of labor in the United States. Nor was the frontier a catalyst that transformed the indolent into the ambitious; squatters who lived on the outer fringes succumbed to indolence amidst the plenty that existed there, many of them victims of malnutrition or hookworm. Yet the mass of the small-propertied farmers who advanced civilization westward did develop a compulsion to labor that became part of the social environment of the successive Wests. Before the pioneer, wrote Alexis de Tocqueville, "lies a boundless continent, and he urges forward as if time pressed him and he was afraid of finding no room for his exertions."[28] All about were riches galore in the form of untapped resources; only his labor was needed to transform them into wealth. So labor he did as he moved westward, knowing that any relaxation, any squandering of time, would only delay the coming of affluence. Expended energy paid higher dividends in an expanding society than in a static one, and this was the realization that unleashed the locomotive tendency in frontiersmen. "All life seems to be more electric, more rapid, and more intense than with us," observed a Briton from the West.[29] By working hard the individual could amass a disproportionate share of nature's abundance; continued hard work was demanded even after the first resources were skimmed off, for technological innovation made their repeated exploitation profitable. So the continuing hope of gain sparked a continuing expenditure of energy in the pursuit of a share of these resources. Work became the gospel of the pioneer, and of the generations that followed.

&§&§ THE QUEST for wealth on America's frontiers contributed to the emergence of another national trait that has persisted into the twentieth century: flagrant wastefulness. No other western nation of the twentieth century so recklessly squanders its resources, or so heedlessly destroys its own creations. The United States, to visiting foreigners, is the land of the throwaway; paper handkerchiefs and paper plates, metal cans and plastic containers, no-deposit–no-return bottles are all made to be used once, then discarded. To a thrifty European the American factory is an assembly line to produce gadgets that will marvelously disintegrate after short use, the American home a reverse assembly line to reduce those gadgets to basic rubble as rapidly as possible. In Britain a man prides himself on the vintage of his car, in America on its recency. Europeans will never cease to be shocked by the extravagant waste of paper bags in an American supermarket, or by the reckless manner in which nearly new machinery is thrown into the dump heap to make room for something better. They are equally astounded by the reluctance of the United States to preserve its dwindling resources, for not until the twentieth century did a conservation movement attract popular support, and even today nature's bounties are squandered with an abandon unknown in other lands.

Wastefulness came naturally to the frontiersman; who would think of preservation amidst overwhelming abundance? In his eyes nature's riches were so plentiful that their exhaustion was beyond comprehension. Why protect trees in a land where they grew by the billions? Why preserve soil when a move to virgin fields was cheaper than fertilizer? To these questions the pioneer had obvious answers. "Nothing on the face of the broad Earth is sacred to him," wrote an Englishman from the Far West. "Nature presents herself as his slave."[30] So the frontiersman felled forests, mined the soil with his wasteful farming methods, slaughtered game, honeycombed mountains with his mining shafts, overcropped pasturage with his herds, drained lakes, and altered the landscape as he moved in quest of wealth.

On the forested frontiers, trees were particular enemies, symbolizing the wilderness that must be destroyed. "He seems to have declared war on the whole species," observed a French traveler in 1817; "he does not spare a single one."[31] All fell before his ax: trees needed for windbreaks, trees that added beauty to the countryside, trees that would have provided cooling shade in summer, even maple groves that would have yielded sweets for the community. Travelers along the Old National Road that after 1818 linked the seaboard and the Ohio River complained of the bleakness of the countryside after the pioneers had passed on, leaving a desolate plain behind them. Everywhere the story was the same, because no pioneer was happy until the land was completely naked. "Then he tells you, it looks handsome," wrote a traveler with amazement.[32]

The soils of America suffered the same fate. With land cheap and both labor and fertilizers expensive, pioneers discovered that they could economize by plundering the soil through successive plantings, then move on. "The American," observed one of many British travelers who described this cycle, "seldom or never looks forward to the future and progressive improvement of his land, he uses it as asses are used in this country, worked while they have a spark of life in them, without one care about their support or preservation."[33] Soils were depleted so rapidly that their exhaustion was a primary factor in the westward movement, leaving behind starved fields as their owners pushed on to new frontiers. "Now lands which at one time would yield with remarkable certainty 30 to 40 bushels of wheat to the acre," wrote a Wisconsonite in the 1870s, "cannot be depended upon to yield 10 or 12."[34] Oldtimers in Nebraska, so the story goes, used to brag to younger men: "Why, son, by the time I was your age I had wore out three farms."[35]

The habit of wastefulness ingrained in the frontiersmen has been transmitted to later generations in somewhat different form. Today reforestation has restored damaged hillsides, and chemical fertilizers have revitalized butchered soils, but exploitive tendencies were too firmly embedded to be abandoned with the passing of the frontier. The pioneer was reckless with nature's riches because their abundance encouraged waste; the twentieth-century American thinks in terms of planned obsolescence because the plentitude of artifacts and the ease with which he acquires them disinclines him to preserve the old. Today's Texan who throws away his Cadillac because the ash trays need cleaning (to quote a modern tall tale) differs only in degree from the Kentucky farmer who told a traveler in 1818 that he was moving to new land rather than carry away the pile of manure that had accumulated near his barn.[36] Today's American who wastes half his plateful of food (or asks for a "Doggie Pack" for the remainder) is comparable to the Ohio landlord who invited a stranger to eat all he wanted without charge as the whole bountiful tableful was to be thrown away.[37] Abundance encourages a modern generation to perpetuate the wasteful habits that abundance bred into the pioneers.

ANY PORTRAIT of the American must depict him not only as a wasteful squanderer but as a consistent innovator, given to experimentation, and inclined to try out new processes or gadgets even when the old are perfectly useful. This inclination was the marvel of the Western world during the nineteenth century. "Would any one but an American," asked an Englishman in the 1860s, "have ever invented a milking machine? or a machine to beat eggs? or machines to black boots, scour knives, pare apples, and do a hundred other things that all other peoples have done with their ten fingers from time immemorial?"[38] Who but an American, he might have added, would have substituted mechanical for human power on the farm by developing gang plows, reapers, threshing machines, seed drills, combines, and a host more? Who but an American would have conceived of the assembly line and the mass-production industries made possible by that labor-saving device? Who but an American would have dreamed of putting the computer to work for mankind so effectively that automation threatened to put half the population out of work? Americans, to Europeans at least, are inventive geniuses whose especial bent is the displacement of men by machines.

Was this the result of the frontiering experience? Visitors from Europe during the eighteenth and nineteenth centuries thought that it was, and Westerners agreed with them. They saw invention as necessary on frontiers, where unique conditions demanded unique artifacts and methods. "The want of those arts and inventions, by which the inhabitants of older countries accomplish their ends," wrote one of the Ohio Valley's most perceptive observers, "renders it necessary for the people of a new state, to invent and substitute others, as emergencies may arise."[39] To Europeans the frontier was "a land of experiment," and the frontiersmen persons with "an extraordinary talent for invention."[40] They acquired those skills through necessity, "having been accustomed to do for themselves in small societies." Lord Bryce believed that these talents had been developed to such an extraordinary degree that the Westerner could turn his hand to any task with an assurance of success beyond the grasp of men from older lands.[41]

In judging the validity of this testimony, we must determine whether conditions in new communities were of the sort to stimulate or retard the inventive process. Innovation, psychologists know, is the achievement of an obstructed wish; an inventor conceives the end that he wishes to achieve, then finds means of overriding the obstacles that stand in his way. These are usually the habits and attitudes acquired by long practice. Past tradition is the most formidable obstacle to creative thought; an inventor seeking a solution is like a chicken running back and forth along a wire fence when a simple detour would let it reach the food beyond. Insomuch as the inventor's obstacle is mental, its influence varies in exact degree that he is weighted by tradition. In a society where the past is venerated, or dominates the present completely, traditionalism becomes an insurmountable obstacle. In a new society, where the opposite is true, a break with precedent is far easier. Frontier communities, where people were recruited from a variety of backgrounds and where a strange environment shattered precedents, provided exceptional breeding grounds for innovation.[42]

The testimony of hundreds of visitors and Westerners agrees that lack of fixed practices along the frontiers stimulated invention. They saw the pioneers as newcomers to a way of life as well as to a new geographic location, so unique as to be "almost the termination of existence." "In flying to the wilderness," wrote a traveler, "they fly a thousand constraints which society must always impose." In doing so they turned their faces from the past to the future, and having little to look back upon, were inclined to devise techniques and artifacts best suited to their new way of life. "Nothing," noted a Missourian, "has been venerated or revered merely because it exists or has endured."[43]

No less a stimulant to frontier inventiveness was the sparseness of population, which ruled out division of labor, forcing each pioneer to satisfy his family's needs. "With the first emigration," announced a guidebook, "there are few mechanics; hence every settler becomes expert in supplying his own necessities."[44] Did he need a home, he could not call in a contractor but must build it himself with the aid of neighbors. Did he require a plow, he must fashion it from local materials, buying only the iron parts from a blacksmith. Did his family need clothing, the cloth must be made and the garments sewed by the housewife. Did illness strike, no doctors could be called and reliance must be placed on the advice of the almanac and common sense. As the frontiersman built, so did he experiment, adapting past artifacts to present needs. The evolution of the "Kentucky" rifle or the American ax from their crude European counterparts testified to his skills. This constant practice endowed the pioneer with the mechanical techniques needed for invention, and encouraged him to think in terms of improvement rather than tradition. Mrs. Trollope found in the national patent office thousands of inventions submitted by persons in remote parts of the country "who had begun by endeavouring to hit upon some contrivance to enable them to *get along* without sending some thousand and odd miles for the thing they wanted."[45]

The physical climate along the frontiers was as conducive to innovation as the social. Changing geographic environments as population shifted westward meant the outmoding of implements and customs. Scythes suitable to the hilly farms of New England were inefficient on the level prairies of Illinois. Plows used for centuries were unworkable on the heavy sod of eastern Nebraska. Techniques originated in Europe and followed in the humid eastern half of the United States proved outmoded in the semiarid western half. Experimentation became a stark necessity if men were to survive, and with each experiment the bonds of custom were loosened. Practices only a decade old were easier to break than those centuries old.[46] Labor shortages in new communities also stimulated the inventive urge; with manpower lacking as cheap lands absorbed potential farm or factory laborers, mechanical power was the only solution. This necessitated new machines and new social concepts. Travelers reported that in the West where workers labored only at their own convenience, and then both badly and ungraciously, mechanical substitutes were necessary as in no other part of the world.[47] The pioneer was the product of a school of experience that taught him to discard tried techniques, and that equipped him to substitute new practices by applying mechanical skill to unique problems.

Although both logic and contemporary testimony suggest that the frontier was an area of innovation unmatched in Europe or the East, some visitors of that day and some scholars of today have argued that the pioneer was less inclined to experimentation than his fellow Americans in the seaboard states. They point out that improved farming techniques were but coldly received along the frontiers; in the pre-Civil War era reformers who urged practices to preserve and improve soils found readier listeners east of the Appalachians than in the Mississippi Valley. "I find a large portion of our farmers prejudiced against every variety of improvement," wrote a salesman for a farm periodical from Illinois, "particularly where the knowledge of that improvement is to be acquired from books."[48] Even during the Civil War, when manpower shortages encouraged farm mechanization, the frontier adopted labor-saving machinery only slowly.[49] Contemporaries and historians who point this out have also emphasized the pioneers' reluctance to venture into untried regions; frontiersmen, they say, resisted the transition from forest to prairie agriculture for a generation even though English immigrants had demonstrated that the grasslands of Indiana and Illinois made ideal farms. Frontiersmen also, it is argued, lagged in the inventive process; not only most industrial but most agricultural improvements were patented by Easterners rather than Westerners.

Those who hold this position fail to grasp one essential point: changes in human behavior must be measured in relative rather than absolute terms. We can label the pioneer an innovator only if we find him *comparatively* more willing to accept and sponsor change than his Eastern or European cousin. Man is by nature a traditionalist, comfortably following established paths until jolted by some unpleasant necessity. No such urgency turned Mississippi Valley farmers of the pre-Civil War period toward improved farming techniques, for their virgin soils produced all that the market could absorb; only the butchered soils of the seaboard states sparked a demand for reform there. Similarly, the slowness of Americans to adjust to prairie agriculture may shock modern scholars, but to Europeans of that day they adapted with startling rapidity; the transition was made in a single generation while on the Continent farm techniques resisted change for centuries. When goaded by necessity, the pioneer proved a willingness to change that contrasted with the relative lethargy of Easterners.

Our concern, moreover, is with the effect of the frontier on the American habit of innovation, not solely with the frontiersman's contribution in that process. The proper question to be asked is not whether the pioneer devised significant inventions, but whether the *existence* of a frontier in the United States made the American people *relatively* more inclined to experimentation than the European, and whether that spirit of experimentation was more noticeable in the West than in the East.

No profound knowledge of mechanical invention is needed to realize that frontiers were ill-suited to produce major contributions. Educational training, wealth, leisure, and the opportunity for intellectual communication among persons of like interests—all essential ingredients in the inventive process—were lacking in pioneer areas. Nor was the frontier's intellectual atmosphere conducive to invention, for the materialistic climate discouraged the abstract theorizing essential to creative thought. Yet the presence of a frontier did stimulate innovation, partly by helping to engender a spirit conducive to experimentation, partly by creating a demand for new products, and partly by fostering an attitude receptive to change as opposed to stability.

On or near the successive frontiers the unique problems facing pioneers forced constant improvisation and experimentation, with a corresponding lessening of traditionalism. No task was too complex or difficult to be undertaken, since there was no alternative. Travelers expressed surprise that untrained men could build a log cabin, fashion furniture, make their own farm implements, and care for the many needs of a growing family with only the help of a few neighbors as untrained as themselves. Equally surprising to Europeans was the ingenuity of the women who spun and wove and sewed their own clothes, tended gardens, molded candles, made soap, and in other ways contributed to the self-sufficiency that was the lot of the pioneer.[50] Living by themselves in a land where division of labor was in its infancy, they had to make do, and "making do" became a way of life. An Illinois farmer returned to his plow on one occasion to find that a mischievous helper had stolen one of the cornhusk collars from the team. Hesitating only a moment he took off his leather trousers, stuffed them with grass, put them about the horse's neck, and plowed all afternoon in his shirt tail.[51] His type of response was not unusual; the whole social atmosphere in which that farmer lived inclined him to face problems and solve them by his own ingenuity.

A no less important function of the frontier in stimulating innovation was to create a demand for new products that could only be met by invention. Constantly changing conditions as population surged westward challenged inventors throughout the eighteenth and nineteenth centuries; a man who could devise a new product or a new technique suitable to a particular need, or who could substitute a mechanical for a hand-powered implement to offset the perennial labor shortage, stood to make a handsome profit for himself. This was the incentive that sent would-be inventors who lived behind the frontier to their drafting boards, and that inspired thousands of inventions. Travelers in the pre-Civil War era often expressed amazement at the labor-saving machinery used in the West or displayed at county fairs: sulky plows that allowed the farmer to ride, seed planters, threshing machines, mechanical clothes washers, and a hundred more.[52] In the postwar years the advance into the Great Plains offered a new incentive to inventors; they responded by producing wire fencing, improved windmills to suck subsurface moisture to the surface, farm machinery needed for the extensive agriculture practiced there, and dry farming techniques. Inventors in Illinois, Indiana, and other states behind the frontier perfected these wonders, but they did so only because they recognized a market on the frontier.[53] The constantly altering demands of a westward-moving population proved a stimulant to innovation lacking in nonfrontier nations.

Such an incentive would not have existed if farmers on successive frontiers had showed a reluctance to accept new machines and untried gadgets. The reception awaiting any invention is as indicative as the invention itself of the flexibility of the society in which it is developed. Invention is like a seed falling on different types of soil; the soil may be too wet, too dry, too sandy, too rocky, for the seed to sprout. In the same fashion, an invention will be accepted in one cultural soil, but not in another. The rate of acceptance is determined by the degree of readiness of any society to absorb a modification or addition to its culture.[54] In firmly established social groups obstacles to acceptance abound: the resistance of established producers whose profits are threatened by a different product, the opposition of organized workers fearful of displacement by labor-saving devices, inertia bred by the long practice of traditional techniques, and political pressures inevitable where vested interests are strongly entrenched. In general, the older and more established the society, the stronger the incentive needed to arouse sentiment for change.

Studies of the acceptance of innovation in rural areas show that the speed with which farmers modify existing practices is influenced by many factors. The increase in profits to be expected from change is all-important, but scarcely less influential is the nature of the leadership structure of the community. Where an elite class exists and accepts innovation, the remainder of the population usually follows. In terms of the speed with which changes are adopted, farmers can be divided into "innovators" who experiment constantly, "adoption leaders" who accept any proven new device, "later adopters" who follow in large numbers, and "nonadopters." In other words, any community equipped with influential leaders and unrestrained by tradition is particularly receptive to innovations, for the leaders are alert to the greater profits promised and the others are willing to follow their example at varying speeds.[55]

Communities fitting this description were normal near the frontiers. The stratification that occurred early in the history of pioneer settlements elevated an informed group of leaders who were especially alert to profits, sufficiently vocal to make their needs known, and able to influence their neighbors. Perhaps even more important was the fact that these leaders combined knowledge and intelligence to a degree that their error judgments were comparatively few, since every innovation was carefully weighed against local conditions before adoption. This meant that the frontier was not an area of change for change's sake, but a region where change was quickly adopted as soon as greater profits were proved probable. Thus frontiersmen before the Civil War ignored Eastern pressures for improved farming techniques simply because poor transportation facilities precluded the export of extensive surpluses. Why bother with special seeds, manuring, careful soil cultivation, and selective livestock breeding when the pioneer's whole purpose was to maintain a subsistence level until he could sell his lands at a speculative profit? The frontiersman who resisted the advice of farm journals and reformers was not opposed to change; he simply knew that his profits would be high enough without change.[56] With the coming of railroads and the opening of world markets the pioneers of the Great Plains country became more interested in improvements; the vogue of mechanized agriculture and bonanza farming in the 1870s and 1880s testified to that. The frontier farmer was eager to accept innovation just as soon as his community leaders convinced themselves that change would be to their advantage.

A case study of one Iowa county between 1855 and 1885 illustrates this fact. There in the early years of settlement, newspapers, farm journals, and agricultural societies all preached the advantages of new crops, new livestock breeds, and new fencing materials; there "drummers" from the highly competitive farm implement industry peddled their wares so effectively that few farmers were unaware of the latest improvements. Some resisted at first, for the investment demanded was large and the risk of proportionately greater profits high. Opposition soon crumbled when the 110 farmers who occupied the upper rungs of society swung into line. These were the natural leaders, holders of offices in the farm organizations, and dictators of social affairs. More important, most of this group could afford to take risks, for some were absentee owners of considerable wealth, others were large resident operators, and still others were merchant-farmers or stock-dealing farmers who supplemented their income in other ways. All could experiment without fear of complete failure if the new breed of cattle or the new power reaper turned out badly. This group was the first to purchase new products or try new techniques. As soon as the success of the experiment was proved, the rest of the farmers fell into line, motivated by the urge to keep pace with their superiors. If the history of this county is typical, the frontier was an area of cautious experimentation in which innovation was somewhat more common than in older areas.[57]

❧❧ THAT THE FRONTIERSMAN was no compulsive experimenter, but that he would change if shown that change was to his advantage, is revealed no less in the history of legal institutions than in that of mechanical inventions. Evidence on this point is ample. Along the frontiers, lawyers and judges alike were usually scantily educated in the common law and distrustful of the pettifogging that seemed designed only to bilk the innocent of their rights. They were inclined to judge issues on the basis of common sense rather than legal precedents. As they applied this philosophy to the unique problems faced in the West, they altered imported practices and in certain areas pioneered a distinctly American law.[58]

One change stemmed from the conflict over land titles that was usual in regions successively occupied by France, Spain, England, and the United States. Untangling this legal skein overtaxed the facilities of the common law; "In many Cases Our practice and policy here, differs widely from their's," observed one justice as he justified the upsetting of an English precedent.[59] Another basic change in procedure stemmed from the need for some legally constituted body to suggest laws that would solve unusual Western problems. The pioneers fastened upon the grand jury to perform this function and expanded its activities in a variety of ways that would have shocked British courts: to relay protests to Washington against actions of the federal government, to voice complaints against territorial officials, to recommend suitable candidates in local elections, as a prod to force legislatures into needed action.[60] Even ordinary juries were endowed with extra power so they could be counted upon to side with debtors against creditors.[61] Beyond the Mississippi the semiarid land required even greater variations of traditional practices, as systems of irrigation law were developed that seriously invaded property rights in the accepted English or Eastern sense. Necessity similarly forced a revolution in legal practices in the mining camps where miners were given the right to use water and extract precious metals without owning a single inch of the land on which they operated—doctrines that Blackstone would have found incomprehensible.[62] All these innovations were eventually given statutory respectability by Congress, and have become an accepted part of American law.

&§&§ THIS ARRAY of evidence leads inevitably to the conclusion that the existence of a frontier in America during its pioneering period did help promote a climate where innovation was more acceptable than in older societies. The frontiersman, like his fellows everywhere, was more comfortable on a beaten path than on an unblazed trail. But the realities of his life forced him to improvise. The absence of economic specialization in sparsely settled regions and the uniqueness of the situations that he encountered on successive frontiers required new techniques, new instruments, new practices. Less encumbered by tradition, he was free to experiment, and to welcome products or ideas that would make life easier for him. His own jack-of-all-trade inclinations and the challenge that he threw before inventors in the settled areas behind the frontier alike helped create in the United States a social environment less restrained by tradition than in England or Europe, and one in which innovation was more acceptable.

9

The Frontier
and the
Migratory Compulsion

IF STUDENTS of the American character can agree upon any one thing, it is that the compulsion to move about has created a nation of restless wanderers unlike any other in the world. The people are forever on the go. They cross from place to place in a room, drive unbelievable distances to consume a meal that they could have obtained nearer home, travel interminably by car to country clubs where they transfer to electric carts from which they emerge occasionally to swat a golf ball, and seemingly spend half their lives in automobiles waiting for traffic jams to clear. They squander their vacations by hurrying to distant points and hurrying home again. They shift from country to town, from town to suburb, and from suburb to country. They abandon one home for another with such predictable frequency that bank statements and dividend checks include for convenience a change of address card. When the fever strikes, the American goes, indifferent to the risks and scornful of that attachment to place that restrains the European.

Sang Stephen Vincent Benét in his *Western Star*

> Americans are always moving on.
> It's an old Spanish custom gone astray,
> A sort of English fever I believe,
> Or just a mere desire to take French leave,
> I couldn't say. I couldn't really say.
> But when the whistle blows, they go away.[1]

Those who resist are not only few but judged slightly strange. Not long ago *The New York Times* believed newsworthy the fact that a man in California had lived in the same house for fifty years—a journalistic judgment incomprehensible to a European. Wrote a midcentury Russian visitor in amazement: "They regard a person who lives in the place where he was born a rarity."[2] Americans live on wheels. They watch motion pictures at drive-in theaters, eat at drive-in restaurants, deposit funds at drive-in banks, sleep in drive-away trailers, and kill each other at the rate of fifty thousand a year by driving too fast and too recklessly. "If God were suddenly to call the world to judgment," wrote a Latin-American statesman after visiting the United States, "He would surprise two-thirds of the American population on the road like ants."[3]

The migratory urge has made tourism a big business, supporting hosts of travel agents, motel and hotel owners, railroads and airlines and steamship companies, restaurateurs and assorted hangers-on needed to keep the tide flowing. The money spent by Americans in their pursuit of pleasure is astronomical. During all the sixteenth century the New World contributed less than a billion dollars in gold and silver to revitalize the economy of the Old, yet in 1960 alone two and one-half times this sum was squandered by American tourists in Europe, threatening the dollar and trade balances of their country. The Great Migration of the 1630s brought 25,000 Puritans to New England; today more than a million vacationers descend on that historically rich land yearly. The South complained that the North ravaged its wealth during the Civil War, yet between 1960 and 1965 Northern tourists visiting Southern states spent more money than both the Union and Confederacy during the entire war. The itching feet of Americans will take them everywhere, anytime, and anyhow.[4]

Vacation travel might signify only an unusual propensity for pleasure seeking, but the readiness of the American people to change their places of residence defies such a simple explanation. Change they do, and with astounding frequency. The recent pattern can be summarized in the following table showing the numbers of Americans moving each year, some locally within the county where they had lived, others to different counties and states:[5]

	DID NOT MOVE	Percent	MOVED WITHIN COUNTY	Percent	MOVED OUTSIDE COUNTY	Percent
1950	119,190,000	81.0	16,476,000	11.2	9,075,000	6.2
1957	131,648,000	79.7	21,566,000	13.1	10,298,000	6.2
1958	133,501,000	79.7	22,023,000	13.1	11,240,000	6.7
1959	137,018,000	80.3	22,313,000	13.0	10,489,000	5.9
1960	139,766,000	80.1	22,564,000	12.9	11,247,000	6.5
1961	140,821,000	79.4	24,289,000	13.7	11,246,000	6.3

Like all statistics, these columns of figures are more confusing than enlightening, but the truths that they reveal are worth extracting. Recently, each year one of every five Americans has changed his residence, one in every sixteen has moved to another county, and one in thirty to another state. Put in another way, in the single year 1961 no less than 35.5 million people shifted from one house to another. If these figures are projected over a decade, the results are even more startling. Of the 176 million people living in the United States at the end of the 1950s, only 30 million had lived in the same house for twenty years, and no less than 82 million had changed residence during the past decade.[6]

This shifting about is partly haphazard—from place to place within cities, from town to country, from city to suburb—but a directional trend is noticeable and not without significance. What Frank Lloyd Wright once puckishly described as the "westward tilt" of the continent is sliding population toward the Pacific Ocean today as it has for two centuries. During the 1950s the Far Western states grew by 38.9 percent while no other section gained more than 16.5 percent; that decade saw the area beyond the Rockies add 7,863,142 souls to its population as three of every five counties there gained in numbers. The entire city of New York would have to be emptied to provide the men, women, and children who inundated the Far Western states between 1950 and 1960.[7]

Within the West, the habit of mobility is so strong that the people there are unusually restless. In 1960 barely one third of all Californians lived in the same house they occupied five years before; northern Californians move about at the rate of one of every three households every year; southern Californians at the rate of one in every two. In the Eastern states, by contrast, only one in every ten householders changes residence yearly. Westerners also apply for 52 percent more passports than the national average, while airlines between Los Angeles and New York carry one fourth more passengers from the former city than the latter. In flights between Los Angeles and Chicago, residents of the City of Angels outnumber Chicagoans two to one.[8] Wandering is a curse for all Americans, but doubly so for those who live in the West.

THAT THE PEOPLE of the United States are unusually migratory is a demonstrable fact. That this tendency is traceable solely to their frontiering heritage is far less certain. To suggest this is to ignore a comparable degree of mobility among western Europeans. At the beginning of the twentieth century the number of European urbanites living in the city where they were born varied from something over 60 percent in London and Antwerp to less than 35 percent in Paris and Vienna; for Europe as a whole, half the urban population had been born outside the city of residence. Fragmentary evidence indicates that mobility has increased since World War II, and that it is correlated with the degree of prosperity of the nation.[9] Improved transportation facilities, and especially opportunities for self-advancement stemming from the growth of industrial-urban complexes have tended to break local ties and prod peoples everywhere into moving. No frontier background is needed to stir populations into movement when a better job awaits at the end of the rainbow.

To trace American mobility to its pioneering connections is similarly to ignore the fact that many population shifts in the eighteenth and nineteenth centuries had nothing to do with the West. Throughout the past, the city has been an attracting force rivaling cheap land; save for one decade, urban population growth has exceeded total population growth since the founding of the Republic. In 1790 one in every twenty Americans lived in a city, in 1860 one in every five, in 1960 five of every eight.[10] Within the cities ever-changing conditions stir the population into movement. Neighborhoods "decline" as their ethnic character changes, causing shifts to other areas. Homes give way to factories, stores, and freeways. Business districts move to keep pace with their labor supply. Suburban areas rise overnight from cow pastures. All of these changes mean moving about as people follow jobs or change from one to another. As areas of most rapid growth, cities have accounted for a major portion of the nation's internal migration since at least the middle of the nineteenth century. Men were infected with the virus of *movingitis* as readily in urban as in rural America.

The American social order can be compared to a pot of boiling water, filled with particles moving up and down, to and fro, in a constant state of agitation. The heat keeping these particles in motion is the opportunity for self-improvement; where gain beckons, men go. In underdeveloped countries, with stratified caste systems, there is no such incentive, and nine-tenths of the people live in the districts where they were born. In eighteenth- and nineteenth-century America the opposite was true, and society was atomized. Men left Eastern farms for cities or Western farms; they moved from farm to farm, from city to city, from frontier village to frontier village. Immigrants from Europe flocked in to take the places of those who shifted westward.[11] All was bustle and motion from the eighteenth century onward. Our concern is with the degree to which the frontier provided the opportunity that kept the pot boiling.

In exploring such a connection, we must focus on the pre-twentieth century years before industrialization stirred the migratory instinct in both Europe and America. In those simpler days Americans did move about more than Europeans. This is indicated by the fragments of statistical data that can be gathered. Thus in the United States of a century ago more people moved from state to state than today; in 1850 more than 23 percent of the population resided outside the state of birth, and in 1860 nearly 25 percent. Europe witnessed no such mobility. Even at the end of the century two-thirds of the Austrians and Bavarians and nearly 60 percent of the rural Frenchmen and Swedes lived in the same community in which they had been born. In Switzerland fewer than 10 percent in 1850 and 14 percent in 1900 were living outside of the canton where they first saw the light of day.[12] These figures are too scattered to be relied upon, but they do suggest that Americans were more mobile than Europeans. In other words, moving about was a trait in a frontier country, but not in countries where pioneering was impossible.

Just as meaningful is the testimony of hundreds of travelers who visited the United States in the eighteenth and nineteenth centuries. Almost to a man, they singled out mobility as a trait that distinguished the American from the European; almost to a man they expressed amazement at the abandon with which people shifted their homes without heed to the local attachments prominent in the Old World. The attention paid this trait suggests that the locomotive habit was peculiar to America, just as repeated comment that the tendency was exaggerated in the West indicates a connection with the frontiering experience.

Visitors saw Americans in general and Westerners in particular as in a "constant state of migration," only tarrying now and then to clear land for others to enjoy or build houses for others to occupy.[13] This was their habit as early as the mid-seventeenth century, nor had they outgrown it at the dawn of the twentieth. Three centuries ago the Reverend Cotton Mather deplored the tendency of his Boston flocks to "*Go out* from the institutions of God, Swarming into New Settlements, where they and their untaught Families are Like to *Perish for Lack of Vision.*" A hundred years later a Virginia governor lamented that the people "acquire no attachment to place: But wandering about Seems engrafted in their Nature; and it is a weakness incident to it, that they Should for ever imagine the Lands further off, are Still better than those upon which they have already settled."[14] In the middle nineteenth century a sensitive observer characterized the United States as "a bivouac rather than a nation, a grand army moving from the Atlantic to the Pacific, and pitching tents along the way." To Lord Bryce the Americans were "almost nomadic," and cursed with a fever in their blood that made them permanently transitory.[15] "After they have passed through every part of the land of promise," predicted one traveler, "they will, for the sake of one more change, return to the seaboard again."[16]

So persistent was the habit of moving that it could not be dislodged, even when the need for moving was absent. Alexis de Tocqueville believed that shifting about had become "a game of chance, which they pursue for the emotions it excites, as much as for the gain it procures." Americans moved for pleasure as well as profit, obeying a slightly mad impulse to be on the way despite comfortable conditions at home. "Many," wrote an observer along the Oregon Trail, "are going there without any other specific object, than simply to be *moving.*"[17] The wandering life was so attractive that it was irresistible. One traveler caught the spirit of the migratory American when he wrote: "If hell lay in the West, they would cross heaven to reach it."[18]

The instinct that has made vacationing a major industry in twentieth-century America astounded visitors no less than the tendency to shift dwellings. During the nineteenth century families thought nothing of embarking on a journey of a thousand miles for no reason save to view the countryside or visit a relative. A father and mother with a brood of children and perhaps a grandmother along, all crowded into a skiff bound down the Ohio or Mississippi to drop in on a brother in a distant city, was not an unusual sight. "The Americans," wrote a British visitor, "are a travelling people."[19] Wandering begat wandering, for the heavy volume of passenger traffic allowed railroad and steamboat lines to lower fares and multiply accommodations, making travel still easier. Some movers seemed to be taking their homes with them, for the ingenious manner in which houses were moved from spot to spot within cities was a perennial source of wonderment to Europeans. "It sounds unbelievable," recorded a Swedish visitor, ". . . but on the other hand, what is there that an American will not try?"[20]

If moving about was a national characteristic, that trait appeared in exaggerated relief along the frontiers. There mobility was a way of life, expected of all energetic people, and as socially acceptable as stability in more mature societies. Charles Dickens saw the West as peopled by a great human army, led by wandering pickets whose lives were spent in extending its outposts, leaving home after home behind. Indeed, most had no homes in the traditional sense, occupying frail, half-finished dwellings until the urge to depart set them journeying farther westward. There, all was constant coming and going, all was turbulence. "Everything shifts under your eye," wrote a pioneer. "The present occupants sell, pack up, depart. Strangers replace them. Before they have gained the confidence of their neighbors, they hear of a better place, pack up, and follow their precursors."[21]

Any one of dozens of impulses could set the usual pioneer to westering, if their own spokesmen and the travelers who recorded their wanderings can be believed. Let the soil begin to lose its "youthful energy," let neighbors press within a few miles, let rumors fly of richer lands ahead, and he was away with the wind. "The country is getting so peopled up I can't live in it no how," a pioneer told a visitor to the Illinois frontier. "Why," came the answer, "the last time I saw you, you told me your next neighbour lived seven miles off." "Yes, but there is one within three miles now, and I can't stand it no longer; one can't go out into the woods but he hears the sound of the axe and the crash of trees."[22] Others needed not even this pressure, but departed when the wanderlust decreed; once the bark began peeling from their rail fences they knew they had stayed in one spot too long, and took off. A traveler in the Western states during the 1850s found every farmer with whom he talked ready to go. "He is," wrote a Westerner of his fellow Westerners, "fond of change for the sake of change; and he will have it, though it brings him new labors and new hardships."[23]

As these wanderers on the fringes of civilization fled ever deeper into the wilderness, their places were taken by succeeding waves of frontiersmen until the whole process resembled the movement of a giant army, with one division following the other from the seaboard onward. As early as 1795 a traveler in the backwoods found the forests teeming with pioneers who had moved many times in their lives, but were looking for good lands for still another move. A generation later another visitor along the road to Pittsburgh reported a steady procession of migrants far more numerous and just as interesting as the Canterbury pilgrims.[24] As these newcomers flocked into the West those already there were eager to move on after selling their "improvements"; emigrants from the East talked of settling in Ohio, Ohioans were eager to move to Missouri, Missourians planned to migrate to Oregon. Such was their restlessness that farms were abandoned before clearing was completed, their owners lured farther west by tales of still richer soils. Travelers near Pittsburgh were told that the "rage for descending the Ohio" explained the deserted dwellings along the road; in Ohio they were informed that abandoned farms had belonged to farmers who had migrated to Illinois; in Illinois and Missouri they heard that the Oregon Fever was attracting former occupants.[25] In the Far West the story was the same; abandoned farms in east Texas were the result of a rush to west Texas, and deserted homes in Kansas testified to the attractions of the plains beyond.[26] Alexis de Tocqueville wrote of the pioneer that "the woods stoop to give him a passage, and spring up again when he is past."[27]

The volume of the westward-moving stream of population can be explained only by the presence of repeated movers: those who shifted westward a half-dozen times or more. These were to be expected among squatters on the outer limits of the settlements, but many could be found among the small-propertied farmers who made up the bulk of the emigrants. Travelers' accounts are sprinkled with tales of men who had moved seven times in the last 300 miles, of oldsters who had lived in eight homes, of a pioneer who had been born in New Hampshire, raised in New York, married in Ohio, and settled "for the present" in Missouri.[28] One met a well-to-do sixty-year-old who had sold a prospering New York state farm to begin anew in Michigan because he missed the excitement of pioneering; another found a Texan who had begun his wanderings with Daniel Boone and had been on the move ever since.[29] An exploring expedition along the Missouri River in 1819 stumbled on a lonely outcast who had settled miles ahead of his nearest neighbor, but who questioned them eagerly about the unoccupied Platte River valley that lay far ahead. "We discovered," wrote the chronicler, "that he had the most serious intention of moving with his family to that river."[30]

This contemporary testimony strongly suggests that the United States appeared to Europeans of the eighteenth and nineteenth century a land of exceptional mobility, and that the migratory urge intensified along the frontiers. "The nearer the border you get," wrote a traveler from Kansas in 1871, "the more you will find who want to sell out and move West."[31] That the visitors who described this trait were attracted by the spectacular rather than the usual, and that they probably exaggerated, makes little difference. What is significant is the universal agreement among hundreds of visiting Britons and Europeans that the American people in general, and the frontiersmen in particular, differed from their overseas counterparts in their unusual propensity for moving about. This was a national characteristic, seemingly originating in the Western settlements, and spreading eastward to infect all Americans.

❧❧ SUCH AN EXPLANATION becomes more meaningful if we can determine *how* the frontier stimulated migration. A clue is provided by the motives that separate today's movers from the nonmovers. Ask those who have shifted residence in today's cities why they did so and they will give a variety of answers: the need of a larger home for a growing family, the changing character of the neighborhood, the dissolution of a family through divorce, the desire among oldsters for sun and a warmer climate.[32] But one motive is stressed by virtually every mover as basic to his decision: the necessity of a better home in a better neighborhood to reflect and improve the higher social status he had recently achieved. The pattern of migration, in other words, is determined largely by social mobility; in the semantics of social science, "residential mobility is often the spatial expression of vertical social mobility." This is all-important. The shift from one job to another seldom demands a move, since modern transportation allows workers to reach most parts of the area in which they reside. But a new job on a higher status level does demand a move, because a larger house in a more elite neighborhood will allow his family to mingle with the "right" people and his children to attend the "proper" schools. It will also help him take the next step up the ladder by associating with influential men who can help him along. Self-glorification and self-improvement are the two basic drives that govern modern migrants.[33]

These motives shed light on those that impelled frontiersmen to adopt the peripatetic life. Few who went west were poor; the financial demands of pioneering excluded the poverty-stricken. Most were established farmers with some capital, and all were governed by a compelling desire for self-improvement. They might be driven westward by worn-out lands, or uncongenial neighbors, or overcrowding; they might be attracted by the thirst for adventure or the thrill of westering. They might be lured by the promotion literature of land speculators, or find the invitation of new roads and riverboats irresistible. But the basic urge was for a better farm, more wealth, and a higher status in life. Upward mobility was as compelling a desire for them as for the fast-rising junior executive who moves to a modern suburb, and somewhat easier to achieve in the relatively open society of pioneer communities. The young men who formed the bulk of the westward-moving tide—the average age of frontiersmen ranged from fifteen to twenty-five years—moved largely because they sensed that status improvement was easier in new than in established settlements.[34]

The compulsion to frontiering as a status escalator is understandable, since the universal dream of the pioneer was the Eden that lay ahead. Always the fields beyond the western horizon were richer and deeper than those being tilled. A traveler talked with a prospering Michigan farmer who planned a move to the western part of the territory because the soil there was 4 feet thick *"and so fat that it will grease your fingers."* Others pictured the West as the land of promise, the plains of Mamre, a paradise of milk and honey that would transmute the laziest dullard into a prosperous gentleman.[35] The pioneer, noted a British visitor, "has always something better in his eye, further west; he therefore lives and dies on hope, a mere gypsy in this particular;" when he finally reached the Pacific he would doubtless sit himself down "and weep for other worlds."[36] Travelers who noted this universal ambition also realized that its achievement was possible, for as long as people continued to move toward frontiers, land prices there would steadily advance. The pioneer who sold his holdings could buy equally good land ahead at one twentieth the price, thus accumulating the fortune that would elevate him to a post as community leader.[37] Upward mobility was the urge that sent men westering, confident that the labors of pioneering would be rewarded by wealth and status.

The existence of a frontier where cheap lands served as a bootstrap in the social hierarchy distinguished America in the eighteenth and nineteenth centuries, and helps explain the restlessness of its people. Europe, with no such frontier, provided lesser opportunities to the young and ambitious. The European was bound to his place of birth simply because he was bound to his class; as long as he was tied to one bit of land or one job, he could not aspire to a higher rung in society and experienced no compulsion to move. Families passed on the place of dwelling and place of business together, for they were inseparably linked. So young members of the family stayed in the ancestral home; continuous residence for two or three centuries was the rule rather than the exception. With no opportunity for vertical mobility there was no incentive to physical mobility.

The changes that have occurred in the moving habits of Europeans in recent years add force to this argument. Beginning in the late nineteenth century, economic diversification opened a variety of new jobs and hence of new opportunities, a trend that has continued and accelerated during the twentieth century. At the same time a lessening of class distinctions before a tide of democratic reform unshackled individuals who had been restrained from self-improvement in the past. Thus a chance for upward social mobility became a reality to thousands of ambitious young men. Throughout the Western world, job opportunities served as a lever to displace persons from traditional home or family situations, and to send them hurrying away in quest of a better life. Migration became a fact in Europe, and migration engendered migration; the more people moved the greater the urge to move. The multiplication of opportunities created a situation in the Old World that the frontier had long since created in the New.

These observations are substantiated by in-depth studies of the migratory process in select Western communities. In one Wisconsin county men with high incomes who had achieved status moved less often during the frontier period than those with low incomes who were seeking status; 85 percent of those who moved had property worth less than $100. Those who moved between 1860 and 1870 possessed livestock worth $365 and reported an annual wheat production of 175 bushels; those who stayed owned $443 worth of livestock and produced an average of 214 bushels of wheat. The urge for improvement affected even recent arrivals from Europe, who were naturally less wealthy than the native population. On the whole they showed a greater tendency to migrate than the native-born. Those who moved away from the country were usually young, with the highest mobility rate among those under twenty. Occupation neither deterred nor stimulated migration, for both the farm and city populations lost about half their numbers to other counties between 1850 and 1880.[38]

Migration in Kansas between 1860 and 1930 underlines these conclusions, as well as supporting other generalizations on frontier mobility. Of the frontiersmen who entered that territory between 1854 and 1860, only 35 percent remained five years later, only 26 percent ten years later, and only 20 percent at the end of twenty-five years, whether they lived in the humid East where agricultural conditions were excellent, or in the semihumid West where farming was more hazardous. Of those living in the state in 1885, 51.4 percent were still there after ten years, and 40.8 percent after twenty. This suggests that the first comers were typically restless pioneers, unwilling to stay no matter how satisfactory the living conditions; notable is the fact that the highest percentage of loss occurred in the first decade after 1860 when the nomads who drifted westward on the fringes of settlement departed; departures steadily declined after that until relative stability was reached after twenty-five years. Even then, however, losses were still high, with few townships retaining more than 40 percent or 50 percent of their farmers for more than ten years.[39] Comparable population turnovers marked the history of a Nebraska township, where 106 of the 190 farmers who purchased land between 1872 and 1892 sold out and departed during the pioneering period, and ten others moved away but retained title to their farms.[40] The coming and going of frontier drifters, and the high percentage of failures among newcomers with insufficient capital or skill to succeed, kept the West in a state of constant ferment. "Like most new places," wrote the editor of a Great Plains newspaper, "we have had many comers and goers."[41]

≈§≈§ THE FRONTIER forces that stimulated mobility played their part in shaping the American character; moving about has helped alter the traits and institutions of the people of the United States. This occurred not through actual migration, which was a short-term process, but because of strains created by departure from a familiar environment and adjustment to an unfamiliar environment. The severing of family and community ties changed behavioral patterns in individuals, just as did the requirements of adapting to the new community in which they settled; pioneers must dovetail into an unfamiliar system of role and status, a new leadership structure, and a changed system of values than the ones to which they had been accustomed. This was a long-term process, and explains why frontier areas remained socially fluid for a decade or more as leaders jockeyed for position, economic functions were distributed, the disillusioned moved on, and later comers drifted in to take their places. This turbulence engendered a social environment unlike that of any other section, and from this stemmed—in part at least—alterations in the traits of the people.

One noticeable result was a by-product of the uprooting that tore migrants from familiar associations that had provided them with emotional security. With friends and sometimes family left behind, the mover found himself in a strange world lacking the sanctuaries into which he had traditionally escaped. Nor did the cooperative enterprises needed for frontier development and defense provide a substitute; they were so obviously temporary expedients that he hesitated to seek in them the attachments essential to internal well being. Having been hurt by the severing of past relationships, he was reluctant to make new permanent friendships or to form deep associations lest he be forced to endure a similar upsetting experience in the future. Instead he tended to fasten upon his immediate family, giving so generously of himself to wife and children that an abnormal home environment resulted. "In his character of pioneer," wrote an able observer, "it is his destiny to attach himself to nothing, to no place, edifice, object, or person, except his wife, to whom he is indissolubly bound night and day."[42] The frontiersman—or the modern migrant— also sought artificial companionship to ease his loneliness; the literary clubs, debating societies, and library groups that blossomed in the newer Wests were emotional stopgaps no less than symbols of cultural interests. This same sense of grouplessness encouraged the pioneer to be unduly inquisitive of strangers and embarrassingly hospitable to visitors, as he sought to substitute acquaintances for the friends on whom he had depended.[43]

Adjustment to a new environment was no less upsetting to the pioneer than departure from the old. Among modern movers tensions springing from a failure to make that adjustment or from rebellion against the strange situation have caused a disproportionate number of emotional breakdowns.[44] Among pioneers inability to adjust to unfamiliar customs and practices often altered personality, leaving some frightened and uncertain, others unduly aggressive as they overcompensated for their insecurity. Travelers condemned frontiersmen for their boastfulness, their incessant bragging, their unpleasant aggressiveness. Not all were guilty, of course, but the exceptional number who unleashed their insecurities in this form gave the whole West a reputation for "puffing."[45]

The natural frontier tendency of wastefulness was strengthened by migration, and grafted into the national character by the continuing mobility that characterized the American people. The pioneer was recklessly wasteful not only because of the abundance of resources surrounding him, but also because he sensed that he would soon be moving on. Why bother to improve or preserve a temporary home? Why guard the soil's riches when a stranger would be handling the plow tomorrow? So the frontiersman butchered the soil and skimmed off the resources with no thought to the future. His descendents are governed by the same impulses even today; modern city dwellers endure unpleasant surroundings because they subconsciously sense that they will soon be moving to something better. Only a stabilized people will exert itself to improve conditions with an eye to the future.[46]

Perhaps the most important result of the habit of mobility has been the strengthening of nationalism at the expense of localism. Migration has broadened vistas, undermined provincialism, and expanded speculative energies. Every move westward meant an uprooting of attachments; loyalty to a state of birth eroded away as the pioneer adapted to his new locality, yet he lacked the traditions that would create new loyalties of equal intensity. His emotional need for some attachment directed his devotion to the national government, for wherever he moved, this stood ready to provide for his needs. This tendency was magnified by the scattering of the habits and customs of peculiar localities as men left to conquer new areas where different habits and customs emerged. From a pragmatic point of view, constant migration doomed localism and perpetuated nationalism.

This result was apparent in the detachment from place that travelers noted as one of the characteristics of frontiersmen. Europeans were almost universally shocked at the readiness with which men abandoned their homes, their relatives, their traditions, and their places of birth to fly westward in quest of opportunity. "They quit the parental roof never to see it again," wrote a French observer, "as naturally and with as little emotion, as young birds desert forever their native nest as soon as they are fledged."[47] Attachment to place suffered no less than attachment to parents among those smitten by the locomotive impulse. "There is nothing," observed a visitor, "more remarkable in the character of the Americans than the indifference with which they leave their old habitations"; another added that what a European called "local attachments" were nonexistent in the United States and that anyone would forsake his most treasured heritage if assured that he could earn $10 rather than $8.[48] "He has," wrote a traveler of the typical Westerner, "no root in the soil, he has no feeling of reverence, and love for the natal spot and the parental roof; he is always disposed to emigrate, always ready to start in the first steamer that comes along, from the place where he has just now landed. He is devoured with a passion for locomotion."[49] Such an erosion of local loyalties prepared the pioneer for a magnification of national loyalties.

Continuing migration in the postfrontier period has increasingly refired nationalism. Constant shifting about has helped standardize both ideas and products; the demand for familiar items voiced by movers has created a national market for standard brands fatal to economic localism. Persistent movement has also played the role that it did in pioneer days, lessening loyalties to the mover's native region or state without substituting equally intense loyalties for his new home. This has meant a steady shifting of allegiance from local and state to national governments, with the populace more and more willing to accept federal officials as the principal arbiters of their economic activities. The result has been a steady intrusion of national authority into spheres previously reserved for the states.[50]

Migration has not only strengthened certain character traits among Americans—family loyalty, nationalism, and wastefulness—but has wrought changes in institutions of equal significance. The adjustment of Protestant and Catholic churches to existence in a mobile social order typifies this impact. These traditional bodies, like all venerable

institutions, could be transplanted only with difficulty, after generations of practice made them less adaptable than the individual. Those
most deeply rooted in tradition were most reluctant to change, and
suffered most from migration. Thus the imported Anglican church
found its rigid structure poorly suited to the environment of colonial
America and lost ground steadily; by the time of the Revolution it was
so weakened that it could scarcely survive the taint of Toryism and
did not regain its strength until generations later. Similarly, when the
frontier crossed the Appalachians, further institutional developments
were necessary, and once more the most tradition-steeped churches
were least able to comply. Congregationalism and Episcopalianism
made few footholds in the West, but the less fettered institutions—the
Methodist and Baptist churches especially—were pliable enough to
adjust to the frontiermen's needs. This was the fate of every institution
that was freighted with past tradition; as men shifted about, their
institutions were changed or rose and fell in direct proportion to their
flexibility.

The Roman Catholic church underwent a similar transmutation as
it adjusted to a migratory society. In the Old World it had perfected
a parish organization suitable to rural communities and had leaned
heavily on state support. In the New World it must minister to a large
population, largely urban after the Civil War, without state support.
The formal structure of the church was too rigid to change before
these demands, but the challenge was met by voluntary organizations
that sprang up to meet the need. The parochial school system, magnified beyond its importance in any other country, and fraternal societies
such as the Knights of Columbus illustrate the extent of the revolution
taking place. Such societies would have been impossible in Europe,
but in America they played an invaluable role by easing the transition
of immigrants and lessening loneliness among newly arrived city
dwellers. Even such a tradition-weighted institution as the Roman
Catholic Church must alter its functions when transplanted to a land
where migration was a way of life.[51]

۶§۶§ THE MOBILITY that persists as a national trait owes much
to the pioneers whose restless feet blazed the trails westward. As they
moved—from Eastern farm to Western farm, from Eastern city to
Western city, from country to town, and from town to country—in

their never-ending quest for greater wealth and higher status, they weakened attachments to place and family, and fastened onto the nation's folklore the belief that movement rather than stability assured success. Cheap lands were the force that set this tide in motion, and the sequential exploitation of the West's natural resources renewed its vigor thereafter. Because men would go everywhere, anytime, for self-improvement, the habit of going became ingrained in the national character. Had this opportunity not existed, in the form of the frontier's virgin riches, Americans of today would be less prone to shift about with nary a thought of the consequences.

Nor does the habit of migrating seem destined to decline as memories of frontier days dim. Mobility generates mobility; change for change's sake has become a trait of the American people. They speak in terms of moving: "Here today and gone tomorrow." "I don't know where I'm going but I'm on my way." "Don't be a stick-in-the-mud." "Anywhere I hang my hat is home sweet home." For migration is not only a means of change but a guarantor of success. Those who have moved—whether pioneers bound for the West, immigrants bound for urban ghettos, or the ambitious bound for the cities—have generally improved their lot, finding better jobs, more pay, improved amenities, and especially higher status. The hero of the Horatio Alger myth was never a stay-at-home, but a venturesome young man willing to go anywhere to win a fortune, and win it he always did. So the impression has grown that the mere act of moving is a good thing, assuring a step up the social ladder. Those who have migrated are more apt to migrate again than those who have not, and they also infect their children and some nonmovers with the disease.[52] Moving has become an American fever; the Americans will continue to be a nation of habitual migrants as long as they hope for a better life and a better world.

10

The Frontier
and American
Behavioral Patterns

VISITORS FROM ABROAD who have commented on the distinctive habits of the American people—their mobility, their wastefulness, their love of experimentation, their devotion to democracy—have also noted a number of attitudes that they find exaggerated in the United States. Americans, they say, are dedicated idealists, willing to offer sacrifices in men and money to the better world of their dreams. They are incurable optimists, sustained by a faith in the future. They are insufferable nationalists, less bound by local loyalties than the people of other lands, and given to insisting loudly and sometimes profanely on the superiority of their own institutions. They are annoyingly curious, prying into matters that are not their concern, and denying their neighbors the privacy normal in civilized countries. Americans, travelers insist, have elevated their women folk to unjustified positions of influence, to a degree that any sensible male would escape to a land where his superiority was recognized. These traits, so apparent in the nineteenth century and persistent in lesser degree today, were observed along the frontiers, and stemmed in part from the social environment prevailing in pioneer communities.

 TO ACCEPT a picture of Americans as impractical idealists is to flirt with a seemingly impossible contradiction. They were, nearly all overseas visitors agree, money-grabbing materialists, condemned to the pursuit of the Almighty Dollar by their acceptance of the Puritan ethic and by work habits bred of a frontiering background. How can a man be a materialist and an idealist at the same time? That Americans accomplished this miracle is abundantly demonstrated. Throughout the nineteenth century a procession of business leaders amassed fortunes by ruthless tactics, then poured their wealth back into projects designed for the public good. "You will find him a close calculator," wrote a French observer during the 1830s, "and yet susceptible of enthusiasm—passionately fond of money, and yet far from being avaricious—nay often very prodigal."[1] In the twentieth century the story is the same. Citizens risk heart attacks by ruthlessly pursuing fortunes, yet labor no less diligently to raise gigantic sums for good works. They engage in speculative practices to pyramid their wealth, but contribute generously to the public welfare through foundations or gifts. Businessmen proclaim their hard-headed practicality, yet head societies to end the threat of nuclear warfare by teaching Esperanto or preaching moral disarmament. "Yes," observed a modern visitor, "the cult of the dollar does exist in America, but in America there are also people who deny themselves a pair of shoes and tickets to the cinema in order to send gifts to Yugoslav children."[2] Taking and giving go hand in hand in the United States.

This apparent contradiction can be explained if we realize that Americans have pursued wealth not for wealth's sake, but as a status symbol. Goading them on, particularly in the nineteenth century, was a subconscious sense of cultural inferiority. Easterners felt insecure as they surveyed the mature civilizations of Europe; Westerners felt insecure as they contrasted their social orders with the older societies to their east. Money meant not only comforts but also culture, not only luxuries but also a place in the ranks of civilized society. This spirit was strongest along the frontiers, where cultural growth was most retarded and the sense of lag especially goading. The Westerner, wrote one, pursues gain "not only of wealth, but also of reputation, of comfort, of happiness, gain of all that is supposed to be desirable."[3] Money was not an end in itself but an escalator to a better life, a better social order, and the satisfactions of self-realization. The pursuit of the Almighty Dollar was idealistic no less than it was materialistic. Once achieved, wealth could be given away; its owner had proven himself and his culture, and could now attend to the poverty from which he had sprung. These attitudes were commonplace in nineteenth-century America, and particularized on the frontier where the sense of cultural lag was strongest.

◄§◄§ THE FRONTIER was also partially responsible for the optimism that was and is a distinguishable American trait. At least from the period of the Revolution, the people were calmly confident of their future, knowing that every man with skill and determination could make a fortune, and probably would. From the eighteenth century on travelers noted that the United States glorified what was to come in the same spirit that Europeans venerated what had been; each tended to exalt what it had the most of. "The Englishman," one wrote, "has built according to his means—the American according to his expectations."[4] To Alexis de Tocqueville there was not a country in the world that "more confidently seizes the future" than the United States; a half century later Lord Bryce found the Americans "more hopeful" than any that he knew.[5] Well into the twentieth century, observers were impressed by the rosy visions that led the people into the future, and of their certainty that every problem would be solved when tomorrow dawned.[6] Nor were these empty dreams only; Americans were ready to back their hope with hard cash in daring speculations. Nowhere in the world was the rags-to-riches myth more universally accepted, and nowhere did the people gamble with greater assurance that rewards were certain, no matter how impossible the odds.

This spirit found particular expression along the frontiers where fortunes could be made with the turn of a shovel, the plotting of a new railroad, or an influx of newcomers to buy off the surplus acreage. There the "go-ahead" atmosphere encouraged speculations that shocked conservative Easterners. Ralph Waldo Emerson, listening to talk among Chicago land speculators of booming prices in the 1850s, heard the price of a parcel advance from $50,000 to $80,000 in a single evening. "Yes," a bystander told him, "that is about the fair growth of Chicago *per hour*."[7] There as elsewhere the certainty of growth encouraged get-rich-quick schemes. Why scrimp and hoard when rising prices for lots of grain or beef were as certain as tomorrow's sunrise? Why look backward when the road ahead was paved with riches? A traveler in frontier Minnesota who asked a toll-bridge operator whether his fee included the right to come back was told: "We don't know anything about coming back; *it's all go ahead in this country*."[8] When Westerners insisted on using the present indicative instead of the future subjunctive, they simply displayed their belief that what might be was as assured as though it actually were.[9]

This optimism found political expression in the confident faith of nineteenth-century Americans that continuous expansion was the God-intended lot of their nation. Thomas Jefferson spoke of the United States as a "standing monument and example" to the rest of the world, sure that its benevolent government would be copied by country after country as peoples shed the chains of tyranny. Andrew Jackson was no less assured when he used the happy phrase, "expanding area of freedom," to describe the future of American political institutions. This, by the 1840s, was the nation's "manifest destiny," decreed by a benevolent Deity as a proper fate for people whose government was worthy of extension to the less fortunate everywhere.[10] Continuous expansion was God's will. Nothing must stand in the way, neither Indian barbarian nor Mexican peon nor British tyrant on his London throne. The red men could be pushed aside, or assigned to the barren wastes of Western reservations, for they had abandoned all rights to justice by hindering the march of progress.[11] So much power, so much good, must never be contained. "Our western boundary will, ultimately, be the Pacific Ocean," declared a pioneer as early as 1818; "our northern, the North Pole; our southern, the Isthmus of Darien; and on the ocean we shall have no competitor."[12]

Amongst an expanding people optimism was inevitable, and as long as a frontier moved westward, expansion would be the way of life for Americans. To the Westerner the vast expanses of the interior had been scooped out by the hand of God and endowed with untold riches to await exploitation by His chosen peoples. Wrote one: "One could as well gaze upon the rising sun and not foresee the splendors of midday, as live in these magnificent plains, and have no vision of their future greatness."[13] Just as long as a frontier of cheap lands lay to the west, just as long as virgin resources awaited use, as long could men be utterly sure that the future would be better than the present. "Their eyes," noted Tocqueville, "are fixed upon another sight."[14] They saw the future, not the past; the rude village rising from scarred fields was a triumph over what had been, and would be soon surpassed by what was destined to be. This was a law of expansion as inflexible as Newton's law of gravity.

Translated into terms of the individual, this meant that the most humble would better his lot as he took advantage of the expanding economy. The Old World might appear to the poet a crumbling ruin, a buried world, but in the American West

> a bursting empire meets the eye,
> The spreading wave of life still onward sweeps,
> And as he views the mighty flood roll by,
> His bosom beats with proud anticipation high.[15]

Why not? Large families were the rule along the frontiers where children were certain of a status higher than their parents. "Mr. Malthus," wrote a traveler from the Ohio Valley backwood, "would not be understood here."[16] In the West no evil was without a remedy that tomorrow would bring. Was life uncomfortable in a crude cabin? A few more acres cleared, a new arrival with cash to buy off the excess 40 acres, and a frame house could be built. Did the new fields fail to produce a proper yield? Better lands lay just ahead and could be reached in a single move. This was as foreordained as the succession of night and day. Wealth to the Westerner was not simply an end in itself, not only a symbol of the higher status that was his true aim, but a lottery prize to be immediately laid out for another lottery ticket that would bring an even more spectacular return.[17] With expansion assured, with population growth inevitable, who could possibly lose?

This was the inevitable belief of Westerners, since all about them were examples of pulsating, dynamic growth. Every pioneer cabin was a symbol of progress, for a year or two later it would be surrounded by extensive fields and young orchards, and within a decade would be replaced by a brick or frame dwelling that mirrored the wealth and status of its owner. That some failed to make this rags-to-riches transition mattered not; their luck had run out for a moment and would return with the next move. Growth was the real order of the day, as forests disappeared, plains succumbed to the plow, farms prospered, and hamlets blossomed into cities almost overnight. These were sights to quicken the blood, and to stir the gambling instinct in any man. Not even the most sluggish could live in the past amidst such an atmosphere; the future mattered, and the future was destined to be better than the present.[18]

So Westerners planned eagerly for the day ahead, stretching their optimism to the breaking point. "A New-England man," wrote an Illinois frontiersman, "can have but a faint conception of the *rage* existing at the west for '*improving*' the country."[19] Everywhere blueprints for new utopias filled the minds of men. A visitor to a backwoods hamlet in Michigan was astounded to find the settlers projecting a railroad and talking of a future metropolis. Another found the handful of citizens in the raw little village of New Athens at the junction of the Mississippi and Missouri rivers anticipating the day when their city would outshine its namesake:

> Again shall Athens bid her columns rise,
> Again her lofty turrets reach the skies,
> Science again shall find a safe retreat,
> And commerce here as in a centre meet.

Still farther west visitors marveled that every crossroads town was called a "city" by its inhabitants; one in 1867 overheard with delight a newcomer ask the proprietor of the only house in La Park, Colorado, "if anyone was talking about building a second house in that city." So persuasive was this atmosphere that a young lawyer, arriving in Grand Island, Nebraska, in 1867, found himself swept along. "I acquired almost by instinct a firm belief in the future of the great plains," he later wrote. ". . . From whatever or wherever it came, I know that I did not try to analyze or explain my early feeling that Nebraska would be a great state and this small settlement a thriving city."[20] The frontier cast a spell that entangled the most skeptical.

The logic of expansion, and the example of constant growth in the West, meant that optimism was the common faith of frontiersmen. Each saw the West's exploitable riches as a personal escalator to a better life. This seemed reasonable when "growing up with the country" meant a frame house to replace the log cabin, and a local judgeship or seat in the assembly to symbolize an elite position in society. Faith in the future became a habit of thought no less persistent than belief in equality. And as the successive Wests merged into Easts, optimism increasingly characterized national thought. If the American of the nineteenth century was an unrealistic optimist, it was largely because his belief in the inevitability of progress through expansion made him so.

◆§◆§ TO TRAVELERS from abroad, optimism was no less characteristic of the nation's ethos than nationalism. They found the people of the United States unabashedly proud of their country, tiresomely boastful of its virtues, and annoyingly eager to depreciate other lands as contrasting unfavorably with their own. Superpatriotism was more marked in the nineteenth century than the twentieth, but it has persisted as a deterrent to the international cooperation essential to survival in the nuclear age. This nationalistic spirit flamed in exaggerated form along the frontiers, and has been often ascribed to the pioneering experience.

If we are to validify this assumption, we must determine when and where nationalism emerged as an identifiable phenomenon in the United States. No people can experience a sense of "nationalism" until they have been welded into a common "nationality." In America this occurred during the years following the Revolution with a dawning awareness that a commonly shared past, a common culture, a common language, common customs, and a common purpose bound the people together.[21] This realization could be translated into a spirit of "nationalism" only when the mass of the people strongly identified themselves with their nation and desired its aggrandizement. Traditions must develop to serve as a cohesive force and erase local jealousies. A shared culture must be created in the form of literature and folklore. Behavioral patterns acceptable to all must cement people of different sections and ethnic background into one.[22] If it can be shown that identification with the national government began in the West, and that cultural and behavioral patterns emerging there served as a cohesive force on all the people of the United States, the influence of the frontier on the nationalistic spirit can be appreciated.

That identification with the national government was by the 1830s loudly and often rudely expressed by the American people as a whole is attested to by virtually every traveler who visited the United States. Let a visitor confess that he was from another land and he was immediately subjected to a barrage of pro-American comment that even the most tolerant found distressing. Not a person in the nation, one Englishman complained, but insisted that his countrymen were "*more* learned, *more* powerful, and altogether *more* extraordinary than any other people in the world." Another found the "constant habit of praising themselves, their institutions, and their country" one of their most annoying traits. After listening for weeks to this self-glorification, one visitor fully expected that Americans would soon boast that their country was not only the most powerful and most learned, but the oldest nation in the world. Even Alexis de Tocqueville, sympathetic though he was, was driven to confess that "nothing is more embarrassing in the ordinary intercourse of life than this irritating patriotism of the Americans."[23]

With spread-eagle boasting about the United States went derogatory remarks about other nations of the world. To the American of the middle nineteenth century Europe was a decadent land, governed by despots, peopled by serfs, and sustained by memories of a dead past. "Europe—what is Europe," asked a stump speaker in the 1840s. "She's nowhar—nothing—a circumstance—a cypher—a bare absolute ideal! We have faster steam-boats, swifter locomotives, larger creeks, bigger plantations, bigger mill privileges, broader lakes, higher mountains, deeper cataracts, louder thunder, forkeder lightning, braver men, handsummer *wee-men*, more money than England dare have."[25] Listening to such "puffing," a traveler understandably resorted to British understatement to remark that American patriotism "was not properly moderated by reflection."[26] The American people were identifying with their federal government, and stoking the fires of nationalism by doing so.

Significantly, the degree of identification intensified along the frontiers; travelers in the 1830s and 1840s reported that superpatriotism was rampant there as in no other part of the country. "In the interior," a French visitor observed, "people talk more often about war and hold heroic deeds in higher esteem than they do on the coast."[27] This seemed logical to Europeans and Westerners alike, for as one observed, "the foreign influences, which dilute and vitiate this virtue in the extremities, cannot reach the heart of the continent, where all that lives and moves is American." Nowhere but along the frontiers could a landlord summon his guests to dinner by shouting "Gentlemen, we are a great people."[28] Nowhere but in the West could leading citizens take pride in their section's role as a binding force for the Union in periods of crisis, such as flamed during the nullification controversy of 1832. "As a people," one wrote at that time, "we are strong for the union, and the whole union." The West's part in the expansionist fever of the 1840s defies exaggeration; a frontiersman summed up the sentiments of his section on the eve of the Mexican War when he told a visitor that "he saw no reason under the sun why a Spaniard should be left on the northern side of Panama. The isthmus, the north pole, and the two great oceans, were in his opinion the only boundaries which the Republic should recognize." A generation later the West was eager to go to war against Mexico to "clean out" the Maximilian crowd.[29] Frontiersmen were proudly, confidently nationalistic. Scarcely a book or magazine printed in the West, hardly a newspaper article or Fourth of July oration, but made clear the section's strong attachment to the Union, its unwavering opposition to any division, and its eagerness to fight all creation to uphold American principles. Identification with the national government was more deeply rooted there, and more loudly expressed, than in any other part of the country.

That this spirit should flame beyond the Appalachians seemed natural to contemporaries. They, like later scholars, saw the frontier as one of a number of cohesive forces, operating in a variety of ways to bind the nation together. It played this role, Americans believed, partly by lessening the divisive strains that threatened the Republic in its formative years, and partly by strengthening allegiance to the national while lessening loyalty to states or regions. The importance of the frontier as a nationalizing influence cannot be appreciated until we analyze its functioning in these different capacities.

As a uniting force, the frontier was particularly significant in the early days of the Republic when conflict between the thirteen states threatened to Balkanize the nation. Such might have been its fate save for the millions of commonly held acres lying west of the Appalachians. The mere existence of this fortune in real estate deterred disunion by promising shared wealth for the future, providing funds from which the states could pay their war debts and veterans' pensions, and assuring all people a reserve of opportunity that few would willingly abandon. The public lands continued to strengthen union in the post-Revolutionary years when the trans-Appalachian West served as a pawn in the power struggles of England, France, and Spain. The diplomatic squabbles over ownership of the Mississippi Valley had a dual effect on nationalistic psychology; on the one hand they intensified the loyalty of Westerners who realized that only the national government stood between them and despotic administration by an alien power, and on the other they quickened the patriotism of

Easterners whose determination to keep the western territories increased proportionately as pressures multiplied to take them away. George Washington mirrored these fears when in 1783 he urged young men to settle on the frontiers and pleaded for improved communication between East and West.[30] So intense were the loyalties bred of these experiences that the nation could overcome the divisive strains generated by the War of 1812 and the early sectional conflicts.

The West, during the remaining years of the nineteenth century, served not only as a bond of union but as the creator of a variety of nationalizing forces that strengthened the national spirit. One of the most important, and least tangible, was the sense of oneness bred of enjoying a common experience; the people developed commonly shared behavioral patterns that differed from those of Europe and made them aware of their own distinctiveness. Few realized that pioneering had placed its stamp upon them, but all knew that Europeans were strange creatures, lacking the "go-ahead" spirit, the restless energy, the speculative urge, the wandering instincts, and the democratic ways of their fellow countrymen. That these distinctions were sensed rather than realized was unimportant; they formed a psychological basis for nationalism that would have been lacking had no frontier existed.

The expansion that went hand-in-hand with pioneering also served as a cohesive force. As successive generations realized that opportunity lay along the frontiers, they turned their backs on Europe and their faces toward the West. Each step that they took weakened ties with the past and strengthened allegiance to the nation. The riches in natural resources found on the frontier fired their patriotism still more by creating the impression that the United States was destined to become the world's most powerful republic. "Westward the course of empire" might well have been the slogan of American nationalism. No red-blooded citizen but swelled with pride as he viewed the future, for the time would soon come when snobbish Europeans who criticized American culture would have their comeuppance.[31] Who could avoid a sense of national pride when he was certain that his country's place was secure as the world's greatest nation?

For the time being, however, the United States, and especially the West, lagged far behind in cultural advance. This mere fact stirred nationalistic sentiments, simply because Americans felt called upon to defend their nation against the criticisms of European visitors. With each new barb they bulged muscles and unleashed torrents of praise for their native land, voicing patriotic platitudes so often that eventually they became nationalistic in belief as well as pronouncement. This was particularly the case with Westerners, whose cultural immaturity inspired the most galling attacks from travelers and who felt called upon to respond most vehemently. Having mouthed the glories of the United States so often, and having heard neighbors join in the chorus, they were bound to believe some of what they said and heard. If they spoke the language of nationalism more vigorously than their cousins in the East, they did so because the frontier had cursed them with a sense of cultural inferiority that required compensation.

The Westerner's nationalistic prejudices were also stimulated by the wandering tendency bred of his frontier experiences. His habit of moving about doomed localism; he was bound to no one place but felt free to journey to any part of the nation as a tourist or prospective settler. Europeans were often amazed by the wide knowledge of their country exhibited even by Americans in humble circumstances, just as they were shocked by the willingness of any person to abandon his home if opportunity beckoned elsewhere.[32] As early as 1796 a South Carolina Congressman could write that his constituents on the remote frontiers were "wholly freed from that local attachment which arises from habit and long residence"; a few years later an English visitor noted of the American that "his feelings are more centered upon his institutions than his mere country. He looks upon himself more in the light of a republican than in that of a native of a particular territory."[33] This detachment from local loyalties meant that Americans in general and frontiersmen in particular would center their patriotism on the national government, just as their constant moving about helped nationalize customs and institutions. In both instances the nationalistic spirit was strengthened.

Finally—and most important of all—the existence of a frontier required the federal government to multiply its functions, with a corresponding decrease in the activity and authority of the states. In certain areas national power was unquestioned; the pioneer looked to Washington for the army that would protect him from Indian attack, the forts that would guard the borderlands, and the mail service that would link him with his departed home. In less clearly defined areas of federal functioning, the states and nation soon developed a partnership concept that had not been envisaged by the framers of the Constitution. This emerged as the westward movement made clear that the problems of one state were the problems of another; the need for national perspective in their solution became increasingly desirable. These were largely Western problems, with local variations but with so many features in common that only intergovernmental cooperation could affect the most rapid and economical solutions. A "partnership" between nation and states became essential if an efficient internal improvements system was to be created, rivers and harbors improved, the public domain distributed equitably, and the widest educational opportunities provided for all. In each of these areas federal power encroached on state power, but with the complete consent of the state leaders and people. And as this occurred, pioneers increasingly centered their loyalties on Washington, rather than on a state capital, which could not supply their needs.[34]

The operation of this partnership can be illustrated in the realms of internal improvements and distribution of the public domain. States entered bravely upon the task of road building early in the history of the Republic, but the rapid spread of population westward soon focused attention on the need for a national plan if the various state systems were to dovetail. Albert Gallatin realized this, and in 1808 announced a blueprint for a national network of internal improvements. As this was debated over the next years, individual states took their cues and began to fit their own programs into the nation-wide pattern. Their acquiescence convinced Congress that they would welcome even more planning, which it provided in 1824 by establishing the National Board of Internal Improvement. From that time on cooperation was usual, with the federal government contributing over-all plans and surveys. Its role was appreciated; stagecoach passengers in the West were heard to praise the national administration —not the local—for providing the fine roads over which they traveled with such reckless speed.[35]

The public domain proved an even more effective device for pyramiding federal power. Not only did the sale of government-owned lands provide funds for a variety of functions that would have been forbidden a less well-endowed government, but administration of the domain gave Washington officials a source of power over the states that could never have existed in a country without a frontier. This was exercised over all land-grant states admitted to the Union. Each wanted to use the lands within its borders to benefit its own economy; the central government was equally eager to prevent the states from taxing its domain. Here was an opportunity for bargaining, and here also was an opportunity for federal officials to use the public domain for national purposes, despite opposition of "strict constructionists." Even the most dedicated constitutionalist was inclined to waver when his state stood to benefit financially from the reservoir of federally owned lands within its borders.

The cooperation between states and nation that resulted allowed federal officials to use the public domain for a variety of purposes in the national interest. Some went in direct grants to the states to support schools, internal improvements, reclamation, public buildings, veterans' benefits, and the like. Land grants were also funneled through the states to private companies that built roads and canals, railroads, colleges, and other improvements that would serve the people of the whole country. Government lands were similarly granted directly to railroads, homesteaders, mining and lumbering interests, and other groups promising to contribute to the nation's economic growth. Between the 1840s and the end of the century these land-grant programs carried federal support—and a degree of federal authority—into every corner of the West. The people there were aware that Washington was their benefactor, offering them transportation, education, welfare, and recreation. To argue from this that the land-grant states were more nationalistic than the older nonland-grant states is to meddle with the unprovable. Yet the newer states did become accustomed to cooperation with the federal government even before their admission to the Union, and this willingness to cooperate continued after statehood. In this manner national authority impressed itself upon a far-flung people.[36]

Both Westerners and overseas visitors who observed them recognized that unusual dependence on the national government had bred unusual loyalties. Alexis de Tocqueville had this in mind when he wrote of the "irritable patriotism" of Americans; so did a traveler who commented on the Westerners in 1818: "Bred up under the eye, and fostered by the care of the national government, they have attached themselves to the national institutions with a devotion of feeling unknown in the older parts of the Republic."[37] During the Civil War Ignatius Donnelly, who spoke for all the West that he knew so well, summed up frontier nationalism when he told the House of Representatives: "We who come . . . from the far West have not that deep and ingrained veneration for State power which is to be found among the inhabitants of some of the older States. We have found that State lines, State names, State organizations, are in most cases, the variest creatures of accident. . . . We feel ourselves to be the offshoots of the nation. We look to the nation for protection. The love of our hearts gathers around the nation."[38] Pioneers who were conscious of having created a state under federal auspices, and nurtured that state with federal funds, were less inclined than Easterners to exhibit local prejudices.

These Western loyalties mirrored sentiments likely to be engendered in a dynamic society. In a static social order, where limits of state and federal authority had been rigidly defined, any attempt on the part of one government to cross into the other's territory would have spelled the collapse of federalism. In the United States, however, situations were constantly altered by problems stemming from population expansion. These challenged older ways of doing things, and outmoded traditional divisions of authority; their very complexity demanded action on both levels of government. Their influence becomes clear when we recognize the large number of innovations in American federalism traceable to the peopling of the West. The constitutional structure was altered as each new generation developed mechanisms for intergovernmental cooperation, and each alteration both extended federal influence and made the people more aware that they lived in a nation, rather than in a state or section.[39]

The frontier, nursing a sense of unity for the American people, nationalizing habits and institutions, weakening local attachments, and broadening the functions and authority of the national government at the expense of the states, served as a powerful catalyst in creating the nationalism that visitors noted as a distinctive trait. That the frontier was solely responsible is emphatically not true. The strong national spirit rested on a number of foundations: the traditions of loyalty to country inherited from Europe, the rise of a native culture, the success of the democratic experiment, the ocean barriers that isolated the nation from world conflicts during its formative years, and a dozen more. Yet these would have been less effective in a static society; the dynamics of expansion breathed new life into American nationalism and fostered the flag-waving loyalty that overseas visitors found both universal and lamentable.

✺ NO MATTER how nationalistic the frontiersmen might be, they were backwoodsmen, living in comparative isolation from the main currents of life, and exhibiting characteristics of the country dweller that have through history proved annoying to the urbanite and the sophisticate. The usual pioneer was largely uneducated, often lonely, and haunted by a subconscious sense of his own cultural inferiority. At the same time he was certain that the future would remedy all ills, and transmute him into a cultured worldling, as rich in learning as in dollars. The internal struggle between the world of reality in which he lived and the world of hope to which he aspired fashioned psychological conflicts within the frontiersman that accounted for some of his most noticeable characteristics. His boastfulness, his prying inquisitiveness, his warm hospitality were all singled out for special comment by those who visited the West. These traits have largely disappeared with the passing of the frontier and the eclipse of rural America, but remnants persist in the braggadocio of some Americans when traveling abroad, the curiosity that they display to strangers, and the friendliness with which they open their doors to visitors from other continents.

Bragging was a universal trait, and as universally condemned by travelers. Scarcely a frontiersman but boasted endlessly to strangers that he had the best gun, the fastest horse, the handsomest wife, the prettiest house, the richest land, and the finest government in all the world. To him every shabby schoolhouse was a college, every rivulet a mighty river capable of freighting the world's commerce, every cluster of shacks a metropolis. Some visitors were wise enough to realize that boasting was a symptom both of the pioneer's hidden insecurity and his lack of education; one found him at that stage of mental culture in which "inflation of language is produced as naturally as weeds on rank soil."[40] Most were not that charitable and longed to escape from a region that they branded "a paradise of puffers."[41]

The curiosity of the Westerner was just as annoying to the visitor. A few understood the malady: thinness of settlement made the pioneer perpetually curious just as thickness of settlement made the British or Japanese unusually polite. Yet no amount of rationalization could persuade them to forgive the "impertinent inquisitiveness" that they found in the West. Every stranger was fair game for a barrage of questions that transcended all bonds of good taste and left the British especially in a state of total dismay.[42]

Understandably, the pioneers developed a knack for personal prying that no one could escape. No task was too important to interfere with this inquisition; a traveler in Texas had a frontiersman drop a plow and run twenty rods to ask him where he came from and where he was going; another in early Kentucky was stopped so abruptly that he imagined a highwayman was about to relieve him of his purse.[43] Once buttonholed, the visitor was expertly quizzed. Charles Dickens had scarcely boarded a Mississippi steamboat when he was fastened upon by a stranger who first fired a fusillade of questions about the author's fur coat—where he bought it, what fur it was, what it weighed, how much it cost—then moved on to his watch "and asked what *that* cost, and whether it was a French watch, and where I got it, and how I got it, and whether I bought it or had it given me, and how it went, and where the keyhole was, and when I wound it, every night or every morning, and whether I ever forgot to wind it at all, and if I did, what then?"[44] An unfortunate botanist in backwoods New York was constantly beset by strangers who not only asked him innumerable questions about the portfolio that he carried for collecting plants, but pawed and poked at his collections until they were endangered.[45] The pioneer was most certainly an ill-mannered inquisitor, showing no respect for privacy as he sought to ease the loneliness of his life and broaden his cultural horizons with a few tidbits of information.

If the pioneer's lonely isolation made him embarrassingly inquisitive, it also made him generously hospitable. Strangers whatever their class and background were warmly welcomed into every frontier cabin, partly because they carried news of the outside world, partly because an unfamiliar face broke the monotony of backwoods life. Harriet Martineau correctly diagnosed the openhanded greetings that met her everywhere in the West as a "virtue of young society." Others saw frontier hospitality as a product of the wealth of a new land that, "showering down her blessings with bountiful hand," taught the pioneer to be liberal rather than niggardly. Still others ascribed the trait to the primitive social order where the absence of rigid rules permitted every man to act according to his own generous whims.[46] Whatever the reason, all travelers agreed that no other country offered such eager hosts as Western America. There the welcome phrase, "Hello, light and tie," was universally used on successive Wests from the Atlantic to the Pacific. A traveler spoke for all of his kind when he reported journeying 10,000 miles in the interior, 2000 of them through a countryside with not a single public accommodation, without once having to sleep in the open or miss a meal.[47]

Even poverty was no excuse for lack of hospitality, as many a visitor found when he knocked at the door of miserable cabins on the fringes of settlements. Often there was little food for man or horse, and usually there was no bed save a blanket in the corner of the hut, but no visitor was ever refused. All that the owner possessed was freely given, and offers to pay were indignantly refused. "I'll have to be a most powerful heap poorer nor I'm now," one was told, "afore I'll take anything for sich a poor shelter to feller critturs what's lost." Another who tried to justify paying for milk by saying that he had plenty of money was politely informed: "Well, I have milk enough, so we're even."[48] Generosity came naturally to frontiersmen whose confidence in the future was limitless, and hospitality was their most common means of exhibiting generosity.

⊸§⊸§ THE FRONTIER encouraged not only man's kindness to man, but to woman as well. To the pioneer, any "female" was an asset, partly because respectable white women were scarce enough to be in unusual demand, partly because they were economically more valuable than in settled communities. Their scarcity is a matter of record; the difficulties and uncertainties of life on the edges of settlement kept them at a minimum. East of the Mississippi most outposts were founded by young men who had left their families temporarily behind; in the Far West the gentler sex was almost unknown among fur trappers, miners, and cattlemen. In the Colorado mines men outnumbered women by twenty to one; in California the proportion was more than ten to one. To men living such a monastic existence, the feminine sex acquired a sanctity and desirability unknown in regions with a more normal male-female ratio. Annals of mining camps are filled with tales of grizzled prospectors who paid a dollar a head to look at a woman's bonnet, or to touch a little girl's skirt, or to dance about a post on which a lady's hat was enshrined.[49]

Their desirability was accentuated by their value, for women normally performed many of the tasks essential to frontier life. They built the fires, milked the cows, cared for a kitchen garden, fetched wood and water, cooked meals, churned butter, spun flax, wove cloth, and fashioned clothes for the entire family. These were essential chores in a land where there was little division of labor.[50] Many a confirmed bachelor who had been content with his lot in the East changed his mind when he reached the West; one explained to a traveler that he was heading back home to find a bride because "there wasn't any stout ones in our settlement, and it takes so long to make up to a *stranger*, that I allowed I mought as well go back and see the old folks, and get somebody that I know'd thar to come with me."[51] That frontiersman had a keen eye for the practical, as he must along the frontiers. One who returned to the East after a life in the West was disgusted with the "weak, feminy, wimmen bodies" he found in the cities, all clearly incapable of managing a dinner pot, killing a bear, or making leather britches for their menfolk.[52]

Both the economic value and the scarcity of women along the frontiers altered masculine attitudes and standards. Marriage became not only desirable but essential; girls of ten or twelve years and spinsters of uncertain antiquity were alike eagerly courted as soon as they reached a Western community. "Matrimony, like death, spares neither age nor condition," wrote a traveler in the Far West.[53] Early marriages were the rule, and divorce less sternly frowned upon than in the East, for judge and jury knew that any mistreated wife would not remain single long. The whole pattern of family life was altered by frontier conditions, although the alterations were less serious than those later wrought by urbanization.

More enduring was the changed attitude toward women originating in the social environment of frontier communities. Pioneers viewed them through different eyes than Europeans; they were to be sought after, venerated, and pampered to a degree unrecognizable in areas with a more equitable ratio of the sexes. "One of the first peculiarities that must strike a foreigner in the United States," wrote a traveler in 1841, "is the deference paid universally to the sex, without regard to station." Charles Dickens noted with surprise that men stood until ladies were seated; other visitors were amazed at the respect with which their every whim was greeted.[54] When one commented on this behavior to a frontier housewife, she sniffed that her husband had better be kind to her for "if he don't, there's plenty will."[55]

This attitude was magnified in the wilder frontiers of the Far West, where pioneers recognized that women—respectable women, that is—were harbingers of civilization as well as desirable helpmates. "From the day when a silk dress and a lace shawl were seen on Main Street," one visitor to the Great Plains observed, "that thoroughfare became passable clean and quiet; oaths were less frequently heard; knives were less frequently drawn; pistols were less frequently fired."[56] The West rewarded women for the civilization that they carried in their handbags by allowing them political as well as social rights denied them in the East. Kansas debated granting them the vote as early as the 1870s, and the Wyoming territorial legislature pioneered in allowing them the franchise in 1869.[57] Here was proof that the gentler sex held a unique position in the eyes of Westerners.

◄§◄§ THE ALTERED relationship between men and women symbolized the changes wrought in American values by the westward movement of the frontier. The American of today is no longer the naïve optimist, the arrogant nationalist, or the boastful, prying, warm-hearted host to strangers pictured by nineteenth-century travelers. These were rural no less than Western traits, and they have dimmed with the advent of industry and urbanization. But despite the growing pattern of conformity that makes the American less distinguishable from all industrialized peoples, traces of these characteristics remain. Optimism has been dealt crippling blows by the Great Depression of the 1930s and by the troubled world scene brought to the nation's attention by World War II. Braggadocio and inquisitiveness have succumbed to increasing sophistication. Nationalism has assumed a new coloration with the advent of the Cold War and the threat of nuclear extermination. But the deference with which the males of America treat their feminine companions, the authority granted them in home and government, and the equality allotted them in the masculine world of business, all testify to the persistence of pioneer traits in twentieth-century society.

11

The
Persistence of
Frontier Traits

THOSE WHO HAVE read this far will agree that the frontier's impact on American traits and institutions can never be exactly defined. This is not surprising. Human behavior defies simple explanation, for man as an individual and man as a social entity reacts to such a variety of forces and responds in such personalized behavioral patterns that laws explaining his conduct can never be formulated. To say that three centuries of westering made the people of the United States more democratic or more nationalistic is to invite the criticism of scholars who can prove that this group or that in America was less democratic or less nationalistic than such and such a group beyond the seas. Yet one generalization seems justified: the pioneering experience helped exaggerate certain traits until the differences were observable to visitors from other lands.

◄§◄§ THE NATURE of the migration process contributed to these differences. Pioneering was selective, attracting those who were unusually insecure at home or who experienced an abnormal desire for adventure or self-betterment. The appeal of the West was to the man of action, willing to gamble the comforts of a known community against the more spectacular but uncertain prospects of an unknown. Those who remained at home were usually the contented, the contemplative, and the timid. Neither poverty nor wealth were determining factors, for while the very poor usually lacked the means to migrate and the very rich lacked the incentive, sprinklings from both groups were found among the frontiersmen. This sifting meant that in the successive Wests were concentrated to an unusual degree middle-class men of action who were bold enough to stake their future against the odds offered by nature and whose zest for adventure and thirst for self-improvement were above average. The grouping of these men on successive frontiers during the early stages of settlement helped create an atmosphere substantially different from that of established communities.

Those who did migrate followed no orderly pattern, although they may be divided into two loosely defined groups. The first comprised advanced pioneers interested in *using* nature: fur trappers, missionaries, herdsmen, and others whose livelihood depended on preserving the wilderness intact. Unwittingly, however, they served as vanguards of civilization, for they spied out the best lands, defined transportation routes, and helped destroy the self-sufficiency of the Indian occupants. Behind them, but sometimes alongside of them, came the second group bent on *subduing* nature: squatters, small-propertied farmers, equipped farmers, town planters, land speculators, merchants, millers, lawyers, printers, distillers, and the dozens more needed to erect a civilization on the ashes of the wilderness. Like their predecessors, they refused to be bound by laws of social evolution, moving helter-skelter as their ambitions and opportunities decreed. At times the first comers on a virgin frontier would be squatters or small-propertied farmers, at others villagers eager to plant a town at some favored site. No orderly procession of "trappers' frontier," "farmers' frontier," and "urban frontier," moved westward across America; the scene rather was of kaleidoscopic patterns constantly changing within a broad zone that was itself slowly advancing with each passing year.

As this went on, pioneers were influenced by two new environments. One was physical; frontiersmen lived in an unfamiliar world where neighbors were relatively few, where division of labor was less advanced than in matured societies, where danger sometimes lurked, and where land was cheaper and labor dearer than in the successive Easts. The other, and far more important, was social, formed by a blending of physical conditions and human beings equipped to capitalize upon them. Physically the frontier was distinctive in offering exceptional opportunity for individual self-advancement. There a man with large ambition and small capital could secure the farm or village lot that might springboard him to greater wealth and higher status as markets emerged and an influx of newcomers nudged prices higher. Yet men wanting to better themselves were essential before the frontier escalator could operate. Spaniards and Portuguese, migrating to Latin America from nations where absolutism curbed individual incentive and where freedom of economic enterprise was almost unknown, lacked the incentives to use the resources spread before them. English pioneers, by contrast, were accustomed to private ownership of land and a degree of economic and political freedom. They were equipped to exploit a physical environment that offered unusual opportunity for the individual to better himself. This combination of land awaiting utilization and a people capable of utilizing it created the distinctive social environment of the American frontier.

The key feature of this environment, it must be emphasized, was the degree of opportunity offered for upward economic and social mobility. This was provided in part by the low man-land ratio, and in part by the relatively fluid state of society. The former allowed the comparatively propertyless individual a chance to better his financial status, whether as farmer extracting wealth from the soil, as speculator capitalizing on the influx of newcomers to multiply his investment, or as townsman providing his neighbors with mercantile and professional services. The fluid social order promised that few roadblocks would be strewn in his path as he journeyed toward success. Frontier societies were less stabilized than those in older areas. Although stratification occurred almost from the beginning, class lines were less tightly drawn and more easily breached; those who aspired to social status or political leadership achieved success more easily than in older communities. Just as important was the fact that the newness of the social order and the variety of backgrounds of those who composed it precluded the imposition of traditional status symbols. Wealth inherited through three generations, or a distinguished lineage, might be essential to social eminence in tradition-governed communities, but on frontiers respect was reserved for those who could contribute most to the group. Each man was free to seek his own level; vertical mobility was a built-in feature of life in the various Wests.

That faith in progress was the basic creed of Anglo-American frontiersmen was demonstrated time and time again by the rebellious spirit that flamed whenever restraints were placed on their freedom of self-advancement. Rebellions occurred surprisingly early in the seventeenth century, as the first pioneers from England realized that the New World required new rules. The Virginia Company sought to operate its preserves as a company estate, manned by paid servants; within a few years the colonists had won the right to till their own farms and to share in their own government through a House of Burgesses. The Massachusetts General Court tried to restrict settlement to designated towns adjacent to older communities; that system broke down completely as the speculative spirit scattered settlers deep in the wilderness in quest of the best lands. An enterprising people, transplanted to an environment where a social escalator was in operation, would stand for no hindrances as they advanced in wealth and status.

This was the atmosphere that helped exaggerate certain traits and value judgments long existent among Europeans and Easterners, but now sharpened until visitors from Britain found the Westerners to be a new breed, so different from their ancestors as to be scarcely recognizable. Travelers during the eighteenth and nineteenth centuries noted these differences among all Americans, but found them most clearly etched along the frontiers, becoming more apparent with each move from the settled toward the unsettled portions of the nation.

That the differences were traceable solely to the pioneering experience is obviously untrue; they stemmed from the mingling of peoples drawn from diverse backgrounds, isolation from European thought currents, the newness of the country, the lack of enervating tradition, and a host more. Nor were these differences of kind rather than degree. Man is by instinct a traditionalist, and the avowed purpose of all frontiersmen was to build in the West a model of the social order that they had known in the East. This urge meant a modification, not a disruption, of established behavioral patterns. It meant also that the successive Wests would remain dependent on the Easts adjacent to them, and that a continual flow of culture westward would offset the degrading influence of the primitive physical environment.

Yet change in the traits and institutions of the pioneers did occur, even though it was relative rather than complete, and even though a majority of the inhabitants were reluctant to accept it. These alterations were traceable largely to the greater degree of opportunity for self-improvement that distinguished the American Wests from the American Easts, and from Europe. Characteristics and patterns of behavior that allowed men to capitalize on this situation, or that recognized the altered social relationships existing in a land where equality of opportunity was greater than in older societies, gradually emerged in frontier communities. These changes meant that the transit of civilization to the successive frontiers was never complete; each move westward accentuated traits and strengthened institutions that differed from those of the East.

৽৽ AMONG THESE changes, none was more pronounced than that which adjusted the political practices and philosophy of the frontiersmen to a world in which grass-roots democracy was a fact of life. True, no revolution in the institutions of government occurred. The pioneers invented few democratic theories or devices, contenting themselves with the constitutional models that lay behind them. Their practice was to borrow the more democratic features of the governments that they imitated, combining these into a system that was completely traditional, but that still moved mankind slightly further toward equalitarianism. By the time of the Revolution, the dispersal of ownership of land had combined with these reforms to open the ballot box to a sizable portion of the population. Democratic progress continued as new states entered the Union, building their constitutions on borrowings from the old, but steadily awarding more power to the people. On the local level this trend was even more apparent, as the franchise was broadened, the responsibility of political leaders to their constituents accentuated, and posts of authority awarded newly risen leaders who would have been denied such an opportunity in less fluid societies.

Social democracy made greater gains on the frontier than political democracy. Belief in the potential equality of all men was the common faith of the pioneers. To them every man was a "gentleman" and every woman a "lady" simply because they were sure to achieve this status soon. Servants in the traditional sense were unknown there; "helpers" expected to eat with the family, and waiters in frontier inns to discard their aprons and join in card games or conversation with the guests. These were symbolic actions, for they mirrored attitudes natural in a social setting where opportunity might elevate the most humble and hazards might dethrone the most affluent. What was more natural than belief in equality in a land where the leveling influence of equal opportunity, the lack of an established leadership structure, and the absence of a tradition-based set of rules governing social conduct opened the door to self-advancement to all. Here was *American* democracy, as distinguished from its European ancestor, most vigorously expressed.

If the frontier altered men's attitudes toward their fellow men, it also forced them to change their beliefs concerning the role that government should play in their lives. To them, every man was a self-dependent individual, capable of caring for himself without the fostering care of society. This seemed just in a land that provided equal opportunity for all to ascend the social ladder. Cooperation was entirely reconcilable with this brand of individualism; the frontiersman who depended on his neighbors to defend him, help build his home, and market his goods was never reluctant to solicit aid from the government, or to accept regulatory measures, when his own betterment was involved. His individualism found voice only when the demands of society threatened his personal self-advancement. With a larger stake in society than his Eastern cousin, and with the promise of an even greater stake as he capitalized on the opportunities available in a new land, he was exceptionally sensitive on this point. Governmental checks upon his real or anticipated upward mobility he protested; government aid to that mobility he welcomed.

Frontier opportunity altered the economic no less than the political and social attitudes of pioneers, and of Easterners as well. Both responded to the wealth that flowed into the nation's trade channels as the resources of successive Wests were utilized. This process continued over many years as technological improvements allowed the sequential exploitation of nature's riches and a recurring revitalization of the national economy. The presence of this usable wealth, and the promise of even more to come, accustomed frontiersmen to a steadily improving standard of living, and this in turn shaped their attitude toward material possessions. Money was the ladder to improved social status, the gateway to political power, the avenue to a more abundant life, the key to cultural improvement. Wealth was essential because wealth would buy status and culture. So important were these goals that leisure and pleasure must be abandoned temporarily; so urgent was the desire for self-advancement that the higher arts must for the time being give way to more practical tasks.

The possibility of progress helped accentuate other traits noticeable among the frontiersmen. They worked hard, scorned indolence, and branded time wasting as immoral. They were shamefully wasteful, destroying the forests and mining the soils as they advanced, because this was the quickest path to wealth and the devil take posterity. They were quick to improvise, scornful of tradition, and adept in jack-of-all-trades skills needed in a land where division of labor was relatively uncommon. Inventors they were not, lacking the training, leisure, and technical facilities needed to produce revolutionary new products. These came from the East in response to the demands of the West, for the recurring needs created by expansion into unfamiliar physical environments called for a constant creation of gadgets, machines, and techniques in the area behind the frontier. The Wests stimulated invention directly, but even more importantly by lessening respect for time-tested techniques and weakening the influence of tradition.

The opportunity for upward social mobility bred the habit of physical mobility. Had the United States in the eighteenth and nineteenth centuries been a static society, in which rigid class lines checked individual advancement, there would have been no more incentive for internal migration than in the Europe of that day. But with progress the order of society, people did move often as they sought better jobs and higher status. As they moved—from East to West, from farm to village, from town to city—others followed filling the vacuums left by their departure, some from abroad as immigrants, others from the seaboard, but all motivated by the will-o'-the-wisp of self-improvement. To some, migration became a habit, to be indulged in whenever the spirit moved, even when conditions at home were satisfactory. Physical mobility was basically a device to achieve social mobility, and as long as opportunity beckoned—whether from frontier or factory—the American would follow.

The quest for betterment, and the dream of a better life as frontier resources were exploited, helped bestow upon the pioneer the optimism that was another of his identifiable attitudes. As long as expansion was a fact of life, improvement was certain. Why scrimp and hoard when rising prices would surely bring affluence? Why be content with a secondary role for the nation when its emergence as a major power was assured? Expansion had given substance to such dreams in the past, and would in the future. This was a law of nature as inflexible as the law of supply and demand. Impatience to realize these dreams tended to speed up life along the frontiers; nowhere was the "go-ahead" spirit so extravagantly shown, and nowhere the speculative urge so strongly exhibited. These were by-products of a faith in the future that was justified as long as westering was the way of the present.

Visions of the United States as the greatest nation on earth helped mold the nationalistic spirit. Everywhere in America during the nineteenth century, but most particularly in the Wests, travelers were buttonholed by natives who assured them that the United States had the best government, the rosiest future, the strongest army, and the handsomest people in the world. This faith was partly an outgrowth of frontier optimism, but it was bolstered by the pioneering experience. The habit of migration helped nationalize characteristics and create nation-wide institutions. The necessity for expansion allowed the federal government to enlarge its power at the expense of local attachments. Demands for internal improvements and problems associated with the disposal of the public domain encouraged a partnership between the nation and the states that undermined provincialism. The ardent nationalism that characterized the United States in the nineteenth century was the product of many forces, but one was the expansion of the frontier. Here, as in other areas of thought and action, the faith in progress that was rooted in the westering experience had altered the value judgments and belief of the American people.

&§«§ TO MEN and women whose characters and way of life had been partially molded by two centuries of expansion, the "closing" of the frontier in 1890 meant a difficult period of readjustment. Generations of Americans had looked to the cheap lands of the West as escalators to wealth and higher status. Now they must accustom themselves to a relatively closed-space existence, with an appropriate reappraisal of the role of government in their lives, and essential shifts in the national psychology. Fortunately time was available for these adjustments, for the pronouncement of the director of the census that "there can hardly be said to be a frontier line" after 1890 was distinctly premature. Actually all the trans-Mississippi West of that day, excluding California, contained only twice as many cultivated acres as the single state of Ohio. So expansion continued, some to fill gaps where cultivable lands remained, some to subdue marginal areas with improved farming techniques, some to open new frontiers by irrigation. Four times as much government land was homesteaded between 1890 and the present as between 1862 and 1890. The national center of population moved steadily toward the Pacific in the twentieth century, from a point in central Indiana where it rested in 1890 to a spot near Centralia, Illinois, in 1960. The "westward tilt" of the continent has continued to spill people toward the Pacific even with the frontier "closed."

Yet the stark fact remained that the opportunity for expansion was declining, and that the social order was evolving from its agricultural to its industrial stage. Everywhere, for all to see, were the physical manifestations of the new order: mushrooming cities, complexes of factories, transportation networks geared to the needs of international markets, a growing labor force increasingly conscious of its class status, a diminishing number of farmers. No longer was the agrarian the solid, steadfast symbol of integrity to American youth; glamorous roles in the new mythology were assigned to business titans, while the farmer became a "hick" or a "hayseed." No longer could wage earners dream of escaping from their factories to the cheap lands of the West. Now they must work as their employers dictated or perish, just as farmers must learn to preserve their soils and lavish capital on permanent improvements, just as industrialists must discover how to exist by digging deeper into known resources rather than exploiting new deposits. These were hard lessons to learn. They required not only new techniques, but a new understanding of the nature of society.

They must be learned, for the age of geographical expansion was drawing to a close throughout the Western world. Since the dawn of the sixteenth century Western man had lived by engulfing new areas and utilizing virgin resources. Columbus and those who followed him had revealed a whole treasure-trove of riches awaiting use by Europeans: the Americas, Africa, Australia, the Pacific Islands. The discovery of this Great Frontier changed overnight the man-land ratio in the Western world from 26.7 to the square mile to 4.8 to the square mile. No longer necessary were the strict controls needed when men lived shoulder to shoulder: absolute monarchs, an authoritarian church, a social order governed by a caste system, the rigid regulation of economic activities. Now men were freer to move about, socially as well as physically, and to improve themselves. During the next four centuries new opportunities opened along the Great Frontier helped increase population by 625 percent and the supply of precious metals by 18,308 percent. This spelled prosperity, and prosperity allowed the Western world to substitute freedom for absolutism. Capitalistic free-enterprise systems replaced serfdom, democratic governments toppled tyrannical rulers, liberal churches rose to challenge religious authoritarianism, legal institutions were recast to impose fewer restraints on individual enterprise, philosophical beliefs were remolded to glorify the individual and the gospel of work by which he succeeded. Freedom sounded its own death knell by stimulating expansion; by 1930 the man-land ratio of 29.5 for the first time in four centuries surpassed that of the year 1500. Not only the United States, but all of the Western world, now had to adjust to a closed-space existence.[1]

Nor could this adjustment be delayed, despite the visions of publicists who conjured up new frontiers to replace the old. Opportunity, they preached, as great as that offered by cheap lands, beckoned along the frontiers of electricity, of automation, of space. That these areas of expansion will provide opportunity for the upward mobility of millions seems indisputable, but equally indisputable is the fact that the form and nature of this opportunity has been forever altered by the passing of the frontier. The new science and technology will create jobs, but they will be jobs in corporations or government bureaucracies where advancement depends on cooperative endeavor. The passing of the geographical frontier doomed the agricultural pioneer or the small entrepreneur who would scale the social ladder by the application of his own energies to untapped resources. The principal distinguishing feature of old America—the opportunity for the self-employed to win personal vertical advancement through individual enterprise—cannot be duplicated in the new America of the twentieth century.

Political realization of the altered circumstances has encouraged a widening of governmental power and activity. President Theodore Roosevelt's "Square Deal" stressed conservation and control of business on the premise that competition for the resources remaining would breed a dog-eat-dog social order unless regulated by national authority. President Woodrow Wilson's "New Freedom" sought to insure continuing economic opportunity to the individual in a frontier-less land by checking the trend toward industrial monopoly. President Franklin D. Roosevelt's "New Deal" was based on the belief that men must live with others in a world where flight to a frontier was impossible, and that the government must offer them the security formerly provided by the "safety valve" of cheap lands. President Harry S Truman's "Fair Deal" and President John F. Kennedy's "New Frontier" were designed to assure comfort and security through welfare legislation rather than through the free enterprise possible in an expanding society. President Lyndon B. Johnson's "Great Society" envisaged governmental activity in a variety of areas that would have been unacceptable to an earlier generation. Rightly or wrongly, the American people have signified their willingness to abandon certain freedoms for security and opportunity that their ancestors believed could be found in the West.

JUST AS the passing of the frontier has wrought a change in political philosophy, so has it slowly altered the national character. With the spread of the industrial-urban complex in the twentieth century, certain traits associated with the rural social order, and others valuable in an expanding society, have eroded, some to disappear, others to persist in somewhat altered form. Yet frontier-bred characteristics still help explain some of the differing character traits that distinguish Americans from other peoples of the world. We can understand their persistence only if we realize *how* the pioneering experience influenced later generations, and *why* it no longer does so in all areas of behavior.

The avenues through which these characteristics were spread over a wide geographic area were many. Continuing communication between the seaboard and successive Wests allowed ideas and attitudes, no less than goods, to flow in both directions; as Eastern culture hurried the maturing of the frontier by transmission westward, Western social attitudes altered the viewpoint of the seaboard by transmission eastward. Their reception was aided by the maternal concern with which the East viewed the West, and by the impact of frontier resources on older economies. The movement of wealth eastward created opportunities for individual self-improvement behind as well as in the areas of exploitation, while the flow of migrants between older societies and new loosened the social structures of established communities. Upward mobility was stimulated in the East, operating on a descending scale from the outposts of civilization to the seaboard, and even affecting Europe. The rags-to-riches vision which endowed the pioneers with so many of their distinctive characteristics inspired much of the Western world during its era of expansion.

The social environment of the Wests was transmittible over time as well as space. In this sense it differed from the physical environment that changed so rapidly under the impact of civilization that its influence was felt only briefly. This was not the case with the social environment, for the sequential exploitation of natural resources continued year after year, maintaining as it did so the atmosphere of progress that underlay alterations in character traits associated with frontier opportunity. Men infected with the "go-ahead" spirit that it engendered remained infected, even after the era of initial opportunity had passed. Children who had been moved frequently from frontier to frontier had less attachment to place than those reared in one community, and were more inclined to move themselves when they reached maturity. Discussions of material values, or anti-intellectualism, or the role of females in society, fastened attitudes on children that persisted through their lives—and were passed on to their children. Thus did the social environment perpetuate itself after the passing of the frontier that gave it birth. Its vestiges are apparent in the mores of modern America, even though they are slowly receding before the advance of urban-industrial values.

The traits that have eroded most rapidly in the twentieth-century United States are those closely associated with rural life and thought. Collectively, Americans are no longer considered boastful "puffers," compensating for their subconscious sense of inferiority by showing a brash face to the world. They are no longer reputed to be inquisitive busybodies, prying into the private lives of strangers obliging enough to submit to their questions. They no longer enjoy reputations for holding wide their doors to every passer-by, as did their pioneer ancestors eager for tidbits of information to enlighten their lonely lives, although the ease with which Americans still greet strangers is supposedly in sharp contrast with the shy aloofness of the Englishman's image. Concern with others has lessened amidst the impersonality of the modern city.

Anticultural prejudices noticeable in frontier America have also weathered away. As machines assume burdens that once busied man, and as mechanization elevates the living standard, time is released for abstract thought and esthetic creativity. This has altered popular attitudes toward work; endless labor is no longer essential to social respectability, and leisure no longer a sin against society. For twentieth-century Americans patronage of the arts is the gateway to elite status, just as was the acquisition of wealth a century ago. Yet relics of past attitudes remain. The amount of time and money devoted to cultural pursuits is less among American businessmen than among their overseas counterparts. Nor have the artist and the abstract thinker (unless he be a physicist) achieved the rank accorded them abroad; anti-intellectualism is still noticeable among a segment of the people who find satisfaction in ridiculing "eggheads." These outworn attitudes, hopefully, are destined for extinction, but their persistence demonstrates a difference between the United States and Europe partly traceable to the frontiering experience.

The optimism that made pioneer life endurable has also been a victim of twentieth-century developments. This was dealt a killing blow by the Great Depression of the 1930s. The collapse of an economic structure believed to be as firm as Gibraltar, the dazed perplexity of the nation's leaders as they tried to explain why, the uncertain groping toward a solution, all offered testimony to the degree to which a benign past fixed the expectations of the people. Before recovering from this blow, they saw their country plunged into a world war and into the strange new world that emerged from that cataclysm. Suddenly they realized that they were no longer masters of their own destiny. The protecting seas around them had been transformed into potential highways for aggressors. Their democratic beliefs were challenged by alien philosophies that unaccountably appealed to emerging nations of the non-Western world. Their monopoly in technological progress disappeared as they lagged behind in the race toward outer space and nuclear destruction. A nightmare present had suddenly replaced a golden dream of the future.[2]

Traditional optimism was scattered by these developments, leaving the people grasping for some alternative. Eventually, perhaps, a philosophy of realism will be substituted for a philosophy of expectation, as it has in older nations of the Western world. In time Americans may learn that men everywhere are more prisoners than masters of the era in which they live, and that no nation, no matter how powerful, can shape global society to its own image. Yet these realizations come slowly and painfully to a people bred in a tradition of frontier optimism.

The arrogant nationalism of the past has also been altered by the erosion of the nation's ego. Internally the United States of today is more tightly united than it was a century ago; the continuing ebb and flow of population, the extension of federal authority and the contraction of local authority, the nationalization of markets and consumer goods distribution, have all contributed to a sense of unity surpassing that of frontier America. In external relations, however, modern events have forced a searching appraisal of the national spirit. The unexpected contraction of the "area of freedom" and the realization that it would contract even more rapidly were not its borders defended by force, have disturbed the equilibrium of the American people no less than the equilibrium of the world. Americans have not questioned the virtues of their own political system, or lessened their loyalties except among extremist groups. But the braggadocio disapproved by travelers a century ago has been displaced by a quieter, more contemplative, type of patriotism. The nationalism known to frontiersmen has given way to another that may prove more enduring, and that certainly is better adjusted to a contracting world.

ᴥᔑᴥᔑ WHILE OPTIMISM, nationalism, and certain rural traits have been abandoned or altered, other frontier characteristics persist and even thrive in the twentieth century, although sometimes in slightly modified form. In general, those that have endured have proven suitable to an industrial-urban environment, and to a prospering social order. The good times that have blessed the United States through most of the postfrontier years have provided a climate for their survival, no less than did the boom era of expansion.

Certainly there has been no slackening of faith in political democracy, and only a slight lessening in the practice of social democracy. Political democracy has been broadened by the extension of federal authority; the expansion of the franchise by the forced removal of poll tax restrictions and the opening of ballot boxes to persons of all races and creeds have registered democratic gains as impressive as those of the Jackson era. Nor has the spirit of egalitarianism in social relations disappeared. Servants may no longer wish to be called "helps," and certainly do not insist on dining with their masters or joining the family bridge game afterward, but they are still difficult to obtain in a land where menial tasks are considered downgrading. A relative lack of class feeling also distinguishes the United States when contrasted with modern Europe; the insistence of people on all social levels that they belong to the "middle class"; the easy familiarity of the taxicab driver or elevator operator in striking up a conversation with the city's bigwigs; the willingness of elite groups to open their ranks to newcomers, all indicate that the spirit of frontier equality has persisted.

Social mobility is similarly a fact of life in today's America no less than in frontier America. Although opportunity has slowly lessened with the stratification of society, both the belief and practice of self-elevation have been kept alive by a variety of factors: the persistence of the rags-to-riches myth, the multiplication of opportunities for jobs in the expanding industrial order, the creation of upper-status posts by the growth of managerial functions, and the prosperity that allowed the United States to maintain a higher standard of living than any other nation. Just as in frontier times the opportunity for advancement offered by successive Wests weakened class distinctions and loosened stratified societies, so now does industrial opportunity ease passage from one level to another. Comparable opportunity in Europe has stimulated social mobility there until the rate of advance is about that in the United States. But in the *belief* that every man of proven ability has the right and duty to scale the ladder of success, and in the manner in which the higher ranks open to receive him, America differs from the Old World. The tradition, if not the fact, of unrestricted progress for the individual was woven into the national consciousness by frontiering, and there it remains.

The same can be said of other characteristics that were etched deeply into the national character during the era of expansion, and that persist in the prosperous mid-twentieth century climate. Wastefulness is still a national trait, for although conservationists have checked the ruthless extermination of wild life and have slowed the wholesale destruction of forest and mineral wealth, the "throw-away" compulsion prevails as it did a century ago. "Disposable" and "planned obsolescence" are key words in the American vocabulary far more than in the European. Popular attitudes supporting these extravagances have not been duplicated overseas; they are products of the frontier heritage and frontier prosperity.

Akin to the habit of wastefulness is the rebellion of the American people against traditionalism. This manifests itself in their lack of attachment to place; they move about today almost as frequently as did their pioneer ancestors who pursued illusive fortune across the continent. It is revealed also in their impatience with time-tested techniques. Anything new or different is viewed by Americans as desirable, just as it is considered by tradition-bound Europeans to be suspect. This has been an important national asset, for constant experimentation and improvement in production techniques have allowed the United States to compete in world markets despite higher wages and living standards. Today this gap is narrowing as the goal of prosperity and the stern fact of competition drives all countries of the Western world into technological experimentation. But the head start enjoyed by the United States can be credited in part to a frontier social environment in which change was the order of the day.

Hard work, and with it a jaundiced view of all who shirk their social obligations, has similarly remained a passion of the American people. A leisure class can and does exist in the twentieth-century United States, but in numbers, in influence, and in public esteem it ranks below its counterparts in older nations. Nor do Americans indulge themselves as do their cousins overseas; they may have a good time on the golf links or at ski resorts, but such luxuries are only for holidays or after hours. The recently introduced "coffee break" is the only permissible interruption in the working day; the leisurely luncheon, the prolonged "tea time," the peaceful siesta, the national custom of closing shops at a respectable hour of the afternoon, are alien to the nation's philosophy. Even the middle-class custom of the "cocktail hour" provides such strong stimulants that a lesser time is needed to achieve a given level of exhilaration than with the *apéritifs* of Europe. Today's American works hard and plays hard not only because his country's prosperity offers opportunity for self-promotion, but more importantly because the respectability of labor has been enshrined in the national consciousness by the frontier past.

Nor has the pioneer era's undue respect for women completely vanished in a world in which equality of the sexes is proclaimed by reformers as a social ideal. Today the man–woman ratio has narrowed, and today the gentler sex jostles the stronger for posts in office and factory, but the frontier tradition of deference is too strong to be dislodged. Despite some indications to the contrary, most males continue to carry the bundles on shopping tours, rise when ladies enter the room, and allow their wives free access to a wonderland of luxuries through the use of charge-a-plates and joint banking accounts —all customs that strike Europeans as indisputable proof of the insanity of men in the United States.

&§&§ THESE, THEN, are the frontier's bequests to the United States of the twentieth century. A new physical environment of machines and cities has changed the face of the land and lessened differences between nations of the Western world. But relics of the pioneer heritage remain to distinguish Americans from their contemporaries beyond the seas. Their faith in democratic institutions, their belief in equality, their insistence that class lines shall never hinder social mobility, their wasteful economy, their unwillingness to admit that automation has lessened the need for hard work, their lack of attachment to place, their eagerness to experiment and to favor the new over the old, all mark the people of the United States as unique. To say that these characteristics and attitudes were solely the result of a pioneering past is to ignore many other forces that have helped shape the American character. But to deny that three centuries of frontiering endowed the people with some of their most distinctive traits is to neglect a basic molding force that has been the source of the nation's greatest strength—and some of its most regrettable weaknesses.

Notes

Chapter 1
The History of a Theory

1 The extent of the literature on this subject is suggested in Michael Mc-Giffert, "Selected Writings on American National Character," *American Quarterly*, XV (Summer 1963), pp. 270–288.

2 Cited in Rush Welter, "The Frontier West as Image of American Society, 1776–1860," *Pacific Northwest Quarterly*, LII (January 1961), pp. 2–3.

3 Francis Parkman, *The Old Régime in Canada* (Boston, 1893), p. 395; Francis Parkman, *History of the Conspiracy of Pontiac* (Boston, 1898), p. xiii.

4 Cited in Harry H. Clark, "Lowell—Humanitarian, Nationalist, or Humanist?" *Studies in Philology*, XXVII (July 1930), pp. 431–432.

5 Alexis de Tocqueville, *Democracy in America* (New York, 1954), II, 371–382; James Bryce, *The American Commonwealth* (New York, 1889), II, 681.

6 The views of Sumner and Marx are summarized in Edith H. Parker,

"William Graham Sumner and the Frontier," *Southwest Review*, XLI (Autumn 1956), p. 359. The author of this article concludes that by the summer of 1893 Sumner had developed the frontier theory virtually as it was later stated by Turner. Actually Sumner's conclusions, while suggestive, fail to recognize the importance of the frontier in molding the American character.

7 Editorial in California *Daily Times*, 1868, quoted in Charles A. Barker, *Henry George* (New York, 1955), p. 96.

8 The comment of 1834 can be found in Robert Baird, *View of the Valley of the Mississippi* (Philadelphia, 1834), pp. 100–102. The others are quoted in Welter, "The Frontier West as Image of American Society," *loc. cit.*, p. 5.

9 Hubert H. Bancroft, *Essays and Miscellany* (San Francisco, 1890), pp. 189, 191. An excellent discussion of the writers who first suggested the frontier's influence is in Herman C. Nixon, "Precursors of Turner in the Interpretation of the American Frontier," *South Atlantic Quarterly*, XXVIII (January 1929), pp. 83–89.

10 Edwin L. Godkin, "Aristocratic Opinions of Democracy," *North American Review*, CCVI (January 1865), pp. 194–232. Turner did not hear of Godkin's article until it was called to his attention by Professor Andrew C. McLaughlin of the University of Michigan. He read it carefully, chuckled, and said: "Godkin has stolen my thunder." This story was told to Dr. Fulmer Mood by Harold R. Shurtless, who had heard it from Professor McLaughlin. It appears in Fulmer Mood, "Turner's Formative Period," in Frederick Jackson Turner, *The Early Writings of Frederick Jackson Turner* (Madison, Wis., 1938), p. 39.

11 The best discussion of this subject is in Lee Benson, "The Historical Background of Turner's Frontier Essay," *Agricultural History*, XXV (April 1951), pp. 59–82. Some additional information is in Nixon, "Precursors of Turner," *loc. cit.*, pp. 87–89.

12 Frederick J. Turner to Carl Becker, December 16, 1925, Frederick Jackson Turner Papers, Henry E. Huntington Library, TU Box 34 (Hereafter cited as Turner Papers, HEH). For an extended discussion of Turner's early life and its influence on his frontier theory see Ray A. Billington, "Young Fred Turner," *Wisconsin Magazine of History*, XLVI (Autumn 1962), pp. 38–48.

13 Turner to Caroline Mae Sherwood, September 5, 1887, Turner Papers, HEH, TU Box A.

14 *Ibid.*, March 25, 1888, Turner Papers, HEH, TU Box A.

15 Commonplace Book for *c.* 1885, Turner Papers, HEH, TU Vol. III, Book I.

16 Turner to Carl Becker, December 16, 1925, Turner Papers, HEH, TU Box 34.

17 Among the most useful volumes on the psychology of creative thought are Jacques Hadamard, *The Psychology of Invention in the Mathematical Field* (Princeton, N.J., 1949); D. M. Johnson, *The Psychology of Thought and Judgment* (New York, 1955); and Robert Thomson, *The Psychology of Thinking* (Baltimore, Md., 1959). A delightful series of descriptions of experiments in the field is in George Humphrey, *Directed Thinking* (New York, 1948).

18 *Catalogue of the University of Wisconsin* (Madison, Wis., 1891), pp. 114–116; (Madison, Wis., 1892), pp. 97–99; (Madison, Wis., 1893), pp. 61–62.

19 The map employed five groups of increasing density: I 2–6 inhabitants to the square mile, II 6–18, III 18–45, IV 45–90, and V over 90. Francis A. Walker, *Statistical Atlas of the United States Based on the Results of the Ninth Census 1870* (n.p., 1874), p. 4, plates XVI–XIX. Accession records of the State Historical Society of Wisconsin, where Turner worked, show that the volume was acquired in the 1880s. Evidence in his manuscript reading notes suggests that he used the volume in 1891. One note, headed "Frontier," begins: "Walker puts body of continuous settlement thus." Turner Papers, HEH, TU 3 x 5 Drawer No. 1. Two learned discussions of the development of map-making techniques essential to understanding Walker's contribution are Fulmer Mood, "A British Statistician of 1854 Analyzes the Westward Movement in the United States," *Agricultural History*, XIX (July 1945), pp. 142–151, and especially Fulmer Mood, "The Rise of Official Statistical Cartography in Austria, Prussia, and the United States, 1855–1872," *Agricultural History*, XX (October 1946), pp. 209–225. The same author's "The Concept of the Frontier, 1871–1898: Comments on a Select List of Source Documents," *Agricultural History*, XIX (January 1945), pp. 24–30, lists and describes twenty census publications of the period whose references to the frontier might have influenced Turner.

Mood's "The Development of Frederick Jackson Turner as a Historical Thinker," Colonial Society of Massachusetts, *Transactions, 1937–1942,* XXXIV (Boston, 1943), pp. 283–352, brilliantly describes this phase of Turner's career.

20 "Review of: 'Statistical Atlas of the United States," *The International Review,* II (January, 1875), p. 133.

21 Fletcher W. Hewes and Henry Gannett, *Scribner's Statistical Atlas of the United States Showing by Graphic Methods Their Present Condition and Their Political, Social and Industrial Development* (New York, c. 1883). This volume was published by Charles Scribner's Sons because Census Bureau funds were exhausted, but was prepared by the Bureau. Accession records of the State Historical Society of Wisconsin show that it was acquired in 1887. For information on the volume see Simon N. D. North, *Henry Gannett, President of the National Geographic Society, 1910–1914* (Washington, D.C., 1915).

22 *Ibid.,* p. xliv. The passage appears in the essay on "Density of Population," pp. xliii–xliv.

23 U.S. Bureau of the Census, 11th Census, 1890, *Census Bulletin No. 12. Population of the United States by States and Territories 1890* (Washington, D.C., 1890), p. 5.

24 U.S. Bureau of the Census, 11th Census, 1890. *Compendium of the Eleventh Census: 1890. Part I, Population* (Washington, D.C., 1892). The essay "Progress of the Nation" appears on pp. xxxv–cxxvii, and the statement on the closing of the frontier on p. xlviii.

25 For speculation on this subject see Rudolf Freund, "Turner's Theory of Social Evolution," *Agricultural History,* XIX (April 1945), pp. 79–80.

26 Turner Papers, HEH, TU 3 x 5 Drawer No. 1. Section: "Frontier."

27 Even as a student Turner may have been influenced by the textbook of an English historian, John A. Doyle, *History of the United States* (New York, 1876). Doyle used Walker's early maps on population density and his text not only stressed the westward movement but suggested its impact on the American character. The book was certainly known to Turner, for it had been reviewed by his mentor, William F. Allen, in the *Nation,* XXII (May 1876), p. 296.

28 Achille Loria, *Analisi della Proprietà Capitalista* (Turin, 1889), 2 volumes. More clearly than any other book that Turner might have read, this stresses the importance of "free" land in the evolution of American society and the significance of the passing of the frontier. Whether or not Turner actually read the volumes before publishing his own essay is not clear. A copy of the 1889 edition, in Italian, was owned by Turner, but he was innocent of any knowledge of that language. Lee Benson, "Achille Loria's Influence on American Economic Thought: Including His Contributions to the Frontier Hypothesis," *Agricultural History,* XXIV (October 1950), pp. 182–199, argues brilliantly that Loria influenced Turner, a viewpoint presented less strongly in James C. Malin, *Essays on Historiography* (Lawrence, Kan., 1953), pp. 14–17. The Turner Papers, HEH, TU File Drawer No. 15. Folder "Notes on A. Loria," contain a number of notes in Turner's hand summarizing Loria, but these are not to the section of the book that Benson maintains most influenced him.

29 Henry George, *Progress and Poverty. Lovell's Library Edition* (New York, 1882). A copy of this edition was owned by Turner, and heavily underlined through page 161. This and other evidence suggests that he read the volume in connection with his work for Professor Ely while a student at the Johns Hopkins University. One significant passage

dealing with the influence of the frontier was copied by Turner, apparently at this period or in the early 1890s, Turner Papers, HEH, TU File Drawer No. 15. That Turner's memory was not infallible was shown by a letter that he wrote to Merle Curti on January 5, 1931: "I never saw his earlier essays and think that I never read his *Progress and Poverty* before writing the 'Frontier.' . . . I have [since] read the *Progress and Poverty* discussion of the public domain and its influence upon the question of labor and capital. It is clear that, so far as the land question and legislation on its taxation goes, he had the idea before my 'Frontier.'" Turner Papers, HEH, TU Box 45.

30 Walter Bagehot, *Physics and Politics* (New York, 1880). A copy of this edition, badly worn and heavily underlined, was owned by Turner and presented to the Huntington Library. Such phrases as "breaking the cake of custom" that Turner later used were noted especially, on pp. 146–147, 150.

31 A clipping from the *Providence Journal*, June 19, 1889, reporting the lecture in full is in the Turner Papers, HEH, TU File Drawer No. 15, Folder "F. A. Walker PBK 1889." Passages pertinent to the frontier theory have been heavily underlined.

32 Emile Boutmy, *Studies in Constitutional Law. France-England-United States* (London, 1891). The notes in which Turner copied extensively from Boutmy are in Turner Papers, HEH, TU File Drawer No. 15.

33 André Churillon, "American Life from the French Point of View," *Review of Reviews*, V (May 1892), p. 488.

34 An excellent analysis of the manner in which Turner fused myths and theories of his day into his frontier thesis is Robert F. Berkhofer, Jr., "Space, Time, Culture and the New Frontier," *Agricultural History*, XXXVIII (January 1964), pp. 21–30.

35 Turner's review of the first two volumes of Roosevelt's history is in *The Dial*, X (August 1889), pp. 71–73. His essay on Von Holst is in the Turner Papers, HEH, TU File Drawer No. 15, Folder: "Essay on History of U.S. by Von Holst." This has been printed for the first time in Wilbur R. Jacobs, ed., *Frederick Jackson Turner's Legacy* (San Marino, Calif., 1965), pp. 85–104. A thirty-page manuscript of the lecture on American Colonization delivered before the Madison Literary Club is also in the Turner Papers, HEH, TU File Drawer No. 15, Folder: "American Colonization."

36 *The Aegis*, VII (November 4, 1892), pp. 48–52. Reprinted in Turner, *Early Writings of Frederick Jackson Turner*, pp. 71–83, and in Ray A. Billington, ed., *Frontier and Section* (Englewood Cliffs, N.J., 1961), pp. 28–36. Turner had earlier published a brilliant essay in which he set forth his views on history in general: "The Significance of History," *Wisconsin Journal of Education*, XXI (October 1891), pp. 230–234, and (November 1891), pp. 235–256. This is also reprinted in the two volumes mentioned above. For a discussion of the significance of these essays see Fulmer Mood, "Turner's Formative Period," in Turner, *Early Writings of Frederick Jackson Turner*, pp. 30–36.

37 Turner's former Johns Hopkins professor, Herbert B. Adams, thought so well of the "Problems" essay that he suggested it be expanded and read before a meeting of the American Historical Association scheduled to meet in connection with the Columbian Exposition at Chicago in July 1893. Herbert B. Adams to Turner, Turner Papers, HEH, TU Box 1. A formal invitation to read the paper was extended by President Charles Kendall Adams of the Uni-

versity of Wisconsin, himself a historian of note. Turner answered that his paper would be entitled "The Significance of the Frontier in American History." Turner to Charles K. Adams, February 23, 1893, University of Wisconsin, Presidents of University, General Correspondence, C. K. Adams, 1891–1901, Series 4/8/1 Box No. 4, Folder T–Z, University of Wisconsin Archives. He almost withdrew in favor of one of his graduate students a short time later, but was persuaded to prepare the paper. Turner to William F. Poole, May 10, 1893, William F. Poole Papers, The Newberry Library, April–June 1893. The letter, with interesting sidelights, is printed in W. L. Williamson, "A Sidelight on the Frontier Thesis: A New Turner Letter," *Newberry Library Bulletin,* III (April 1953), pp. 46–49.

38 The essay was first printed in the *Proceedings of the Forty-first Annual Meeting of the State Historical Society of Wisconsin* (Madison, Wis., 1894), pp. 79–112. It has been reprinted many times since. A note on the changes made by Turner in the early reprintings is in Fulmer Mood, "A Comparison of Differing Versions of 'The Significance of the Frontier,'" in Turner, *Early Writings of Frederick Jackson Turner,* pp. 275–292. The essay was included in the first volume of collected essays of Turner, *The Frontier in American History* (New York, 1920), pp. 1–38. The quotation is on p. 1.

39 Andrew Jackson Turner to Helen M. Turner, July 23, 1893, Turner Papers, HEH, TU Box B. The paper was mentioned by the Chicago *Tribune,* July 13, 1893. William F. Poole, who arranged the program, did not mention the paper in the official reports that he prepared for the *Dial,* XV (August 1, 1893), p. 60, or the *Independent,* XLV (July 20, 1893), p. 12. President Charles K. Adams,

in a private evaluation of Turner written for the publishers of *Johnson's Universal Encyclopedia* in July 17, 1893, also failed to mention the paper. Williamson, "Sidelight on the Frontier Thesis," *loc. cit.,* p. 49.

40 Hale to Turner, April 21, 1894; Walker to Turner, January 31, 1894; Andrews to Turner, February 6, 1894; Turner Papers, HEH, TU Box 1. Roosevelt to Turner, February 10, 1894, Frederick Jackson Turner Papers, The Houghton Library, Harvard University.

41 Frederick J. Turner, "The Problem of the West," *Atlantic Monthly,* LXXVIII (September 1896), pp. 289–297. An extended correspondence over this article between Turner and Walter Hines Page is in the Turner Papers, Houghton Library, covering the period May 29 to August 6, 1896. Clippings of favorable editorials from the Chicago *Tribune,* August 30, 1896, the Boston *Herald,* August 22, 1896, and other newspapers are in the Turner Papers, HEH, TU Box 54. The article's popularity, of course, was linked with the excitement over the election of 1896.

42 "Dominant Forces in Western Life," *Atlantic Monthly,* LXXIX (April 1897), pp. 433–443; "The Middle West," *International Monthly,* IV (December 1901), pp. 794–820; "Contributions of the West to American Democracy," *Atlantic Monthly,* XIC (January 1903), pp. 83–96. All of these essays are reprinted in Turner, *The Frontier in American History.*

43 For an impressive list of Turner's students see Mood, "Development of Frederick Jackson Turner as a Historical Thinker," *loc. cit.,* pp. 350–351.

44 A brief discussion of the introduction of the frontier theme into schoolbooks is in Oscar O. Winther, "The Frontier Hypothesis and the Historian," *Social Education,* XXI (November 1957), pp. 294–295. Its

first appearance, Professor Winther maintains, was in Mary P. Parmele, *The Evolution of an Empire* (1896).

45 Woodrow Wilson, "The Proper Perspective of American History," *Forum*, XIX (July 1895), pp. 544–559; "The Making of the Nation," *Atlantic Monthly*, LXXX (July 1897), pp. 1–14.

46 Ethel F. Fiske, ed., *The Letters of John F. Fiske* (New York, 1940), p. 693. Fiske writes of a lecture on this subject given in Missouri on March 14, 1895.

47 James Westfall Thompson, "Profitable Fields of Investigation in Medieval History," *American Historical Review*, XVIII (April 1913), p. 495. Professor Thompson later illustrated this point in a number of articles, and especially in his *An Economic and Social History of the Middle Ages, 300–1300* (New York, 1928), which devotes a whole chapter to comparing the process of expansion in medieval Germany and the United States.

48 Turner to Carl Becker, December 1, 1925, Turner Papers, HEH, TU Box 34. Earle D. Ross, "A Generation of Prairie Historiography," *Mississippi Valley Historical Review*, XXXIII (December 1946), pp. 391–410, explores the extent of Turner's influence on midwestern historians. As late as 1941 a survey showed that the great majority of Turner's students were unwilling to listen to a single criticism of their master's work. George W. Pierson, "American Historians and the Frontier Hypothesis in 1941," *Wisconsin Magazine of History*, XXVI (September 1942), pp. 40–43.

49 Norman Foerster, "American Literature," *Saturday Review of Literature*, II (April 3, 1926), pp. 677–679, pleaded for a reinterpretation of American literature that would recognize the "frontier spirit" as defined by Turner. The books mentioned were written by Ralph L.

Rusk (1925), Dorothy Dondore (1926), and Lucy L. Hazard (1927).

50 *Capital Times* (Madison, Wis.), January 15, 1931.

51 New York *Times*, September 24, 1932. A discussion of Turner's influence on New Deal thought is Curtis Nettels, "Frederick Jackson Turner and the New Deal," *Wisconsin Magazine of History*, XVII (March 1934), pp. 257–265.

52 James T. Adams, "Rugged Individualism Analyzed," *New York Times Magazine*, March 8, 1934, pp. 1–2, 11. For similar discussion on a scholarly level see James C. Malin, "Mobility and History," *Agricultural History*, XVII (October 1943), pp. 177–178, and "Space and History: Reflections on the Closed-Space Doctrines of Turner and Mackinder," *Agricultural History*, XVIII (July 1944), pp. 107–126.

53 This subject is explored in William A. Williams, "The Frontier Thesis and American Foreign Policy," *Pacific Historical Review*, XXIV (November 1955), pp. 379–395. A less searching discussion is in Lawrence S. Kaplan, "Frederick Jackson Turner and Imperialism," *Social Science*, XXVII (January 1952), pp. 12–16.

54 A brilliant analysis of the impact of the Turner thesis on intellectuals is in Warren I. Susman, "The Useless Past: American Intellectuals and the Frontier Thesis: 1910–1930," *Bucknell Review*, XI (March 1963), pp. 1–20.

55 Although the mass assault on Turner's theories began in the 1930s, a few attacks had been mounted a decade before, or even earlier. One of his friends, Edmond S. Meany, challenged Turner's statement that trading posts grew into towns in "The Towns of the Pacific Northwest Were Not Founded on the Fur Trade," American Historical Association, *Annual Report for 1909*

(Washington, 1911), pp. 165–172. Another close friend, Clarence W. Alvord, held in his review of the collected essays (1920) that the orderly procession of trappers, herdsmen, and farmers oversimplified a complex migration process. "The Frontier in American History," *Mississippi Valley Historical Review*, VII (March 1921), pp. 403–407. The first general assault came in 1925 with the publication of John C. Almack, "The Shibboleth of the Frontier," *Historical Outlook*, XVI (May 1925), pp. 197–202. Almack branded the frontier thesis as a "diluted type of Marxian determinism," and argued that the frontier itself had degraded American culture, harmed the economy, and contributed little to political development. Characteristically and prophetically, Turner wrote, on reading this article, that he had been surprised at the little criticism "that I got when historians began to take note of the interpretation, so that a reaction was to be expected." Turner to Arthur M. Schlesinger, May 5, 1925, Turner Papers, HEH, TU Box 34.

56 The most competent and effective critic on this score was George W. Pierson, "The Frontier and Frontiersmen of Turner's Essays," *Pennsylvania Magazine of History and Biography*, LXIV (October 1940), pp. 449–478, and "The Frontier and American Institutions. A Criticism of the Turner Theory," *New England Quarterly*, XV (June 1942), pp. 224–255. These arguments, and those of other critics, are repeated in Richard Hofstadter, "Turner and the Frontier Myth," *American Scholar*, XVIII (Autumn 1949), pp. 433–443.

57 Pierson, "Frontier and Frontiersmen," *loc. cit.*, p. 478, "Frontier and American Institutions," *loc. cit.*, pp. 247–251, 254.

58 Comment on Turner's tendency to be misled by metaphors is in Henry

Nash Smith, *Virgin Land: The American West as Symbol and Myth* (Cambridge, Mass., 1950), and Harold P. Simonson, "Frederick Jackson Turner: Frontier History as Art," *Antioch Review*, XXIV (Summer 1964), pp. 201–211.

59 Murray Kane, "Some Considerations on the Frontier Concept of Frederick Jackson Turner," *Mississippi Valley Historical Review*, XXVII (December 1940), pp. 386–391; David M. Potter, *People of Plenty: Economic Abundance and the American Character* (Chicago, 1954), pp. 23–24.

60 James C. Malin, "Ecology and History," *Scientific Monthly*, LXX (May 1950), p. 296; James C. Malin, "The Turner-Mackinder Space Concept of History," in Malin, *Essays on Historiography* (Lawrence, Kan., 1946), pp. 23–24; Malin, "Space and History," *loc. cit.*, pp. 65–74.

61 Kane, "Some Considerations on the Frontier Concept," *loc. cit.*, pp. 395–398. Ray A. Billington, "The Origin of the Land Speculator as a Frontier Type," *Agricultural History*, XIX (October 1945), pp. 204–222, points out Turner's failure to include speculators in his list of frontier types. He was berated for his neglect of religious factors in Gilbert J. Garraghan, "Non-Economic Factors in the Frontier Movement," *Mid-America*, XXIII (October 1941), pp. 263–271.

62 Kane, "Some Considerations on the Frontier Concept," *loc. cit.*, pp. 382–386; Pierson, "Frontier and American Institutions," *loc. cit.*, pp. 254–255; Morris Zaslow, "The Frontier Hypothesis in Recent Historiography," *Canadian Historical Review*, XXIX (June 1948), p. 156.

63 Potter, *People of Plenty*, pp. xxvi, 146–160, 161–165.

64 Arthur M. Schlesinger, "The City in American Civilization," *Mississippi Valley Historical Review*, XXVII (June 1940), pp. 43–67.

65 Charles A. Beard, "The Frontier in American History," *New Republic,* XXV (February 16, 1921), pp. 349–350; Louis M. Hacker, "Sections—or Classes," *Nation,* CXXXVII (July 26, 1933), pp. 108–110; Louis M. Hacker, "Frederick Jackson Turner: Non-Economic Historian," *New Republic,* LXXXIII (June 5, 1935), p. 108. Hacker's criticisms were challenged by Benjamin Stolberg, "Turner, Marx and the A.F. of L.," *Nation,* CXXXVII (September 1933), pp. 302–303.

66 This was the theme of the presidential address before the American Historical Association in 1945: Carlton J. H. Hayes, "The American Frontier—Frontier of What?" *American Historical Review,* LI (January 1946), pp. 199–216. The quotation is from p. 206. The concept of the United States as a frontier of Europe had been earlier developed by Dixon Ryan Fox, *Ideas in Motion* (New York, 1935).

67 Turner to Mrs. William Hooper, February 13, 1921, Turner Papers, HEH, TU-H Box 5.

68 Thomas C. Chamberlin's article, "The Method of Multiple Working Hypotheses," *Journal of Geology,* V (November–December 1897), pp. 837–848, revolutionized scientific research.

69 Frederick J. Turner, "The Development of American Society," [Illinois] *Alumni Quarterly,* II (July 1908), pp. 120–121.

70 Merle Curti to Turner, August 13, 1928, Turner Papers, IIEH, TU Box 38.

71 Turner to Carl Becker, February 13, 1926, Turner Papers, HEH, TU Box 35.

72 Turner, "Significance of History," in *Early Writings of Frederick Jackson Turner,* pp. 53–54.

73 Turner to Marcus L. Hansen, August 21, 1927, Turner Papers, HEH, TU Box 37. A modern student calls Turner the true father of immigration history. Edwin Mims, Jr., *American History and Immigration* (Bronxville, N.Y., 1950), pp. 13–56. Turner to A. C. McLaughlin, June 8, 1927, Turner Papers, HEH, TU Box 36, urged McLaughlin to establish a chair in "American population history" at the University of Chicago.

74 Turner to Arthur M. Schlesinger, April 18, 1922, Turner Papers, HEH, TU Box 31.

75 Turner to Kenneth Colgrove, July 31, 1912; Turner to Carl Becker, March 25, 1909, Turner Papers, HEH, TU Boxes 18, 12. When John F. Jameson accepted the chair in history at the Library of Congress in 1927, Turner urged him to develop the study of social history, which he felt would "help the new generation." J. F. Jameson to Turner, November 25, 1927, in Elizabeth Donnan and Leo F. Stock, eds., *An Historian's World: Selections from the Correspondence of John Franklin Jameson* (Philadelphia, 1956), p. 327.

76 Turner to Carl Becker, October 3, 1925, Turner Papers, HEH, TU Box 34.

77 Turner to Isaiah Bowman, December 24, 1931, Turner Papers, HEH, TU Box 53.

78 Turner to Marcus L. Hansen, January 7, 1926, Turner Papers, HEH, TU Box 35.

79 Turner to E. M. Violette, January 18, 1907, Turner Papers, HEH, TU Box 8.

80 Address delivered in 1901, reprinted in Frederick J. Turner, *The Significance of Sections in American History* (New York, 1932), p. 193. See also his "Notes for Talk to Thursday Club, Boston, March 17, 1921," in Turner Papers, HEH, TU File Drawer No. 15.

81 "Significance of History," in Turner, *Early Writings of Frederick Jackson Turner,* p. 57; Turner, "Development of American Society," *loc. cit.,* p. 121.

82 Turner to Arthur H. Buffinton,

October 20, 1926, Turner Papers, HEH, TU Box 35.

83 "Notes for Opening Remarks at the Beginning of Course in History of US 1880–1920," Turner Papers, HEH, TU Box 56; "Notes for Essay on the Significance of the Middle West, 1830–1850," Turner Papers, HEH, TU File Drawer No. 15; Turner to Merle Curti, August 27, 1928, Turner Papers, HEH, TU Box 38.

Chapter 2 How and Why Pioneers Moved Westward

1 This dual meaning was retained in the first major dictionary published in the United States, Noah Webster's *A Compendious Dictionary of the English Language* (1806), which defined a frontier as "furthest settlements," as well as a "limit, boundary, border on another country." In his 1828 *magnum opus, An American Dictionary of the English Language,* Webster defined the word only as a border or line between countries. For excellent discussions of this subject see Fulmer Mood, "Notes on the History of the Word *Frontier," Agricultural History,* XXII (April 1948), pp. 78–83, and especially, John T. Juricek, "American Usage of the Word 'Frontier' from Colonial Times to Frederick Jackson Turner," *Proceedings of the American Philosophical Society,* CX (February, 1966), pp. 10–34.

2 *The Century Dictionary,* published in six volumes between 1889 and 1891, and *Webster's International Dictionary of the English Language,* published in 1890, included these definitions among several others.

3 Turner attempted to define the word in an article on "Frontier" in *Johnson's Universal Cyclopaedia* (New York, 1894), III, 606–607. This article has been reproduced in Ful-

mer Mood, "Little Known Fragments of Turner's Writings," *Wisconsin Magazine of History,* XXIII (March 1940), pp. 338–341. He also struggled with a definition in his essay, "The First Official Frontier of the Massachusetts Bay," *The Frontier in American History* (New York, 1920), pp. 41, 52, and in an article on "Frontier in American Development," prepared for Andrew C. McLaughlin and Albert B. Hart, eds., *Cyclopedia of American Government* (New York, 1914), II, 61.

4 Turner to John C. Parish, April 14, 1926, Turner Papers, HEH, TU Box 35. Turner to L. L. Bernard, November 24, 1928, Turner Papers, HEH, TU Box 40.

5 This subject is explored in Fulmer Mood, "Studies in the History of American Settled Areas and Frontier Lines: Settled Areas and Frontier Lines, 1625–1790," *Agricultural History,* XXVI (January 1952), pp. 16–34.

6 For an understanding defense of Turner's use of the word "frontier" see H. C. Allen, "F. J. Turner and the Frontier in American History," in H. C. Allen and C. P. Hill, eds., *British Essays in American History* (London, 1957), p. 146. Both Turner's definitions, and those in this paragraph, can be attacked on two grounds. Some scholars claim that they ignore the Spanish-American frontier, others that they fail to recognize the importance of the Indian frontier in westward expansion. These viewpoints are clearly set forth in T. M. Pearce, "The 'Other' Frontiers in the American West," *Arizona and the West,* IV (Summer 1962), pp. 105–112, and Jack D. Forbes, "Frontiers in American History," *Journal of the West,* I (July 1962), pp. 63–73.

7 A convenient collection of diverse treatments of the wide variety of topics relating to motivation is in David C. McClelland, ed., *Studies*

in Motivation (New York, 1955). A standard work on an important phase of the subject is David C. McClelland, et. al., *The Achievement Motive* (New York, 1953).

8 Timothy Dwight, *Travels in New-England and New-York* (New Haven, Conn., 1821), II, 458.

9 Tyrone Power, *Impressions of America during the Years 1833, 1834, and 1835* (London, 1836), I, 304–305.

10 Quoted in Julia C. Altrocchi, *The Old California Trail* (Caldwell, Idaho, 1945), p. 25.

11 George P. Garrison, ed., "A Memorandum of M. Austin's Journey," *American Historical Review*, V (April 1900), pp. 525–526.

12 Morris Birkbeck, *Notes on a Journey in America* (London, 1818), p. 34.

13 Henry R. Schoolcraft, *Journal of a Tour into the Interior of Missouri and Arkansaw* (London, 1821), p. 93.

14 John E. Baur, "The Health Seekers in the Westward Movement, 1830–1900," *Mississippi Valley Historical Review*, XLVI (June 1959), pp. 91–110, John E. Baur, *The Health Seekers of Southern California* (San Marino, Calif., 1959), *passim*. The quest for health did not influence migrations until the Far West, with its dry climate, was being occupied. An observer in 1796 noted that migrants "seldom or ever consider whether the part of the country to which they are going is healthy or otherwise, at least they are scarcely ever influenced in their choice of a place of residence either by its healthiness or unhealthiness." Isaac Weld, *Travels through the United States of North America* (London, 1807), II, 93–94.

15 Charles J. Latrobe, *The Rambler in North America* (London, 1835), I, 84–87; Baynard Rush Hall, *The New Purchase; or, Seven and a Half Years in the Far West* (New York, 1843), I, 1.

16 Timothy Flint, *Recollections of the Last Ten Years* (Boston, 1826), pp. 241–242; Henry David Thoreau, "Walking," in *The Writings of Henry David Thoreau* (Boston, 1906), V, 217.

17 An example of the manner in which Easterners divided when offered an opportunity to move to the frontier was provided by the German Palatines who settled in the Hudson River valley in the early eighteenth century. When offered an opportunity to escape poverty and intolerable living conditions by moving to the Schoharie Valley frontier, only about one fourth responded. Walter A. Knittle, *Early Eighteenth Century Palatine Emigration* (Philadelphia, 1937), p. 221.

18 These concepts and illustrations are borrowed by permission from an unpublished essay by Dorothy Johansen, "Pacific Northwest Immigration," pp. 1–16. Professor Johansen shows that the image of law and order projected by the first Oregon pioneers attracted a different type of settler from that moving to California or Texas, where an image of lawlessness was created by Anglo-Spanish conflicts.

19 Quoted in Carl Bridenbaugh, *Myths and Realities: Societies of the Colonial South* (Baton Rouge, La., 1952), p. 122.

20 Douglass North, "International Capital Flows and the Development of the American West," *Journal of Economic History*, XVI (December 1956), pp. 493–505.

21 Albert H. Smyth, ed., *Writings of Benjamin Franklin* (New York, 1905–1907), II, 65; J. C. Fitzpatrick, ed., *Writings of George Washington* (Washington, 1931–1944), XXVIII, 206; A. A. Liscomb and A. L. Bergh, eds., *Writings of Thomas Jefferson* (Washington, 1903–1904), XI, 55.

22 Sidney Smith, *The Settler's New Home; or the Emigrant's Location* (London, 1849), p. 1; Hugh S. R. Elliott, ed., *Letters of John Stuart*

Mill (London, 1919), II, 299; Karl Marx, *Capital* (London, 1930), II, 857–858; Thomas Carlyle, quoted in Ernest Marchand, "Emerson and the Frontier," *American Literature,* III (May 1931), pp. 152–153.

23 W. Stull Holt, "Hegel, the Turner Hypothesis, and the Safety-Valve Theory," *Agricultural History,* XXII (July 1948), pp. 175–176.

24 For typical comments see Michael Chevalier, *Society, Manners and Politics in the United States* (Boston, 1839), p. 144, and Harriet Martineau, *Society in America* (New York, 1837), I, 292–293.

25 Edward Everett, "Flint's Condensed Geography and History," *North American Review,* XXVIII (January 1829), p. 82; Caleb Atwater in *Sangamo Journal* (Illinois), September 28, 1832, quoted in R. Carlyle Buley, *The Old Northwest* (Indianapolis, Ind., 1950), II, 45.

26 Roy M. Robbins, "Horace Greeley: Land Reform and Unemployment, 1837–1862," *Agricultural History,* VII (January 1933), pp. 18–41. *Congressional Globe,* 32nd Cong., 1st Sess., Appendix, p. 737 (April 22, 1852). For a thorough discussion of this subject see Helene S. Zahler, *Eastern Workingmen and National Land Policy, 1829–1862* (New York, 1941).

28 For a typical opinion see Edwin L. Godkin, "Aristocratic Opinions of Democracy," *North American Review,* CCVI (January 1865), pp. 194–232. The best discussion of the popular belief in a safety valve during this period is in Henry Nash Smith, *Virgin Land: The American West as Symbol and Myth* (Cambridge, Mass., 1950), pp. 165–173, 195–200.

29 Frederick J. Turner, "Contributions of the West to American Democracy," *Frontier in American History,* p. 259, and "Significance of the Mississippi Valley in American History," *ibid.,* p. 192.

30 Handwritten draft of lecture prepared about 1924, Turner Papers, HEH, TU File Drawer No. 14, unmarked folder.

31 In the first draft of a lecture on "The United States and Its Sections" prepared for delivery at the College of New Hampshire in 1922 he included the line: "the safety-valve of unoccupied free lands in the West has disappeared." In a draft prepared some time later, this line was crossed out. Turner Papers, HEH, TU File Drawer No. 14, unmarked folder. The whole paragraph was omitted when the lecture was published as "Sections and Nation," *Yale Review,* XII (October 1922), pp. 1–21.

32 Frederick J. Turner, *The United States, 1830–1850: the Nation and Its Sections* (New York, 1935), p. 278. Turner's students remembered that he paid no attention to the doctrine in his late teaching years. Rufus S. Tucker, quoted in George W. Pierson, "American Historians and the Frontier Hypothesis in 1941," *Wisconsin Magazine of History,* XXVI (September 1942), p. 53; E. E. Dale, "Memories of Frederick Jackson Turner," *Mississippi Valley Historical Review,* XXX (December 1943), pp. 356–357.

33 See for example John R. Commons, *History of Labour in the United States* (New York, 1926), I, 4; Victor S. Clark, *History of Manufactures in the United States, 1607–1860* (Washington, D.C., 1916), pp. 155, 364; Frederic L. Paxson, *When the West Is Gone* (New York, 1930), p. 123.

34 A brief discussion of the operation of the "resources" safety valve is in Chester W. Wright, "The Significance of the Disappearance of Free Land in Our Economic Development," *American Economic Review Supplement,* XVI (March 1926), p. 265. On the "sociopsychological" safety valve see Carter Goodrich, "The Australian and American Labor Movement," *The Economic*

Record, IV (November 1929). Goodrich shows that Australian workmen early developed a high degree of class consciousness and unionization, despite exceptionally high wages. This can be explained, he believes, by the fact that Australian workers *knew* they had no outlet to the West, while American workers *believed* they did.

35 Flint, *Recollections of the Last Ten Years,* p. 10; Power, *Impressions of America,* I, 304–305; Charles F. Hoffman, *A Winter in the West, by a New-Yorker* (New York, 1835), I, 286–287.

36 New York *Tribune,* April 8, 1857.

37 Nor did the Homestead Act of 1862 alter the situation, for speculators appropriated all of the best land, which was sold at a price beyond the reach of the average worker. Paul W. Gates, "The Homestead Act in an Incongruous Land System," *American Historical Review,* XLI (July 1936), pp. 652–681; Fred A. Shannon, "The Homestead Act and the Labor Surplus," *ibid.,* pp. 637–651. Clarence H. Danhof, "Farm-Making Costs and the 'Safety Valve'; 1850–1860," *Journal of Political Economy,* XLIX (June 1941), pp. 317–359, is the most thorough treatment of this subject.

38 See for example: Smith, *Settler's New Home,* pp. 87–88, and Nathan H. Parker, *The Iowa Handbook for 1856* (Boston, 1856), pp. 159–161.

39 Data to substantiate these generalizations are in the numerous studies attacking the safety-valve concept that appeared during the 1930s and 1940s. Among the most useful of these are Anne Bezanson, "Some Historical Aspects of Labor Turnover," in *Facts and Factors in Economic History* (Cambridge, Mass., 1932), pp. 692–708; Clarence H. Danhof, "Economic Validity of the Safety-Valve Doctrine," *Journal of Economic History Supplement* (December 1941), pp. 96–106; Carter Goodrich and Sol Davison, "The

Wage-Earner in the Westward Movement," *Political Science Quarterly,* LI (March 1936), pp. 64–66; and Murray Kane, "Some Considerations on the Safety Valve Doctrine," *Mississippi Valley Historical Review,* XXIII (September 1936), pp. 176–185.

40 An excellent study of this subject is Carl N. Degler, "The West as a Solution to Urban Unemployment," *New York History,* XXXVI (January 1955), pp. 63–85.

41 Goodrich and Davison, "Wage-Earner in the Westward Movement," *loc. cit.,* pp. 80–85. These data were gathered from newspapers in several Massachusetts and New York towns.

42 U.S. Bureau of the Census, *Eighth Census. Population* (1860), pp. xxxiv–xxxv. Fragmentary evidence to support this view is provided by the "letters of removal" given migrating New England Congregationalists by their pastors. Of eighteen such letters issued in Shutesbury only two were destined for the frontier; of thirty-eight given at Leverett between 1828 and 1845 only one was to a migrant bound for the West. Margaret R. Pabst, *Agricultural Trends in the Connecticut Valley Region of Massachusetts, 1800–1900* (Northampton, Mass. 1941), pp. 44–46.

43 Fred A. Shannon, "A Post Mortem on the Labor–Safety-Valve Theory," *Agricultural History,* XIX (January 1945), pp. 32–34, is the standard argument against the operation of an "indirect" safety valve after 1860.

44 Norman J. Simler, "The Safety-Valve Doctrine Re-Evaluated," *Agricultural History,* XXXII (October 1958), p. 253.

45 Herbert Heaton, "Other Wests Than Ours," *Journal of Economic History, Supplement* VI (December 1946), pp. 61–62.

46 Simler, "Safety-Valve Doctrine Re-Evaluated," *loc. cit.,* pp. 250–252.

47 *Ibid.,* pp. 252–257.

48 Ellen von Nardroff, "The American Frontier as Safety Valve—The Life,

Death, Reincarnation, and Justification of a Theory," *Agricultural History*, XXXVI (July 1962), pp. 138–142. For a criticism of this point of view see Henry M. Littlefield, "Has the Safety Valve Come Back to Life?" *Agricultural History*, XXXVIII (January 1964), pp. 47–49.

49 George G. S. Murphy and Arnold Zellner, "Sequential Growth, the Labor–Safety-Valve Doctrine and the Development of American Unionism," *Journal of Economic History*, XIX (September 1959), pp. 402–414.

50 *Ibid.*, pp. 414–419; Nardroff, "American Frontier as Safety Valve," *loc. cit.*, pp. 129, 137–138.

51 C. Warren Thornthwaite, *Internal Migration in the United States* (Philadelphia, 1934), pp. 8–10.

52 Liscomb and Bergh, eds., *Writings of Thomas Jefferson*, XVI, 74–75.

53 Mrs. Steele, *A Summer Journey in the West* (New York, 1841), p. 139. For similar comments by other travelers see Martineau, *Society in America*, I, 159, and Dwight, *Travels in New-England and New-York*, II, 459. The same observation is made by a careful contemporary observer in John L. McConnel, *Western Characters or Types of Border Life in the Western States* (New York, 1853), p. 271.

54 Ely had borrowed this concept from Friedrich List, *National System of Political Economy* (Philadelphia, 1856), p. 72. Ely's views, virtually as he imparted them in his Johns Hopkins lectures, are in his *An Introduction to Political Economy* (New York, 1889), pp. 40–41. This whole subject is admirably explored in Fulmer Mood, "The Development of Frederick Jackson Turner as a Historical Thinker," Colonial Society of Massachusetts, *Transactions, 1937–1942*, XXXIV (Boston, 1943), pp. 305–307.

55 Turner, *Frontier in American History*, p. 12. In a later essay, published in 1914, Turner noted that the colonial New England frontier did not advance by orderly stages, but by the mingling of various frontier types. Turner, "First Official Frontier of the Massachusetts Bay," *loc. cit.*, pp. 43–44.

56 Many travelers in the pre-Civil War era described these three frontier types, distinguishing clearly between them. Among the most thorough of these accounts are William N. Blane, *An Excursion through the United States and Canada, during the Years 1822–23* (London, 1824), pp. 179–180; Victor Collott, *A Journey in North America* (Paris, 1826), I, 109–114; Dwight, *Travels in New-England and New-York*, I, 459; Henry B. Fearon, *Sketches of America* (London, 1818), pp. 224–225; James Flint, *Letters from America* (Edinburgh, 1822), pp. 206–209; John H. Logan, *A History of the Upper Part of South Carolina* (Columbia, S.C., 1859), I, 149–151; Achille Murat, *A Moral and Political Sketch of the United States of North America* (London, 1833), pp. 45–79; and John M. Peck, *A New Guide for Emigrants to the West* (Boston, 1836), pp. 114–116. Turner's reading notes indicate that he used most of these works before 1893. Gerald G. Steckler, S.J., "North Dakota versus Frederick Jackson Turner," *North Dakota History*, XXVIII (Winter 1961), pp. 330–43, argues that the settlement process in North Dakota was more complex than suggested by Turner.

57 George W. Ogden, *Letters from the West* (New Bedford, Mass., 1823), pp. 16–17. Descriptions of the squatters abound in accounts of travelers to the West. Among the fullest are Thomas L. McKenney and James Hall, *History of the Indian Tribes of North America* (Philadelphia, 1838–1844), III, 87–88; Fortescue Cuming, *Sketches of a Tour to the Western Country* (Pittsburgh, Pa., 1810), p. 118; Elias P. Fordham, *Personal Narrative of Travels* (Cleveland,

Ohio, 1906), pp. 127–128; James Hall, *Sketches of History, Life, and Manners in the West* (Philadelphia, 1835), II, 54–56; and Martineau, *Society in America,* I, 162–163.

58 Birkbeck, *Notes on a Journey in America,* p. 122. For further comment on the health of the squatters see Dwight, *Travels in New-England and New-York,* II, 459, 462; John Melish, *Travels through the United States of America* (London, 1818), p. 373; and Francois M. Perrin du Lac, *Travels through the Two Louisianas and Among the Savage Nations of the Missouri* (London, 1807), pp. 38–39.

59 Travelers' testimony on the indolence of the squatters is plentiful. See for example: J. H. Beadle, *The Undeveloped West; or, Five Years in the Territories* (Philadelphia, 1873), p. 229; Eliza W. Farnham, *Life in Prairie Land* (New York, 1846), p. 330; Fordham, *Personal Narrative,* p. 156; Frederick Gerstaecker, *Wild Sports in the Far West* (Boston, 1859), p. 164; James Hall, *Letters from the West* (London, 1828), pp. 271–272; and Weld, *Travels through the States of North America,* I, 206.

60 Birkbeck, *Notes on a Journey in America,* p. 92; J. D. Borthwick, *Three Years in California* (Edinburgh, 1857), p. 2.

61 For evidence of the existence of squatters on the prairies and plains of the trans-Mississippi West see Samuel Bowles, *Across the Continent* (Springfield, Mass., 1866), pp. 20–21; Thomas Nuttall, *Journal of Travels into the Arkansas Territory* (Philadelphia, 1821), pp. 47, 51, 214–215; Frederick L. Olmsted, *A Journey Through Texas* (New York, 1857), p. 284; and especially Henry R. Schoolcraft, *Journal of a Tour into the Interior of Missouri and Arkansaw* (London, 1821), pp. 5–6, 15, 30–32, 37, 43–51.

62 The most thorough study of this sub-

ject is J. L. Moreno, *Who Shall Survive* (Washington, 1934). A classic study of the effect of anomie on one group of immigrants to America is in William I. Thomas and Florian Znaniecki, *The Polish Peasant in Europe and America* (New York, 1927), II, 1692–1701.

63 Thaddeus M. Harris, *The Journal of a Tour into the Territory Northwest of the Alleghany Mountains* (Boston, 1805), p. 59.

64 Most travelers in the West distinguished between squatters and small-propertied farmers. See as typical Francis Baily, *Journal of a Tour in the Unsettled Parts of North America* (London, 1856), p. 218; Hall, *Sketches of History, Life, and Manners in the West,* II, 66; McConnel, *Western Characters,* p. 108; and Alexander Mackay, *The Western World* (Philadelphia, 1849), II, 138–139.

65 Excellent descriptions of life on this frontier are in Baily, *Journal of a Tour,* pp. 217–219; Collot, *A Journey in North America,* I, 109–114; Flint, *Letters from America,* pp. 206–209; Fordham, *Personal Narrative,* pp. 125–127; Hall, *Letters from the West,* pp. 306–307; and Francois A. Michaux, *Travels to the Westward of the Alleghany Mountains* (London, 1805), p. 139.

66 Avery Craven, "The 'Turner Theories' and the South," *Journal of Southern History,* V (August 1939), pp. 291–314, shows that these successive stages operated in the advance of the Southern frontier, but with variations traceable to the labor and agricultural systems.

67 New York *Daily Tribune,* June 3, 1859, quoted in James C. Malin, "Mobility and History," *Agricultural History,* XVII (October 1943), p. 180. An indication of the success of speculators can be found in the fact that of 36 million acres of the public domain sold in Iowa, 27 million passed through the hands of jobbers.

Ray A. Billington, "The Garden of the World: Fact and Fiction," in John J. Murray, ed., *The Heritage of the Middle West* (Norman, Okla., 1958, pp. 48–49. No competent history of land speculation has been written, but information on speculators as a frontier type is in Ray A. Billington, "The Origin of the Land Speculator as a Frontier Type," *Agricultural History,* XIX (October 1945), pp. 204–222, and Paul W. Gates, "The Role of the Land Speculator in Western Development," *Pennsylvania Magazine of History and Biography,* LXVI (July 1942), pp. 314–333. Allan G. and Margaret B. Bogue, " 'Profits' and the Frontier Land Speculator," *Journal of Economic History,* XVII (March 1957), carefully analyzes profits made by two groups of speculators, one in Illinois and one in Nebraska, to conclude that their returns were somewhat greater than would have been received on other investments. This conclusion is bolstered in an excellent statistical study of Iowa land sales by Robert P. Swierenga, "Land Speculator 'Profits' Reconsidered: Central Iowa as a Test Case," *Journal of Economic History,* XXVI (March 1966), pp. 1–28, which reveals far larger profits than hitherto believed.

68 Thomas James, *Three Years Among the Indians and Mexicans* (St. Louis, Mo., 1916), pp. 101–102.

69 Latrobe, *Rambler in North America,* II, 139. An excellent study of the city as a frontier institution in the Ohio Valley is Richard C. Wade, *The Urban Frontier. The Rise of Western Cities, 1790–1830* (Cambridge, Mass., 1959).

70 George Booth, "Frontier Folk," *International Review,* IX (July 1880), p. 34. The best discussion of the westward migration of urban institutions is Bayard Still, "Patterns of Mid-Nineteenth Century Urbanization in the Middle West," *Missis-*sippi Valley Historical Review, XXVIII (September 1941), pp. 187–206.

Chapter 3 The Frontier and the American Character

1 This literary device is shamelessly borrowed from George R. Stewart, *American Ways of Life* (Garden City, N.Y., 1954), pp. 11–12.

2 For able discussions of this subject see Clyde Kluckhohn and M. A. Murray, *Personality in Nature, Society and Culture* (New York, 1949), pp. 41–45, and E. B. Taylor, *Primitive Culture* (New York, 1924), pp. 1–2. The historian attempting to summarize findings of social or physical scientists faces an impossible problem. He must either use the technical language of the discipline at the risk of proving incomprehensible to his lay readers, or he must try to translate their concepts into nontechnical language with the certainty of offending the scientists. The latter course has been followed in the pages that follow, with the realization that the inexact terminology fails to reflect the shades of meaning that the books and articles on which they are based do express.

3 George P. Murdock, "The Cross-Cultural Survey," *American Sociological Review,* V (June 1940), pp. 361–370; Logan Wilson and William L. Kolb, *Sociological Analysis* (New York, 1940), p. 69.

4 W. D. Wallis, "Geographical Environment and Culture," *Social Forces,* IV (June 1926), pp. 702–708.

5 W. N. and L. A. Kellogg, *The Ape and the Child* (New York, 1933); Kingsley Davis, "Extreme Isolation of a Child," *American Journal of Sociology,* XLV (May 1940), pp. 554–565; Kingsley Davis, "Final Note on a Case of Extreme Isola-

tion," *American Journal of Sociology,* LII (March 1947), pp. 432–437.

6 H. H. Newman, "Identical Twins," *Scientific Monthly,* XXXIV (February 1932), pp. 169–171; Robert S. Woodworth, "Heredity and Environment: A Critical Survey of Recently Published Material on Twins and Foster Children," *Social Science Research Bulletin No. 47* (New York, 1941); Horatio H. Newman, *Multiple Human Births* (New York, 1940), pp. 189–199.

7 Romanzo Adam, *Inter-Racial Marriage in Hawaii* (New York, 1937).

8 Edward A. Ross, "Ossification," *American Journal of Sociology,* XXV (March 1920), pp. 529–538.

9 Charles Loomis, *Social Relationships and Institutions in Seven New Rural Communities* (Washington, 1940), pp. 9, 15–16, 32. Loomis' conclusions are summarized and appraised in Allan G. Bogue, "Social Theory and the Pioneer," *Agricultural History,* XXXIV (January 1960), pp. 24–30. A second method of testing— by examining social customs in pioneer communities throughout the world—was made by James G. Leyburn, *Frontier Folkways* (New Haven, Conn., 1935). Unfortunately the author's evidence is not reliable, nor is his analysis thorough. Far more research on comparative frontiers is needed before conclusions can be drawn.

10 This subject is well discussed in Richard L. Power, *Planting Corn Belt Culture* (Indianapolis, Ind., 1953), which describes the mingling of Yankees and Southerners in Indiana.

11 Bogue, "Social Theory and the Pioneer," *loc. cit.,* pp. 33–34.

12 Victor A. Belaúnde, "The Frontier in Hispanic America," *Rice Institute Pamphlets,* X (1923), pp. 202–213. For a similar argument see Carlton J. H. Hayes, "The American Frontier—Frontier of What?" *American Historical Review,* LI (January, 1946), pp. 206–210.

13 For an elaboration of this argument see Ray A. Billington, "The Frontier in American Thought and Character," in Archibald R. Lewis and Thomas F. McGann, eds., *The New World Looks At Its History* (Austin, Texas, 1963), pp. 78–81.

14 An interesting study by Vianna Moog, *Bandeirantes and Pioneers* (New York, 1964), argues that the failure of Portugal to develop Brazil was due to the spirit of the conquerors who sought surface wealth without personal labor and were handicapped by feudal economic institutions and theories. He feels that the *bandeirantes,* or flag carriers, who roamed early Brazil as the *conquistadores* roamed New Spain, symbolized the reasons for this failure. This same point was made many years ago in Michael Chevalier, *Society, Manners and Politics in the United States* (Boston, 1839), pp. 425–427. This astute French visitor pointed out that between the Spanish and English occupation, the Reformation had unleashed new forces in Europe. "Her children," he goes on, "carried with them the germ of these principles and institutions, which were to secure to them the same supremacy in the New." Chevalier also speculates that if the English had met sturdy native foes, as did the Spaniards with the Aztecs, they would have developed a rigid military autocracy founded on the servitude of inferior races. Instead they could do away with all military establishments after the fall of Quebec.

15 For good descriptions of the French settlements and settlers in the Mississippi Valley see: John Bradbury, *Travels in the ·Interior of America, in the Years 1809, 1810, and 1811* (Liverpool, England, 1817), pp. 263–264; Chevalier, *Society, Manners and Politics in the United States,* pp. 276–281; Timothy Flint, *Recollections of the Last Ten Years* (Boston, 1826), p. 236; **Charles F.**

Hoffman, *A Winter in the West* (New York, 1835), I, 120–122; James Stuart, *Three Years in North America* (New York, 1833), II, 313–314, 324; and Isaac Weld, *Travels through the States of North America, and the Provinces of Upper and Lower Canada* (London, 1807), II 8–9.

16 Discussions of the Pennsylvania Germans in this context are in Richard H. Shryock, "British Versus German Traditions in Colonial Agriculture," *Mississippi Valley Historical Review*, XXVI (June 1939), pp. 39–54, and John G. Gagliardo, "Germans and Agriculture in Colonial Pennsylvania," *Pennsylvania Magazine of History and Biography*, LXXXIII (April 1959), pp. 192–218. The latter is descriptive rather than analytical. The failure of the Wisconsin Germans to follow frontier practices is stressed in Joseph Schafer, "The Yankee and Teuton in Wisconsin," *Wisconsin Magazine of History*, VI (December 1922), pp. 131–135; (March 1923), pp. 261–279; (June 1923), pp. 386–402. Travelers who commented on the persistence of Old World customs among the Germans included, for Pennsylvania, Francois A. Michaux, *Travels to the Westward of the Alleghany Mountains* (London, 1805), pp. 63–64, and Charles A. Murray, *Travels in North America during the Years 1834, 1835, and 1836* (London, 1839), I, 187; and, for the Midwest, Reginald Aldridge, *Ranch Notes in Kansas, Colorado, the Indian Territory, and Northern Texas* (New York, 1884), p. 35, Frederick L. Olmsted, *A Journey through Texas* (New York, 1857), pp. 145–147, and Harriet Martineau, *Society in America* (New York, 1837), I, 298–299.

17 James Caird, *Prairie Farming in America* (New York, 1859), p. 97. Similar observations on national differences are in Flint, *Recollections of the Last Ten Years*, pp. 236–237,

and Charles Lyell, *Travels in North America* (London, 1845), II, 70.

18 Hoffman, *Winter in the West*, I, 106–107. Peter Kalm, *Travels into North America* (London, 1772), I, 350, points out that when Swedes first arrived in America they built barns as was their custom, but soon abandoned the practice in imitation of the Yankees. As a result many of their cattle froze to death.

19 Richard C. Wade, *The Urban Frontier* (Cambridge, Mass., 1959), pp. 316–318. For a similar argument see Earl W. Hayter, "Sources of Early Illinois Culture," *Transactions of the Illinois State Historical Society*, XLIII (1936), pp. 84–86.

20 Charles L. Camp, ed., *James Clyman, American Frontiersman, 1792–1881* (San Francisco, Calif., 1928), p. 35.

21 Samuel Bowles, *Across the Continent* (Springfield, Mass., 1866), pp. 256–257.

22 Hoffman, *A Winter in the West*, I, 107.

23 Martineau, *Society in America*, I, 338. For comment on this point see Richard H. Shryock, "Cultural Factors in the History of the South," *Journal of Southern History*, V (August 1939), pp. 242–243. A penetrating psychological study of two fictional characters as they respond to the Dakota environment after migration from northern Europe is in Ole Edvart Rölvaag, *Giants in the Earth*. For a discussion of this theme in the novel see Robert Steensma, "Rölvaag and Turner's Frontier Thesis," *North Dakota Quarterly*, XXVII (Autumn 1959), pp. 100–104.

24 E. Stanley, *Journal of a Tour in America, 1824–1825* (n.p., 1930), pp. 181–182; Timothy Flint, *History and Geography of the Mississippi Valley* (Cincinnati, Ohio, 1832), I, 137.

25 Caroline M. Kirkland, *Western Clearings* (New York, 1845), p. vi.

26 Anonymous writer in *Biblical Rep-*

ertory and Theological Review, III (July 1836), pp. 381–382.

27 Frederick Marryat, A Diary in America (London, 1839), I, 17–18; Simon A. O'Ferrall, A Ramble of Six Thousand Miles Through the United States of America (London, 1832), pp. 228–229.

28 Flint, History and Geography of the Mississippi Valley, I, 135; James Hall, Sketches of History, Life and Manners in the West (Philadelphia, 1835), I, 216.

29 James Bryce, The American Commonwealth (Chicago, 1891), II, 697. James Hall, Letters from the West (London, 1828), pp. 236–246, is a particularly full contemporary discussion of this transformation.

30 John L. McConnel, Western Characters or Types of Border Life in the Western States (New York, 1853), pp. 110–116.

31 William A. Baillie-Groham, Camps in the Rockies (New York, 1882), pp. 22–23.

32 Bryce, American Commonwealth, II, 696–706.

33 Alexander Mackay, The Western World (Philadelphia, 1849), II, 119. Another British traveler expressed this sentiment somewhat more strongly when he wrote: "If you prefer cleanliness to filth, modesty to inquisitiveness, honesty to theft, civility to vulgar effrontery of men who mistake lawless license for liberty," do not go West. E. Howitt, Selections from Letters Written during a Tour through the United States, in the Summer and Autumn of 1819 (Nottingham, England [1820]), p. 200.

34 Daniel Blowe, A Geographical, Historical, Commercial, and Agricultural View of the United States of America (London, 1820), p. 741.

35 Diary entry of June 7, 1831. George W. Pierson, Tocqueville and Beaumont in America (New York, 1938), p. 118.

36 An excellent summary of historical views on national character is in David M. Potter, People of Plenty: Economic Abundance and the American Character (Chicago, 1954), pp. 3–31. See also Karl W. Deutsch, Nationalism and Social Communication (New York, 1953), pp. 4–6.

37 Abraham Kardiner, The Psychological Frontiers of Society (New York, 1945), passim, concludes that the forces molding a basic personality are both primary (maternal care, early discipline) and secondary (folklore, religion, dogmas, value systems).

38 Reinhold Niebuhr, A Study of the American Character (Washington, D.C., 1961), pp. 1–7, defines the American character as "a pattern of consistency that is woven by historical circumstances." He pictures the American character as a product of the interplay between a frontier physical environment and the strong sense of purpose inherited from Puritanism.

39 Erich Fromm, "Individual and Social Origins of Neurosis," American Sociological Review, IX (August 1944), pp. 380–383.

40 This interpretation was advanced by Margaret Mead, And Keep Your Powder Dry (New York, 1942). It is summarized in Potter, People of Plenty, pp. 47–50.

41 David Riesman, The Lonely Crowd: A Study of the Changing American Character (New Haven, Conn., 1950), passim.

42 Karen Horney, The Neurotic Personality of Our Time (1937), summarized in Potter, People of Plenty, loc. cit., pp. 54–56.

43 Francis L. K. Hsu, Americans and Chinese: Two Ways of Life (New York, 1953), pp. 10–11.

44 The following discussion of the manifestations of national character is based on a number of excellent modern works, including Denis W. Brogan, The American Character (New York, 1944); Roger Burlingame, The American Conscience (New York, 1957); Marcus Cunliffe,

"The American Character," in *The Nation Takes Shape, 1789–1837* (Chicago, 1959), pp. 186–197; Howard Mumford Jones, *America and French Culture* (Chapel Hill, N.C., 1927); Max Lerner, *America as a Civilization* (New York, 1957); and Arthur M. Schlesinger, "What Then Is the American, This New Man?" *American Historical Review*, XLVIII (January 1943), pp. 225–244. Among the travelers the most useful in this respect are Bryce, *American Commonwealth*, Chevalier, *Society, Manners and Politics in the United States*, and Alexis de Tocqueville, *Democracy in America* (Cambridge, Mass., 1863).

45 Bryce, *American Commonwealth*, II, 280.

46 Merle Curti, "American Philanthropy and the National Character," *American Quarterly*, X (Winter 1958), pp. 420–437.

47 This viewpoint is staunchly defended in Owen Lattimore, "The Frontier in History," *Relazioni del X Internazionale di Scienze Storiche* (Florence, 1955), I, pp. 105–138.

48 Schlesinger, "What Then Is the American, This New Man?" *loc. cit.*, pp. 227–232, 241–244.

49 Ilya Ehrenburg, "Ilya Ehrenburg's America," *Harper's Magazine*, CXCIII (December 1946), pp. 562–576.

50 The case for this interpretation is in Louis Hartz, *The Liberal Tradition in America* (New York, 1955).

51 This viewpoint is persuasively presented in Potter, *People of Plenty*.

52 The best statement of this thesis is George W. Pierson, "A Restless Temper . . . ," *American Historical Review*, LXIX (July 1964), pp. 969–989. The same author argues the case for mobility as a molding trait in "The Moving American," *Yale Review*, XLIV (Autumn 1954), pp. 99–112; "The M-Factor in American History," *American Quarterly*, XIV (Summer 1962), pp. 275–289; and "Under a Wandering Star," *Virginia*

Quarterly Review, XXXIX (Autumn 1963), pp. 621–638.

Chapter 4 The Frontier: Cradle of Barbarism or Civilization?

1 E. Howitt, *Selections from Letters Written during a Tour through the United States* (Nottingham, England [1820]), p. 46; William Faux, *Memorable Days in America* (London, 1823), p. 206. Travelers noticed that the decay of civilized manners was especially apparent in children who had not had the advantages of an eastern background. Zerah Hawley, *A Journal of a Tour through Connecticut, Massachusetts, New York, the North Part of Pennsylvania and Ohio* (New Haven, Conn., 1822), p. 63.

2 Peter Kalm, *Travels into North America* (London, 1772), II, 711.

3 Richard J. Hooker, ed., *The Carolina Backcountry on the Eve of the Revolution: The Journal and Other Writings of Charles Woodmason, Anglican Itinerant* (Chapel Hill, N.C., 1953), pp. 15, 16–17.

4 Morris Birkbeck, *Letters from Illinois* (London, 1818), p. 96; Timothy Flint, "The Kentuckian in New York," *Western Monthly Review*, I (1827), p. 88.

5 Quoted in Ralph Rusk, *The Literature of the Middle Western Border* (New York, 1925), I, 75n.

6 J. E. Alexander, *Transatlantic Sketches, Comprising Visits to the Most Interesting Scenes in North and South America and the West Indies* (London, 1833), II, 107.

7 Baynard R. Hall, *The New Purchase: or, Seven and a Half Years in the Far West* (New York, 1843), II, 158–159. Eye-gouging stories are plentiful in the travel literature of the West. Among the most colorful are Fortescue Cuming, *Sketches of a Tour in the Western Country* (Pittsburgh, Pa., 1810), pp. 118–119;

Ashe, *Travels in America*, I, 225–231; Simon O'Ferrall, *A Ramble of Six Thousand Miles Through the United States of America* (London, 1832), pp. 169–170; and Charles Sealsfield, *The Americans As They Are; Described in A Tour through the Valley of the Mississippi* (London, 1828), pp. 23–27.

8 For typical descriptions, some of which may be believed, see such travel accounts as Thomas Ashe, *Travels in America, Performed in 1806* (London, 1808), I, 232; William N. Blane, *An Excursion through the United States and Canada, during the Years 1822–3* (London, 1824), p. 161; Faux, *Memorable Days in America*, p. 231; Henry B. Fearon, *Sketches of America* (London, 1818), p. 264; Elias Fordham, *Personal Narrative of Travels* (Cleveland, Ohio, 1906), pp. 148–149; John Melish, *Travels through the United States of America* (London, 1818), p. 372; and Charles A. Murray, *Travels in North America during the years 1834, 1835, and 1836* (London, 1839), I, 213–215. Colorful but sketchy information on this subject is in Robert V. Haynes, "Law Enforcement in Frontier Mississippi," *Journal of Mississippi History*, XXII (January 1960), pp. 41–42.

9 Sidney Smith, *The Settler's New Home: or The Emigrant's Location* (London, 1849), pp. 96–97; George W. Featherstonhaugh, *A Canoe Voyage up the Minnay Sotor* (London, 1847), I, 152.

10 Charles Dickens, *American Notes* (London, 1842), II, 52; Andrew F. Muir, ed., *Texas in 1837: An Anonymous, Contemporary Narrative* (Austin, Texas, 1958), p. 92.

11 "The Journey of Lewis David von Schweinitz to Goshen, Bartholomew County in 1831," *Indiana Historical Society Publications*, VIII (Indianapolis, Ind., 1927), p. 230.

12 Excellent contemporary descriptions are in J. H. Beadle, *The Undeveloped West; or, Five Years in the Territories* (Philadelphia, 1873), pp. 434–435, and William A. Bell, *New Tracks in North America* (London, 1869), I, 18. Disorder in one cow town is described in Norbert R. Mahnken, "Ogallala—Nebraska's Cowboy Capital," *Nebraska History*, XXVIII (April–June 1947), pp. 85–109.

13 Bell, *New Tracks in North America*, I, 90.

14 Quoted in Ernest Marchand, "Emerson and the Frontier," *American Literature*, III (May 1931), pp. 154–155.

15 Travelers were prone to exaggerate tales of frontier violence because they saw what they wanted to see. Those with anti-American prejudices saw a savage land; those with opposite views painted a picture of peace and prosperity. One British traveler noted that if Americans recorded their impressions of Europe in the same way, "they would be singling out not the best, not the average, but the worst classes of the population," and could if they wished, provide "a very harrowing calendar of crime." William A. Baillie-Grohman, *Camps in the Rockies* (New York, 1882), p. 27. For similar frank statements by travelers see Blane, *An Excursion through the United States*, p. 147; and Abner D. Jones, *Illinois and the West* (Boston, 1838), pp. 25–26.

16 Smith, *The Settler's New Home*, p. 95.

17 The classic treatment of this subject is William I. Thomas and Florian Znaniecki, *The Polish Peasant in Europe and America* (New York, 1927), II, 1647–1652, which studies the effect on individuals of moving from one environment to another.

18 Franklin D. Scott ed., *Baron Klinkowstrom's America, 1818–1820* (Evanston, Ill., 1952), p. 191.

19 Quoted in Dixon Wecter, "Instruments of Culture on the Frontier,"

Yale Review, XXXVI (Winter 1947), p. 246.

20 R. L. Hartt, "The Ohioans," *Atlantic Monthly,* LXXXIV (November 1899), p. 682.

21 Samuel Bowles, *Across the Continent* (Springfield, Mass., 1866), pp. 327–328.

22 Elise D. Isely, *Sunbonnet Days* (Caldwell, Idaho, 1935), p. 180.

23 Alexis de Tocqueville, *Democracy in America* (New York, 1945), I, 406–407.

24 The best case for the thesis that Eastern civilization advanced almost unchanged to the frontier has been made by Louis B. Wright, "The Westward Advance of the Atlantic Frontier," *Huntington Library Quarterly,* XI (May 1948), pp. 261–275, and *Culture on the Moving Frontier* (Bloomington, Ind., 1955), *passim.* Briefer explorations of the theme are in Howard M. Jones, *America and French Culture* (Chapel Hill, N.C., 1927), pp. 50–51, and Earl Pomeroy, "Toward a Reorientation of Western History: Continuity and Environment," *Mississippi Valley Historical Review,* XLI (March 1955), pp. 582–583, 591–592.

25 Benjamin Thomas, *Lincoln's New Salem* (Springfield, Ill., 1934), pp. 29–36.

26 Descriptions of Lexington's cultural growth are in Bernard Mayo, "Lexington: Frontier Metropolis," in Eric F. Goldman, ed., *Historiography and Urbanization. Essays in American History in Honor of W. Stull Holt* (Baltimore, Md., 1941), pp. 31–40; Richard C. Wade, *The Urban Frontier. The Rise of Western Cities, 1790–1830* (Cambridge, Mass., 1959), pp. 233–239; and Wright, *Culture on the Moving Frontier,* pp. 60–63. The quotation is from Richard C. Wade, "Urban Life in Western America, 1790–1830," *American Historical Review,* LXIV (October 1958), p. 25.

27 John Bakeless, *Daniel Boone* (New York, 1939), p. 55.

28 Osburne Russell, *Journal of a Trapper, or Nine Years in the Rocky Mountains* (Boise, Idaho, 1921), pp. 55, 109; Frances F. Victor, *The River of the West* (Hartford, Conn., 1870), pp. 83–84. An interesting argument to show that the mountain men not only longed to return to civilization but usually did so is in William H. Goetzmann, "The Mountain Man as Jacksonian Man," *American Quarterly,* XV (Fall 1963), pp. 402–415.

29 Don D. Walker, "Reading on the Range: The Literary Habits of the American Cowboy," *Arizona and the West,* II (Winter 1960), pp. 307–318, deals amusingly with this subject.

30 Charles H. Shinn, *The Story of the Mine* (New York, 1898), pp. 67–68. A similar case study of cultural demands in a remote Nevada mining district is in W. Turrentine Jackson, *Treasure Hill. Portrait of a Silver Mining Camp* (Tucson, Ariz., 1963), pp. 26–27.

31 LeRoy R. Hafen, ed., *Colorado and Its People* (New York, 1948), I, 192–194, 231–235.

32 Timothy Flint, *Recollections of the Last Ten Years* (Boston, 1826), p. 48.

33 Hooker, ed., *Carolina Backcountry on the Eve of the Revolution,* p. 226.

34 Othman A. Abbott, *Recollections of a Pioneer Lawyer* (Lincoln, Nebr., 1929), p. 152.

35 D. Griffiths, Jr., *Two Years' Residence in the New Settlements of Ohio* (London, 1835), pp. 83–84.

36 This jumble of information has been assembled from such diverse sources as an article in *Niles' Weekly Register,* XI (February 8, 1817), p. 392; Adam Hodgson, *Letters from North America, Written during a Tour in the United States and Canada* (London, 1824), I, 269; James B. Finley, *Autobiography of Rev. James B. Finley: or, Pioneer Life in the West*

(Cincinnati, Ohio, 1853), pp. 113–114; Robert G. Athearn, *High Country Empire* (New York, 1960), pp. 232–233; Merle Curti, *The Making of an American Community* (Stanford, Calif., 1959), pp. 384–385; William W. Ferrier, *Ninety Years of Education in California, 1846–1936* (New York, 1927), pp. 36–40; Everett Dick, *The Sod House Frontier, 1854–1890* (New York, 1937), p. 315; and Edward A. Miller, "The History of Educational Legislation in Ohio from 1803 to 1850," *Ohio Archaeological and Historical Society Publications*, XXVII (1918), pp. 1–27.

37 *Western Review*, III (1820), p. 145.

38 R. E. Banta, *The Ohio. Rivers of America Series* (New York, 1949), p. 409; Finley, *Autobiography*, pp. 113–114. For the extensive use of classics in colonial education see Frank Klassen, "Persistence and Change in Eighteenth Century Colonial Education," *History of Education Quarterly*, II (June 1962), pp. 83–99. On the national period an excellent brief account is in Walter A. Agard, "Classics on the Midwest Frontier," in Walker D. Wyman and Clifton B. Kroeber, eds., *The Frontier in Perspective* (Madison, Wis., 1957), pp. 165–183.

39 James C. Olson, *History of Nebraska* (Lincoln, Nebr., 1955), pp. 84–85; Athearn, *High Country Empire*, p. 239; Dick, *Sod House Frontier*, pp. 419–420.

40 Robert Baird, *View of the Valley of the Mississippi, or the Emigrant's and Traveller's Guide to the West* (Philadelphia, 1834), p. 324. Information on the popularity of newspapers on the Ohio Valley frontier is in R. Carlyle Buley, *The Old Northwest: Pioneer Period, 1815–1840* (Indianapolis, Ind., 1950), II, 489–496; Rusk, *Literature of the Middle Western Frontier*, I, 131–164; and William H. Venable, *Beginnings of Literary Culture in the Ohio Valley* (Cincinnati, Ohio, 1891), pp.

38–39, which lists those published. A fine case study of one frontier newspaper is in Curti, *Making of an American Community*, pp. 409–412. For the story of magazine publishing see Buley, *Old Northwest*, II, 523–533; Wade, *Urban Frontier*, pp. 251–254; and Venable, *Beginnings of Literary Culture*, pp. 58–128.

41 Typical traveler's comments are in Beadle, *The Undeveloped West*, p. 438; and George W. Featherstonhaugh, *Excursion through the Slave States* (New York, 1844), p. 96. Cecil Howes, "Pistol-Packin' Pencil Pushers," *Kansas Historical Quarterly*, XIII (May 1944), pp. 115–138, is both colorful and informative on journalism in the Far West.

42 James Bryce, *The American Commonwealth* (Chicago, 1891), II, 898.

43 Francois A. Michaux, *Travels to the Westward of the Alleghany Mountains* (London, 1805), pp. 160–161.

44 Typical comments are in Karl Bernhard, *Travels Through North America, During the Years 1825 and 1826* (Philadelphia, 1828), II, 25; Charles G. B. Daubney, *Journal of a Tour through the United States, and in Canada, Made during the Years 1837–38* (Oxford, England, 1843), pp. 143–144; James Flint, *Letters from America* (Edinburgh, 1822), p. 272; Timothy Flint, *Recollections of the Last Ten Years*, p. 67; Hall, *The New Purchase*, I, 199; Hodgson, *Letters from North America*, I, 142, 286–287; Frederick L. Olmsted, *A Journey through Texas* (New York, 1857), pp. 48, 430; and John Palmer, *Journal of Travels in the United States of America, and in Lower Canada, Performed in the Year 1817* (London, 1818), p. 127.

45 Daubney, *Journal of a Tour*, pp. 143–144; Flint, *Recollections of the Last Ten Years*, p. 229.

46 Ethel F. Fiske, *The Letters of John J. Fiske* (New York, 1940), p. 543.

47 John Parsons, *A Tour Through In-*

diana in 1840 (New York, 1920), pp. 120–121; Jones, *Illinois and the West*, pp. 102–103.

48 An excellent discussion of this subject is in William Charvat, *Literary Publishing in America, 1790–1850* (Philadelphia, 1959), pp. 18–25.

49 Howard H. Peckham, "Books and Reading on the Ohio Valley Frontier," *Mississippi Valley Historical Review*, XLIV (March 1958), pp. 652–653. By the end of the 1830s, Cincinnati's presses alone produced a half million volumes yearly, most of them schoolbooks. Rusk, *Literature of the Middle Western Frontier*, I, 70–71.

50 A brief biography of this bookseller, James D. Bemis, is in Madeleine B. Stern, *Imprints on History: Book Publishers and American Frontiers* (Bloomington, Ind., 1956), pp. 5–23.

51 Peckham, "Books and Reading on the Ohio Valley Frontier," *loc. cit.* p. 652; Wright, *Culture on the Moving Frontier*, pp. 71–75; Wade, *The Urban Frontier*, p. 140. Comparable information on frontier Pittsburgh is in Edward P. Anderson, "Intellectual Life of Pittsburgh, 1786–1836," *Western Pennsylvania Historical Magazine*, XIV (April 1931), pp. 101–105.

52 Joseph S. Schick, *The Early Theater in Eastern Iowa* (Chicago, 1939), pp. 161–165; Stern, *Imprints on History*, pp. 137–138.

53 Numerous studies of private libraries owned by Westerners testify to the cultural interests of a surprising number of frontiersmen. Thus in St. Louis, the 669 inhabitants in 1803 collectively owned between 2000 and 3000 books. See John F. McDermott, "Private Libraries in Frontier St. Louis," *Papers of the Bibliographical Society of America*, LI (1957), pp. 19–37; John F. McDermott, *Private Libraries in Creole St. Louis* (Baltimore, Md., 1938), pp. 1–23; and Flora H. Apponyi, *Libraries of California* (San Francisco, Calif., 1878), *passim*.

54 The history of subscription libraries on the Mississippi Valley frontier is told in such works as Eleanora A. Baer, "Books, Newspapers, and Libraries in Pioneer St. Louis, 1808–1842," *Missouri Historical Review*, LVI (July 1962), pp. 358–360; W. T. Norton, "Early Libraries in Illinois," *Journal of the Illinois State Historical Society*, VI (July 1913), pp. 246–251; Venable, *Beginnings of Literary Culture*, pp. 263–264; and Wade, *The Urban Frontier*, pp. 254–256. An excellent case study of one library is in J. F. Waring, *Books and Reading in Hudson, 1800–1954: A History of the Hudson Literary and Historical Society* (Hudson, Ohio, 1954).

55 Henry Howe, *Historical Collections of Ohio* (Cincinnati, Ohio, 1847), p. 349.

56 Sarah J. Cutler, "The Coonskin Library," *Ohio Archaeological and Historical Quarterly*, XXVI (January 1917), pp. 58–77.

57 *The Genius of the West*, quoted in Venable, *Beginnings of Literary Culture*, pp. 251–252.

58 Albert D. Richardson, *Beyond the Mississippi* (Hartford, Conn., 1867), p. 51.

59 Edward E. Dale, "The Frontier Literary Society," *Nebraska History*, XXXI (September 1950), pp. 167–182, is based on the records of a pioneer Nebraska society.

60 John Turner, *Pioneers of the West* (Cincinnati, Ohio, 1903), p. 62.

61 Reading tastes on the Ohio Valley frontier are discussed in James M. Miller, *The Genesis of Western Culture: the Upper Ohio Valley, 1800–1825* (Columbus, Ohio, 1938), pp. 147–151; and Rusk, *Literature of the Middle Western Frontier*, II, 1–38.

62 Peckham, "Books and Reading on the Ohio Valley Frontier," *loc. cit.*, pp. 657–660.

63 Logan Esarey, "The Literary Spirit Among the Early Ohio Valley Settlers," *Mississippi Valley Historical Review*, V (September 1918), pp.

148–153, gives many examples of this type of writing. Others are in Buley, *The Old Northwest*, II, 558–562, and Rusk, *Literature of the Middle Western Frontier*, II, 272–351.

64 Anderson, *Intellectual Life of Pittsburgh*, pp. 225–231; Buley, *The Old Northwest*, II, 573–576; Wade, *The Urban Frontier*, pp. 143–146.

65 Douglas L. Hunt, "The Nashville Theatre, 1830–1840," *Birmingham-Southern College Bulletin*, XXVIII (Birmingham, Ala., 1935), pp. 3–8; Bruce E. Mahan, "The Iowa Thespians," *Palimpsest*, IV (January 1923), pp. 14–24. Rusk, *Literature of the Middle Western Frontier*, II, pp. 352–357, also deals with the Ohio Valley theater.

66 Robert D. Harper, "Theatrical Entertainment in Early Omaha," *Nebraska History*, XXXVI (June 1955), pp. 93–104; Harold E. and Ernestine B. Briggs, "The Early Theater on the Northern Plains," *Mississippi Valley Historical Review*, XXXVII (September 1950), pp. 231–264; George R. MacMinn, *The Theater of the Golden Era in California* (Caldwell, Idaho, 1941), pp. 21–34, 38–42; Hafen, ed., *Colorado and Its People*, I, 261–263; Jerry Bryan, *An Illinois Gold Hunter in the Black Hills* (Springfield, Ill., 1960), pp. 32, 34.

67 Esther C. Dunn, *Shakespeare in America* (New York, 1939), pp. 175–204, deals with Shakespeare on the Mississippi Valley frontier.

68 *Ibid.*, pp. 205–218; MacMinn, *Theater of the Golden Era*, pp. 86, 196.

69 Rusk, *Literature of the Middle Western Border*, I, 56–57.

70 Prentice Mulford, *Prentice Mulford's Story* (New York, 1889), pp. 145–146.

71 Fearon, *Sketches of America*, pp. 252–253; Flint, *Recollections of the Last Ten Years*, p. 185.

72 Quoted in Carl Bridenbaugh, *Myths and Realities: Societies of the Colonial South* (Baton Rouge, La., 1952), p. 191; and in F. Garvin Davenport, "Culture versus Frontier in Tennessee, 1825–1850," *Journal of Southern History*, V (February 1939), p. 24.

73 Flint, *Letters from America*, p. 146.

74 Frederick Marryat, *A Diary in America* (London, 1839), I, 24.

75 Timothy Flint, *The History and Geography of the Mississippi Valley* (Cincinnati, Ohio, 1832), I, 134; Michael Chevalier, *Society, Manners and Politics in the United States* (Boston, 1839), p. 220.

76 This thesis is advanced in A. H. Maslow, *Motivation and Personality* (New York, 1954).

77 James H. Lanman, "The Progress of the Northwest," *Hunt's Merchants' Magazine*, III (July–December 1840), p. 39; Caroline M. Kirkland, *A New Home—Who'll Follow? or, Glimpses of Western Life* (New York, 1839), p. 135. Similar observations are in Morris Birkbeck, *Notes on a Journey in America* (London, 1818), p. 81, and Henry McMurtrie, *Sketches of Louisville* (Louisville, Ky., 1819), pp. 119, 125.

78 Quoted in Wecter, "Instruments of Culture on the Frontier," *loc. cit.*, p. 243.

79 Hall, *The New Purchase*, I, 141.

80 Merle Curti, "Intellectuals and Other People," *American Historical Review*, LX (January 1955), pp. 259–282, deals with the frontier as one influence on American anti-intellectualism. See also; Richard Hofstadter, *Anti-Intellectualism in American Life* (New York, 1963), and Arthur K. Moore, *The Frontier Mind: A Cultural Analysis of the Kentucky Frontiersman* (Lexington, Ky., 1957), pp. 5–7.

81 Quoted in Davenport, "Culture versus Frontier in Tennessee," *loc. cit.*, pp. 23–24.

82 Quoted in Buley, *The Old Northwest*, II, 563.

83 Since the 1920s, one school of literary historians has assigned the frontier a major role in reshaping the character of American writing. For statements of this case see J. B. Hubbell, "The Frontier in American Literature," *Southwest Review*, X (January 1925), pp. 84–92; Percy Boynton, *The Rediscovery of the Frontier* (Chicago, 1931), and Arlin Turner, "Seeds of Literary Revolt in the Humor of the Old Southwest," *Louisiana Historical Quarterly*, XXXIX (April 1956), pp. 143–151. The quotation is from John S. Robb, *Streaks of Squatter Life and Far Western Scenes* (Philadelphia, 1846), p. viii.

84 Hall, *The New Purchase*, II, 171.

85 *Ibid.*, II, 83. For similar comments see Harriet Brown, *Grandmother Brown's Hundred Years, 1827–1927* (Boston, 1929), p. 133, and Eliza W. Farnham, *Life in Prairie Land* (New York, 1846), pp. 330–331.

86 James H. Rodabaugh, "Robert Hamilton Bishop," *Ohio Historical Society Collections*, IV (Columbus, Ohio, 1935), p. 65; Buley, *The Old Northwest*, II, 389–390; Merle Curti, *The Making of an American Community* (Stanford, Calif., 1959), p. 283.

87 Hall, *The New Purchase*, II, 173.

Chapter 5 The Structure of Frontier Society

1 T. C. C., "Western Prairies," *The American Whig Review*, XXVIII (May 1850), p. 526.

2 Merle Curti, *The Growth of American Thought* (2nd edn., New York, 1951), p. 292.

3 Baynard R. Hall, *The New Purchase: or, Seven and a Half Years in the Far West* (New York, 1843), p. 72.

4 A study of passenger lists on ships sailing from Bristol to America in the second half of the seventeenth century shows that about 36 percent of the immigrants were yeoman farmers, 22 percent artisans and tradesmen, 10 percent laborers, and only 1 percent gentlemen and professional men. Thus farmers and skilled workers outnumbered all others by five to one. Mildred Campbell, "Social Origins of Some Early Americans," in James M. Smith, ed., *Seventeenth-Century America. Essays in Colonial History* (Chapel Hill, N.C., 1959), pp. 66–76.

5 An excellent study of aristocratic impulses is Arthur M. Schlesinger, "The Aristocracy in Colonial America," *Massachusetts Historical Society Proceedings*, LXXIV (1962), pp. 3–21. The quotation is on pp. 6–7.

6 Egon E. Bergel, *Social Stratification* (New York, 1962) pp. 249–256; R. Carlyle Buley, *The Old Northwest: Pioneer Period, 1815–1840* (Indianapolis, Ind., 1950), I, 140–141; Richard C. Wade, *The Urban Frontier* (Cambridge, Mass., 1959), pp. 105–106.

7 Edward N. Saveth, "The American Patrician Class: A Field for Research," *American Quarterly*, XV (Summer 1963), pp. 240–241; Wade, *The Urban Frontier*, pp. 203–230.

8 Fortescue Cuming, *Sketches of a Tour to the Western Country* (Pittsburgh, 1810), p. 71; Samuel Jones, *Pittsburgh in 1826* (Pittsburgh, 1826), p. 43.

9 Simon A. O'Ferrall, *A Ramble of Six Thousand Miles Through the United States of America* (London, 1832), pp. 230–231; Frances Trollope, *Domestic Manners of the Americans* (London, 1832), modern edition, New York, 1949), p. 155.

10 Mrs. Houston, *Hesperos: or, Travels in the West* (London, 1850), II, 220–221. For other testimony on this point see Abner D. Jones, *Illinois and the West* (Boston, 1838), pp. 145–146; Frederick Marryat, *A Diary in America* (London, 1839), I, 208; and Catherine Stewart, *New Homes in the West* (Nashville, Tenn., 1843), pp. 12–13.

11 Merle Curti, *The Making of an American Community: A Case Study of Democracy in a Frontier County* (Stanford, Calif., 1959), pp. 107–112.

12 Houston, *Hesperos*, I, 175–176. 176.

13 Franklin G. Adams, *The Homestead Guide* (Waterville, Kan., 1873), p. 113.

14 John Woods, *Two Years' Residence in the Settlement on the English Prairie in the Illinois Country* (London, 1822), p. 295. Travelers' accounts of the use of titles in the backwoods are numerous. See especially, Thomas Ashe, *Travels in America* (London, 1808), I, p. 298; James Flint, *Letters from America* (Edinburgh, 1822), p. 144; Zerah Hawley, *Journal of a Tour through Connecticut, Massachusetts, New York, and North Part of Pennsylvania and Ohio* (New Haven, Conn., 1822), pp. 47–48; Charles J. Latrobe, *The Rambler in North America* (London, 1835), p. 260; and Woods, *Two Years' Residence,* p. 295.

15 Timothy Flint, *Recollections of the Last Ten Years* (Boston, 1826), p. 52.

16 Wade, *The Urban Frontier*, pp. 106, 111, 312–313.

17 Henry McMurtrie, *Sketches of Louisville* (Louisville, Ky., 1819), p. 119.

18 Caleb Atwater, *Remarks Made on a Tour to Prairie du Chien* (Columbus, Ohio, 1831), p. 180; Frederick J. Gustorf, "Frontier Perils Told By an Early Illinois Visitor," *Journal of the Illinois State Historical Society,* LV (Summer 1962), p. 154; Charles F. Hoffman, *A Winter in the West, by a New-Yorker* (New York, 1935), II, 3; and Caroline M. Kirkland, *Western Clearings* (New York, 1845), p. 38.

19 Bergel, *Social Stratification*, pp. 22–23; Pitirim Sorokin, *Social Mobility* (New York, 1927), pp. 12–13, 337–341.

20 Kingsley Davis and Wilbur E. Moore, "Some Principles of Stratification," *American Sociological Review,* X (April 1945), pp. 242–249. This "Davis-Moore Reward Theory" is widely accepted as a logical explanation of stratification. A similar theory on the necessity of stratification to society is in Talcott Parsons, "A Revised Analytical Approach to the Theory of Social Stratification," in R. Bendix and S. M. Lipset, *Class, Status and Power* (Glencoe, Ill., 1953), pp. 92–128, and a comparable hypothesis in W. Lloyd Warner, Marchia Meeker, and Kenneth Eells, *Social Class in America* (Chicago, 1949), pp. 3–32. For an opposite theory, which holds that in the United States positions of the highest social good (in religion, education, and government) are not rewarded as well as those of lesser value to society (in entertainment, liquor dispensing, and athletics) see Melvin Tumin, "Some Principles of Social Stratification: A Critical Analysis," *American Sociological Review,* XVIII (August 1953), pp. 378–394.

21 "Ascribed status," as distinguished from "achieved status," is that assigned to individuals without reference to their abilities, as kingship or membership in a hereditary caste. The standard work on this subject is Ralph Linton, *The Study of Man* (New York, 1936), pp. 113–121.

22 Bergel, *Social Stratification,* pp. 180–201, 208–209.

23 Leonard Reissman, *Class in American Society* (Glencoe, Ill. 1959), p. 115. An excellent explanation of the methodology employed in determining the nature of classes is in *ibid.,* pp. 115–166.

24 W. Lloyd Warner and Paul S. Lunt, *The Social Life of a Modern Community* (New Haven, Conn., 1941); *The Status System of a Modern Community* (New Haven, Conn., 1942); W. Lloyd Warner and Leo

Srole, *The Social Systems of American Ethnic Groups* (New Haven, Conn., 1945); and W. Lloyd Warner and J. O. Low, *The Social System of the Modern Factory* (New Haven, Conn., 1947).

25 John Useem, Pierre Tangent, and Ruth Useem, "Stratification in a Prairie Town," *American Sociological Review*, VII (June 1942), pp. 331–342.

26 James West, *Plainville, U.S.A.* (New York, 1945). A similar study of "Elmtown," a corn-belt community of 6000 inhabitants, reaches virtually these same conclusions. See August B. Hollingshead, *Elmtown's Youth* (New York, 1949).

27 John F. Cuber and William F. Kenkel, eds., *Social Stratification in the United States* (New York, 1954), pp. 303–309, argue for the continuum theory, holding that class divisions in the United States are so ill defined that the upper-upper, upper-middle, and similar designations are meaningless.

28 Reissman, *Class in American Society*, pp. 11–22; Bergel, *Social Stratification*, pp. 413–415.

29 A distinction is made between "vertical mobility" and "horizontal mobility," which designates a movement from one job to another on the same socioeconomic level. For a good discussion of this subject see Sorokin, *Social Mobility*, pp. 133–134.

30 The most impressive marshalling of evidence to show that vertical mobility differs little between modern industrial nations is Seymour M. Lipset and Reinhard Bendix, *Social Mobility in Industrial Society* (Berkeley, Calif., 1959), *passim.* Specific discussion of the points noted in this paragraph are on pp. 11–13, 57–64, 236–237, 366–368, and 414–440. A thorough discussion of social mobility in modern Britain is in David V. Glass, ed., *Social Mobility in Britain* (London, 1954).

31 Bergel, *Social Stratification*, pp. 337–340. Rowland Berthoff, "The American Social Order: A Conservative Hypothesis," *American Historical Review*, LXV (April 1960), pp. 510–511, argues that the post depression government efforts to provide security have solidified class lines, even to creating a leadership class of Roosevelts, Tafts, Rockefellers, and Kennedys.

32 A study of some 8000 business leaders in 1928 and a similar study of executives in 1952 showed that the number recruited from upper-class backgrounds grew from 50 percent to 66 percent during those years. A similar survey of names in the *National Cyclopedia of American Biography* showed that between 1771 and 1800 about 65 percent of those famous enough to be included came from upper-class families; by 1891–1920 the percentage had grown to 74 percent. W. Lloyd Warner and James C. Abegglen, *Occupational Mobility in American Business and Industry, 1928–1952* (Minneapolis, Minn., 1955), p. 45; W. Lloyd Warner, *American Life: Dream and Reality* (Chicago, 1962), pp. 145–152.

33 Art Buchwald, *Is It Safe to Drink the Water* (Cleveland, Ohio, 1961), pp. 74–76.

34 Berthoff, "The American Social Order," *loc. cit.*, pp. 503–505.

35 *North American Review*, III (May, 1816), p. 20.

36 Reissman, *Class in American Society*, pp. 306–308. In 1850 67.2 percent of the American people were engaged in primary production, 16.2 percent in secondary, and 16.6 percent in tertiary. By 1935 the number engaged in primary had fallen to 24.8 percent, while those engaged in secondary had increased to 28.1 percent and in tertiary to 47.1 percent.

37 George G. S. Murphy and Arnold Zellner, "The Turnerian Frontier

Process: Generator of Social and Economic Opportunity," paper read at meeting of American Historical Association, 1959 (unpublished), pp. 18–22.

38 A poll of high school students taken in 1942 showed that of those who preferred a risky job and high income over a secure job with lower income, 14 percent came from the lower class, 16 percent from the working class, 29 percent from the upper-middle class, and 31 percent from the upper class. Quoted in Reissman, *Class in American Society*, p. 362. Many of the theories in this paragraph are advanced in Allan G. Bogue, "Social Theory and the Pioneer," *Agricultural History*, XXXIV (January 1960), p. 31, based on his study of pioneer settlements in Illinois and Iowa.

39 Cuber and Kenkel, eds., *Social Stratification in the United States*, pp. 15–17; Bergel, *Social Stratification*, pp. 334–337. A visitor to the Indiana frontier in 1819 reported that would-be lawyers had only to read Blackstone's *Commentaries* and to serve for a few weeks under another lawyer to qualify for the bar. Flint, *Letters from America*, pp. 168–169.

40 William A. Reavis, "The Maryland Gentry and Social Mobility, 1637–1676," *William and Mary Quarterly*, XIV (July 1957), pp. 418–428.

41 Quoted in Carl Bridenbaugh, *Myths and Realities: Societies of the Colonial South* (Baton Rouge, La., 1952), p. 195.

42 Norman H. Dawes, "Titles as Symbols of Prestige in Seventeenth-Century New England," *William and Mary Quarterly*, VI (January 1949), pp. 69–83; Robert E. Brown, *Middle-Class Democracy and the Revolution in Massachusetts, 1691–1780* (Ithaca, N.Y., 1955), pp. 18–19.

43 Quoted in Alice M. Earle, *Customs and Fashions in Old New England* (New York, 1893), p. 317.

44 L. G. Tyler, ed., *Narratives of Early Virginia, 1606–1626* (New York, 1907), pp. 284–285.

45 Ann Hulton, *Letters of a Loyalist Lady* (Cambridge, Mass., 1927), pp. 49–50.

46 Gustorf, "Frontier Perils Told By an Early Illinois Visitor," *loc. cit.*, p. 144. For similar comments by travelers see William A. Bell, *New Tracks in North America* (London, 1869), I, 13; James Bryce, *The American Commonwealth* (Chicago, 1891), II, 806; and John Melish, *Travels through the United States of America* (London, 1818), p. 421.

47 Atwater, *Remarks Made on a Tour to Prairie du Chien*, p. 39.

48 Roy P. Basler, ed., *The Collected Works of Abraham Lincoln* (New Brunswick, N.J., 1953–1955), I, 344.

49 Trollope, *Domestic Manners of the Americans*, I, 159–160.

50 *Cincinnati Literary Gazette*, III (June 18, 1925), p. 193; Daniel Drake, *Discourse on the History, Character, and Prospects of the West* (1834, reprinted Gainsville, Fla., 1955), p. 9; Jones, *Illinois and the West*, pp. 103–104; Flint, *Letters from America*, p. 177.

51 John L. McConnel, *Western Characters or Types of Border Life in the Western States* (New York, 1853), p. 110.

52 Curti, *The Making of an American Community*, pp. 57–65, 154–162, 187–221.

53 Nancy C. Robertson, "Social Mobility in Ante-Bellum Alabama," *Alabama Review*, XIII (April 1960), pp. 135–145. Two statistical studies of "horizontal" or "occupational" mobility suggest that in the East at this time there was far greater movement from job to job than in England. A study of labor turnover in a Delaware River shipyard for the period 1854–1870 shows a greater shifting about than today; a similar study of a textile mill in Holyoke,

Massachusetts, reveals that less than 35 percent of the workers in 1860 had been employed for three years or more. These figures, although by no means conclusive, seem to indicate a more turbulent society than in Europe or modern times. Anne Bezanson, "Some Historical Aspects of Labor Turnover," in *Facts and Factors in Economic History: Articles by Former Students of Edwin Francis Gay* (Cambridge, Mass., 1932), pp. 692–708; Ray Ginger, "Labor in a Massachusetts Cotton Mill, 1853–60," *Business History Review*, XXVIII (1954), pp. 67–91.

54 Alexander Mackay, *The Western World* (Philadelphia, 1849), II, 68; Jones, *Illinois and the West*, pp. 102–104.

55 Quoted in Robert G. Athearn, *Westward the Briton* (New York, 1953), p. 151. Further testimony on this point is in Atwater, *Remarks Made on a Tour to Prairie Du Chien*, p. 35; and Trollope, *Domestic Manners of the Americans*, p. 121.

56 In 1940 79.2 percent of those polled in one poll and 88 percent in another said they belonged in the middle class, in 1943 the number was 87 percent in a third poll. "The People of the United States—a Self-Portrait," *Fortune*, XXI (February 1940), p. 21; George Gallup and Saul F. Rae, *The Pulse of Democracy* (New York, 1940), p. 169; Hadley Cantril, "Identification with Social and Economic Class," *Journal of Abnormal and Social Psychology*, XXXVIII (1943), pp. 74–80.

57 Of those interviewed, 3 percent said they belonged in the upper class, 43 percent to the middle class, 51 percent to the working class, and only 1 percent to the lower class. Richard Centers, *The Psychology of Social Classes* (Princeton, N.J., p. 180.

58 Kurt B. Mayer, *Class and Society* (New York, 1955), p. 69; Reissman, *Class in American Society*, pp. 293–294; Warner, *American Life: Dream*

and Reality, pp. 129–131; and Lipset and Bendix, eds., *Social Mobility in Industrial Society*, pp. 76–78.

Chapter 6 Frontier Democracy: Political Aspects

1 Frederick J. Turner, "The West and American Ideals," (1914), in *The Frontier in American History* (New York, 1920), p. 293.

2 Turner's writings and unpublished manuscripts contain many references to frontier democracy. His views on the subject are summarized in Avery Craven, *Democracy in American Life* (Chicago, 1941), pp. 38–67.

3 George W. Pierson, "The Frontier and Frontiersmen of Turner's Essays," *Pennsylvania Magazine of History and Biography*, LXIV (October 1940), pp. 468–472; Benjamin F. Wright, Jr., "American Democracy and the Frontier," *Yale Review*, XX (December 1930), pp. 354–355.

4 *Ibid.*, pp. 355–363; Richard Hofstadter, "Turner and the Frontier Myth," *American Scholar*, XVIII (Autumn 1949), pp. 339–340.

5 John C. Almack, "The Shibboleth of the Frontier," *Historical Outlook*, XVI (May 1925), pp. 197–202; George W. Pierson, "The Frontier and American Institutions. A Criticism of the Turner Theory," *New England Quarterly*, XV (June 1942), pp. 240–247.

6 Wright, "American Democracy and the Frontier," *loc. cit.*, pp. 351–353. Morris Zaslow, "The Frontier Hypothesis in Recent Historiography," *Canadian Historical Review*, XXIX (June 1948), pp. 158, 164–165, accepts the view that frontier conditions have fostered social but not political democracy, and that the degree of democracy varied with the background of the settlers.

7 Wright, "American Democracy and the Frontier," *loc. cit.*, pp. 363–364;

Benjamin F. Wright, "Political Institutions and the Frontier," in Dixon R. Fox, ed., *Sources of Culture in the Middle West* (New York, 1934) pp. 22–33. Thomas P. Abernethy, "The Southern Frontier, an Interpretation," in Walker D. Wyman and Clifton B. Kroeber, eds., *The Frontier in Perspective* (Madison, Wis., 1957), argues that the Southern experience fails to show that the frontier served as a democratizing influence.

8 Wright, "Political Institutions and the Frontier," *loc. cit.*, pp. 24–25; Chilton Williamson, *American Suffrage from Property to Democracy, 1760–1860* (Princeton, N.J., 1960), pp. 208–209.

9 That this was Turner's intention is amply demonstrated in his correspondence. "What I was dealing with," he wrote a friend after the passage had been critically attacked, "was in the first place, the *American* character of democracy as compared with that of Europe or of European philosophers." Turner to Frederick Merk, January 9, 1931, Turner Papers, HEH, TU Box 45. An excellent discussion of the term "American democracy" as used by Turner in his published works is in John D. Barnhart, *Valley of Democracy: The Frontier versus the Plantation in the Ohio Valley, 1775–1818* (Bloomington, Ind., 1953), pp. 233–234.

10 Denis W. Brogan, *The American Character* (New York, 1944), pp. 16–17, argues convincingly that while the Americans of today are famed for their lawlessness, they are unusually respectful of the law and of the authority of their state and nation.

11 Quoted in Herman C. Nixon, "Precursors of Turner in the Interpretation of the American Frontier," *South Atlantic Quarterly*, XXVIII (January 1929), p. 85.

12 Alexis de Tocqueville, *Democracy in America* (New York, 1945), I, 371–372.

13 Charles Sealsfield, *The Americans As They Are; Described in a Tour through the Valley of the Mississippi* (London, 1828), p. 16.

14 Tocqueville, *Democracy in America,* I, 1, 65.

15 Baynard R. Hall, *The New Purchase: or, Seven and a Half Years in the Far West* (New York, 1843), I, 237. For other examples see *ibid.*, I, 208; J. Richard Beste, *The Wabash: or Adventures of an English Gentleman's Family in the Interior of America* (London, 1855), II, 166–175; James Flint, *Letters from America* (Edinburgh, 1822), p. 172; and Robert Dale Owen, "Recollections from a Public Life: Western People and Politicians Forty Years Ago," *Scribner's Monthly Magazine*, XV (December 1877), pp. 256–257.

16 Research on contemporary communities suggests that in areas of homogeneous cultural background, political activity is less marked than that in mixed neighborhoods. This would indicate that the mingling of peoples in frontier areas would stimulate such activity. John H. Kolb, *Emerging Rural Communities: Group Relations in Rural Society* (Madison, Wis., 1959), p. 17.

17 George C. Homans, *The Human Group* (New York, 1950), p. 169.

18 Edwin L. Godkin, "Aristocratic Opinions of Democracy," *North American Review*, CCVI (January 1865), p. 219. Similar views are expressed in "Uses and Abuses of Lynch Law," *American Whig Review*," XI (May 1850), pp. 460–461, and Tocqueville, *Democracy in America*, I, 258–259.

19 Hall, *The New Purchase*, I, 236.

20 Quoted in Richard H. Luthin, "Some Demagogues in American History," *American Historical Review*, LVII (October 1951), p. 34, and Simon A. O'Ferrall, *A Ramble of Six Thousand Miles Through the United States of America* (London, 1832), p. 224.

21 Michael Chevalier, *Society, Manners*

and Politics in the United States (Boston, 1839), p. 225.

22 A survey of extensive historical materials on the history of Free-masonry in the United States indicates that lodges were founded in every Western community very soon after the first settlement, and that the founding lodge members usually included the most prominent men. Thus Lewis Cass was an organizer of the first lodge in Muskingum, Ohio, along with a leading merchant, the sheriff, the hotel keeper, and a lawyer. The lodge at Cedar Rapids, Iowa, was established by eight men who were also responsible for organizing the lyceum and collegiate institute. In Texas twenty of the fifty-nine signers of the Declaration of Independence were Masons, seven of the first nine speakers of the assembly, eight of the fourteen supreme court justices, and all four presidents during the republican period. These examples can be multiplied almost indefinitely in the published literature. The subject deserves further study by someone with access to the manuscript sources. Among the published materials, the following are useful: Erik M. Eriksson, "Masons in the Building of Iowa," *Grand Lodge Bulletin*, XXVII (October–December, 1926), pp. 259–267; 300–312, 349–356, and (January–March, 1927), pp. 18–23, 135–141; Charles W. Ferguson, *Fifty Million Brothers* (New York, 1937), p. 21; Robert F. Gould, ed., *A Library of Freemasonry* (Philadelphia, 1911), IV, 258–268; Thomas E. Green, *The Mason as a Citizen* (Cedar Rapids, Iowa, [1926]), pp. 9–11; Joseph W. Hale, "Masonry in the Early Days of Texas," *Southwestern Historical Quarterly*, XLIX (January 1946), pp. 374–379; Daniel McDonald, *A History of Freemasonry in Indiana* (Indianapolis, Ind., 1898), p. 32; Albert G. Mackay, *The Mystic Tie* (New York, 1856), pp. 109–110;

John C. Smith, *History of Free-masonry in Illinois, 1804–1829* (Chicago, 1903), p. 40; and Oliver P. Stidger, "Our Masonic Pioneers," *Quarterly of the Society of California Pioneers*, VI (March 1929), pp. 30–33.

23 Tocqueville, *Democracy in America*, I, 64–65. This theme is also developed in Godkin, "Aristocratic Opinions of Democracy," *loc. cit.*, pp. 219–220. An example was the refusal of the Carolina pioneers to accept the blueprint for a quasi-feudal society prepared by John Locke. On this subject see Arthur M. Schlesinger, "The Aristocracy in Colonial America," *Massachusetts Historical Society Proceedings*, LXXIV (1962), pp. 3–4.

24 Francis J. Grund, *The Americans, in their Moral, Social, and Political Relations* (Boston, 1837), p. 211.

25 This theme is admirably developed in Roy F. Nichols, "The Territories: Seedbeds of Democracy," *Nebraska History*, XXXV (September 1954), pp. 159–172.

26 These findings are summarized in Stanley Elkins and Eric McKitrick, "A Meaning for Turner's Frontier. Part I: Democracy in the Old Northwest," *Political Science Quarterly*, LXIX (July 1954), pp. 325–330. This article was the first to explore the validity of this problem by using the tools of the social scientist.

27 Evelyn Page, "The First Frontier— the Swedes and Dutch," *Pennsylvania History*, XV (October 1948), pp. 290–304.

28 Thomas P. Abernethy, *Three Virginia Frontiers* (Baton Rouge, La., 1940), pp. 20–27.

29 Bernard Bailyn, "Politics and Social Structure in Virginia," in James M. Smith, ed., *Seventeenth-Century America. Essays in Colonial History* (Chapel Hill, N.C., 1959), pp. 90–98, 108–110; Richard B. Morris, *Studies in the History of American Law* (New York, 1930), pp. 73–82.

30 Stanley Elkins and Eric McKitrick,

"A Meaning for Turner's Frontier, II, The Southwest Frontier and New England," *Political Science Quarterly,* LXIX (December 1954), pp. 585–594. The authors illustrate their point by a case study of the town of Hadley, pp. 595–601.

31 These are the conclusions of Robert E. Brown, *Middle-Class Democracy and the Revolution in Massachusetts, 1691–1780* (Ithaca, N.Y., 1955), pp. 21–37, 401–403. An opposite conclusion is reached by Elisha Douglas, *Rebels and Democrats* (Chapel Hill, N.C., 1955), who argues that little progress was made toward democracy in the Revolutionary period, due to a lack of leadership, the wide dispersal of the majority of people on farms, and the fact that the reform impulse was satisfied by the achievement of the ideals of the Revolution. A case study of voting in Cambridge, Massachusetts, tends to support the first conclusion. B. Katherine Brown, "Puritan Democracy: A Case Study," *Mississippi Valley Historical Review,* L (December 1963), pp. 377–396.

32 These conclusions are based on such careful studies as Bailyn, "Politics and Social Structure in Virginia," *loc. cit.,* pp. 114–115; Robert E. Brown, "Democracy in Colonial Massachusetts," *New England Quarterly,* XXV (September 1952), pp. 291–313; Richard P. McCormick, *A History of Voting in New Jersey: A Study of the Development of Election Machinery, 1664–1911* (New Brunswick, N.J., 1953); and Charles S. Sydnor, *Gentlemen Freeholders* (Chapel Hill, N.C., 1952).

33 Kirk H. Porter, *A History of Suffrage in the United States* (Chicago, 1918), pp. 20–26; Williamson, *American Suffrage,* pp. 92–137.

34 Barnhart, *Valley of Democracy,* pp. 106–120.

35 *Ibid.,* pp. 80–90; Thomas P. Abernethy, "Democracy and the Southern Frontier," *Journal of Southern History,* IV (February 1938), pp. 8–11;

George F. Taylor, "Suffrage in Early Kentucky," *Register of the Kentucky Historical Society,* LXL (January 1963), pp. 22–29. An excellent contemporary analysis of the Kentucky social structure is in James Hall, *Sketches of History, Life, and Manners in the West* (Philadelphia, 1835), II, 93–96.

36 Barnhart, *Valley of Democracy,* pp. 91–105; Taylor, "Suffrage in Early Kentucky," *loc. cit.,* pp. 30–32. An example of the confusion resulting from delayed surveys is in C. N. Howard, *British Development of West Florida, 1763–1769* (Berkeley, Calif., 1947), pp. 43–44. There so few voters could qualify by proving themselves freeholders that Britain had to abandon self-government or admit all householders to the franchise. The latter course was chosen.

37 Taylor, "Suffrage in Early Kentucky," *loc. cit.,* pp. 32–37, claims that by 1799 Kentucky had achieved a completely democratic government. Abernethy, *Three Virginia Frontiers,* pp. 78–88, reaches the exactly opposite conclusion on the basis of the same evidence. For additional information on Kentucky's first two constitutions see E. Merton Coulter, "Early Frontier Democracy in the First Kentucky Constitution," *Political Science Quarterly,* XXXIX (December 1924), pp. 665–677, and Pratt Byrd, "The Kentucky Frontier in 1792," *Filson Club Historical Quarterly,* XXV (July–October, 1951), pp. 181–203, 286–294.

38 Hall, *The New Purchase,* I, 209–210.

39 Beverley W. Bond, Jr., *The Civilization of the Old Northwest* (New York, 1934), pp. 102–104.

40 Elkins and McKitrick, "A Meaning for Turner's Frontier. Part I," *loc. cit.,* pp. 331–336, 339–353; William F. Vogel, "Home Life in Early Indiana," *Indiana Magazine of History,* X (September 1914), p. 309. Travelers almost universally

commented on the extraordinary interest of the Westerner in politics and on his surprising knowledge in the field. See, for example, Abner D. Jones, *Illinois and the West* (Boston, 1838), pp. 77–87; Caroline M. Kirkland, *A New Home—Who'll Follow? or, Glimpses of Western Life* (New York, 1839), p. 82; James Logan, *Notes of Journey through Canada, the United States of America, and the West Indies* (Edinburgh, 1838), p. 78; Morleigh [pseud.], *Life in the West: Backwoods Leaves and Prairie Flowers* (London, 1842), pp. 206–211; and Tyrone Power, *Impressions of America, during the Years 1833, 1834, and 1835* (London, 1836), I, 388–389. On the other hand, Richard P. McCormick, "New Perspectives on Jacksonian Politics," *American Historical Review*, LXV (January 1960), pp. 288–301, demonstrates with impressive statistical evidence that voters in the West did not participate in elections for the presidency as frequently as those in the East.

41 These data are gathered from the excellent study by Barnhart, *Valley of Democracy*, pp. 138–215. Other information is in Porter, *History of Suffrage in the United States,* pp. 36–40; Bayrd Still, "An Interpretation of the Statehood Process, 1800–1850," *Mississippi Valley Historical Review*, XXIII (September 1936), pp. 192–193; and Williamson, *American Suffrage*, pp. 219–220.

42 Hall, *The New Purchase*, I, 209.

43 Still, "Interpretation of the Statehood Process," *loc. cit.*, pp. 189–192, 199–202; Porter, *History of Suffrage in the United States*, pp. 77–107.

44 Bayrd Still, "Patterns of Mid-Nineteenth Century Urbanization in the Middle West," *Mississippi Valley Historical Review*, XXVIII (September 1941), pp. 194–196; Richard C. Wade, *The Urban Frontier* (Cambridge, Mass., 1959), pp. 74–75.

45 Merle Curti, *The Making of an American Community: A Case Study of Democracy in a Frontier County* (Stanford, Calif., 1959), pp. 259–268, 293–302, 320–323.

46 *Ibid.*, pp. 338–344, 416–426, 440–441.

47 Elkins and McKitrick, "A Meaning for Turner's Frontier, II," *loc. cit.*, pp. 566–575.

48 John D. Hicks, *The Constitutions of the Northwest States* (Lincoln, Nebr., 1923).

49 Hall, *Sketches of History, Life, and Manners In the West*, II, 196–197.

50 Wrote Alexis de Tocqueville in *Democracy in America*, I, 318: "Everything is in motion around you; here, the people of one quarter or a town are met to decide upon the building of a church; there, the election of a representative is going on; a little further, the delegates of a district are posting to the town in order to consult upon some local improvement; in another place, the laborers of a village quit their ploughs to deliberate upon the project of a road or a public school." A traveler boarding an Ohio River flatboat was amused to find the passengers holding an election to choose leaders, cooks, and dishwashers. Hall, *The New Purchase*, I, 47–48. That these democratizing forces could operate even in the early Mormon community at the Great Salt Lake, where both a hostile nature and a powerful church operated against popular participation in decision making, is shown in Alexander Evanoff, "The Turner Thesis and Mormon Beginnings in New York and Utah," *Utah Historical Quarterly*, XXXIII (Spring 1965), pp. 157–173.

Chapter 7 Frontier Democracy: Social Aspects

1 Alexis de Tocqueville, *Democracy in America* (Cambridge, Mass., 1863), II, 121.

2 This section summarizes an important article by John W. Ward, "Individualism Today," *Yale Review*, XLIX (Spring 1960), pp. 380–387. For another discussion of the subject see W. Lloyd Warner, *American Life: Dream and Reality* (Chicago, 1962), pp. 138–146.

3 Francis L. K. Hsu, *Americans and Chinese: Two Ways of Life* (New York, 1953), pp. 149–151.

4 Quoted in Art Buchwald, *Is It Safe to Drink the Water* (Cleveland, Ohio, 1961), p. 78.

5 Ilya Ehrenburg, "Ilya Ehrenburg's America," *Harper's Magazine*, CXCIII (December 1946), p. 565.

6 Quoted in Robert G. Athearn, *Westward the Briton* (New York, 1953), p. 100. These points are discussed in Mody C. Boatright, "The Myth of Frontier Individualism," *Southwestern Social Science Quarterly*, XXII (June 1941), pp. 14–32, and more briefly in Ralph Turner, "The Cultural Setting of American Agricultural Problems," *Farmers in a Changing World: 1940 Yearbook of Agriculture* (Washington, D.C., 1941), Pt. V, 1005–1014.

7 William Faux, *Memorable Days in America: Being a Journal of a Tour to the United States* (London, 1823), p. 194.

8 James Flint, *Letters from America* (Edinburgh, 1822), p. 85; George Featherstonhaugh, *Excursion through the Slave States* (New York, 1844), p. 114; Lewis H. Garrard, *Wah-to-Yah, and the Taos Trail* (Cincinnati, Ohio, 1850), pp. 270–271.

9 Michael Chevalier, *Society, Manners and Politics in the United States* (Boston, 1839), p. 224.

10 Frederick Marryat, *A Diary in America* (London, 1839), I, 228; Tocqueville, *Democracy in America*, I, 242.

11 George Flower, *The Errors of Emigrants* (London, 1841), p. 35; Francis Hall, *Travels in Canada and the United States in 1816 and 1817* (London, 1818), p. 28.

12 Caroline M. Kirkland, *Western Clearings* (New York, 1845), p. 217; Charles Dickens, *American Notes* (London, 1842), II, 108.

13 Charles McKnight, *Our Western Border* (Philadelphia, 1875), p. 185; David Thomas, *Travels through the Western Country in the Summer of 1816* (Auburn, N.Y., 1819), p. 124. Good descriptions of cooperative enterprise in the West are in Everett Dick, *The Dixie Frontier* (New York, 1948) and *The Sod House Frontier* (New York, 1937).

14 Noah Smithwick, *Texas Frontiersman: The Evolution of a State* (Austin, Texas, 1910), pp. 239–240, gives some examples.

15 Charles J. Latrobe, *The Rambler in North America* (London, 1835), I, 136–137. These events are described by countless travelers, whose observations are conveniently summarized in R. Carlyle Buley, *The Old Northwest: Pioneer Period, 1815–1840* (Indianapolis, Ind., 1950), I, 322–327. Merle Curti, *The Making of an American Community: A Case Study of Democracy in a Frontier County* (Stanford, Calif., 1959), pp. 115–116, shows that the cooperative spirit was high in the area that he studied, and cites examples.

16 William F. Vogel, "Home Life in Early Indiana," *Indiana Magazine of History*, X (September 1914), p. 297.

17 Contemporary descriptions of Claim Clubs are in Charles W. Dilke, *Greater Britain* (London, 1868), I, 201–202, and George W. Featherstonhaugh, *A Canoe Voyage up the Minnay Sotor* (London, 1847), II, 135–136.

18 Marvin Hunter, ed., *Trail Drivers of Texas* (Nashville, Tenn., 1925), p. 481.

19 J. D. Borthwick, *Three Years in California* (Edinburgh, 1857), p. 369. A case study of a remote mining

area in Nevada substantiates these conclusions. W. Turrentine Jackson, *Treasure Hill. Portrait of a Silver Mining Camp* (Tucson, Ariz., 1963), pp. 223–224.

20 Bayard Taylor, *Eldorado: Or Adventures in the Path of Empire* (New York, 1850), I, 101. A thorough contemporary description of Regulator activity in the West is in John L. McConnel, *Western Characters or Types of Border Life in the Western States* (New York, 1853), pp. 171–176, 244–245. Lynn I. Perrigo, "Law and Order in Early Colorado Mining Camps," *Mississippi Valley Historical Review,* XXVIII (June 1941), pp. 41–62, argues that there was little lawlessness in the region he describes.

21 Buley, *The Old Northwest,* I, 367–369.

22 Bayard Still, "Patterns of Mid-Nineteenth Century Urbanization in the Middle West," *Mississippi Valley Historical Review,* XXVIII (September 1941), pp. 192–194, 204–205.

23 Boatright, "The Myth of Frontier Individualism," *loc. cit.,* pp. 29–30.

24 *Overland Monthly,* II (December 1883), p. 657.

25 For an excellent presentation of this point of view see Earl Pomeroy, "Toward a Reorientation of Western History: Continuity and Environment," *Mississippi Valley Historical Review,* XLI (March 1955), pp. 588–589.

26 Charles A. Murray, *Travels in North America during the Years 1834, 1835, and 1836* (London, 1839), II, 85.

27 Louise A. K. S. Clappe, *The Shirley Letters from California Mines in 1851–52* (San Francisco, Calif., 1922), p. 159.

28 Caleb Atwater, *Remarks Made on a Tour to Prairie du Chien* (Columbus, Ohio, 1831), p. 24. For a similar observation see Isaac Candler, *A Summary View of America* (London, 1824), pp. 466–467.

29 Quoted in Edward E. Dale, "Turner

—The Man and Teacher," *University of Kansas City Review,* XVIII (Autumn 1951), p. 26. For other examples see William A. Baillie-Grohman, *Camps in the Rockies* (New York, 1882), p. 364, and Harriet Martineau, *Society in America* (New York 1837), II, pp. 163, 168.

30 Franklin D. Scott, ed., *Baron Klinkowstrom's America, 1818–1820* (Evanston, Ill., 1952), p. 132.

31 Chevalier, *Society, Manners and Politics in the United States,* pp. 219–220. Additional testimony on this point appears often in the observations of travelers. See for example, Morris Birkbeck, *Letters from Illinois* (London, 1818), pp. 70–71; Elias P. Fordham, *Personal Narrative of Travels* (Cleveland, Ohio, 1906), pp. 219–220; and "Western Prairies," *American Whig Review,* XI (May 1850), p. 526. Curti, *Making of an American Community,* pp. 112–113, concludes that social relationships in the frontier county studied were more democratic than in Eastern states.

32 Timothy Flint, *The History and Geography of the Mississippi Valley* (Cincinnati, Ohio, 1832), I, 188.

33 Francis Baily, *Journal of a Tour in the Unsettled Parts of North America in 1796 and 1797* (London, 1856), p. 132.

34 Baillie-Grohman, *Camps in the Rockies,* pp. 321–322; Flint, *Letters from America,* pp. 266–267; Murray, *Travels in North America,* II, 300–301.

35 James Stuart, *Three Years in North America* (New York, 1833), II, 125.

36 William Cobbett, *A Year's Residence in the United States of America* (London, 1822), p. 194. Other examples are in Baillie-Grohman, *Camps in the Rockies,* pp. 322–323; James Hall, *Letters from the West* (London, 1828), pp. 9–10; and Alexander Mackay, *The Western World* (Philadelphia, 1849), II, 296–297.

37 Many travelers commented on the fact that all Westerners looked and

dressed alike. See for example: Chevalier, *Society, Manners and Politics in the United States*, pp. 302–303, 431; Mrs. Houston, *Hesperos: or, Travels in the West* (London, 1850), I, 97; Stuart, *Three Years in North America*, II, 386–387, 430; and Isaac Weld, *Travels through the States of North America* (London, 1807), I, 232–233.

38 Adlard Welby, *A Visit to North America and the English Settlements in Illinois* (London, 1821), p. 73.

39 Cornelius C. Felton, "Review of Forest Life in North America," *North American Review*, LV (October 1842), p. 511.

40 Mackay, *The Western World*, II, 29; J. H. Beadle, *The Undeveloped West; or, Five Years in the Territories* (Philadelphia, 1873), p. 222.

41 Charles Lyell, *Travels in North America* (London, 1845), I, 49. Other examples are in Frederick J. Gustorf, "Frontier Perils Told by an Early Illinois Visitor," *Journal of the Illinois State Historical Society*, LV (Summer 1962), p. 149; Simon A. O'Ferrall, *A Ramble of Six Thousand Miles Through the United States of America* (London, 1832), p. 308; Lyell, *Travels in North America*, I, 49.

42 Frances Trollope, *Domestic Manners of the Americans* (London, 1832), p. 100.

43 Abner D. Jones, *Illinois and the West* (Boston, 1838), p. 156; Kirkland, *Western Clearings*, pp. 221–222.

44 Faux, *Memorable Days in America*, p. 202; Patrick Shirreff, *A Tour through North America* (Edinburgh, 1835), p. 276. Similar remarks are quoted in Baillie-Grohman, *Camps in the Rockies*, pp. 30–31; George Combe, *Notes on the United States of North America* (Edinburgh, 1841), III, 282; and Tocqueville, *Democracy in America*, I, 228–229.

45 Murray, *Travels in North America*, I, 120; J. E. Alexander, *Transatlantic Sketches, Comprising Visits to the Most Interesting Scenes in North and South America and the West Indies* (London, 1833), II, 64; Frederick L. Olmsted, *A Journey through Texas* (New York, 1857), p. 301.

46 Stuart, *Three Years in North America*, II, 428.

47 Adam Hodgson, *Letters from North America, Written during a Tour in the United States and Canada* (London, 1824), I, 184; Francois A. Michaux, *Travels to the Westward of the Alleghany Mountains* (London, 1805), p. 112; Howard K. Beale, "Theodore Roosevelt's Ancestry, A Study in Heredity," *New York Genealogical and Biographical Record*, LXXV (1954), pp. 196–205.

48 Susan D. Smedes, *Memorial of a Southern Planter* (Baltimore, Md., 1887), p. 67; Duke de La Rochefoucault-Liancourt, *Travels through the United States of North America* (London, 1799), I, 39–40.

49 Baillie-Grohman, *Camps in the Rockies*, p. 6.

50 Baynard R. Hall, *The New Purchase: or, Seven and a Half Years in the Far West* (New York, 1843), I, 94; Harriet Brown, *Grandmother Brown's Hundred Years, 1827–1927* (Boston, 1929), p. 112; Clappe, *The Shirley Letters from California Mines*, p. 182; Caroline M. Kirkland, *A New Home—Who'll Follow? or, Glimpses of Western Life* (New York, 1839), p. 309.

51 O'Ferrall, *A Ramble of Six Thousand Miles*, pp. 243–244.

52 Testimony on this point is abundant in nearly all travel accounts dealing with the frontiers. See, for example, Morris Birkbeck, *Notes on a Journey in America* (London, 1818), pp. 156–157; Samuel Bowles, *Across the Continent* (Springfield, Mass., 1866), p. 62; Charles G. B. Daubney, *Journal of a Tour through the United States, and Canada, Made during the Years 1837–38* (Oxford, England, 1843), p. 192; Faux, *Memorable Days in America*, p. 224;

Fordham, *Personal Narrative of Travels*, p. 229; and Francis Wright, *Views of Society and Manners in America* (London, 1821), p. 228.

53 Quoted in Athearn, *Westward the Briton*, pp. 80–81. Other examples are in Daniel Blowe, *A Geographical, Historical, Commercial, and Agricultural View of the United States of America* (London, 1820), p. 74; Chevalier, *Society, Manners and Politics in the United States*, p. 431; E. Howitt, *Selections from Letters Written during a Tour through the United States* (Nottingham, England [1820]), p. 227; and Richard Parkinson, *A Tour in America in 1798, 1799, and 1800* (London, 1805), I, 19.

54 Combe, *Notes on the United States of North America*, I, 143; Basil Hall, *Travels in North America, in the Years 1827 and 1828* (Edinburgh, 1829), I, 142–143; Harriet Martineau, *Society in America* (New York, 1837), II, 254–255; and Shirreff, *A Tour through North America*, p. 287.

55 Trollope, *Domestic Manners of the Americans*, pp. 54–55. Many other examples are quoted in Athearn, *Westward the Briton*, pp. 83–89. One well-to-do English family that imported its own servants to a Western ranch found that the servants were being invited to tea by a neighboring rancher, who urged them to insist on being treated as equals, even to having dinner with the family and sitting in the parlor with them afterward.

56 Flint, *Letters from America*, pp. 142–143; Marryat, *A Diary in America*, II, 155–156.

57 Featherstonhaugh, *A Canoe Voyage up the Minnay Sotor*, II, 178; Parkinson, *A Tour in America*, I, 31–32; Shirreff, *A Tour through North America*, p. 269.

58 Marryat, *A Diary in America*, II, 156; James F. Muirhead, *America; The Land of Contrasts* (London, 1898), p. 235; Parkinson, *A Tour in*

America, I, 30–31; Welby, *A Visit to North America*, p. 35.

59 William A. Baillie-Grohman. *Fifteen Years' Sport and Life in the Hunting Grounds of Western America and British Columbia* (London, 1900), pp. 4–5.

60 Kirkland, *A New Home*, p. 86.

61 William T. Harris, *Remarks Made during a Tour Through the United States of America, in the Years 1817, 1818, and 1819* (Liverpool, 1819), p. 49. Good descriptions of frontier inns are in Buley, *The Old Northwest*, I, 483, and Ellen Garwood, "Early Texas Inns: A Study in Social Relationships," *Southwestern Historical Quarterly*, LX (October 1956), pp. 219–244.

62 Flint, *Letters from America*, p. 162. For further examples see Alexander, *Transatlantic Sketches*, II, 76; Baillie-Grohman, *Camps in the Rockies*, p. 65; Hodgson, *Letters from North America*, I, 169; and Edouard de Montulé, *Travels in America, 1816–1817* (Bloomington, Ind., 1950), p. 129.

63 Olmstead, *A Journey through Texas*, p. 26; Ferdinand M. Bayard, *Travels of a Frenchman in Maryland and Virginia* (Ann Arbor, Mich., 1950), p. 36.

64 William Kelly, *A Stroll through the Diggings of California* (London, 1852), p. 47.

Chapter 8   The Economic Impact of the Frontier

1 The distinction between these two frontiers is discussed in Benjamin H. Higgins, *Economic Development: Principles, Problems and Policies* (New York, 1959), p. 189.

2 George G. S. Murphy and Arnold Zellner, "Sequential Growth, the Labor-Safety-Valve Doctrine and the Development of American Unionism," *Journal of Economic History*, XIX (September 1959), pp.

402–421, is the best discussion of the subjects treated in this paragraph.

3 George G. S. Murphy and Arnold Zellner, "The Turnerian Frontier Process: Generator of Social and Economic Opportunity," Paper read at meeting of American Historical Association, December 1959, pp. 1–3, 10–12.

4 Alvin H. Hansen, *Fiscal Policy and Business Cycles* (New York, 1941), p. 360, estimates that about one half of the nation's net capital formation during the nineteenth century was traceable to population growth and territorial expansion.

5 An excellent case study of the effect of Ohio's canal system on adjacent regions is in Carter Goodrich *et al., Canals and American Economic Development* (New York, 1961). The subject is more broadly discussed in Walter Isard, "Transportation Development and Business Cycles," *Quarterly Journal of Economics,* LVII (November 1942).

6 Murphy and Zellner, "Turnerian Frontier Process," *loc. cit.,* pp. 13–18.

7 Convincing statistical evidence on this point is in Karl W. Deutsch, *Nationalism and Social Communication* (Boston, 1953), pp. 36–45.

8 The best discussion of these subjects is in David M. Potter, *People of Plenty: Economic Abundance and the American Character* (Chicago, 1954), pp. 78–90.

9 On the publication of this announcement, the New York *Herald Tribune* wryly asked: "What, no caviar?"

10 Frances Trollope, *Domestic Manners of the Americans* (London, 1832), I, 43; Frederick Marryat, *A Diary in America* (London, 1839), I, 22. This subject is admirably discussed in Marcus Cunliffe, *The Nation Takes Shape, 1789–1837* (Chicago, 1959), pp. 188–189.

11 James Bryce, *The American Commonwealth* (Chicago, 1891), II, 315; Ilya Ehrenburg, "Ilya Ehrenburg's America," *Harper's Magazine,*

CXCIII (December 1946), pp. 562–576.

12 This theory is advanced in A. H. Maslow, *Motivation and Personality* (New York, 1954).

13 John L. McConnel, *Western Characters or Types of Border Life in the Western States* (New York, 1853), p. 288. For similar comments see George Combe, *Notes on the United States of North America* (Edinburgh, 1841), II, 197–198; E. Howitt, *Selections from Letters Written during a Tour through the United States, in the Summer and Autumn of 1819* (Nottingham, England, [1820]), p. 222; Alexander Mackay, *The Western World* (Philadelphia, 1849), II, 296; and Marryat, *Diary in America,* I, 23.

14 Combe, *Notes on the United States of North America,* II, 197–198.

15 Caroline M. Kirkland, *Western Clearings* (New York, 1845), p. 88. Another traveler wrote: "Every moment, of every day, the mind, the ingenuity, the exertion, of the settler, are on the stretch, merely to procure just enough to support existence." Howitt, *Selections from Letters,* pp. 44–45.

16 Charles White, "Influence of Colleges, Especially on Western Education and Civilization," *Biblical Repository and Classical Review,* IV (July 1848), p. 383.

17 Isaac Weld, *Travels through the States of North America, and the Provinces of Upper and Lower Canada, during the years 1795, 1796, and 1797* (London, 1807), I, 292.

18 George W. Featherstonhaugh, *Excursion through the Slave States* (New York, 1844), p. 69.

19 George W. Barnes, "Pioneer Preacher —An Autobiography," *Nebraska History,* XXVII (April–June 1946), pp. 79–80; Mrs. Houston, *Hesperos: or, Travels in the West* (London, 1850), I, 107–108.

20 Quoted in Robert G. Athearn, *Westward the Briton* (New York, 1953), pp. 93–94.

21 Marryat, *A Diary in America*, I, 209; Trollope, *Domestic Manners of the Americans*, pp. 372–373.

22 Adam Hodgson, *Letters from North America, Written during a Tour in the United States and Canada* (London, 1824), I, 304–305.

23 Samuel Bowles, *Across the Continent* (Springfield, Mass., 1866), pp. 201–202.

24 Michael Chevalier, *Society, Manners and Politics in the United States* (Boston, 1839), pp. 283–284. For a similar comment see Harriet Martineau, *Society in America* (New York, 1837), II, 136–137.

25 Hodgson, *Letters from North America*, I, 153. Observations on the pace of life in the West are also in Basil Hall, *Travels in North America, in the Years 1827 and 1828* (Edinburgh, 1829), I, 138, and Dwight L. Dumond, ed., *Letters of James Gilespie Birney, 1831–1837* (New York, 1938), I, 69.

26 Marryat, *A Diary in America*, I, 18; Francis Lieber, ed., *Letters to a Gentleman in Germany* (Philadelphia, 1834), p. 287.

27 Houston, *Hesperos*, I, 149.

28 Quoted in Frederick J. Turner, "Pioneer Ideals and the State University," in *The Frontier in American History* (New York, 1920), p. 275.

29 John Leng, *America in 1876* (London, 1877), p. 317.

30 William A. Baillie-Grohman, *Camps in the Rockies* (New York, 1882), p. 21.

31 Edouard de Montulé, *Travels in America, 1816–1817* (Bloomington, Ind., 1950), p. 170.

32 Francis Wright, *Views of Society and Manners in America* (London, 1821), p. 197. Comparable observations are in Thomas Ashe, *Travels in America, Performed in 1806* (London, 1808), II, 238–239; William N. Blane, *An Excursion through the United States and Canada, during the Years 1822–23* (London, 1824), p. 125; Francis Hall, *Travels in Canada and the United States in 1816*

and *1817* (London, 1818), p. 46; Charles J. Latrobe, *The Rambler in North America* (London, 1835), I, 135; Charles Lyell, *Travels in North America* (London, 1845), I, 20–21; and E. Stanley, *Journal of a Tour in America, 1824–1825* (n.p., 1930), pp. 71, 182.

33 Howitt, *Selections from Letters*, p. 200. Similar comments are in Combe, *Notes on the United States of North America*, II, 334; D. Griffiths, Jr., *Two Years' Residence in the New Settlements of Ohio* (London, 1835), p. 65; Frederick L. Olmstead, *A Journey in the Back Country* (New York, 1860), p. 20; and Weld, *Travels through the States of North America*, II, 328.

34 James E. Jones, *A History of Columbia County, Wisconsin* (Chicago, 1914), I, 125.

35 William W. Johnson, *Kelly Blue* (New York, 1960), p. 122.

36 Thomas Hulme, "Journal of a Tour in the Western Countries of America," in William Cobbett, *A Year's Residence, in the United States of America* (London, 1822), p. 287.

37 Adlard Welby, *A Visit to North America and the English Settlements in Illinois* (London, 1821), p. 145. For a similar experience see Hodgson, *Letters from North America*, II, 37–38.

38 Thomas Nichols, *Forty Years of American Life, 1820–1861* (New York, 1937), p. 63.

39 Daniel Drake, *Discourse on the History, Character, and Prospects of the West* (Cincinnati, Ohio, 1834), pp. 8–9.

40 Baillie-Grohman, *Camps in the Rockies*, pp. 20–21; Mackay, *The Western World*, II, 296.

41 John Woods, *Two Years' Residence in the Settlement on the English Prairie in the Illinois Country, June 25, 1820–July 3, 1821* (London, 1822), 244; Bryce, *The American Commonwealth*, II, 893.

42 This paragraph is summarized from an extensive discussion in Abbott P.

Usher, *A History of Mechanical Inventions* (2nd edn., New York, 1954), pp. 56–83.

43 William T. Harris, *Remarks Made during a Tour Through the United States of America, in the Years 1817, 1818, and 1819* (Liverpool, 1819), p. 48; Wright, *Views of Society and Manners in America*, p. 190; John J. Ingalls, *The Writings of John Ingalls* (Kansas City, Kan., 1902), pp. 465–466. Similar comments are in Houston, *Hesperos*, I, 116–117, and Kirkland, *Western Clearings*, p. vii.

44 John M. Peck, *A New Guide for Emigrants to the West* (Boston, 1836), pp. 122–123.

45 Trollope, *Domestic Manners of the Americans*, p. 219. See also Ferdinand M. Bayard, *Travels of a Frenchman in Maryland and Virginia* (Ann Arbor, Mich., 1950), p. 24; Cobbett, *A Year's Residence in the United States*, p. 181; James Hall, *Letters from the West* (London, 1828), p. 290; Caroline M. Kirkland, *A New Home—Who'll Follow? or, Glimpses of Western Life* (New York, 1839), p. 79; and James Stuart, *Three Years in North America* (New York, 1833), II, 299.

46 Clarence H. Danhof, "American Evaluations of European Agriculture," *Journal of Economic History. Supplement IX* (1949), pp. 61–71.

47 Chevalier, *Society, Manners and Politics in the United States*, p. 313. Similar comments are in Ashe, *Travels in America*, II, 224–226; Joseph Doddridge, *Notes on the Settlement and Indian Wars, of the Western Parts of Virginia and Pennsylvania* (Wellsburg, Virginia, 1824), pp. 140–147; and François A. Michaux, *Travels to the Westward of the Alleghany Mountains* (London, 1805), p. 152.

48 *Western Farmer*, May 1835, quoted in R. Carlyle Buley, *The Old Northwest: Pioneer Period, 1815–1840* (Indianapolis, Ind., 1950), I, 197–198.

49 Earle D. Ross, "Retardation in Farm Technology Before the Power Age," *Agricultural History*, XXX (January 1956), pp. 11–14.

50 Baillie-Grohman, *Camps in the Rockies*, pp. 21–22; Barnes, "Pioneer Preacher—An Autobiography," *loc. cit.*, p. 78; James Hall, *Sketches of History, Life, and Manners in the West* (Philadelphia, 1835), II, 67; Charles F. Hoffman, *A Winter in the West, by a New-Yorker* (New York, 1835), I, 196–197; Trollope, *Domestic Manners of the Americans*, p. 49.

51 Everett Dick, *The Dixie Frontier* (New York, 1948), p. 32.

52 James Caird, *Prairie Farming in America* (New York, 1859), pp. 56–57.

53 Walter P. Webb, *The Great Plains* (Boston, 1931), pp. 510–515 describes the impact of the Great Plains on invention. His conclusions are challenged in Fred A. Shannon, "An Appraisal of Walter Prescott Webb's *The Great Plains*," *Critiques of Research in the Social Sciences: III* (New York, 1940), pp. 79–97, which points out that inventions were made behind, not on the frontier. Shannon does not dispute the stimulus to invention provided by the Great Plains frontier.

54 This theme is developed in two works by William F. Ogburn, *Social Change with Respect to Culture and Original Nature* (New York, 1922), pp. 99–103, and *Technology and International Relations* (Chicago, 1949), pp. 16–27.

55 This material is drawn from the excellent article by Allan G. Bogue, "Pioneer Farmers and Innovation," *Iowa Journal of History*, LVI (January 1958), pp. 1–36.

56 Earle D. Ross, *Iowa Agriculture: An Historical Survey* (Iowa City, Iowa, 1951), p. 49.

57 Hamilton County, Iowa, was the subject of this study, the results of which are summarized in Bogue, "Pioneer Farmers and Innovation," *loc. cit.*, pp. 6–36.

58 The best discussions of the frontier's impact on the common law are in Roscoe Pound, *The Spirit of the Common Law* (Boston, 1921), and Francis R. Aumann, *The Changing American Legal System: Some Selected Phases* (Columbus, Ohio, 1940), pp. 9–152 and especially pp. 14–16. Both credit the frontier with major importance as a molding force. The opposite viewpoint is argued in a biography of a frontier judge: William B. Hamilton, *Anglo-American Law on the Frontier: Thomas Rodney and His Territorial Cases* (Durham, N.C., 1953). Further discussion of the transfer of legal institutions to the West is in the introduction to the following collections of documents: Francis S. Philbrick, "The Laws of Indiana Territory, 1801–1809," *Illinois State Historical Library Collections*, XXI (Springfield, Ill., 1930); Francis S. Philbrick, ed., "The Laws of Illinois Territory, 1809–1818," *Illinois State Historical Library Collections*, XXV (Springfield, Ill., 1950); and William W. Blume, ed., *Transactions of the Supreme Court of Michigan, 1805–1837*, 5 volumes (Ann Arbor, Mich., 1935–1940). Some additional information is in John H. Bickett, Jr., "Origin of Some Distinctive Features of Texan Civilization," Philosophical Society of Texas, *Proceedings of the Annual Meeting, Dallas, December 1, 1945* (Dallas, Texas, 1946), pp. 9–48. A competent review article summarizing works on the subject is Clarence E. Carter, "The Transit of Law to the Frontier: A Review Article," *Journal of Mississippi History*, XVI (July 1954), pp. 183–192.

59 Quoted in Carter, "The Transit of Law to the Frontier," *loc. cit.*, p. 191.

60 Richard D. Younger, "The Grand Jury on the Frontier," *Wisconsin Magazine of History*, XL (Autumn 1956), pp. 3–8.

61 Pound, *Spirit of the Common Law*, pp. 120–127.

62 Brief discussions of changes in irri-

gation and mining law are in Webb, *Great Plains*, pp. 431–446. On mining law see also Rodman W. Paul, *California Gold: The Beginning of Mining in the Far West* (Cambridge, Mass., 1947), pp. 210–216.

Chapter 9 The Frontier and the Migratory Compulsion

1 Stephen Vincent Benét, *Western Star* (New York, 1943), p. 3.

2 *The New York Times*, June 14, 1942; Ilya Ehrenburg, "Ilya Ehrenburg's America," *Harper's Magazine*, CXCIII (December 1946), p. 564.

3 Quoted in George W. Pierson, "The Moving American," *Yale Review*, XLIV (Autumn 1954), p. 103. This excellent article, and three others on mobility by the same author, have been the source of many of the quotations and some of the ideas expressed in this chapter. Professor Pierson, however, is concerned only with the nature and results of American mobility, not its origin in the frontiering experience. See "The M-Factor in American History," *American Quarterly*, XIV (Summer 1962), pp. 275–289; "Under a Wandering Star," *Virginia Quarterly Review*, XXXIX (Autumn 1963), pp. 621–638, and "A Restless Temper," *American Historical Review*, LXIX (July 1964), pp. 969–989.

4 Rembert W. Patrick, "The Mobile Frontier," *Journal of Southern History*, XXIX (February 1963), pp. 3–18. Despite its title, this is a discussion of modern tourism in the United States.

5 Compiled from figures in United States Bureau of the Census, *Statistical Abstract of the United States* (Washington, D.C., 1960), pp. 36–37; (Washington, D.C., 1961), pp. 33–34; (Washington, D.C., 1962), p. 34.

6 *Ibid.* (Washington, D.C., 1961), p. 34; Everett S. Lee, "The Turner

Thesis Re-examined," *American Quarterly*, XIII (Spring 1961), p. 79; Carter Goodrich *et. al.*, *Migration and Economic Opportunity* (Philadelphia, 1936), p. 503; and C. Warren Thornthwaite, *Internal Migration in the United States* (Philadelphia, 1934), p. 3, have information on recent migration patterns.

7 Neil Morgan, "The Great Westward Tilt," *Saturday Review*, XLV (October 20, 1962), p. 40. The term "Western States" includes the Mountain and Pacific states, including Alaska and Hawaii.

8 Morgan, "Great Westward Tilt," *loc. cit.*, p. 64.

9 Pitirim Sorokin, *Social Mobility* (New York, 1927), pp. 383–387. Statistics on comparative mobility are impossible to find. The Central Statistical Office, *Annual Abstract of Statistics* (London, 1960 and 1961), has no information on British migration.

10 United States Bureau of the Census, *Census of Population: 1960. Volume I Characteristics of Population. Part A Number of Inhabitants* (Washington, D.C., 1961), p. xiii. This volume contains useful tables on recent mobility.

11 Sorokin, *Social Mobility*, pp. 381–383.

12 Clarence H. Danhof, "Economic Validity of the Safety-Valve Doctrine," *Journal of Economic History Supplement* (December 1941), p. 99.

13 Washington Irving, *A History of New York* (New York, 1809), I, 175.

14 Cotton Mather, *The Short History of New-England. A Recapitulation of Wonderful Passages Which Have Occur'd* (Boston, 1694), p. 45, contains the quotation from Mather. That from the Virginia governor is borrowed from Pierson, "The Moving American," *loc. cit.*, p. 100.

15 Albert D. Richardson, *Beyond the Mississippi* (Hartford, Conn., 1867); p. 23; James Bryce, *The American*

Commonwealth (Chicago, 1891), I, 383.

16 Estwick Evans, *A Pedestrious Tour, of Four Thousand Miles, through the Western States and Territories* (Concord, N.H., 1819), p. 39.

17 Alexis de Tocqueville, *Democracy in America* (Cambridge, Mass., 1863), I, 376–377; David M. Coyner, *The Lost Trappers* (Cincinnati, Ohio, 1847), pp. 248–249.

18 William A. Baillie-Grohman, *Camps in the Rockies* (New York, 1882), p. 330.

19 John Leng, *America in 1876* (London, 1877), p. 312. Incidents of travel are in such works as Morris Birkbeck, *Notes on a Journey in America* (London, 1818), p. 102; Daniel Blowe, *A Geographical, Historical, Commercial, and Agricultural View of the United States of America* (London, 1820), p. 64; and Fortescue Cuming, *Sketches of a Tour to the Western Country* (Pittsburgh, Pa., 1810), p. 146.

20 Franklin D. Scott, ed., *Baron Klinkowstrom's America, 1818–1820* (Evanston, Ill., 1952), p. 75. Similar comments are in Richard G. A. Levinge; *Echoes of the Backwoods; or Sketches of Transatlantic Life* (London, 1846), II, 14, and Harriet Martineau, *Retrospect of Western Travel* (London, 1838), II, 38.

21 Timothy Flint, *Recollections of the Last Ten Years* (Boston, 1826), p. 76. See also Charles Dickens, *American Notes* (London, 1842), II, 145; G. Imlay, *A Topographical Description of the Western Territory of North America* (London, 1792), p. 149; and James Hall, *Sketches of the History, Life, and Manners in the West* (Philadelphia, 1835), I, 22.

22 William Oliver, *Eight Months in Illinois* (Newcastle-upon-Tyne, England, 1843), p. 190.

23 John L. McConnel, *Western Characters or Types of Border Life in the Western States* (New York, 1853), p. 112. Instances of such restlessness are in Blowe, *Geographical, Histori-*

cal, Commercial, and Agricultural View of the United States, p. 63; Irving, *History of New York*, I, 178; and Patrick Shirreff, *A Tour through North America* (Edinburgh, 1835), p. 81.

24 Isaac Weld, *Travels through the States of North America* (London, 1807), I, 126; James Flint, *Letters from America* (Edinburgh, 1822), pp. 48–49.

25 James Caird, *Prairie Farming in America* (New York, 1859), p. 117; Elias P. Fordham, *Personal Narrative of Travels in Virginia, Maryland, Pennsylvania, Ohio, Indiana, Kentucky* (Cleveland, Ohio, 1906), p. 105; Thomas Hulme, "Journal of a Tour in the Western Countries of America," in William Cobbett, *A Year's Residence, in the United States of America* (London, 1822), p. 286; David Thomas, *Travels through the Western Country in the Summer of 1816* (Auburn, N.Y., 1819), p. 49.

26 J. H. Beadle, *The Undeveloped West; or, Five Years in the Territories* (Philadelphia, 1873), p. 229; Frederick L. Olmsted, *A Journey through Texas* (New York, 1857), p. 82.

27 Tocqueville, *Democracy in America*, I, 377.

28 Flint, *Recollections of the Last Ten Years*, p. 242; Francois A. Michaux, *Travels to the Westward of the Alleghany Mountains* (London, 1805), pp. 137–138; Francois M. Parrin du Lac, *Travels through the Two Louisianas and Among the Savage Nations of the Missouri* (London, 1807), p. 37. One traveler in the West explained the process in these words: "A man removes from the eastern border to the West of Pennsylvania. Perhaps he there erects a house and in a few years sees a good farm around him; another wishing to remove west offers him a sum for it, so much larger than his original outlay that he is tempted to sell, and emigrate farther west. He with his money purchases a place of a man in Ohio, who sells in the same way and passes on. In a few years the Pennsylvania man sells again, and again removes, so that there is a constant stream going step by step to fill up the immense plains and valleys which here abound." Mrs. Steele, *A Summer Journey in the West* (New York, 1841), p. 152.

29 Basil Hall, *Travels in North America, in the Years 1827 and 1828* (Edinburgh, 1829), I, 147–148; Amos A. Parker, *Trip to the West and Texas* (Concord, N.H., 1835), pp. 20–21, both report on the Michigan pioneer. The Texas move is reported in Andrew F. Muir, ed., *Texas in 1837: An Anonymous, Contemporary Narrative* (Austin, Texas, 1958), p. 70. A similar instance is reported in John Parsons, *A Tour through Indiana in 1840* (New York, 1920), pp. 225–226.

30 Edwin James, *Account of an Expedition from Pittsburgh to the Rocky Mountains, Performed in the Years 1819 and '20* (Philadelphia, 1823), I, 106. One of Frederick Jackson Turner's students, Professor E. E. Dale of the University of Oklahoma, reports that his own father migrated as a boy from Kentucky to Missouri, then to California in the 1850 rush, returned home via Panama, joined the Pike's Peak miners in 1858–1859, moved to Nebraska in the early 1870s, then from Nebraska to Texas, and finally from Texas to Oklahoma. A year before his death he considered moving to Oregon to raise prunes. E. E. Dale, "Turner—The Man and Teacher," *University of Kansas City Review*, XVIII (Autumn 1951), p. 27.

31 Beadle, *The Undeveloped West*, p. 229.

32 Edward Ullman, "Amenities as a Factor in Regional Growth," *The Geographical Review*, XLIV (January 1954), pp. 119–132, explores the amenities factor as a motive for migration.

33 Peter H. Rossi, *Why Families Move* (Glencoe, Ill., 1955), pp. 9, 43–44, 96–98, 120–122.

34 Lee, "The Turner Thesis Re-examined," *loc. cit.*, pp. 80–81; Pierson, "The M-Factor in American History," *loc. cit.*, p. 281.

35 Flint, *Recollections of the Last Ten Years*, p. 202; Charles F. Hoffman, *A Winter in the West, by a New-Yorker* (New York, 1835), I, 183–184; Parker, *Trip to the West and Texas*, p. 20.

36 William Faux, *Memorable Days in America: Being a Journal of a Tour to the United States* (London, 1823), pp. 179–180; Flint, *Recollections of the Last Ten Years*, p. 203.

37 J. E. Alexander, *Transatlantic Sketches* (London, 1833), II, 114. A traveler in Kansas in 1871 talked with a prospering farmer who believed he was living in a real heaven on earth, but was about to move because he could "get twice as much [land] out on the Wichita, and have enough left to stock it." Beadle, *The Undeveloped West*, p. 224.

38 Merle Curti, *The Making of an American Community: A Case Study of Democracy in a Frontier County* (Stanford, Calif., 1959), pp. 65–83, 141–143, 443–444.

39 James C. Malin, "The Turnover of Farm Population in Kansas," *Kansas Historical Quarterly*, IX (November 1935), pp. 339–372.

40 Arthur F. Bentley, *The Condition of the Western Farmer as Illustrated by the Economic History of a Nebraska Community* (Baltimore, Md., 1893), pp. 34–39.

41 James C. Malin, *Winter Wheat in the Golden Belt of Kansas* (Lawrence, Kan., 1944), p. 4. Today, as in pioneer days, the first to leave a community are the last to arrive. An analysis of Farm Security Administration projects during the 1930s showed that families who had been most mobile prior to their settlement were the ones most likely to move on.

Allan Bogue, "Social Theory and the Pioneer," *Agricultural History*, XXXIV (January 1960), pp. 24–25.

42 Michael Chevalier, *Society, Manners and Politics in the United States* (Boston, 1839), p. 298.

43 The best discussion of the effect of migration on the American character and institutions is Pierson, "A Restless Temper . . .", *loc. cit.*, pp. 969–989.

44 Benjamin Malzberg and Everett S. Lee, *Migration and Mental Disease* (New York, 1956), is the standard work on this subject.

45 Lee, "The Turner Thesis Re-examined," *loc. cit.*, p. 82.

46 *Ibid.*, p. 82; Pierson, "A Restless Temper . . . ," *loc cit.*, pp. 16–17.

47 Chevalier, *Society, Manners and Politics in the United States*, p. 415.

48 Simon A. O'Ferrall, *A Ramble of Six Thousand Miles Through the United States of America* (London, 1832), p. 167; Hall, *Travels in North America*, I, 147. Similar comments are in Duke de La Rochefoucault-Liancourt, *Travels through the United States of North America* (London, 1799), I, 107; and Charles A. Murray, *Travels in North America during the Years 1834, 1835, and 1836* (London, 1839), I, 148.

49 Chevalier, *Society, Manners and Politics in the United States*, p. 286.

50 Pierson, "A Restless Temper . . . ," *loc. cit.*, pp. 5–10; Lee, "The Turner Thesis Re-examined," *loc. cit.*, p. 81; Rowland Berthoff, "The American Social Order: A Conservative Hypothesis," *American Historical Review*, LXV (April 1960), p. 499–502.

51 An appraisal of the frontier's impact on Protestant churches, with emphasis on the Methodists and Baptists, is in T. Scott Miyakawa, *Protestants and Pioneers* (Chicago, 1964). The effects of migration on the Roman Catholic Church are described in Stanley Elkins and Eric McKitrick, "Ideas in Motion," *American Quar-*

terly, XII (Summer 1960), pp. 188–197.

52 Pierson, "M-Factor in American History," *loc cit.*, p. 288.

Chapter 10 The Frontier and American Behavioral Patterns

1 Michael Chevalier, "The Western Steamboats," *Western Monthly Magazine*, IV (December 1835), p. 414.

2 Ilya Ehrenburg, "Ilya Ehrenburg's America," *Harper's Magazine*, CXCII (December 1946), p. 564.

3 D. Griffiths, Jr., *Two Years' Residence in the New Settlements of Ohio* (London, 1835), p. 54.

4 Frederick Marryat, *A Diary in America* (London, 1836), I, 214–215. For a similar viewpoint see Francis Hall, *Travels in Canada and the United States in 1816 and 1817* (London, 1818), p. 192.

5 George W. Pierson, *Tocqueville and Beaumont in America* (New York, 1938), pp. 118–119; James Bryce, *The American Commonwealth* (Chicago, 1891), II, 290.

6 An excellent discussion of this subject is in Boyd C. Shafer, "The American Heritage of Hope," *Mississippi Valley Historical Review*, XXXVII (December 1950), pp. 427–450.

7 Quoted in Ernest Marchant, "Emerson and the Frontier," *American Literature*, III (May 1931), p. 159.

8 Christoper C. Andrews, *Minnesota and Dacotah: Or Letters Descriptive of a Tour through the North-West* (Washington, D.C., 1857), p. 40. Other examples are in Washington Irving, *A History of New York* (New York, 1809), I, 176–177, and Frank Marryat, *Mountains and Molehills or Recollections of a Burnt Journal* (London, 1855), p. 23.

9 Morris Birkbeck, *Notes on a Journey in America* (London, 1818), pp. 40–41.

10 Frederick Merk, *Manifest Destiny and Mission in American History: a Reinterpretation* (New York, 1963), presents evidence to show that the spirit of manifest destiny was less widely diffused than formerly believed. The existence of such a spirit, no matter how widely held, testifies to American optimism.

11 This attitude is explored in Arthur A. Ekirch, *The Idea of Progress in America, 1815–1860* (New York, 1944), pp. 41–51, 86–90.

12 Estwick Evans, *A Pedestrious Tour, of Four Thousand Miles, through the Western States and Territories* (Concord, N.H., 1819), p. 192.

13 Eliza Farnham, *Life in Prairie Land* (New York, 1846), pp. 90–91.

14 Alexis de Tocqueville, *Democracy in America* (New York, 1945), II, 74.

15 Timothy Flint, *Recollections of the Last Ten Years* (Boston, 1826), p. 360.

16 William T. Harris, *Remarks Made during a Tour through the United States of America* (Liverpool, England, 1819), p. 36.

17 George W. Featherstonhaugh, *Excursion through the Slave States* (New York, 1844), pp. 61–62; Flint, *Recollections of the Last Ten Years*, p. 185; James Hall, *The West: Its Commerce and Navigation* (Cincinnati, Ohio, 1848), p. 12; J. H. Ingraham, *The South West. By a Yankee* (New York, 1835), II, 51.

18 Impressive evidence on this point is in Merle Curti, *The Making of an American Community: A Case Study of Democracy in a Frontier County* (Stanford, Calif., 1950), pp. 116–118, which shows that the idea of progress was more firmly emplanted in a typical Wisconsin frontier county than in the East. For additional comment by travelers see Harriet Martineau, *Society in America* (New York, 1837), II, 164, and Catherine Stewart, *New Homes in the West* (Nashville, Tenn., 1843), p. 105.

19 Abner D. Jones, *Illinois and the West* (Boston, 1838), p. 165.
20 Charles F. Hoffman, *A Winter in the West, by a New-Yorker* (New York, 1835), I, 187–189; Foster B. Zincke, *Last Winter in the United States* (London, 1868), p. 109; Othman A. Abbott, *Recollections of a Pioneer Lawyer* (Lincoln, Nebr., 1929), p. 122.
21 The traditional concept of "nationality" as a group of peoples bound by a common culture, language, religion, and usually race has been upset by the rise of twentieth-century nations in Africa and Asia that have no cultural homogeneity. This whole subject is admirably explored in Philip L. White, "The Origins of American Nationality," unpublished essay in possession of author, pp. 1–6. Much of the section that follows is based on this penetrating analysis of early American nationalism.
22 This concept is developed in Hans Kohn, *American Nationalism* (New York, 1957), pp. 41–89.
23 Mrs. Houston, *Hesperos: or, Travels in the West* (London, 1850), II, 24–25; Basil Hall, *Travels in North America, in the Years 1827 and 1828* (Edinburgh, 1829), I, 109; Adam Hodgson, *Letters from North America, Written during a Tour in the United States and Canada* (London, 1824), II, 31; Tocqueville, *Democracy in America*, I, 249. For similar comments see John Palmer, *Journal of Travels in the United States of America* (London, 1818), pp. 79–81; Isaac Weld, *Travels through the States of North America* (London, 1807), I, 125; and Francis Wright, *Views of Society and Manners in America* (London, 1821), p. 352.
24 Frances Trollope, *Domestic Manners of the Americans* (London, 1832), 160–161; Michael Chevalier, *Society, Manners and Politics in the United States* (Boston, 1839), p. 188.
25 Houston, *Hesperos*, II, 86.
26 Isaac Candler, *A Summary View of*

America (London, 1824), p. 476. Reports of travelers on conversations with natives on nationalism must be accepted with caution. The typical Westerner loved nothing better than to "humbug" a greenhorn; undoubtedly many of the spread-eagle remarks heard by visitors were deliberately designed to take them in. Yet even if this caution is used, a sturdy nationalistic spirit is manifested in every report on conversations with frontiersmen.
27 Edouard de Montulé, *Travels in America, 1816–1817* (Bloomington, Ind., 1950), p. 172. See also Trollope, *Domestic Manners of the Americans*, p. 157.
28 Daniel Drake, *Discourse on the History, Character, and Prospects of the West* (Cincinnati, Ohio, 1834), pp. 40–41; Charles Lyell, *A Second Visit to the United States of North America* (New York, 1849), II, 160.
29 Timothy Flint, *The History and Geography of the Mississippi Valley* (Cincinnati, Ohio, 1832), I, 135; Alexander Mackay, *The Western World* (Philadelphia, 1849), II, 139; Samuel Bowles, *Across the Continent* (Springfield, Mass., 1866), pp. 220–221.
30 These paragraphs are based on the brilliant interpretation of the Revolutionary era in terms of nationalism and localism in William T. Hutchinson, "Unite to Divide; Divide to Unite: The Shaping of American Federalism," *Mississippi Valley Historical Review*, XLVI (June 1959), pp. 3–18, and especially pp. 9–11.
31 A typical Western attitude is expressed in Flint, *Recollections of the Last Ten Years*, pp. 251–252. See also Kohn, *American Nationalism*, pp. 21–23.
32 James Hall, *Letters from the West* (London 1828), pp. 173–174; Palmer, *Journal of Travels in the United States of America*, pp. 152–153.
33 Robert G. Harper of South Carolina, quoted in *Observations on the North-*

American Land Company, Lately Instituted in Philadelphia (London, 1796), p. 113; Mackay, *The Western World*, II, 288.

34 The discussion that follows on the federal-state "partnership" is based on the fresh interpretations advanced in the excellent study by Daniel J. Elazar, *The American Partnership: Intergovernmental Co-operation in the Nineteenth-Century United States* (Chicago, 1962). The thesis is advanced on pp. 11–24 and 304–307.

35 Andrews, *Minnesota and Dacotah*, pp. 58–59.

36 Elazar, *The American Partnership*, pp. 131–134, 278–293, 317–323.

37 Tocqueville, *Democracy in America*, I, 310–311; Wright, *Views of Society and Manners in America*, pp. 396–397.

38 *Congressional Globe*, 38th Cong. 1st Sess., p. 2037.

39 Elazar, *The American Partnership*, pp. 323–325.

40 Edwin L. Godkin, "Aristocratic Opinions of Democracy," *North American Review*, CCVI (January 1865), pp. 220–223.

41 Flint, *Recollections of the Last Ten Years*, pp. 185–189.

42 John Bradbury, *Travels in the Interior of America, in the Years 1809, 1810, and 1811* (Liverpool, England, 1817), p. 305; Candler, *Summary View of America*, pp. 482–483; Palmer, *Journal of Travels in the United States of America*, pp. 129–130.

43 Amos A. Parker, *Trip to the West and Texas* (Concord, N.H., 1835), pp. 116–117; Weld, *Travels through the States of North America*, 1, 234–235. Comparable comments are in most of the travel accounts originating in the West at this time.

44 Charles Dickens, *American Notes* (London, 1842), II, 55–56.

45 E. Howitt, *Selections from Letters Written during a Tour through the United States, in the Summer and Autumn of 1819* (Nottingham, England [1820]), pp. 223–224.

46 Martineau, *Society in America*, I, 229; Parker, *Trip to the West and Texas*, p. 90; Elias P. Fordham, *Personal Narrative of Travels* (Cleveland, Ohio, 1906), p. 145.

47 Bradbury, *Travels in the Interior of America*, pp. 306–307.

48 Baynard R. Hall, *The New Purchase: or, Seven and a Half Years in the Far West* (New York, 1843), II, 70; Hall, *Letters from the West*, p. 124.

49 John M. Letts, *California Illustrated* (New York, 1852), p. 89; Sarah Royce, *A Frontier Lady. Recollections of the Gold Rush and Early California* (New Haven, 1932), pp. 80–81.

50 Ernest R. Groves, *The American Woman* (Greenberg, N.Y., 1937), pp. 92–93, deals inadequately with this subject. A more searching study by David M. Potter, "American Women and the American Character," *Stetson University Bulletin*, LXII (January 1962), pp. 3–6, challenges the view that women were essential to the frontier economy.

51 Farnham, *Life in Prairie Land*, p. 37.

52 Hall, *The New Purchase*, II, 12.

53 Isabelle Randall, *A Lady's Ranch Life in Montana* (London, 1887), p. 117. An identical appraisal is in Hoffman, *A Winter in the West*, II, 51–53.

54 Charles Lyell, *Travels in North America* (London, 1845), I, 57; Dickens, *American Notes*, II, 47; Chevalier, *Society, Manners and Politics in the United States*, p. 430.

55 William H. Dixon, *White Conquest* (London, 1876), I, 166.

56 William H. Dixon, *New America* (Philadelphia, 1867), I, 136. A similar observation is in Iza Duffus Hardy, *Through Cities and Prairie Lands* (Chicago, 1882), p. 93.

57 William A. Bell, *New Tracks in North America* (London, 1869), I, 16; Abbott, *Recollections of a Pioneer Lawyer*, pp. 152–153.

Chapter 11 The
Persistence of Frontier Traits

1 This paragraph is based on the stimulating hypothesis presented in Walter P. Webb, *The Great Frontier* (Boston, 1952).

2 Material on the decline of optimism is drawn from a challenging article by Robert L. Heilbroner, "The Impasse of American Optimism," *The American Scholar*, XXIX (Winter 1959–1960), pp. 13–20.

Bibliographical Notes

Travelers
View the American Frontier

Of the hundreds of travelers from overseas who visited the successive American frontiers during the eighteenth and nineteenth centuries, a small number were particularly acute observers of the forming societies about them. Noting the differences between their own countrymen and the pioneers, they described the Americans in general and Westerners in particular as exhibiting the traits and characteristics that historians have ascribed to the frontier experience. Mobility, an easy-going social democracy, inquisitiveness, nationalism, inventiveness, wastefulness, and respect for the feminine sex were paid particular attention as pioneer characteristics, somehow associated with life in the thinly settled West.

Three of these travelers, two from France and one from Britain, made the American character their especial concern. Alexis de Tocqueville, *Democracy in America*, 2 vols. (London, 1835), Michael Chevalier, *Society, Manners and Politics in the United States* (Boston, 1839), and James Bryce, *The American Commonwealth*, 2 vols. (New York, 1888), deal with the United States as a whole rather than with the frontier, but are essential in understanding the emergence of distinctly American traits.

Relatively few Europeans ventured into the back country during the eighteenth century. Francis Baily, *Journal of a Tour in the Unsettled Parts of North America in 1796 and 1797* (London, 1856), contains sensible observations on the habits of pioneers in western Pennsylvania and along the Ohio, as does Michel-Guillaume St. Jean de Crèvecoeur, *Eighteenth-Century Travels in Pennsylvania and New York* (Lexington, Ky., 1961). The same author's classic *Letters from an American Farmer* (London, 1782) also contains penetrating observations. Scarcely less valuable are Francisco de Miranda, *The New Democracy in America: Travels of Francisco de Miranda in the United States, 1783–1784* (Norman, Okla., 1963), and Isaac Weld, *Travels through the States of North America*, 2 vols. (London, 1807). Weld visited the Virginia and Pennsylvania frontiers, as well as journeying across New York to Detroit.

The first quarter of the nineteenth century witnessed a rapid increase in the number of visitors, and a growing interest in the Western character. Thomas Ashe, *Travels in America, Performed in 1806*, 3 vols. (London, 1808) record the impressions of a hostile aristocrat but a good observer; an opposite prejudice is apparent in Morris Birkbeck, *Notes on a Journey in America* (London, 1818), which describes Birkbeck's visit to Illinois where he later settled. John Bradbury, *Travels in the Interior of America, in the Years 1809, 1810, and 1811* (Liverpool, 1817) contains the impressions of a well-trained British botanist who visited the Ohio Valley and the Louisiana Territory. More concerned with Western characteristics were James Flint, *Letters from America* (Edinburgh, 1822) who visited Kentucky and the Ohio Valley in 1818–1820, and Elias P. Fordham, *Personal Narrative of Travels* (Cleveland, Ohio, 1906), written following an extended visit to those areas and to the Illinois frontier. Of comparable skill as observers of the new society were Adam Hodgson, *Letters from North America*, 2 vols. (London, 1824) and John Melish, *Travels through the United States of America* (London, 1818). The account of the latter, who traveled through the Kentucky and Ohio backcountry in 1810 and 1811, was probably the most widely read book of its kind. Similar journeys were made by André François Michaux, *Travels to the Westward of the Alleghany Mountains* (London, 1805) and John Palmer, *Journal of Travels in the United States of America* (London, 1818). Adlard Welby, author of *A Visit to North America and the English Settlements in Illinois* (London, 1821), was a staunch monarchist' who disliked western democracy so intensely that he described it often and well. The comments of a sensitive Swedish visitor are in Franklin D. Scott, ed., *Baron Klinkowstrom's America, 1818–1820* (Evanston, Ill., 1952).

European travelers were attracted in even larger numbers during the quarter century preceding the Civil War. One of the most famous was Charles Dickens, whose *American Notes* (London, 1842) record the impressions of a hostile observer after a trip to St. Louis. Three exceptionally fine travel accounts that stress Western character traits are D. Griffiths, Jr., *Two Years' Residence in the New Settlements of Ohio* (London, 1835); Basil Hall, *Travels in North America*, 3 vols. (Edinburgh, 1829); and Alexander Mackay, *The Western World*, 2 vols. (Philadelphia, 1849). All three authors visited the Mississippi Valley frontier and prepared sympathetic versions of what they saw. Justly famous as two of the most observing visitors with particular interest in the differences between English and American society are Frederick Marryat, *A Diary in America*, 3 vols. (London, 1839) and Harriet Martineau, *Society in America*, 2 vols. (2nd edn., New York, 1837). Others who shared this interest and provided comparable analyses were Charles A. Murray, *Travels in North America during the Years 1834, 1835, and 1836*, 2 vols. (London, 1839); Simon A. O'Ferrall, *A Ramble of Six Thousand Miles through the United States of America* (London, 1832); and William Oliver, *Eight Months in Illinois* (Newcastle-upon-Tyne, 1843). Two ladies who reacted differently to the western environment but wrote revealing studies of the western character were Mrs. Houston, *Hesperos: or, Travels in the West*, 2 vols. (London, 1850) and Frances Trollope, *Domestic Manners of the American*, 2 vols. (London, 1832). Mrs. Houston visited the Texas frontier, which she enjoyed; Mrs. Trollope spent two years in the Ohio Valley, which she detested.

Sensitive observers seeking to isolate national characteristics were less common in the post-Civil War trans-Mississippi West, partly because improved transportation facilities were beginning to make travel less leisurely. Their observations have been well summarized in Robert G. Athearn, *Westward the Briton* (New York, 1953). Of the visitors who did stress this point of view, two of the most dependable were William A. Baillie-Grohman, *Camps in the Rockies* (New York, 1882) and John Lang, *America in 1876* (London, 1877).

Not only travelers from overseas but visiting Easterners, recently arrived settlers, and Westerners themselves occasionally produced books that emphasized the uniqueness of frontier civilization. For the early nineteenth century, one of the most useful travel books is by a prejudiced New Englander whose dislike of the West stimulated extensive descriptions of the life and character of the people: Timothy Dwight, *Travels in New-England and New-York*, 4 vols. (New Haven, Conn., 1821). The Mississippi Valley frontier was visited by numerous American travelers. Christopher C. Andrews, author of *Minnesota and Dacotah: Or Letters Descriptive of a Tour through the North-west* (Washington, D.C., 1857), found the Minnesota Territory especially attractive. The Western class structure and social mobility there are stressed in Caleb Atwater, *Remarks Made on a Tour to Prairie du Chien* (Columbus, Ohio, 1831). A more remote frontier is described in John J. Audubon, *Delineations of American Scenery and Character* (New York, 1926), which provides one of the best descriptions of squatters beyond the Mississippi. Travelers more commonly visited the Old Northwest during the pre-Civil War years. Among the most useful of their accounts are: Zerah Hawley, *A Journal of a Tour through Connecticut, Massachusetts, New-York, and North Part of Pennsylvania and Ohio* (New Haven, 1822); James Hall, *Letters from the West* (London, 1828), written by a well-educated American judge; Abner D. Jones, *Illinois and the West* (Boston, 1838); and Amos A. Parker, *Trip to the West and Texas* (Concord, N.H., 1835). Three well-known travelers left classic accounts of frontier life beyond the Mississippi: Samuel Bowles, *Across the Continent* (Springfield, Mass., 1866); Horace Greeley, *An Overland Journey,*

from New York to San Francisco (New York, 1860); and Albert D. Richardson, *Beyond the Mississippi* (Hartford, Conn., 1867).

No less interesting than the impressions of travelers are the reminiscences or observations of Easterners who moved to the frontier and recorded their opinions of the life they found there. The diary of an Anglican minister who spent two years among the Presbyterian pioneers in the Carolina backcountry of the eighteenth century is in Richard J. Hooker, ed., *The Carolina Backcountry on the Eve of the Revolution: The Journal and Other Writings of Charles Woodmason, Anglican Itinerant* (Chapel Hill, N.C., 1953). This same period is graphically described in the reminiscences of a backwoods settler: Joseph Doddridge, *Notes on the Settlement and Indian Wars, of the Western Parts of Virginia and Pennsylvania* (Wellsburgh, Va., 1824). A few unusually skilled observers played a similar role during the first half of the nineteenth century. Timothy Flint, *The History and Geography of the Mississippi Valley*, 2 vols. (2nd edn., Cincinnati, Ohio 1832) and *Recollections of the Last Ten Years* (Boston, 1826) record the impressions of a minister from the East who spent the years between 1815 and 1824 largely on the Missouri frontier. Equally valuable, although grossly prejudiced, are the observations of a New Englander who taught school in Indiana during the 1820s: Bayard Rush Hall, *The New Purchase: or, Seven and a Half Years in the Far West*, 2 vols. (New York, 1843). Two housewives who moved to Illinois and Michigan left readable impressions of Western society as seen through women's eyes: Eliza W. Farnham, *Life in Prairie Land* (New York, 1846) and Caroline M. Kirkland whose two books describe the Michigan frontier of the 1830s: *A New Home—Who'll Follow? or, Glimpses of Western Life* (New York, 1839) and *Western Clearings* (New York, 1845).

Finally, Westerners occasionally wrote vigorous defenses of their section in which they emphasized the differences between their kind and Easterners. Guidebook authors sometimes resorted to this device; among the best of those who did so are Robert Baird, *View of the Valley of the Mississippi, or the Emigrant's and Traveller's Guide to the West* (2nd edn., Philadelphia, 1834); John M. Peck, *A New Guide for Emigrants to the West* (Boston, 1836); and J. H. Perkins, *Annals of the West* (Cincinnati, Ohio, 1846). Other Westerners in books or addresses speculated on the reasons for the distinctive Western character. A typical lecture on this subject is Daniel Drake, *Discourse on the History, Character, and Prospects of the West* (Cincinnati, Ohio, 1834). Books emphasizing these themes include James Hall, *Sketches of History, Life, and Manners in the West*, 2 vols. (Philadelphia, 1835) and John L. McConnel, *Western Characters or Types of Border Life in the Western States* (New York, 1853). For the Far West a useful book is Josiah Royce, *California, A Study of American Character* (Boston, 1886).

The History of a Theory

That the frontier had altered the American character was recognized by a few thinking Americans long before Frederick Jackson Turner formulated the "frontier hypothesis" in 1893. A brief sampling of the early theorists is in Herman C. Nixon, "Precursors of Turner in the Interpretation of the American Frontier," *South Atlantic Quarterly*, XXVIII (1929), pp. 83–98.

The evolution of Turner's theories may be studied both in his manuscripts and published works. The bulk of his manuscripts are in the Frederick Jackson Turner Papers, Henry E. Huntington Library and Art Gallery; this collection contains thirty-four file drawers of notes and nearly eighty boxes of correspondence. Smaller collections are in the Archives of the University of Wisconsin, Wisconsin Memorial Library (six boxes), the Wisconsin State His-

torical Society Library (three boxes and one volume of manuscripts), and the Houghton Library of Harvard University (one box). Turner's essays in which he advanced and developed the frontier thesis have been collected into three volumes, two of them published posthumously: *The Early Writings of Frederick Jackson Turner* (Madison, Wis., 1938); *The Frontier in American History* (New York, 1920); and *The Significance of Sections in American History* (New York, 1932). The first of these contains a complete bibliography of his writings, compiled by Everett E. Edwards, and printed on pp. 233–272. The essays most important for frontier theory have been gathered in Ray A. Billington, ed., *Frontier and Section: Selected Essays of Frederick Jackson Turner* (Englewood Cliffs, N.J., 1961). A number of previously unpublished essays and letters by Turner have been edited by Wilbur R. Jacobs and published as *Frederick Jackson Turner's Legacy* (San Marino, Calif., 1965), and *The Historical World of Frederick Jackson Turner* (New Haven, Conn., 1966). Why Turner produced so few published works is examined in Ray A. Billington, "Why Some Historians Rarely Write History: A Case Study of Frederick Jackson Turner," *Mississippi Valley Historical Review*, L (1963), pp. 3–27.

The most searching analysis of the evolution of the frontier thesis in Turner's mind is in Fulmer Mood, "The Development of Frederick Jackson Turner as a Historical Thinker," Colonial Society of Massachusetts, *Transactions, 1937–1942*, XXXIV (1943), pp. 283–352. Less valuable is a detailed textual analysis of Turner's writings to show the emergence of his theory: Per Sveaas Anderson, *Westward is the Course of Empires: A Study in the Shaping of an American Idea: Frederick Jackson Turner's Frontier* (Oslo, Norway, 1956). Lee Benson, in two stimulating articles, has examined the historical atmosphere in which Turner wrote and has appraised the influence of one theorist on his writing: "The Historical

Background of Turner's Frontier Essay," *Agricultural History*, XXV (1951), pp. 59–82, and "Achille Loria's Influence on American Economic Thought: Including His Contributions to the Frontier Hypothesis," *Agricultural History*, XXIV (1950), pp. 182–199. Both essays are reprinted in Lee Benson, *Turner and Beard: American Historical Writing Reconsidered* (Glencoe, Ill., 1960). Gilman M. Ostrander, "Turner and the Germ Theory," *Agricultural History*, XXXII (1958), pp. 258–261 shows that Turner was influenced by, as well as against, this theory of history; in a similar study Robert E. Lerner, "Turner and the Revolt Against E. A. Freeman," *Arizona and the West*, V (1963), pp. 101–108 suggests that his concepts were shaped by a rebellion against political emphasis common among younger historians of his day. Rudolf Freund, "Turner's Theory of Social Evolution," *Agricultural History*, XIX (1945), pp. 78–87 examines the concept of social evolution as understood by Turner at the time he formulated his beliefs.

A number of scholars have appraised the influence of Turner and his frontier theory on the historical profession. An unusually competent, but brief, biographical sketch is in Merle Curti, *Frederick Jackson Turner* (Mexico, D.F., 1949). This has been reprinted in O. Lawrence Burnette, Jr., comp., *Wisconsin Witness to Frederick Jackson Turner. A Collection of Essays on the Historian and the Thesis* (Madison, Wis., 1961), pp. 175–204. The same author has examined Turner's methodology in "The Section and the Frontier in American History: The Methodological Concepts of Frederick Jackson Turner," in Stuart A. Rice, ed., *Methods in Social Science. A Case Book* (Chicago, 1931), pp. 353–367. Other competent discussions of the methods that he employed in historical analysis include: Norman D. Harper, "Frontier and Section, a Turner 'Myth'?" *Historical Studies, Australia and New Zealand*, No. 18 (1952), pp. 1–19, and John H. Randall, Jr., and George Haines IV, "Controlling Assumptions in the

Practice of American Historians," *Theory and Practice in Historical Study; A Report of the Committee on Historiography* [of the Social Science Research Council] (New York, 1946), pp. 43–50. Friendly appraisals of Turner's theory by former students are numerous; two of the best are Carl Becker, "Frederick Jackson Turner," in Howard W. Odum, ed., *American Masters of Social Science* (New York, 1927), pp. 273–318, and Avery Craven, "Frederick Jackson Turner, Historian," *Wisconsin Magazine of History*, XXV (1942), pp. 408–424. Professor Craven has produced two other thoughtful studies dealing primarily with the frontier theory, "Frederick Jackson Turner and the Frontier Approach," *University of Kansas City Review*, XVIII (1951), pp. 3–17, and "The 'Turner Theories' and the South," *Journal of Southern History*, V (1939), pp. 291–314. Among the extensive writings on Turner, other essays that deserve mention are Edwin Mims, Jr., *American History and Immigration* (Bronxville, N.Y., 1950), which deals largely with Turner and is unique in showing the changing evolution of his concepts as he matured; and Wilbur R. Jacobs, "Frederick Jackson Turner," *The American West*, I (1964), pp. 32–35, 78–79, which is a perceptive re-examination of his beliefs based on the study of his unpublished manuscripts. This has been reprinted in slightly expanded form in Wilbur R. Jacobs, John W. Caughey, and Joe B. Frantz, *Turner, Bolton, and Webb. Three Historians of the American Frontier* (Seattle, Wash., 1965).

The attack on the Turner theories that began in the 1930s took two directions. Some historians examined aspects of the theory and denied that the frontier contributed to the growth of democracy, individualism, and the like; these studies will be considered later in this bibliography. Others struck at the basic assumptions or quarreled with Turner's presentation of his thesis. This assault began with John C. Almack, "The Shibboleth of the Frontier," *The Historical*

Outlook, XVI (1925), pp. 197–202, a discursive article arguing that the frontier had hindered rather than stimulated cultural progress. More to the point were two brief articles by Louis M. Hacker, "Sections—or Classes?" *Nation,* CXXXVII (July 26, 1933), pp. 108–110, and "Frederick Jackson Turner: Non-Economic Historian," *New Republic,* LXXXIII (June 5, 1935), p. 108, which castigated Turner for ignoring the class struggle and other economic forces. Frederic L. Paxson, "A Generation of the Frontier Hypothesis," *Pacific Historical Review,* II (1933), pp. 34–51, answered some of these criticisms, but was itself mildly critical. The attack gained momentum with the appearance of two searching studies by George W. Pierson, "The Frontier and Frontiersmen of Turner's Essays," *Pennsylvania Magazine of History and Biography* LXIV (1940), pp. 449–478, and "The Frontier and American Institutions. A Criticism of the Turner Theory," *New England Quarterly,* XV (June 1942), pp. 224–255, both discrediting Turner for the expression of his theory as well as questioning the theory itself. In the same tone was Murray Kane, "Some Considerations on the Frontier Concept of Frederick Jackson Turner," *Mississippi Valley Historical Review,* XXVII (1940), pp. 379–400. Other writers argued that Turner's hypothesis had harmed the American people. James C. Malin in a searching article "Space and History: Reflections on the Closed-Space Doctrines of Turner and Mackinder," *Agricultural History,* XVIII (1944), pp. 65–74, 107–126, charged that his stress on a spatial frontier had blinded the United States to other frontiers in science and technology; and Carlton J. H. Hayes, "The American Frontier—Frontier of What?" *American Historical Review,* LI (1946), pp. 199–216 insisted that his emphasis on national traits had contributed to isolationism and nationalism. Most of these criticisms were repeated in a general attack on the frontier hypothesis by Richard Hofstadter, "Turner and the

Frontier Myth," *American Scholar,* XVIII (1949), pp. 433–443.

These attacks on Turner and his thesis, and a far larger literature on the subject that cannot be listed here, are described and appraised in numerous bibliographical articles. Two early attempts in this direction were Roy L. Lokken, "The Turner Thesis: Criticism and Defense," *Social Studies,* XXXII (1941), pp. 356–365, and J. A. Burkhart, "The Turner Thesis: A Historian's Controversy," *Wisconsin Magazine of History,* XXXI (1947), pp. 70–83. More complete are Gene M. Gressley, "The Turner Thesis—a Problem in Historiography," *Agricultural History,* XXXII (1958), pp. 227–249; Walter Rundell, Jr., "Concepts of the 'Frontier' and the 'West,'" *Arizona and the West,* I (1959), pp. 13–41; and Ray A. Billington, *The American Frontier* (2nd edn., Washington, 1965).

More useful than the assaults on Turner's presentation of his thesis have been studies suggesting areas of investigation that Turner ignored. One germinal book of this sort was Henry Nash Smith, *Virgin Land: The American West as Symbol and Myth* (Cambridge, Mass., 1950), which called attention to the existence of two frontiers, one the actual frontier and the other the frontier present in the imagination of Europeans and Easterners. Both affected American development. Some of Professor Smith's findings have been questioned in two articles by Rush Welter, "The Frontier West as Image of American Society. Conservative Attitudes before the Civil War," *Mississippi Valley Historical Review,* XLVI (1960), pp. 593–614, and "The Frontier West as Image of American Society, 1776–1860," *Pacific Northwest Quarterly,* LII (1961), pp. 1–6. Other writers insisted that Turner ignored religious factors; typical of this school is W. Eugene Shiels, "The Frontier Hypothesis: A Corollary," *Mid-America,* XVII (1935), pp. 3–9. Still others attempted to test the frontier hypothesis by comparing developments in the United States with those in other countries where expansion took place. The literature on this subject is extensive, but is conveniently summarized in two review articles: Dietrich Gerhard, "The Frontier in Comparative View," *Comparative Studies in Society and History,* I (1959), pp. 205–229, and Marvin Mikesell, "Comparative Studies in Frontier History," *Annals of the Association of American Geographers,* L (1960), pp. 62–74.

During the 1950s and 1960s the attack on Turner's theories lessened as scholars turned increasingly to testing rather than condemning his assumptions. This trend is noted in William H. Lyon, "The Third Generation of the Frontier Hypothesis," *Arizona and the West,* IV (1962), pp. 45–50. Typical of the more favorable reappraisals of Turner resulting is H. C. Allen, "F. J. Turner and the Frontier in American History," in H. C. Allen and C. P. Hill, *British Essays in American History* (London, 1957), pp. 145–166.

The full story of the impact of the frontier hypothesis on American thought remains to be told. Curtis Nettels, "Frederick Jackson Turner and the New Deal," *Wisconsin Magazine of History,* XVII (1934), pp. 257–265 is suggestive rather than definitive, as its date of publication indicates. More searching is William A. Williams, "The Frontier Thesis and American Foreign Policy," *Pacific Historical Review,* XXIV (1955), pp. 379–395, although this too lacks proof for many of the statements. Far less convincing is Lawrence S. Kaplan, "Frederick Jackson Turner and Imperialism," *Social Science,* XXVII (1952), which attempts to show that the hypothesis was used as a tool by advocates of imperialism. Other brief studies of this subject are in Walter LaFeber, *The New Empire: An Interpretation of American Expansion, 1860–1898* (Ithaca, N.Y., 1963), which analyzes Turner's writings to show their impact on the psychology of expansion; and David H. Burton, "The Influence of the American West on the Imperialist Philosophy of Theodore Roosevelt," *Arizona and the West,* IV (1962), pp. 5–26, which maintains that Roosevelt's imperialist views originated in his frontier experiences. More convincing is the thoughtful discussion of the manner in which intellectuals reacted to the frontier concept in Warren I. Sussman, "The Useless Past: American Intellectuals and the Frontier Thesis: 1910–1930," *Bucknell Review,* XI (1963), pp. 1–20.

How and Why
Pioneers Moved Westward

The changing meaning of the word "frontier" during the century before Frederick Jackson Turner prepared his essay is the theme of Fulmer Mood, "Notes on the History of the Word *Frontier,*" *Agricultural History,* XXII (1948), pp. 78–83, and especially John T. Juricek, "American Usage of the Word 'Frontier' from Colonial Times to Frederick Jackson Turner," *Proceedings of the American Philosophical Society,* CX (1966), pp. 10–34. Many nonhistorians, and some historians, have quarreled with the Turnerians on this point, insisting that too little attention has been paid the Indian and Spanish-Mexican frontiers of the Far West. The most lucid argument in favor of greater emphasis on the Indian frontier is Jack D. Forbes, "Frontiers in American History," *Journal of the West,* I (1962), pp. 63–73. On the need for more stress on the Spanish-Mexican frontier see T. M. Pearce, "The Other' Frontiers of the American West," *Arizona and the West,* IV (1962), pp. 105–112, and Donald J. Lehmer, "The Second Frontier; The Spanish," in Robert G. Ferris, ed., *The American West: An Appraisal* (Santa Fé, N.Mex., 1963), pp. 141–150.

Material on the motives that impelled pioneers to move westward are widely scattered; a study of this subject based on the diaries and letters of those who 'did move would be useful. Modern motivation theory as developed by sociologists and social psychologists is conveniently summarized in the articles collected in David C. McClelland, ed., *Studies in Motivation* (New York, 1955). A brief discussion of the influence of price cycles on migration is in Douglass C. North, "International Capital Flows and the Development of the American West," *Journal of Economic History*, XVI (1956), pp. 493–505.

The theory that the frontier served as a safety valve for dispossessed Eastern workers has had a long and complex history. During the nineteenth century nearly all Americans believed the West to be an outlet for laborers displaced by depressions or technological unemployment; typical of this faith was the long review article by Edward Everett, "Flint's Geography and History," *North American Review*, XXVIII (1829), pp. 80–103, which makes this point firmly in its opening pages. These views were almost universally held at the time that Turner wrote his early essays.

They were first seriously questioned during the 1930s when the whole frontier concept was under attack. Two simultaneous articles opened the assault: Carter Goodrich and Sol Davison, "The Wage-Earner in the Westward Movement," *Political Science Quarterly*, L (1935), pp. 161–185, and LI (1936), pp. 61–116; and Murray Kane, "Some Considerations on the Safety Valve Doctrine," *Mississippi Valley Historical Review*, XXIII (1936), pp. 169–188. Both used extensive empirical data to show that migration slowed rather than intensified in depression eras, and that few actual wage earners became Western farmers. They were answered by one of Turner's staunchest defenders in three articles: Joseph Schafer, "Some Facts Bearing on the Safety Valve Theory," *Wisconsin Magazine of History*, XX (1936), pp. 216–232; "Concerning the Frontier as Safety Valve," *Political Science Quarterly*, LII (1937), pp. 407–420; and "Was the West a Safety Valve for Labor?" *Mississippi Valley Historical Review*, XXIV (1937),

pp. 299–314. In all, the author advanced opinions of nineteenth-century Americans to show that they believed in a safety valve, as well as scattered data to prove that many Mississippi Valley farmers had been wage-earners in Europe before migrating. His methodology was questioned in a rejoinder by Carter Goodrich and Sol Davison, "The Frontier as Safety Valve: A Rejoinder," *Political Science Quarterly*, LIII (1938), pp. 268–271.

Over the next years, additional evidence was advanced to support the anti-safety-valve argument. Rufus S. Tucker, "The Frontier as an Outlet for Surplus Labor," *Southern Economic Journal*, VII (1940), pp. 158–186, used census data to demonstrate that after 1840 urban areas gained more population than rural. One reason for this was suggested by Clarence H. Danhof, "Farm-Making Costs and the 'Safety Valve': 1850–1860," *Journal of Political Economy*, XLIX (1941), which argued that the cost of moving west was greater than the workingman could bear. That same author summarized most of the arguments against the operation of a direct safety valve in "Economic Validity of the Safety-Valve Doctrine," *Journal of Economic History Supplement* (1941), pp. 96–106. A study by Carl N. Degler, "The West as a Solution to Urban Unemployment," *New York History*, XXXVI (1955), pp. 63–85 advanced convincing proof that the philanthropic societies formed to transport workers west during the pre-Civil War period never operated successfully. The climax to the attack on the safety-valve doctrine came with the publication of Fred A. Shannon, "A Post Mortem on the Labor-Safety-Valve Theory," *Agricultural History*, XIX (1945), pp. 31–37. Using census statistics, Professor Shannon argued that neither a direct nor an indirect safety valve had operated during the nineteenth century, and that beyond the Mississippi, cities acted as a safety valve to relieve farm pressures.

More recently, economists have taken a fresh look at the doctrine, and have concluded that the critics erred. This re-evaluation began with the publication of Norman J. Simler, "The Safety-Valve Doctrine Re-Evaluated," *Agricultural History*, XXXII (1958), pp. 250–257, a searching article maintaining that the critics failed to distinguish between a social and an economic safety valve, and that the latter had operated effectively as an indirect outlet for surplus workers. This argument was carried a step further by George G. S. Murphy and Arnold Zellner, "Sequential Growth, the Labor–Safety-Valve Doctrine and the Development of American Unionism," *Journal of Economic History*, XIX (1959), pp. 402–421, who showed that the sequential exploitation of Western resources had so stimulated the total economy that an effective safety valve did operate, although not exactly as understood during the nineteenth century. This line of reasoning reached a climax in Ellen von Nardroff, "The American Frontier as a Safety Valve—The Life, Death, Reincarnation, and Justification of a Theory," *Agricultural History*, XXXVI (1962), pp. 123–142, which argued convincingly on the basis of economic theory that the frontier did operate as a potential and sociopsychological safety valve, with measurable effects on the American labor movement as well as on the entire economy. A brief answer to Mrs. Nardroff, based largely on semantic differences, was Henry M. Littlefield, "Has the Safety Valve Come Back to Life?" *Agricultural History*, XXXVIII (1964), pp. 47–49.

Turner's belief in the orderly progression of frontier types was first questioned in Edmond S. Meany, "The Towns of the Pacific Northwest Were Not Founded on the Fur Trade," American Historical Association, *Annual Report for 1909* (Washington, 1911), pp. 165–172, which pointed out that in the Northwest trading posts did not evolve into towns as in the Midwest. Gerald G. Steckler, S.J., "North Dakota Versus Frederick Jackson Turner," *North Dakota History*, XXVIII (1961), pp. 33–43 also showed that settlement

processes were more complex than depicted by Turner.

Two frontier types not recognized by Turner have been studied in several scattered works. On land speculators see Ray A. Billington, "The Origin of the Land Speculator as a Frontier Type," *Agricultural History*, XIX (1945), pp. 204–222, and Paul W. Gates, "The Role of the Land Speculator in Western Development," *Pennsylvania Magazine of History and Biography*, LXVI (1942), pp. 314–333. The manner in which speculators appropriated choice sites is shown in William L. Morton, "The Significance of Site in the Settlement of the American and Canadian Wests," *Agricultural History*, XXV (1951), pp. 97–104. Allan G. and Margaret B. Bogue, " 'Profits' and the Frontier Land Speculator," *Journal of Economic History*, XVII (1957), pp. 1–24 show that returns were greater for speculators than earlier investiations had indicated as does Robert P. Swierenga, "Land Speculator 'Profits' Reconsidered: Central Iowa as a Test Case," *Journal of Economic History*, XXVI (1966), pp. 1–28. The standard work on the town dweller as a frontiersman is Richard C. Wade, *The Urban Frontier* (Cambridge, Mass., 1959), which shows the influence of cities in the occupation of the Ohio Valley.

The Frontier and the American Character

Both the volume and complexity of social science literature on the study of national character are indicated in the bibliography prepared by Michael Mc-Giffert, "Selected Writings on American National Character," *American Quarterly*, XV (1963), pp. 271–288.

Social scientists have explored many aspects of personality and character. A basic work in the field is Abram Kardiner, *The Psychological Frontiers of Society* (New York, 1945); the same author has edited with Henry A. Murray and David M. Schneider, *Personality in Nature, Society, and Culture* (2nd edn., New York, 1953), a valuable collection of documents directed to the question of what makes an American an American and an Englishman an Englishman. Another essential treatment is Ralph Linton, *The Cultural Background of Personality* (New York, 1945). Recent studies on the subject are embodied in H. C. J. Duijker and N. H. Frijda, *National Character and National Stereotypes: A Trend Report Prepared for the International Union of Scientific Psychology* (Amsterdam, The Netherlands, 1960), which also contains an extensive bibliography. Particularly useful to the historian is Walter P. Metzger, "Generalizations about National Character: An Analytical Essay," in Louis Gottschalk, ed., *Generalizations in the Writing of History: A Report of the Committee on Historical Analysis of the Social Science Research Council* (Chicago, 1963).

The distinctiveness of the American national character has interested both social scientists and historians. Among the former Lee Coleman, "What is American? A Study of Alleged American Traits," *Social Forces*, XIX (1941), pp. 492–499, is a pioneer effort to isolate traits that are distinctly American, reaching the conclusion that they are too complex to be categorized. Reuel Denney, "How Americans See Themselves," *Annals of the American Academy of Political and Social Science*, CCXCV (1954), pp. 12–20, deals with the problems involved in studying the American character and with definitions. Three book-length studies of importance are Geoffrey Gorer, *The American People: A Study in National Character* (New York, 1948), an interpretation by a Freudian anthropologist; Margaret Mead, *And Keep Your Powder Dry: An Anthropologist Looks at America* (New York, 1943), a pioneer anthropological study; and David Riesman, Reuel Denney, and Nathan Glazer, *The Lonely Crowd: A Study of the Changing American Character* (New Haven, Conn.,

1950), a controversial analysis stressing twentieth-century adjustments. Professor Riesman in "The Study of National Character: Some Observations on the American Case," *Harvard Library Bulletin*, XIII (1959), pp. 5–24, comments on the relations of history to the American character.

The national character has also been analyzed by numerous historians and social scientists from overseas. Among the most useful studies resulting are: D. W. Brogan, *The American Character* (New York, 1944, revised edn., 1956); Marcus Cunliffe, "The American Character," in the same author's *The Nation Takes Shape, 1789–1837* (Chicago, 1959); and Francis L. K. Hsu, *Americans and Chinese: Two Ways of Life* (New York, 1953).

American historians have similarly attempted to appraise the national character, either incidentally or directly. An indispensable pioneer study is Arthur M. Schlesinger, "What Then Is the American, This New Man?" *American Historical Review*, XLVIII (1943), pp. 225–244, which uses travel accounts to identify traits deemed distinctly American by visitors. More general works that pay particular attention to the shaping of the national character include Daniel J. Boorstin, *The Americans: The Colonial Experience* (New York, 1958) and *The Americans: The National Experience* (New York, 1965); Roger Burlingame, *The American Conscience* (New York, 1957); Howard Mumford Jones, *America and French Culture* (Chapel Hill, N.C., 1927); and Max Lerner, *America as a Civilization: Life and Thought in the United States Today* (New York, 1957). A thoughtful essay on the nature of the American character is David M. Potter, "The Quest for the National Character," in John Higham, *The Reconstruction of American History* (New York, 1962), pp. 197–220. Perry Miller, "The Shaping of the American Character," *New England Quarterly*, XXVIII (1955), pp. 435–454, concentrates on the New

England character more than on the national.

Historians have also written extensively on specific aspects of the American national character. Useful are Merle Curti, "American Philanthropy and the National Character," *American Quarterly*, X (1958), pp. 420–437, emphasizing the unusual generosity of the people, and David M. Potter, "American Women and the American Character," *Stetson University Bulletin*, LXII (1962), pp. 1–22, stressing the treatment of women in the United States. Other historians have suggested reasons for the unusual features of the national character, just as did Frederick Jackson Turner in arguing that the frontier experience had altered certain traits. Prominent among such studies are Louis Hartz, *The Liberal Tradition in America: An Interpretation of American Political Thought since the Revolution* (New York, 1955), which ascribes differences to the lack of a medieval heritage; and David M. Potter, *People of Plenty: Economic Abundance and the American Character* (Chicago, 1954), which stresses the continuing abundance made possible by the sequential exploitation of resources. A historian and a demographer have found a basis for unique American traits and institutions in the migratory habits of the people: George W. Pierson, "A Restless Temper . . . ," *American Historical Review*, LXIX (1964), pp. 969–989, and Everett S. Lee, "The Turner Thesis Re-examined," *American Quarterly*, XIII (1961), pp. 77–83. Many of the findings of students of national character are applied to frontier studies in a stimulating article by Allan G. Bogue, "Social Theory and the Pioneer," *Agricultural History*, XXXIV (1960), pp. 21–34.

Students of the frontier since the days of Frederick Jackson Turner have recognized that individuals responded in different ways to different physical environments. This theme has been developed by studying the reaction of differing ethnic or national groups to the New World environment. Ray A. Billington, "The Frontier in American Thought and Character," in Archibald R. Lewis and Thomas F. McGann, eds., *The New World Looks At Its History* (Austin, Texas, 1963), pp. 77–94, argues that cultural tradition helps explain the differences between English and Spanish frontiersmen. Vianna Moog, *Bandeirantes and Pioneers* (New York, 1964) similarly holds that in Brazil the conquistador tradition was more important than the physical environment in shaping civilization. Comparable studies of ethnic pockets within the United States demonstrate the manner in which certain peoples failed to respond to the frontier environment. Two basic examinations of the Germans in Pennsylvania are Richard H. Shryock, "British Versus German Traditions in Colonial Agriculture," *Mississippi Valley Historical Review*, XXVI (1939), pp. 39–54, and John G. Gagliardo, "Germans and Agriculture in Colonial Pennsylvania," *Pennsylvania Magazine of History and Biography*, LXXXIII (1959), pp. 192–218. A similar study of the Wisconsin Germans is Joseph Schafer, "The Yankee and Teuton in Wisconsin," *Wisconsin Magazine of History*, VI (1922–1923), pp. 125–145, 261–279, 386–402. Richard L. Power, *Planting Corn Belt Culture: The Impress of the Upland Southerner and Yankee in the Old Northwest* (Indianapolis, Ind., 1953) reveals the different reactions of Southerners and New Englanders to the Indiana environment.

The Frontier: Cradle of Barbarism or Civilization?

The best interpretation of the problem discussed in this chapter is Earl Pomeroy, "Toward a Reorientation of Western History: Continuity and Environment," *Mississippi Valley Historical Review*, XLI (1955), pp. 579–600, a stimulating appraisal of the relative weight of these two forces in shaping frontier civilization. Among the several studies holding that the Western movement degraded culture is Arthur K. Moore, *The Frontier Mind: a Cultural Analysis of the Kentucky Frontiersman* (Lexington, Ky., 1957). Of lesser scope is F. Garvin Davenport, "Culture versus Frontier in Tennessee, 1825–1850," *Journal of Southern History*, V (1939), pp. 18–33. The best argument in the opposite direction, holding that Eastern civilization was transplanted intact to the successive Wests is Louis B. Wright, *Culture on the Moving Frontier* (Bloomington, Ind., 1955). An amusing article by Dixon Wecter, "Instruments of Culture on the Frontier," *Yale Review*, XXXVI (1947), pp. 242–256, holds to this same position. Two studies of the Ohio frontier by Kenneth V. Lottick apply this thesis: "Culture Transplantation in the Connecticut Reserve," *Historical and Philosophical Society of Ohio Bulletin*, XVII (1959), pp. 154–166, and "The Western Reserve and the Frontier Thesis," *Ohio Historical Quarterly*, LXX (1961), pp. 45–57.

Regional studies of cultural transplant are also helpful. Among those most useful in appraising the frontier's influence, the following deserve mention: for western Pennsylvania, Solon J. and E. H. Buck, *The Planting of Civilization in Western Pennsylvania* (Pittsburgh, Pa., 1939), and Edward P. Anderson, "Intellectual Life of Pittsburgh, 1786–1836," *Western Pennsylvania Historical Magazine*, XIV (1931), pp. 9–27, 92–114, 225–236, 288–309; for the Ohio Valley frontier, Beverley W. Bond, Jr., *The Civilization of the Old Northwest* (New York, 1934), Dixon R. Fox, ed., *Sources of Culture in the Middle West* (New York, 1934), and James M. Miller, *The Genesis of Western Culture: The Upper Ohio Valley, 1800–1825* (Columbus, Ohio, 1938); for the Mississippi Valley, John F. McDermott, "The Enlightenment and the Mississippi Frontier, 1763–1804," *Studies on Voltaire and the Eighteenth Century*, XXIX–XXVII (1963), pp. 1129–1142.

Western literary tastes are considered in such works as William Charvat,

Literary Publishing in America, 1790–1850 (Philadelphia, 1959) and Howard H. Peckham, "Books and Reading on the Ohio Frontier," *Mississippi Valley Historical Review*, XLIV (1958), pp. 649–663. The sectional loyalties of the West as an influence on literary development are the theme of David Donald and Frederick A. Palmer, "Toward a Western Literature, 1820–1860," *Mississippi Valley Historical Review*, XXXV (1948), pp. 413–428. A leading literary figure on the Ohio Valley frontier is studied in two biographies: James T. Flanagan, *James Hall: Literary Pioneer of the Ohio Valley* (Minneapolis, Minn., 1941) and Randolph C. Randall, *James Hall: Spokesman of the New West* (Columbus, Ohio, 1964). Walter A. Agard, "Classics on the Midwest Frontier," in Walker D. Wyman and Clifton B. Kroeber, eds., *The Frontier in Perspective* (Madison, Wis., 1957), pp. 165–183, demonstrates the desire of some frontiersmen to transplant traditional values to their new homes. Don D. Walker, "Reading on the Range: The Literary Habits of the American Cowboy," *Arizona and the West*, II (1960), 307–318, amusingly describes the reading tastes of some cowboys, and Doyce B. Nunis, Jr., *Books in Their Sea Chests: Reading Along the Early California Coast* (San Francisco, Calif., 1964) shows that the California pioneers demanded traditional literary fare.

Works on frontier theaters are numerous. A basic work is Esther C. Dunn, *Shakespeare in America* (New York, 1939), which reveals the bard's popularity in the West. Among the most usable regional histories of the theater are: Joseph S. Schick, *The Early Theater in Eastern Iowa* (Chicago, 1939), which is actually a cultural history of the area; Elbert R. Bowen, *Theatrical Entertainments in Rural Missouri before the Civil War* (Columbia, Mo., 1959); Harold E. and E. B. Briggs, "The Early Theater on the Northern Plains," *Mississippi Valley Historical Review*, XXXVII (1950), pp. 231–264; George R. MacMinn, *The Theater of the Golden Era in California* (Caldwell, Idaho, 1941); and Margaret G. Watson, *Silver Theater: Amusements of the Mining Frontier in Early Nevada, 1850–1864* (Glendale, Calif., 1964).

Material on Western journalism will be found in the standard histories of newspaper publishing in the United States. A book of particular importance is William H. Lyon, *The Pioneer Editor in Missouri, 1808–1860* (Columbia, Mo., 1965). David Kaser, *Joseph Charless: Printer in the Western Country* (Philadelphia, 1963) tells the story of a typical Western editor. An amusing description of the journalism in vogue on the Kansas frontier during the 1850s and 1860s is Cecil Howes, "Pistol-Packin' Pencil Pushers," *Kansas Historical Quarterly*, XIII (1944), pp. 115–138.

The best study of the relationship of the frontier to later anti-intellectualism in America is Merle Curti, "Intellectuals and Other People," *American Historical Review*, LX (1955), pp. 259–282. The same author explores the subject in *American Paradox: The Conflict of Thought and Action* (New Brunswick, N.J., 1956). Richard Hofstadter, *Anti-Intellectualism in American Life* (New York, 1963) is less concerned with the frontier background. An entertaining reappraisal of the nature of anti-intellectualism in the United States, arguing that neither the intellectual nor the anti-intellectual existed until the twentieth century, is J. Rogers Hollingsworth, "American Anti-Intellectualism," *South Atlantic Quarterly*, LXIII (1964), pp. 267–274.

The Structure of Frontier Society

Social scientists have written extensively on stratification and vertical mobility, and much of what they have written is useful to the historian. On stratification basic works include Egon E. Bergel, *Social Stratification* (New York, 1962), which deals with the nature of the class structure, mobility, and the cultural aspects of class division; and John F. Cuber and William F. Kenkel, eds., *Social Stratification in the United States* (New York, 1954), which cogently summarizes most of the case studies on which stratification theory is based. Essential also is a pioneering article by Kingsley Davis and W. E. Moore, "Some Principles of Stratification," *American Sociological Review*, X (1945), pp. 242–249, setting forth the functionalist position in understandable form. Reinhard Bendix and Seymour M. Lipset, eds., *Class, Status and Power, a Reader in Social Classification* (Glencoe, Ill., 1953) conveniently collects most of the important articles dealing with the subject.

The nature of the American class system has also interested social science investigators. Of particular use in this area are such works as Joseph Kahl, *The American Class Structure* (New York, 1957), and Leonard Reissman, *Class in American Society* (Glencoe, Ill., 1959). Both discuss the methodology and results of analyses of the American class system. W. L. Warner, Marchie Meeker, and Kenneth Eells, *Social Class in America* (Chicago, 1949) is a pioneering work particularly in dealing with methods of evaluating the nature of classes. Also important is Richard Centers, *The Psychology of Social Classes* (Princeton, N.J., 1949), which stresses the problem of self-evaluation and shows that most people in the United States consider themselves part of the middle class. The argument that a rising living standard in twentieth-century America is further erasing class lines is advanced in Gideon Sjoberg, "Are American Social Classes Becoming More Rigid?" *American Sociological Review*, XVI (1951), pp. 775–783.

The classic pioneer study of social mobility is Pitirim Sorokin, *Social Mobility* (New York, 1927), which is still useful. It has been largely displaced, however, by Seymour M. Lipset and Reinhard Bendix, *Social Mobility in Industrial Society* (Berkeley, Calif., 1959), which demonstrates through an impressive use of statistics that the rate of vertical mobility is about the same in all industrialized nations. David V. Glass, ed., *Social Mobility in Britain* (London, 1954) is useful for comparative purposes, while the relationship between social and occupational mobility in the United States is stressed in Ray Ginger, "Occupational Mobility and American Life," *Explorations in Entrepreneurial History*, VI (1954), pp. 234–244. The rags-to-riches dream as a factor in causing vertical mobility is appraised in W. Lloyd Warner, *American Life: Dream and Reality* (2nd edn., Chicago, 1962), which stresses the contemporary scene but uses concepts applicable to the earlier period, and in Irvin G. Wyllie, *The Self-Made Man in America* (New Brunswick, N.J., 1954), which uses impressive historical examples.

Sociologists have built many of their theories concerning stratification and social mobility on case studies of various types of American communities. W. Lloyd Warner was responsible for the pioneering study of this sort, that of "Yankee City" as the investigators renamed the city of 17,000 persons they were studying. This resulted in a four-volume report prepared with various collaborators: *The Social Life of a Modern Community* (New Haven, Conn., 1941), *The Status System of a Modern Community* (New Haven, Conn., 1942), *The Social Systems of American Ethnic Groups* (New Haven, Conn., 1945), and *The Social System of the Modern Factory* (New Haven, Conn., 1947). Later studies employing the techniques developed by Warner include John Useem, Pierre Tangent and Ruth Useem, "Stratification in a Prairie Town," *American Sociological Review*, VII (1942), pp. 331–342; James West, *Plainville, U.S.A.* (New York, 1945); and Wayne Wheeler, "Frontiers, Americanization, and Romantic Pluralism," *Journal of the Midcontinent American Studies Association*, III (1962), pp. 27–41.

Both the methodology and conclusions of these studies have been challenged in an important book by Stephan Thernstrom, *Poverty and Progress: Social Mobility in a Nineteenth Century City* (Cambridge, Mass., 1964). The author bases his findings on a study of Newburyport, Massachusetts, between 1850 and 1880. He concluded that vertical mobility was limited, and that common laborers were rarely able to achieve middle-class status. These findings, based on the analysis of hundreds of unskilled laborers, cannot be applied elsewhere until further study determines whether or not the community and the group were representative of the United States of that day.

A few historical studies of the class structure and mobility at isolated places in America tend to substantiate the view that stratification was less rigid than in Europe. These, however, are too few to justify any generalizations. For the colonial period Carl Bridenbaugh, *Myths and Realities: Societies of the Colonial South* (Baton Rouge, La., 1952) grapples with the whole nature of the colonial class structure. Two suggestive articles are Mildred Campbell, "Social Origins of Some Early Americans," in James M. Smith, ed., *Seventeenth-Century America. Essays in Colonial History* (Chapel Hill, N.C., 1959), pp. 63–89, which surveys passenger lists in seventeenth-century England to conclude that most of those departing for America were of the "middling" sort, and William A. Reavis, "The Maryland Gentry and Social Mobility," *William and Mary Quarterly*, 3rd ser., XIV (1957), pp. 418–428, which shows that the rate of vertical mobility was unusually high in colonial Maryland. A healthy corrective to those seeking to prove that democracy was the rule of the day as a result of these changes is Arthur M. Schlesinger, "The Aristocracy in Colonial America," *Massachusetts Historical Society Proceedings*, LXXIV (1962), pp. 3–21, which demonstrates the continuing importance of the upper classes. For the early nineteenth-century South, Nancy C. Robertson, "Social Mobility in Ante-Bellum Alabama," *Ala-*

bama Review, XIII (1960), pp. 135–145, shows the high percentage of marriages between nonslaveholders and slaveholders.

Frontier Democracy: Social and Political Aspects

The case against the frontier as a democratizing influence is clearly stated in two pioneering articles by Benjamin F. Wright, Jr., "American Democracy and the Frontier," *Yale Review*, XX (1930), pp. 349–365, and "Political Institutions and the Frontier," in Dixon R. Fox, ed., *Sources of Culture in the Middle West* (New York, 1934), pp. 15–38. Both argue that democracy was well developed in theory and practice before the settlement of America, and that the principal innovations since that time have been in Europe or the Eastern cities of the United States. Additional evidence that the frontier, at least in the early South, failed to stimulate political democracy is advanced by Thomas P. Abernethy, "Democracy and the Southern Frontier," *Journal of Southern History*, IV (1938), pp. 3–13, and *Three Virginia Frontiers* (Baton Rouge, La., 1940).

These attacks against a theory popularized by Frederick Jackson Turner inspired the inevitable rebuttals. Of these the most eloquent was Avery Craven, "The West and Democracy," in the same author's *Democracy in American Life* (Chicago, 1941), pp. 38–67, a restatement of the traditional position. More effective were two detailed case studies of democratic growth in pioneer communities. Stanley Elkins and Eric McKitrick, "A Meaning for Turner's Frontier," *Political Science Quarterly*, LXIX (1954), pp. 321–353, 565–602, using materials drawn from the records of communities in New England, the Old Northwest, and the ante-bellum South, maintained that the frontier did have a positive effect on democratic growth at the local level. Employing the same methodology, but delving deeper in statistical evidence, Merle Curti, *The Making of an American Community: A Case Study of Democracy in a Frontier County* (Stanford, Calif., 1959), demonstrated that in Trempeleau County, Wisconsin, between 1850 and 1880 progress toward democracy was measurably greater than in a comparable county in Vermont.

The case for frontier democracy was furthered by a detailed study of constitution making on the Ohio Valley frontier by John D. Barnhart, *Valley of Democracy: The Frontier versus the Plantation in the Ohio Valley, 1775–1818* (Bloomington, Ind., 1953). Although showing that pioneer constitution makers tended to borrow rather than innovate, Professor Barnhart demonstrated that they usually adopted the more liberal features of the frames of government that they copied. He also properly stressed the fact that Turner had spoken of "American" democracy, not democracy in general, and showed deviations to justify this distinction. The democratizing effect of the frontier as a region where governmental experimentation was possible was shown in Bayrd Still, "An Interpretation of the Statehood Process," *Mississippi Valley Historical Review*, XXIII (1936), pp. 189–204, and especially in Roy F. Nichols, "The Territories: Seedbeds of Democracy," *Nebraska History*, XXXV (1954), pp. 159–172. A general statement of the frontier spirit as a stimulator of freedom is in Richard A. Bartlett, "Freedom and the Frontier: A Pertinent Re-Examination," *Mid-America*, XXIX (1958), pp. 131–138.

The degree of democracy achieved in pioneer areas has attracted the interest of some historians. One important study of this trend in the Dutch and Swedish settlements of the early seventeenth century is Evelyn Page, "The First Frontier—The Swedes and the Dutch," *Pennsylvania History*, XV (1948), pp. 276–304. For the early Virginia frontier a significant article is Bernard Bailyn, "Politics and Social Structure in Virginia," in James M. Smith, ed., *Seventeenth-Century America. Essays in Colonial History* (Chapel Hill, N.C.,

1959), pp. 90–115, which describes the changes in leadership structure making possible democratic innovation. A more general study of eighteenth-century Virginia, attempting to show that the ordinary people did have political power at the time of the Revolution, is Robert E. and B. K. Brown, *Virginia: 1705–1786: Democracy or Aristocracy* (East Lansing, Mich., 1964). Somewhat more convincing is an earlier study by Robert E. Brown, *Middle-Class Democracy and the Revolution in Massachusetts, 1691–1780* (Ithaca, N.Y., 1955), which uses voting lists and other evidence to show that most people had sufficient property to qualify for the franchise. A sample of the evidence on which these conclusions are based is in B. Katherine Brown, "Puritan Democracy: A Case Study," *Mississippi Valley Historical Review*, L (December 1963), pp. 377–396.

The extent of the popular franchise in the nineteenth century can be learned from such works as Kirk H. Porter, *A History of Suffrage in the United States* (Chicago, 1918) and especially Chilton Williamson, *American Suffrage from Property to Democracy, 1760–1860* (Princeton, N.J., 1960). The latter argues that the West was imitative rather than creative in the realm of government, and that suffrage reform was more a product of the philosophy of natural rights than of the frontier. In an interesting article tending to substantiate this conclusion, Richard P. McCormick, "New Perspectives on Jacksonian Politics," *American Historical Review*, LXV (1960), pp. 288–301, shows that Andrew Jackson inspired no upsurge of interest in the West and that Westerners did not flock to the polls as eagerly as Easterners.

Frontier individualism has been questioned in Mody C. Boatright, "The Myth of Frontier Individualism," *Southwestern Social Science Quarterly*, XXII (1941), pp. 14–32, which stresses the fact that the pioneers were particularly dependent on cooperative enterprise. Most of his examples are drawn from the Great Plains frontier. This point is reinforced in Bayrd Still, "Patterns of Mid-Nineteenth Century Urbanization in the Middle West," *Mississippi Valley Historical Review*, XXVIII (1941), pp. 187–206, presenting an impressive array of evidence to show that frontier communities accepted regulatory measures beneficial to society more readily than Eastern communities. T. Scott Miyakawa, *Protestants and Pioneers* (Chicago, 1964), argues that the frontier churches played a major part in enforcing conformity and restraining individualism. John W. Ward, "Individualism Today," *Yale Review*, XLIX (1960), pp. 380–392, examines the sources of individualism, with proper attention to its unique expression on the frontier.

The Economic Impact of the Frontier

The role of the frontier as a stimulant to the national and world economies has not been properly studied by either historians or economists. Chester W. Wright, "The Significance of the Disappearance of Free Land in Our Economic Development," *American Economic Review Supplement*, XVI (1929), pp. 265–271, is uncritical and speculative, and adds little to actual knowledge of the manner in which the frontier economy operated. Far more important are two articles that outline the theory of sequential growth as applied to Western development: George G. S. Murphy and Arnold Zellner, "Sequential Growth, The Labor–Safety-Valve Doctrine and the Development of American Unionism," *Journal of Economic History*, XIX (1959), pp. 402–421, and Robert F. Berkhofer, Jr., "Space, Time, Culture and the New Frontier," *Agricultural History*, XXXVIII (1964), pp. 21–30. Both, however, consider the frontier's economic role only incidentally. The subject is also touched upon in Benjamin H. Higgins, *Economic Development: Principles, Problems and Policies* (New York, 1959). In-depth studies of the manner in which the frontier contributed to capital growth would be welcomed.

More attention has been paid to the effect of the pioneering process on innovation. That Western farmers were slow to respond to opportunities offered by improved techniques or machinery has been amply demonstrated. Albert L. Demaree, *The American Agricultural Press, 1819–1860* (New York, 1941), shows that the urge for improvement was centered in the East, not the West, during this period. Clarence H. Danhof, "American Evaluations of European Agriculture," *Journal of Economic History Supplement*, IX (1949), pp. 61–71 traces the spread of knowledge of European innovations among American farmers before 1860, and shows the high rate of rejection. The same task is performed less ably for a later period in Earle D. Ross, "Retardation of Farm Technology before the Power Age," *Agricultural History*, XXX (1956), pp. 11–17. By far the most capable study of the subject is Allan G. Bogue, "Pioneer Farmers and Innovation," *Iowa Journal of History*, LVI (1958), pp. 1–36, which uses Hamilton County, Iowa, between 1855 and 1885 as a case study of the readiness with which farmers adopted new inventions.

Regional studies also shed some light on this problem. Walter P. Webb, *The Great Plains* (Boston, 1931) argues persuasively that the frontier's advance over the unfamiliar Great Plains environment stimulated invention, a viewpoint challenged in Fred A. Shannon, "An Appraisal of Walter Prescott Webb's *The Great Plains*," *Critiques of Research in the Social Sciences: III* (New York, 1940). The readiness of Great Plains farmers to use improved brands of wheat is touched upon, although sometimes only incidentally, in James C. Malin, *Winter Wheat in the Golden Belt of Kansas: A Study in Adaptation to a Subhumid Geographic Environment* (Lawrence, Kansas, 1944).

Changes in the legal system necessitated by the advance of civilization into unfamiliar environments also await their chroniclers. Roscoe Pound, *The Spirit of the Common Law* (Boston, 1921), in a chapter on "Pioneers and the Law," pp. 112–138, outlines certain adjustments made in court systems and procedure under the impact of the "pioneer spirit," but advances only slight evidence, as does Francis R. Aumann, *The Changing American Legal System: Some Selected Phases* (Columbus, Ohio, 1940). Much of the other scant writing on the subject is summarized in a review article, Clarence E. Carter, "The Transit of Law to the Frontier: A Review Article," *Journal of Mississippi History*, XVI (1954), pp. 183–192. Examples of the opportunities awaiting legal scholars in this field are Richard D. Younger, "The Grand Jury on the Frontier," *Wisconsin Magazine of History*, XL (1956), pp. 3–8, 56, which shows the radical changes made in that institution; and the several books of James Willard Hurst on legal history, the latest of which is *Law and Economic Growth: The Legal History of the Lumber Industry in Wisconsin, 1836–1915* (Cambridge, Mass., 1964).

The Frontier and American Behavioral Patterns

Of the numerous traits ascribed by historians to the frontier experience, American mobility has attracted the greatest amount of attention. The subject has not been extensively studied by social scientists, although such books on social mobility as Pitirim Sorokin, *Social Mobility* (New York, 1927) and Seymour M. Lipset and Reinhard Bendix, *Social Mobility in Industrial Society* (Berkeley, Calif., 1959), contain some information. An informative study on modern mobility is Peter H. Rossi, *Why Families Move* (Glencoe Ill., 1955). In recent years the importance of mobility as a molding force has been appreciated by a historian and a demographer who have begun intensive studies of its impact on society. The historian, George W. Pierson, has contributed four readable articles to the literature: "The Moving American," *Yale Review,* XLIV (1954), pp. 99–112; "The M–Factor in American History," *American Quarterly,* XIV (1962), pp. 275–289; "Under a Wandering Star," *Virginia Quarterly Review,* XXXIX (1963), pp. 621–638; and "A Restless Temper . . . ," *American Historical Review,* LXIX (1964), pp. 269–289. The demographer, Everett S. Lee, has projected several books on the subject, and has suggested the lines to be investigated in "The Turner Thesis Reexamined," *American Quarterly,* XIII (1961), pp. 77–83. Less general, but of some significance in showing the effect of migration on institutions, is Stanley Elkins and Eric McKitrick, "Ideas in Motion," *American Quarterly,* XII (1960), pp. 188–197. Some light on the amount of mobility among Westerners is shed in a few regional studies, of which the following are typical: Arthur F. Bentley, *The Condition of the Western Farmer as Illustrated by the Economic History of a Nebraska Community* (Baltimore, Md., 1893); James C. Malin, "The Turnover of Farm Population in Kansas," *Kansas Historical Quarterly,* IV (1935), pp. 339–372; and James C. Malin, "Mobility and History," *Agricultural History,* XVII (1943), pp. 177–191.

Whether the frontier engendered optimism or pessimism has been disputed by historians; they agree, however, that the United States did have unusual faith in progress and the future. The extent of this belief is revealed in Arthur A. Ekirch, *The Idea of Progress in America, 1815–1860* (New York, 1944) and for a later period in Boyd C. Shafer, "The American Heritage of Hope," *Mississippi Valley Historical Review,* XXXVII (1950), pp. 427–450. Robert L. Heilbroner, "The Impasse of American Optimism," *American Scholar,* XXIX (1949–1960), pp. 13–20, traces part of the current temper of the people of today to the collapse of their optimistic beliefs.

A strong case for the frontier's influence on American nationalism is made in Hans Kohn, *American Nationalism* (New York, 1957). More searching is an article by William T. Hutchinson, "Unite to Divide; Divide to Unite; The Shaping of American Federalism," *Mississippi Valley Historical Review,* XLVI (1959), pp. 3–18, which shows the manner in which the West stimulated a nationalistic spirit during the early days of the Republic. For the nineteenth century the best analysis of the frontier's role in this respect is Daniel J. Elazar, *The American Partnership: Intergovernmental Co-operation in the Nineteenth-Century United States* (Chicago, 1962), a stimulating and original book. David W. Noble, *Historians Against History: The Frontier Thesis and the National Covenant in American Historical Writing since 1830* (Minneapolis, 1966), analyses the works of several historians, and especially of Turner, to show the manner in which they have sharpened the nationalistic spirit in America.

The effect of the closing of the frontier on American life and thought awaits adequate study. Frederic L. Paxson, *When the West is Gone* (Boston, 1930), touches briefly on the problem, which is explored more fully in Walter P. Webb, *Divided We Stand: The Crisis of a Frontierless Society* (New York, 1937). The broader implications of the problem are brilliantly discussed in Walter P. Webb, *The Great Frontier* (Boston, 1952), a book that has inspired an extended controversy. For arguments for and against the Webb thesis see G. Barraclough, "Metropolis and Macrocosm," *Past and Present,* III (1954), pp. 77–93, and four articles by as many eminent scholars in Archibald R. Lewis and Thomas F. McMann, eds., *The New World Looks at Its History* (Austin, Texas, 1963), pp. 135–169. Rowland Berthoff, "The American Social Order: A Conservative Hypothesis," *American Historical Review,* LXV (1960), pp. 495–514, is a stimulating discussion of present-day society as the aftermath of a period of pioneering and immigration. The impact of the frontier past on the present will be fully explored in a later volume in this series by Allan G. Bogue.

Index

Adams, Herbert Baxter, influence of, on Frederick Jackson Turner, 7.
Alabama, social mobility in, 112.
Alger, Horatio, personifies rags-to-riches myth, 113, 197.
Allen, William Francis, influence of, on Frederick Jackson Turner, 7.
American character, appraisal of influences on, 222–226; effect of frontier on, 59–61; effect of physical mobility on, 181–184, 193–197; elements of, 62–66; enduring impact of frontier on, 229–235; explanation of, 47–53; explanations of uniqueness of, 66–67; foreign observers on, 1–2; idealism as element of, 200–201; nationalism as element of, 202–212; optimism as element of, 201–205; place of women in, 215–217; rural traits in, 212–215; scientific definitions of, 61–62.
"American dream," influence of frontier on, 113–114.
American Historical Association, effect of Frederick Jackson Turner on, 14; 1893 meeting, 13.
American literature, effect of frontier on, 92–94; influence of frontier hypothesis on, 14–15; in West, 85.
Andrews, Charles M., reaction of, to frontier hypothesis, 13–14.

Anomie, among backwoodsmen, 42–43; as frontier trait, 53–54.
Anti-intellectualism, effects of frontier on, 94–95; existence of, on frontier, 90–91; persistence of, in modern America, 230–231.
Austin, Moses, on westward migration, 27.

Backwoodsmen, as frontier type, 41–43; lawlessness among, 72.
Bacon's Rebellion, 127.
Bagehot, Walter, influence of, on Frederick Jackson Turner, 11.
Baldwin, Joseph G., as frontier author, 93.
Beard, Charles, rejects frontier hypothesis, 14.
Beecher, Henry Ward, on western culture, 74.
Benét, Stephen Vincent, quoted on mobility, 182.
Boastfulness, decline of, in modern America, 230; as frontier trait, 194, 213.
Bookstores, spread of, on frontier, 82–83.
Boone, Daniel, as frontier hero, 91; interest in reading, 76–77.
Boutmy, Emile, influence of, on Frederick Jackson Turner, 11.

Bragging. See Boastfulness.

Bridger, Jim, reading tastes of, 77.

Brown, Samuel, helps found Coonskin Library, 83–84.

Bryce, Lord James, on American innovation, 171; on American materialism, 164; on American optimism, 201; on American physical mobility, 186; on American work habits, 64; on distinctiveness of frontier, 60; quoted on frontier influence, 4, 6.

California, law enforcement in, 147; mobility in, 182–184; settlement of, 50; theaters in, 86–87.

Carlyle, Thomas, on safety-valve, 30.

Cattlemen, cooperation among, 146; as frontier types, 40–41.

Census Bureau, use of, by Frederick Jackson Turner, 8–10.

Chamberlin, Thomas E., influence of, on Frederick Jackson Turner, 19.

Channing, Edward, rejects frontier hypothesis, 14.

Channing, William Ellery, on migration, 27.

Character, American. See American character.

Cheyenne, Wyoming, theaters in, 86.

Chicago, economic controls in, 147; land speculation in, 201–202.

Churillon, André, influence of, on Frederick Jackson Turner, 11.

Cincinnati, Ohio, bookstores in, 82; class divisions in, 100–101; cultural activities in, 76; social mobility in, 111; theaters in, 85.

Claim clubs, as frontier institutions, 146.

Class structure, effect of frontier egalitarianism on, 151–153; effect of frontier on, 97–101, 108–113; in modern America, 113–116; nature of, in United States, 102–106.

Classics, popularity of, on frontier, 79–80; 94.

Colorado, cultural activities in, 77–79; lawlessness in, 71; optimism in, 204; treatment of women in, 215.

Competition, as element in American character, 63–64.

Conservation movement, effect of frontier on, 169.

Constitution. See Democracy.

Coonskin Library, founding of, 83–84.

Cooper, James Fenimore, reaction of frontiersmen to, 82, 85, 93.

Cooperation, prevalence of, on frontier, 143–146.

Cowboys, cooperation among, 146; reading tastes of, 77.

Creative process, use of, by Frederick Jackson Turner, 8–12.

Crockett, Davy, as frontier hero, 91.

Culture, anthropological definition of, 49; changes in American, 50–52; as element in American character, 61–62.

Curiosity, decline of, 230; as frontier trait, 213–214.

Dabney, Thomas, 154.

Davenport, Iowa, bookstores in, 82–83; libraries in, 83.

Davis, C. Wood, on closing of frontier, 6.

Deadwood, South Dakota, theaters in, 86.

Defense, as cooperative endeavor on frontier, 144–145.

Democracy, among early settlers, 54–56; appraisal of frontier influences on, 223–224; belief in, as American trait, 64–65; changed by frontier, 121–126; effect of closing of frontier on, 228–229; effect of frontier on, 117–120; nature of, in United States, 120–121; persistence of, in twentieth century, 232–233; practice of, on frontiers, 126–137; social aspects of, on frontier, 139–157.

Denver, Colorado, class divisions in, 101; cultural activities in, 77–79; newspapers in, 80.

Depressions, effect of, on migration, 32–34.

Dickens, Charles, on American inquisitiveness, 214; on American materialism, 164; on American mobility, 187; on frontier conformity, 144; on frontier lawlessness, 71; on treatment of women, 216.

Donnelly, Ignatius, on frontier nationalism, 211–212.

Drake, Daniel, lack of appreciation for, 91; on social mobility, 111.

Drinking, excess of, on frontier, 71–72; on mining frontier, 77–78.

Dunning, William A., rejects frontier hypothesis, 14.
Dutch colonies, democracy in, 126–127; primitivism in, 70.
Dwight, Timothy, on backwoodsmen, 41–42; on migration, 27.

Economy, appraisal of effect of frontier on, 224–225; effect of frontier on, 160–163.
Education, demand for, on frontier, 78–79; effect of frontier on, 88–89, 93–94.
Ely, Richard T., influence of, on Frederick Jackson Turner, 7; on social evolution on frontier, 39.
Emerson, Ralph Waldo, on frontier optimism, 201–202.
England, effect of, on American democracy, 118–119, 120; nature of colonization from, 54–56.
Englishmen, as frontiersmen, 57, 58–59.
Environment, physical, effect of, on frontiersmen, 48–58; nature of, in America, 221.
Environment, social, defined, 49; effect of, on ethnic groups, 56–57; impact of, on national character, 58–61; nature of, 49–54.
Equality, as frontier creed, 150–151; nature of, in America, 153–157; reasons for, 151–153.
Erie Canal, effect of, on migration, 34.
Europe, mobility in, 184–185.
Everett, Edward, on frontier safety valve, 31.
Eye gouging, on frontier, 71.

Farm machinery, effect of frontier on, 175–178.
Farmers, as frontiersmen, 43–44.
Farming techniques, effect of frontier on, 173–178.
Fiske, John, as spokesman for frontier hypothesis, 14.
Flint, James, on social mobility, 111.
Flint, Timothy, as editor, 88; lack of appreciation of, 91; on migration, 28; on western culture, 78.
Foerster, Norman, applies frontier hypothesis to literature, 14.
Foreign policy, effect of frontier thesis on, 15, 18.

Franklin, Benjamin, on frontier as safety valve, 30; quoted on frontier, 4; on use of leisure, 167.
Freemasons, as elite groups on frontiers, 124.
Frontier, alternate frontiers, 228; appraisal of ' impact of, on American character, 223–226; appraisal of influence of, 219–223; closing of, 226–229; cooperative spirit on, 143–146; as cradle of barbarism, 70–73; description of, 3–6; economic impact of, 159–163; effect of, on American individualism, 142–143; effect of, on concept of equality, 150–157; effect of, on literature and education, 87–94; effect of, on national character, 52–58; effect of, on physical mobility, 184–189; effect of, on social mobility, 106–113; effect of, on social structure, 97–101, 105–106; encourages hospitality, 214–215; encourages idealism, 200–201; enduring effects of, 229–235; Frederick Jackson Turner's definition of, 16; impact of, on newcomers, 59–61; innovation on, 171–178; materialism on, 163–166; modern definitions of, 23–25; as molding force in United States, 67–68; as nationalizing force, 205–212; nature of individualism on, 148–150; nature of migration to, 29–39; perpetuation of civilization on, 73–87; reasons for migration to, 26–29; regulatory activities on, 146–148; sequence of migration to, 39–40; as stimulant to physical mobility, 189–192; stimulates boastfulness, 212–213; stimulates curiosity, 213–214; stimulates optimism, 201–205; treatment of women on, 215–217; types of settlers on, 39–45; wastefulness on, 168–170.
Frontier hypothesis, atmosphere in which formulated, 5–6; as explanation of aspects of American character, 67–68; evolution of, in Frederick Jackson Turner's mind, 8–12; reaction against, 15–18; reception of, among scholars, 13–15; stated, 3; statement of, by Turner, 12, 13.
Fur trappers, as frontier types, 40–41; individualism among, 143. *See* Mountain men.

Gallatin, Albert, urges internal improvements, 210.

Gannett, Henry, influence of, on Frederick Jackson Turner, 9.

Geographic determinism, defended against, 21–22; Frederick Jackson Turner accused of, 17.

George, Henry, influence of, on Frederick Jackson Turner, 11; quoted on frontier influence, 4.

Germans, on American frontier, 56–57, 58.

Godkin, E. L., on frontier as molding force, 5.

Greeley, Horace, on backwoodsmen, 42; on frontier as safety valve, 31–32; on speculators, 44.

Hale, Edward Everett, reaction of, to frontier hypothesis, 13.

Hall, James, as frontier editor, 88.

Hamilton, Alexander, on the frontier as safety valve, 30.

Hegel, Wilhelm Friedrich, on safety valve doctrine, 30.

Hewes, Fletcher W., influence of, on Frederick Jackson Turner, 9.

Homestead Act, influence of, on speculation, 44; passed, 31.

Hooper, Johnson J., as frontier author, 93.

Hospitality, decline of, 230; as frontier trait, 214–215.

Idealism, as frontier trait, 66, 200–201.

Illinois, class divisions in, 101; cost of pioneering in, 33; democracy in, 132–133; innovation in, 173, 175–176; mobility in, 187; optimism in, 204; regulatory laws in, 147; settlement patterns in, 45.

Indiana, class divisions in, 101; cooperation in, 145–146; democracy in, 120, 123; educational practices in, 79; higher education in, 94; newspapers in, 80; political practices in, 131, 132–133; reading tastes in, 81; religion in, 91; tastes in, 81.

Indians, treatment of, on frontier, 202.

Individualism, as an American characteristic, 65; appraisal of frontier influence on, 224; effect of frontier on, 143–150; nature of American individualism, 140–142.

Ingenuity, as frontier trait, 175.

Innovation, extent of, on frontier, 171–178; as frontier trait, 65; in governmental practices, 121; persistence of, 233–234.

Inns, as democratic institutions, 156–157.

Inquisitiveness. See Curiosity.

Institutions, effect of frontier mobility on, 195–196.

Internal improvements, effect of on nationalism, 210.

Inventiveness. See Innovation.

Investment, effect of frontier on, 161–162.

Iowa, as center of lawlessness, 71; democracy in, 133; innovation in, 177–178.

Irish, as frontiersmen, 57.

Irrigation, effect of, on legal doctrine, 178–179.

Irving, Washington, on American materialism, 163.

Jefferson, Thomas, on American optimism, 202; on frontier class structure, 98; on frontier types, 39; quoted on frontier patterns, 4; on safety valve doctrine, 30.

Johns Hopkins University, influence of, on Frederick Jackson Turner, 7.

Johnson, Lyndon B., effect of closing of frontier on, 229.

Kansas, cultural activities in, 74; education in, 79; equality in, 153; grants political rights to women, 217; mobility in, 192; newspapers in, 80; use of titles in, 100.

Kentucky, bookstores in, 82; class divisions in, 101; cultural activities in, 76; democracy in, 119; 129–131; educational developments in, 88; equality in, 152; individualism in, 142; lawlessness in, 70–71; reading tastes in, 81; schools in, 79; wastefulness in, 170.

Kipling, Rudyard, on American lawlessness, 65.

Knights of Columbus, effect of frontier on, 196.

La Follette, Philip, use of frontier hypothesis by, 15.

Land, conflict over titles, 178–179; influence of, on social development, 4, 6; nationalizing influence of, 210.

Land grants, effect of, on nationalism, 211.

Land speculators. *See* Speculators.

Latin America, nature of settlement in, 54–55.

Law, effect of frontier on, 178–179.

Lawlessness, as American trait, 65; effect of women on, 216–217; and frontier individualism, 141; on frontiers, 146–147; as frontier trait, 70–73; reasons for, on frontier, 53–54.

Leadville, Colorado, cultural activities in, 77–78.

Lexington, Kentucky, cultural activities in, 76; bookstores in, 82; libraries in, 83; class structure in, 99.

Libraries, in Ohio Valley, 88; spread of on frontier, 83–84.

Lincoln, Abraham, on frontier preaching, 91; as frontiersman, 76; on social mobility, 111.

Literary societies, spread of, on frontier, 84.

Literature, effect of frontier on, 14–15; emergence of, on frontier, 92–93; reading of, on frontier, 76–78, 81–84.

Little Rock, Arkansas, newspapers in, 80.

Longstreet, August Baldwin, as frontier author, 93.

Loria, Achille, influence of, on Frederick Jackson Turner, 11.

Los Angeles, mobility of population in, 184.

Louisville, Kentucky, cultural beginnings in, 58.

Lowell, Henry Wadsworth, as frontier author, 82.

Lowell, James Russell, quoted on nature of frontier, 4; on use of leisure, 167.

McLaughlin, Andrew C., rejects frontier hypothesis, 14.

Manifest Destiny, as expression of frontier optimism, 202.

Marriage, frequency of, on frontier, 216.

Martineau, Harriet, on frontier hospitality, 214.

Marx, Karl, quoted on frontier's influence, 4, 6; on safety valve doctrine, 30.

Massachusetts, abolition of property qualifications in, 136; democracy in, 128–129; social mobility in, 110.

Materialism, as American trait, 64; effect of, on frontier culture, 90–91; as frontier characteristic, 163–166.

Mather, Cotton, quoted on mobility, 186.

Michigan, belief in equality in, 153–154; cooperation among settlers, 144; cultural activity in, 91; growth of, 33; optimism of people, 204; physical mobility in, 190; reaction of settlers to, 59; social democracy in, 156; work habits of settlers, 165.

Migration, effect of, on immigrants, 17; effects of, 220; nature of, 29–39; reasons for, 26–29; sequential pattern of, 39–45. *See* Mobility, physical.

Miners, books among, 83; cooperative activities among, 146; effect of legal practices of, 178–179; law enforcement among, 146–147; reading tastes of, 77–78; theaters in mining camps, 86; treatment of women, 215.

Minnesota, optimism in, 202.

Missionaries, as frontier types, 40.

Mississippi Valley, class divisions in, 101; conformity in, 144; effect of, on nationalism, 207–208; individualism in, 143; lack of innovation in, 173–174; newspapers in, 80; social mobility in, 110–111; theaters in, 85–86.

Mobility, physical, as American characteristic, 65, 181–184; appraisal of frontier influence on, 225; among backwoodsmen, 42; effect of, on American character, 67, 193–195; effect of, on American nationalism, 209; effect of, on institutions, 195–197; reasons for, 187–192.

Mobility, social, as American characteristic, 62–63, 64–65; comparison of, in United States and Europe, 106–107; effect of frontier on, 108–115; effect of, on franchise, 136; effect of, on frontier democracy, 122–123; effect of, on physical mobility, 189–192; extent of, on frontier, 37–38; importance of, on frontier, 221–222; persistence

Mobility (*continued*)
of, in United States, 233; reasons for, in United States, 108.
Mountain men, interest in reading, 77; refusal to abandon civilization, 58.
Multiple causation, use of, by Frederick Jackson Turner, 18–20.

Nashville, Tennessee, lawlessness in, 71; theaters in, 85.
National Board of Internal Improvements, 210.
National character. *See* American character.
Nationalism, as American characteristic, 205–206; appraisal of frontier influence on, 226; decline of, 232; definitions of, 205; effect of physical mobility on, 194–195; strengthened by frontier, 207–212.
Nebraska, educational activities in, 78; innovation in, 173; literary societies in, 84; newspapers in, 80; optimism in, 204; physical mobility in, 192; soil depletion in, 170.
New England, migration from, 32–34; social mobility in, 110; social stratification in, 103.
New Salem, Illinois, cultural activities in, 76.
New York State, voting patterns in, 126–127.
Newspapers, popularity of, on frontier, 80–81.
Natural wealth, influence of frontier on, 162.

Ohio, blue laws in, 147; class divisions in, 101; class structure in, 99; cultural activities in, 74; education in, 78–79, 93–94; growth of democracy in, 122, 132–133; lack of democracy in first constitution, 119; libraries in, 83–84; newspapers in, 80; reading in, 89; wastefulness in, 170.
Ohio Valley, democratic practices in, 131–133; education in, 88; expansion in, 59, 203; libraries in, 88; publishing in, 82; reading tastes in, 84–85.
Old Northwest, democracy in, 131–133; local government in, 133–135.
Old Southwest, government in, 135.

Omaha, Nebraska, newspapers in, 80; theater in, 86.
Omnibus states, democracy in, 136.
Opera, on mining frontier, 77–78.
Optic, Oliver, on rags-to-riches myth, 113.
Optimism, as American characteristic, 66; appraisal of frontier influence on, 225–226; decline of, in United States, 231–232; as frontier trait, 201–205.

Parkman, Francis, quoted on frontier, 4.
Personality, as element in American character, 61–62.
Pittsburgh, class structure in, 99; early laws in, 58; mobility in, 188; publishing in, 82; theaters in, 85.
Plows, evolution of, on frontier, 173.
Populists, urge regulation of railroads, 148.
Primitivism, as frontier condition, 70–73.
Principle of Association. *See* Cooperation.
Publishing, effect of frontier on, 81–82; products of western publishers, 84; in West, 82.

Reading, effect of social environment on, 92–93; among frontiersmen, 76–77, 81–85, 88–89; in Illinois, 76; on Kansas frontier, 74; in Lexington, Kentucky, 76.
Regulators, as law enforcement agencies, 146.
Religion, effect of mobility upon, 195–196; effect of, on frontier culture, 91.
Rhode Island, voting in, 136.
Roman Catholic Church, effect of mobility on, 196.
Roosevelt, Franklin D., effect of closing of frontier on, 229; use of frontier thesis by, 15.
Roosevelt, Theodore, effect of closing of frontier on, 228–229; reaction of, to frontier hypothesis, 13; review of, by Frederick Jackson Turner, 11; as westerner, 154.

Sacramento, California, theater in, 86.
Safety Valve Doctrine, definitions of, 32; effect of, on franchise, 136; history of, 30–31; modern interpretations of, 35–39; operation of, 34–35; use of, by Frederick Jackson Turner, 31–32.

San Francisco, libraries in, 83; newspapers in, 80; theaters in, 86–87.

Schoolcraft, Henry, quoted on frontier, 27.

Sequential growth, effect of, on economy, 37; effect of, on frontier, 160–163.

Servants, treatment of, on frontier, 155–156.

Shakespeare, William, as frontier playwright, 76, 77, 81, 86.

Shirley, Dame, on frontier equality, 150.

Smith, Captain John, on social mobility, 110.

Smith, Sidney, on frontier lawlessness, 72–73.

Social democracy, appraisal of frontier influences on, 223–224; importance of, on frontier, 139–157; persistence of, in United States, 233. See Democracy.

Social environment, appraisal of, 221; effect of, on class structure, 105–106; effect of, on frontier culture, 92–94; influenced by physical mobility, 193–195; persistence of, in United States, 229–230.

South Dakota, social stratification in, 103–104.

Spanish colonies, lack of democracy in, 119–120; nature of, 54–55.

Speculators, effect of optimism on, 201–202; as frontier type, 44–45; as product of frontier environment, 222.

Spencer, Herbert, read on frontier, 81.

Squatters. See Backwoodsmen.

Stratification, definition of, 101–102; effect of egalitarianism on, 151–153; effect of, on innovation, 176–177; effect of, on mobility, 185; in frontier society, 98–101; nature of, in United States, 102–106.

Sumner, William Graham, quoted on influence of frontier, 4.

Suffrage, in America, 119–120; expansion of, on frontier, 126–137; extension of, to frontier women, 216–217. See Democracy.

Swedish colonies, democracy in, 126–127; primitivism in, 70.

Tennessee, democracy in, 119, 129; lack of culture in, 89, 92; lawlessness in, 71; schools in, 78.

Texas, cooperation in, 146; equality of people in, 154; individualism in, 143; regulation of economy in, 148.

Theater, as frontier institution, 85–87.

Thompson, James W., use of frontier hypothesis by, 14.

Thoreau, Henry David, quoted on mobility, 28.

Titles, use of, on frontier, 100, 110, 154–155.

Tocqueville, Alexis de, on American mobility, 186, 188; on American nationalism, 206, 211; on American optimism, 201, 203; on American work habits, 168; on frontier civilization, 74; on frontier cooperation, 144; on frontier democracy, 122, 124; on frontier individualism, 140; on national character, 61.

Towns, as frontier institutions, 45.

Trempeleau County, Wisconsin, democracy in, 134–135.

Truman, Harry S., effect of closing of frontier on, 229.

Turner, Frederick Jackson, acceptance of frontier thesis, 13–15; attacks on frontier thesis, 15–18; definitions of frontier by, 24; early life of, 6–7; evolution of frontier hypothesis, 8–12; on frontier democracy, 117, 120; on frontier types, 39; historical concepts, 19–22; influences on, 7–8; on nature of settlement process, 46; statement of frontier thesis, 12–13; use of safety valve doctrine by, 24, 31–32, 39; validity of theories of, 67–68.

Urban frontier, described, 45.

Urbanization, as stimulant to physical mobility, 184–185.

Ustinov, Peter, quoted on individualism, 141.

Vertical mobility. See Mobility, social.

Vigilantes, as law enforcement agencies, 146–147.

Vincennes, Indiana, cultural activities in, 79; theater in, 85.

Virginia, democracy in, 127–128; physical mobility in, 186; social mobility in, 110.

Virginia City, Nevada, cultural activities in, 77; schools in, 79.

Von Holst, Hermann, disagreement with, by Frederick Jackson Turner, 11.
Voting. *See* Suffrage, Democracy.

Walker, Francis A., influence of, on Frederick Jackson Turner, 9–10, 11; reaction of, to frontier hypothesis, 13.
Washington, George, on safety valve doctrine, 30; urges national unity, 208.
Wastefulness, as American characteristic, 65; effects of physical mobility on, 194; as frontier trait, 168–170; persistence of, in United States, 233.
Webster, Daniel, on American materialism, 164
Wilson, Woodrow, effect of closing of frontier on, 229; influence of, on Frederick Jackson Turner, 7; as popularizer of frontier hypothesis, 13.
Winthrop, John, on safety valve doctrine, 30.

Wisconsin, democracy in local government of, 133–134; mobility in, 191–192; schools in, 94; social mobility in, 112; soil depletion in, 170.
Wisconsin, University of, influence of, on Frederick Jackson Turner, 7–8.
Women, changed status in United States, 65; respect for, in modern America, 234–235; treatment of, on frontier, 215–216.
Work, as American characteristic, 64; effect on frontier culture, 90–91; as frontier trait, 166–168; persistence of habit of, in United States, 234.
Workingmen, migration of, to frontier, 32–39.
World frontier, passing of, 227–228.
Wright, Frank Lloyd, quoted on mobility, 183.
Wyoming, democratic innovations in, 156; grants franchise to women, 217.